CW01662766

Post-war Japan as a Sea Power

Bloomsbury Studies in Military History

Series Editor: Jeremy Black

Bloomsbury Studies in Military History offers up-to-date, scholarly accounts of war and military history. Unrestricted by period or geography, the series aims to provide free-standing works that are attuned to conceptual and historiographical developments in the field while being based on original scholarship.

Published:

The 56th Infantry Brigade and D-Day, Andrew Holborn (2010)
The RAF's French Foreign Legion, G. H. Bennett (2011)
Empire and Military Revolution in Eastern Europe, Brian Davies (2011)
Reinventing Warfare 1914-1918, Anthony Saunders (2011)
Fratricide in Battle, Charles Kirke (2012)
The Army in British India, Kaushik Roy (2012)
The 1711 Expedition to Quebec, Adam Lyons (2013)
Britain, Germany and the Battle of the Atlantic, Dennis Haslop (2013)
Military Transition in Early Modern Asia, 1400-1750, Kaushik Roy (2014)
The Role of the Royal Navy in South America, Jon Wise (2014)
Scotland and the British Army 1700-1750, Victoria Henshaw (2014)
War and State-Building in Modern Afghanistan, edited by Scott Gates and Kaushik Roy (2014)
Conflict and Soldiers' Literature in Early Modern Europe, Paul Scannell (2014)
Youth, Heroism and Naval Propaganda, Douglas Ronald (2015)
William Howe and the American War of Independence, David Smith (2015)

Forthcoming:

Reassessing the British Way in Warfare, K. A. J. McLay (2015)
The D-Day Landing on Gold Beach, Andrew Holborn (2015)
Australasian Propaganda and the Vietnam War, Caroline Page (2015)
Australian Soldiers in the Boer and Vietnam Wars, Effie Karageorgos (2016)
English Landed Society and the Great War, Edward Bujak (2018)

Post-war Japan as a Sea Power

Imperial Legacy, Wartime Experience and the Making of a Navy

Alessio Patalano

Bloomsbury Academic
An imprint of Bloomsbury Publishing Plc

B L O O M S B U R Y
LONDON • OXFORD • NEW YORK • NEW DELHI • SYDNEY

Bloomsbury Academic
An imprint of Bloomsbury Publishing Plc

50 Bedford Square
London
WC1B 3DP
UK

1385 Broadway
New York
NY 10018
USA

www.bloomsbury.com

BLOOMSBURY and the Diana logo are trademarks of Bloomsbury Publishing Plc

First published 2015
Paperback edition first published 2016

© Alessio Patalano, 2015

Alessio Patalano has asserted his right under the Copyright, Designs and Patents Act, 1988, to be identified as Author of this work.

All rights reserved. No part of this publication may be reproduced or transmitted in any form or by any means, electronic or mechanical, including photocopying, recording, or any information storage or retrieval system, without prior permission in writing from the publishers.

No responsibility for loss caused to any individual or organization acting on or refraining from action as a result of the material in this publication can be accepted by Bloomsbury or the author.

British Library Cataloguing-in-Publication Data
A catalogue record for this book is available from the British Library.

ISBN: HB: 978-1-4725-2651-9
PB: 978-1-3500-1108-3
ePDF: 978-1-4725-2232-0
ePub: 978-1-4725-2682-3

Library of Congress Cataloging-in-Publication Data
Patalano, Alessio.
Post-war Japan as a sea power: imperial legacy, wartime experience and the making of a navy/Alessio Patalano.
pages cm. – (Bloomsbury studies in military history)
Includes bibliographical references and index.
ISBN 978-1-4725-2651-9 (hbk.) – ISBN 978-1-4725-2232-0 (.pdf) – ISBN 978-1-4725-2682-3 (.epub) 1. Japan. Kaigun.
2. Sea-power – Japan. 3. Japan – History, Naval. I. Title.
VA653.P47 2015
359'.03095209045–dc23
2014042343

Series: Bloomsbury Studies in Military History

Typeset by Deanta Global Publishing Services, Chennai, India

This book is dedicated to Julie,
the 'captain' of my life and the 'lighthouse' of my heart,
and to the sea that made us meet on a summer day.

Contents

Abbreviations and Acronyms

AAW	Anti-Air Warfare
AEW	Airborne Early Warning
AIP	Air Independent Propulsion
ASROC	Anti-Submarine Rocket
ASW	Anti-Submarine Warfare
AWACS	Airborne Warning and Control System
BMD	Ballistic Missile Defence
C4I	Command, Control, Communications, Computers and Information
CDS	Combat Direction System
CIC	Combat Information Centre
CinC	Commander in Chief
CIWS	Close-In Weapons System
CMS	Chief of Maritime Staff, JMSDF
CO	Commanding Officer
CODAG	Combined Diesel and Gas Turbine
CODOG	Combined Diesel or Gas Turbine Engine
COGAC	Combined Gas Turbine and Gas Turbine
COGOC	Combined Gas Turbine or Gas Turbine
CVH	Helicopter Carrier (Japan)
DSP	Democratic Socialist Party
EEZ	Exclusive Economic Zone
FY	Financial Year (1 April – 31 March)
GDP	Gross Domestic Product
IJA	Imperial Japanese Army
IJN	Imperial Japanese Navy
JASDF	Japan Air Self-Defence Force
JCG	Japan Coast Guard
JCP	Japan Communist Party
JDA	Japan Defence Agency
JGSDF	Japan Ground Self-Defence Force
JMoD	Japan Ministry of Defence
JMSDF	Japan Maritime Self-Defence Force
JNA	Japanese naval Association
JSDF	Japan Self-Defence Forces
JSP	Japan Socialist Party
KI	Kodansha International
LDP	Liberal Democratic Party
MAAG-J	Military Assistance and Advisory Group – Japan

MCM	Mine Counter Measures
MOF	Ministry of Finance
MOFA	Ministry of Foreign Affairs
MOOTW	Military Operations Other Than War
MSA	Maritime Safety Agency
MSC	Maritime Staff College, JMSDF
MSF	Maritime Safety Force
MSO	Maritime Staff Office, JMSDF
MTDP	Mid-Term Defence Programme
MW	Mine Warfare
NATO	North Atlantic Treaty Organisation
NCO	Non-Commissioned Officer
NDA	National Defence Academy
NDC	National Defence Council
NDPG	National Defence Programme Guideline
NDPO	National Defence Programme Outline
NGS	Naval Gunfire Support
NIDS	National Institute for Defence Studies
NPR	National Police Reserve
NSC	Naval Staff College, IJN
NSF	National Safety Force
NTDS	Naval Tactical Data System
OCS	Officer Candidate School, JMSDF
ONUMOZ	United Nations Operations in Mozambique
OPD	Operations and Plans Department, MSO, JMSDF
PED	Personnel and Education Division, MSO, JMSDF
PKO	Peacekeeping Operations
PLAN	People's Liberation Army Navy
PPD	Plans and Programmes Division, MSO, JMSDF
PPS	Plans and Policy Section, MSO, JMSDF
PR	Public Relations
PSI	Proliferation Security Initiative
RIMPAC	Rim of the Pacific Exercise
SA	Safety Agency
SAM	Surface-to-Air Missile
SAREX	Search and Rescue Exercise
SAU	Search Attack Unit
SIGINT	Signal Intelligence
SLOCs	Sea Lanes of Communication
SOSUS	Sound Surveillance Sonar System
SSM	Surface-to-Surface Missile
SSN	Nuclear-powered Attack Submarine
SURTASS	Surveillance Towed Array Sonar System
SVTOL	Short and Vertical Take-Off and Landing
TACAN	Tactical Antenna

TIU	Tokyo Imperial University (present Tokyo University)
UNCLOS	United Nations Convention for the Law of the Sea
UNTAC	United Nations Transitional Authority in Cambodia
USN	United States Navy
USSBS	United States Strategic Bombing Survey
VLS	Vertical Launch System
WPNS	Western Pacific Naval Symposium

JMSDF Ship Classification

Japanese	English
護衛艦 (Goeikan) DD	Destroyer
護衛艦 (Goeikan) DDH	Helicopter Destroyer
護衛艦 (Goeikan) DDG	Guided Missile Destroyer
護衛艦 (Goeikan) DDA	All Purpose Destroyer
護衛艦 (Goeikan) DDK	Anti-Submarine Destroyer
護衛艦 (Goeikan) DE	Escort Vessel
潜水艦 (Sensuikan) SS	Submarine
掃海艦 (Sōkaikan) MSO	Ocean Minesweeper
掃海艇 (Sōkaitei) MSC	Coastal Minesweeper
掃海管制艇 (Sōkaikanseitei) MCL	Minesweeper Controller
掃海艇 (Sōkaitei) MSB	Minesweeper Boat
掃海母艦 (Sōkaibokan) MST	Minesweeper Tender
魚雷艇 (Gyoraitei) PT	Motor Torpedo Boat
ミサイル艇 (Misairutei) PG	Patrol Gunboat
哨戒艇 (Shōkaitei) PB	Patrol Boat
輸送艦 (Yusōkan) LST	Tank Landing Ship
輸送艦(Yusōkan) LSU	Landing Ship Utility
輸送艇(Yusōtei) LCU	Landing Craft Utility
エアクション艇 (Eakushontei) LCAC	Landing Craft Air Cushion
練習艦 (Renshūkan) TV	Training Vessel
練習潜水艦 (Renshū Sensuikan) TSS	Training Submarine
練習支援艦 (Renshū Shienkan) ATS	Training Support Ship
多用途支援艦 (Tayōto Shienkan) AMS	Aux. Multipurpose Support
海洋観測艦 (Kaiyō Kansokukan) AGS	Oceanographic Research Ship
潜水艦救難艦 (Sensuikan Kyūnankan) ASR	Submarine Rescue Vessel
潜水艦救難母艦 (Sensuikan Kyūnanbokan) AS	Submarine Rescue Tender
試験艦 (Shikenkan) ASE	Auxiliary Ship Utility
補給艦 (Hokyūkan) AOE	Fast Combat Support Ship

Source: Japan Maritime Self-Defence Force, *Ships and Aircraft of the JMSDF* (Tokyo: Kaijōjieitai Shimbunsha, 2007), 4.

Figures, Maps and Photos

Figures

Maps

Photos

Photos 5.2, 5.4 and 5.5 are courtesy of the author. All other photos are courtesy of the Photographic Archive of the Public Affairs Office, Maritime Staff Office, Japan Maritime Self-Defence Force.

Conventions

This book adopts the revised Hepburn Romanisation system. Macrons are used to indicate long vowels in Japanese, except for place names (e.g. Tokyo) of common use in English language publications. Italics are used for ship names in all cases.

Japanese names are given with family names preceding first names. In bibliographical references, names of Japanese authors are given according to Western practice. Names of Japanese authors in English language publications are reported according to the original text and therefore appear in some cases without macron (e.g. Koda instead of Kōda), or with different spelling (e.g. Kazutomi instead of Kazuomi).

The reference system has been conceived to be as comprehensive as possible for specialists, while giving readers unfamiliar with the Japanese language some indication of the character of the sources used. When a Japanese publication is referred to for the first time a full bibliographical description is given, including characters, phonetic reading, and English translation. Thereafter, references report the author's surname, the phonetic reading of the title or an abbreviated version of it.

In the text, reference is made to the conventional periodisation of Japanese modern history, the system of 'era names',[1] which is used in Japan instead of the Gregorian calendar. *Nengō* derive their names from the ruling Emperor. Since 1868, Japanese history has been distinguished by four eras:

Meiji (1868–1912);
Taishō (1912–26);
Shōwa (1926–89);
Heisei (1989–Present).

Acknowledgements

This book represents the culminating stage of a journey that started on an autumn evening in November 2004. I had just landed in Tokyo and a senior JMSDF officer who had studied the previous year at the Royal College of Defence Studies came to greet me and discuss my plans over a meal. That evening, a mix of disorientation, jet lag, curiosity and genuine excitement made me realise that the journey I was about to begin would be very different from the one I had just completed. I felt disoriented and curious because I knew little of where the journey would land me. I was excited because right there I was taking my first step into it.

Like any intellectual journey of this kind, many deserve recognition for their contribution to it. Over the past decade, I have met countless individuals who stimulated my knowledge, widened my horizons, tested my skills, and disagreed with my findings. All, in their own way, contributed to the making of this book. Some have become inspiring mentors; others, esteemed colleagues; more than a few, close friends. It would take more than the pages of this text to name them all, though my gratitude towards them is a source of constant strength and makes me look forward to continuing on the next stop of this journey with the same excitement of that November night of ten years ago.

I am particularly indebted to those who, at the various stages of the manuscript, provided me with invaluable feedback and advice. My original supervisors at King's College London, Andrew Lambert and the late Saki Dockrill, shouldered most of the burden of getting this project to stand on its own feet. They constantly encouraged my research endeavours and unquestionably supported my fieldwork activity. Andrew eventually became my next-door colleague at the Department of War Studies, and our chats today are less on the history of the Japanese navy. Yet, he remains my intellectual 'lighthouse'. Saki was prematurely taken from the love of family, friends, and colleagues. Yet, the memory of our discussions about Japan's strategic shortcomings during the Pacific War accompanied me as I reviewed the history of the Imperial Navy. Reinhard Drifte and Eric Grove were invaluable in consolidating the foundations of this project, drawing upon their complementary expertise to sharpen my thoughts on Japanese defence policy and naval affairs. Equally important, Carol Gluck, Elizabeth Guran, John T. Kuehn, Barak Kushner, Peter Mauch, Rana Mitter, Andrew Oros, Peter Roberts, Richard Samuels and Geoffrey Till, all acted with great generosity offering constructive comments and helpful suggestions on specific chapters. James E. Auer offered me intellectual shelter with his encyclopaedic knowledge of US–Japan naval alliance matters and Japanese politics when I knew little about either subject. I wish to thank also John Bradford for sharing with me his perspective on Japan as a naval officer deployed in the archipelago.

At the Department of War Studies, many colleagues contributed to this project. Marcus Faulkner and Alan James have, over the years, patiently engaged with me in countless hours of discussions on Japan, naval history, and on the teaching of East Asia in a non-area studies context. Joe Maiolo showed me the virtues of being an academic when he first encouraged me to become one. Today, they all remind me just how invaluable friendships are in life. Mervyn Frost was exquisitely supportive of my work on Japan as I took the first steps as a young lecturer in the department. Together with his wife Lola, they created the most welcoming working atmosphere a young academic could wish for. Recently, renewed support and intellectual stimulus came from a new colleague, Thomas Rid, and from Theo Farrell who, notwithstanding a very busy schedule as Head of Department, took the time to offer insightful comments on the original proposal for the book. Altogether, these individuals embodied and continue to embody the compass of my intellectual and professional growth. For the past five years, I had the privilege to partake in some of the most stimulating discussions on East Asian security and on Japan's role in it with my students. Their support and contribution to my development as an expert on this subject and as a teacher is beyond price.

In Japan, I have a great many deal of individuals to thank. The Hashiramoto family, who hosted me during my first visit to Japan in 1999, introduced me to the beauty of Kansai's culture and traditions and shaped the affection I developed for the country. In the world of academia, I wish to thank my 'mentors' and generous hosts at the National Graduate Institute for Policy Studies and at Aoyama Gakuin Daigaku, Watanabe Akio, Iwama Yoko, Aoi Chiyuki, and Takagi Seiichiro. They opened the doors to their universities' resources and aided a number of crucial introductions that were instrumental in developing a network in the Japanese defence policy circles. Robert Dujarric, Michishita Narushige, Tohmatsu Haruo, Yamaguchi Noboru, Tadokoro Masayuki, Agawa Naoyuki, and Hikotani Takako regularly took time to engage with me in stimulating discussions on Japanese defence politics and military history. Kaneko Yuzuru, National Institute for Defence Studies (NIDS), kindly agreed to grant me special access to the main library, while Ishizu Tomoyuki arranged on more occasions seminar opportunities at NIDS where I presented parts of the findings of this book. More broadly, I wish to express my deepest gratitude to the numerous colleagues and friends at NIDS who, over the years, welcomed my work and helped me push the boundaries of my knowledge. NIDS is an invaluable source of understanding for foreign scholars like myself seeking to comprehend Japanese military history and defence policy. I feel nonetheless privileged because among the research staff at NIDS, Kotani Ken and Moriyama Ayumi proved to be invaluable friends as well as insightful fellow scholars.

This book would not exist without the cooperation of the Japan Maritime Self-Defence Force. Many officers have dedicated countless hours to patiently explain the value of Japanese naval traditions, and showed me how they are practised on a daily basis. In particular, Rear Admirals Ike Taro and Otsuka Umio gave me the unique opportunity to integrate the knowledge and passion of a young academic with the wisdom and friendship of experienced professionals. Vice Admiral Koda Yoji guided me through the navy's inner thinking with some of the most thought-provoking discussions on the history of the Imperial Japanese Navy, even though some of them gave numerous headaches to his junior aides at fleet headquarters. Vice Admiral Fukumoto Izuru opened the doors of the Maritime Staff College, allowed me to feel the vibrant intellectual atmosphere among his instructors and research specialists, and shared with me his personal experience in the Great Eastern Japan Earthquake in 2011. Captain Kitagawa Keizo was never too far whenever I had a last minute question. The daily commitment of these officers to their profession is the most invaluable legacy of Japan's imperial past.

From 2004 to 2012, financial support provided by the Japan Foundation and the AHRC award schemes, by the Coles Foundation, and by the small grant schemes of the Great Britain Sasakawa Foundation and the Department of War Studies enabled me to visit Japan to conduct fieldwork activity on a regular basis. Needless to say, without these grants it would have been impossible to complete this book.

At Bloomsbury, I am grateful to Claire Lipscomb, for her genuine enthusiasm for, and support to, the project at a time when publishers thought that writing on East Asian naval subjects mostly meant writing about China's naval modernisation. Emma Goode was equally supportive and patient, guiding me towards the completion of the manuscript. From beginning to end, they made the process of finishing this book a true delight.

Finally, I have one other major debt to acknowledge to my family. Despite geographical distance, I always feel them close to my heart and if today I am what I am it is because of their unquestioned emotional support throughout the years. Since 2012, this support has widened thanks to my in-laws and their parents. Their joy for life allowed me to experience a most regenerating time as I discovered Nice and its crystal blue waters whenever I visited them.

Alessio Patalano
London, 7 October 2014

1

Japanese Sea Power: From Kaigun to Kaiji

If we admit that history is a study and not a romance, it is the province of whatever claims the name of history, not only to teach the glories or the misfortunes of the past, but to point out the causes which induced them, and the way in which they are to be imitated or avoided.[1]

John K. Laughton
('The Scientific Study of Naval History', 1874)

By maritime strategy we mean the principles which govern a war in which the sea is a substantial factor.[2]

Naval strategy does not exist as a separate branch of knowledge. It is only a section of a division of the art of war.[3]

Julian S. Corbett
(The 'Green Pamphlet', 1909)

A fleet is like a hand of cards at poker or bridge. You don't see it as aces and kings and deuces. You see it as a hand, a unit. You see a fleet as a unit, not carriers, battleships and destroyers. You don't play individual cards, you play the hand.[4]

William F. Halsey
(Fleet Admiral, United States Navy)

Re-enacting the past

A pale sun was shining over the island of Etajima.[5] The midshipmen about to graduate from the Officer Candidate School – the Japanese Naval Academy – were getting ready for the formal ceremony. The landscape, the buildings, all contributed to make this event very special and 'traditional'. The island, located in the Inland Sea, set the academy just twenty-five minutes by ferry from the nearby shipbuilding city of Kure, birthplace of the Imperial Navy's leviathan battleship *Yamato*. The cherry and pine trees girdling the avenue leading to the Great Hall[6] added extra light to the 'red-bricks'[7] used in 1893 to mould the cadets' quarters after the Royal Naval Academy in Portsmouth.[8] In a place where seismic activities forced a constant renovation of space, the academy stood as an enduring reminder of the Meiji success in creating a modern navy.[9]

In the Great Hall, the traditional character of the ceremony did not overshadow the obvious differences with the pre-war era, when the awarding of the diplomas took place in the presence of the Crown Prince and occasionally, of the Emperor himself. Then, the graduating students knelt, bringing their heads to the floor in a slow movement to pay their homage to the imperial authority. After honour graduates had received ceremonial daggers, they would all perform another deep bow to celebrate the relationship linking the naval 'limbs' to their imperial 'head'.[10] Now, the ritual silence was replaced by the singing of the Japanese National Anthem and by the remarks of the Superintendent of the school, the Commandant of Kure Naval District, and the retired senior officer representing the Japanese Naval Association.[11] In their respective roles of educator, commanding officer, and 'living memory of the service', they delivered speeches following a practice[12] used by the Imperial Navy to instil in young cadets desired values.[13] Some of the ritualism had changed since the pre-war era, but the aim of its content had not.

This became apparent when the three senior naval figures described the role of the Japanese Naval Academy. Since the days of the First Sino-Japanese (1894–95) and the Russo-Japanese (1904–5) Wars, the academy had the responsibility to forge classes of skilled professionals entrusted with national security. They stressed the academy's prime challenge in pursuing this goal, which was the need to adapt to social and political changes to meet the requirements of a country with increasing international responsibilities and cogent regional strategic concerns. Commitments to the coalition operations in the Indian Ocean and the daily operations to deter military intrusions in Japanese territorial waters and to counter North Korea's nuclear and missile threats were the examples they used to present the plethora of the JMSDF's missions.[14] In the remarks, the qualities expected by Japanese officers were presented with the same clarity as those of naval leaders worldwide: discipline, authority, responsibility, loyalty and will to perform to the best standards.[15]

Moments later, marching under the flag that signals 'Bravo – Zulu' (i.e. 'well done') flying from the academy's yard mast, the graduates left the Great Hall and arrived at the pier. There, they boarded crafts taking them to one of three *Hatsuyuki* class destroyers, soon to leave for a three-month training cruise overseas. The senior officer supervising the ceremony ashore shouted the word 'bōfure'[16] and the other officers joined him in the traditional send-off of 'cap-waving'. To the Japanese naval officer, this moment is particularly significant, as the departing boats are a metaphor for the midshipman's decision to leave behind his previous life for a stricter, severe[17] path of service to the nation.[18] The newly appointed midshipmen responded by adding one last profound bow, sealing the re-enactment of a ceremony largely codified during the early days of the Imperial Navy and that had cradled generations of naval leaders in Japan since 1888.[19]

The navy and Japan: Explaining the core argument

This book is about history. It is about the history of the post-war Japanese navy, also known as Japan Maritime Self-Defence Force (JMSDF).[20] It is about how history is remembered, memorialised and displayed for the purpose of national defence. It starts by asking a simple question. Why did the Imperial Navy seem to matter so much at the graduation ceremony of the JMSDF, an organisation that does not even share the same name? This book provides the answer to this question. An answer of great relevance that requires, however, a brief preliminary explanation of the relationship linking navies to national security in general, and of their importance in East Asia and in Japan in particular.

Alfred Mahan was among the first scholars to investigate this relationship. He argued that naval supremacy could empower a country with undisputed command of the sea; this, in turn, allowed government authorities the strategic flexibility to choose how to best counter possible threats. His study of British history proved this point.[21] British contemporary Julian Corbett did not disagree with Mahan, but he specified that navies served states best when they were part of a 'maritime strategy', one seeking to harmonise geography, military power and economic resources.[22] For an island nation like Britain, the ideal maritime strategy minimised its vulnerability to attacks from the sea and maximised deterrence to prevent disruptions to trade and commerce essential for its economic survival.[23] Naval supremacy had served this purpose, but implicit to Corbett's views was the notion that this did not mean that a superior naval force was a 'mandatory' strategy. As another British strategist later remarked, throughout modern British history, the pursuit of strong naval allies to prevent an invasion and protect commerce, or indeed the maintenance of a strong fleet, represented two of four possible options open to authorities in London.[24] The key point was that the fleet was 'the hand of poker' that governments played to 'shape events both at sea and on land' to enhance national security.[25]

This notion is certainly not lost on East Asia. In this region, navies matter, for the sea is the primary regional connective fabric, allowing maritime capabilities to play a primary role in influencing regional security and power structures. Empirical evidence of how maritime capabilities are deployed to enhance the national security of the various regional state actors abounds. Across the past decade, incidents in the East and South China Seas involving the use of maritime forces (including navies and coast guards) to patrol, deter or coerce opponent state actors have shown the growing importance of the maritime realm to regional security.[26] In this context, analysts have drawn much attention to Chinese naval modernisation and growing capabilities to assess Beijing's ability to replace the United States as the dominant regional player.[27] In such examinations, one factor is often left unaccounted for: the JMSDF.

This is rather surprising given that the navy has long played a crucial role in the rise of Japan as a modern state. A quick glance at the history of the Imperial Navy would confirm this statement. In the early stages of the Meiji era, after Japanese authorities agreed that the possession of a degree of naval power was a strategic imperative, they endeavoured to build a strong navy. In less than half a century, this force became a 'symbol of national progress and power, one which instilled pride and heralded Japan's "modern emergence"'.[28] In 1905, the staggering victory at Tsushima against the Russian Baltic Fleet became a statement of an accomplished naval mastery that 'justified the cost and sacrifice of Japanese modernisation'.[29] In the following forty years, the Imperial

Navy sought to fulfil a Mahanian destiny, expanding the empire to the most remote corners of the Pacific before its eventual dramatic demise. In Japanese, this staggering experience is reflected in the fact that the word *kaigun* – used normally to translate the word 'navy' – is charged with evocative images of one of the finest fleets in naval history. As doyen naval historians Mark Peattie and David Evans pointed out, as the country emerged onto the world stage, the navy was its shield and spear, its 'agent for projection of Japanese power abroad'.[30] The Imperial Navy was, in this respect, symptomatic of the Japanese attempt to pursue a strategy of naval supremacy in the waters of the Sea of Japan and the China Seas.

Some would argue that the Japanese naval power never fully recovered from the demise of the Imperial Navy. The normative context that constrained the size and shape of the post-war navy was evidence of the relative decline in Japanese status. In the post-war era, the Japanese no longer employed the term *kaigun* to indicate their navy. Instead, they used the word *kaiji*, an abbreviation for *Kaijōjieitai* (literally, maritime force for self-defence). Compared to *kaigun*, the word *kaiji* had few, if any, evocative images. On this subject, Peattie and Evans too remarked that, compared to the pre-war Imperial Navy, the JMSDF had 'a modest role in cooperating with the U.S. Navy to preserve the security of Japan's home waters'. As they concluded, 'Never again will Japanese naval power be so visually impressive.'[31] Significantly, the use of a different term for the JMSDF reflected the normative limitations of the post-war Japanese military apparatus underlining the divide between the two naval forces. The implicit idea seemed to be that for Japan there was no alternative strategy to seeking naval supremacy, and no substitute for a navy that could not nurture Mahanian aspirations.

Yet, if the name and size of the navy had changed, the centrality of the navy to Japanese security had not. Today's JMSDF constitutes a vital component of one of the world's largest defence apparatus. Officials at the Japanese Ministry of Defence[32] stress that the navy constitutes Japan's 'first line of defence', for the archipelago's core strategic security concerns are determined by its archipelagic geography and its dependence on overseas supply of raw materials.[33] Naval power represents a core feature of Japanese security as it is essential to avoid disruptions of the sea lanes of communication (SLOCs) transporting the majority of the country's trade by value and volume, and more than 80 per cent of its energy – a dependence further increased in recent times after the shutdown in 2011 of the country's nuclear power plants.[34]

In contemporary Japan, the relevance of the navy to protect the nation's maritime economic arteries has the highest political recognition. In December 2012, only days after he had come into power, Japanese Prime Minister Abe Shinzō pointed out that 'Japan, as one of the oldest sea-faring democracies in Asia' was to 'play a greater role in preserving the common good' in the Indo-Pacific area.[35] A few months later, he further articulated on this idea, stressing that 'the peace and prosperity of Japan as a maritime nation have their origins in free, open, and peaceful seas. Based on a shift in thinking from "a country protected by the sea" to "a country that protects the sea," Japan is determined to maintain stable sea-lanes and defend our maritime interests within our territorial waters and EEZ while also upholding the order of free and open seas on the basis of the rule of law, opposing changes to the status quo predicated by force.'[36] In connecting the requirements of national security to the country's maritime geography, Prime Minister Abe re-emphasised a post-war understanding of Japan's dependence on the sea for its economic survival that draws its origins in the policies first set by Prime Minister Yoshida Shigeru.[37] As a recently retired Japanese flag officer put it, in post-war Japan the pursuit of a degree of sea power was 'a matter of national survival in a crisis or wartime'.[38]

The significance of the Japanese navy to national security pertains also to its contribution to other core functions of national defence, first and foremost, deterrence. The centrality of the fleet in preventing military incursions and missile threats in Japanese air and maritime spaces underscores this point.[39] The navy also sets the tone for national contributions to alliance requirements with the United States and international security. From the decades-long activities to patrol the Sea of Japan and the East China Sea in tandem with the United States Navy (USN), to the first deployment of minesweepers in the Persian Gulf in 1991, to the refuelling activities in the Indian Ocean and the anti-piracy operations in the Gulf of Aden in the 2000s, naval assets shaped the boundaries of Japan's contribution to regional and international stability. In a similar fashion, the promotion of navy-to-navy relations and confidence-building measures such as visit exchanges, joint exercises and maritime cooperation with other regional actors empowered the Japanese governments with an important means for cooperative forms of diplomacy.[40] Indeed, throughout the past decade and a half, the increased role of the Japanese navy as a tool of statecraft and its potential contribution to the evolving maritime balance of power in East Asia has not passed unnoticed in specialised literature.[41]

The core argument set forth in this book is that the success of the JMSDF in articulating its role as a tool of statecraft within a national maritime strategy rested on its ability to re-examine the imperial experience and the wartime defeat. Indeed, the book contends that the post-war navy cannot be understood outside the context of its process of interaction with the imperial past. This interaction between past and present informed matters of ethos and organisational culture; it shaped approaches to service strategy and national policy; it offered relevant doctrinal concepts and principles to maximise ship designs; it guided the development of public relations and professional education; and it offered the lenses the leadership of the Japanese navy used to process its working partnership with the US Navy. This book tells the story of how, throughout a period of sixty years, the post-war navy met the challenges of rearmament and modernisation to create a modern naval force that today stands as one of the pillars of the country's security policy. The book does not challenge the well-established idea that the working partnership with the United States was crucial in the material development of the navy. Rather, it seeks to complement this view by opening a window into the internal organisational dynamics of the JMSDF, offering a context to understand how the Japanese processed American assistance. In so doing, the book suggests that in the making of the post-war navy, the United States provided in many cases the bricks and the Imperial Navy the mortar and the blueprints.

The navy and its history: Uncovering new source materials

Investigating what exactly 'the mortar' and 'the blueprints' were about represented the single major challenge for this book, one that was only possible to overcome with access to new primary sources never made available to any researcher before and since. In Japan, there is no public access to post-war military archives. The historical research centre at the National Institute for Defence Studies (NIDS) in Tokyo contains archival materials on the modern period from the Meiji era to the end of the Pacific War. In the past, this meant that only James E. Auer – the first scholar to write on the JMSDF – was granted special access to Japanese naval documents from the occupation period and the 1950s by means of direct contacts between American and Japanese naval elites. Auer's ground-breaking work, however, did not lead to the establishment of a systematic archive for consulting Japanese naval documents. In a not too dissimilar fashion, I was granted exclusive, personal access to documentation held by the Education Section of the Personnel and Education Division of the JMSDF's Maritime Staff Office – the navy's governing body.

Personal ties developed with senior staff officers enabled me to have unfettered access to files on the navy's educational system, recruitment data, photographic materials, and copies of the Chiefs of Staff *New Instructions* for the period 1961–2012. The *New Instructions*, though not classified, have never been circulated outside the JMSDF. These documents proved to be invaluable in comprehending the extent to which the traditions and legacy of the Imperial Navy informed post-war naval policy, strategy and doctrine. In particular, their standing in the navy is equivalent to what is known as 'higher-level doctrine'. They served (and continue to serve) to establish the navy's material, human and spiritual priorities, to provide service members with a sense of common purpose and an understanding of the role of the organisation in national defence, and to motivate them to fight and defeat an enemy.[42] This set of documents enabled this book not merely to update the original research conducted by James Auer in the 1970s, but, more significantly, to uncover the internal dynamics governing the decision-making of the JMSDF to a depth unknown to previous research.

A second significant source of understanding of how service members – both individually and as an organisation – view their history and the influences upon it were the hundreds of hours spent in interaction and conducting interviews with the JMSDF. Across the navy, between November 2004 and July 2012, senior officers at the top of the command structure – including several Chiefs of Maritime Staff – and crews and officers of numerous surface units, at the Naval Academy in Etajima and at the Maritime Staff College in Tokyo, offered their precious time to answer my questions. In particular, formal interviews with four former chiefs of staff who introduced key organisational reforms between the end of the 1980s and 2005 were equally crucial. During the fieldwork activity, a number of events made me appreciate the support in terms of the time I was being given. On 9 April 2010, I was invited on board a Japanese destroyer in Sasebo for an interaction with its officers on the subject of Japanese maritime strategy and Sino-Japanese relations. Shortly after, Japanese news reported that on 8 April, a Chinese naval helicopter had flown just 90 m from another Japanese destroyer deployed in the East China Sea.[43] The event had happened only hours before my visit, yet the officers showed the utmost respect for our exchange. Last but by no means least, my interactions with the JMSDF benefited from a survey and focused interviews carried out with the students of the 2005 Command and Staff Course of the Maritime Staff College.

In terms of published documentation, the NIDS main library, which is located in a different part of the same military compound, though not open to the general public, contains the entire collection of the official histories published by the JSDF. In particular, on the occasion of the navy's fifty-year celebrations, the JMSDF produced a series of updated official histories of some of its key branches, including those of key institutions like the Maritime Staff College.[44] In addition, the library holds a number of unpublished research papers produced by the staff colleges, official and semi-official publications on military affairs in both English and Japanese and a multi-volume series of collected documents from different bodies of the American administration concerning US–Japan military relations, covering the period 1955–71. The ensemble of these sources contributed to the substance, depth and quality of this book. In particular, this book analysed these sources employing the methodology for the study of navies pioneered by authors like John Laughton and Julian Corbett, and applied to contemporary cases by Eric Grove and John Hattendorf.[45]

This wealth of new source materials sets this book apart from prior work on the subject. James Auer's *The Post-war Rearmament of Japanese Maritime Forces, 1945-71*, Peter Woolley's *Japan's Navy: Politics and Paradox, 1971-2000*, and Euan Graham's *Japan's Sea Lane Security, 1940-2004: A Matter of Life or Death?* looked at selective aspects of Japan's post-war naval problems to engage specific debates on East Asian security. In the works by Auer and Woolley, the JMSDF represented a case study to investigate the role of the US–Japan alliance in Japan's early post-war rearmament (Auer), and Japan's contribution through the alliance to regional security (Woolley). Both books highlighted the role of senior US Navy leaders in the Japanese naval rearmament and the centrality of navy-to-navy relations in the security partnership. These books – combined with other Japanese language secondary sources – offered invaluable information on the mechanics of the US–Japan naval relationship.[46] In more recent times, Elizabeth Guran's doctoral thesis *The Dynamics and Institutionalisation of the Japan-US Naval Relationship (1976-2001)* added an extra layer to the understanding of the cooperation between the two navies. In particular, it reviewed the impact of personalities against the process of institutionalisation of defence cooperation, making the point that the strength of the bilateral relationship owned more to the shared threat perceptions and agreed ways to tackle them than previously credited. Graham's book complemented these studies by exploring the role of sea-lane defence as a key notion in the wider Japanese national debate on security.

The existence of a solid literature analysing the US–Japan naval alliance, and the impact of the US navy on the development of the JMSDF, allowed this book to open a new avenue of research, focusing on the JMSDF as an organisation. The book departs from the existing research agenda to widen the understanding of the Japanese navy beyond the relational aspect with its American counterpart. It proposes a shift in the analytical focus by investigating the navy from within to understand the ways in which this key Japanese state institution debated the utility of the relationship with the United States. It further explores how the JMSDF weighted the importance of this relationship against the service overall priorities. In this context, the book examines how the imperial naval experience affected the way the JMSDF approached its roles and missions and, within that context, its relationship with the US Navy. One of the advantages of this approach concerns the possibility to place the experience of the JMSDF in the wider context of the impact of war on the transformation of military forces, offering an in-depth perspective on how one of the United States' closest military allies in East Asia looks at its strategic options and pursues its capabilities.

The naval focus of this book also meant that I did not include the Japan Coast Guard (JCG) in the analysis. Recently, the increasing role of the JCG in ensuring the safety of and access to the country's vast Exclusive Economic Zone (EEZ) prompted political scientists from the fields of Japanese and international security to shift the focus onto the impact of this organisation on Japan's overall military power. Richard Samuels' article '"New Fighting Power!" Japan's Growing Maritime Capabilities and East Asian Security' published in the Winter 2007 issue of *International Security*, Chris Hughes' *Japan's Remilitarisation*, and more recently, Lindsay Black's *Japan's Maritime Security Strategy: The Japan Coast Guard and Maritime Outlaws* are three prominent examples of academic interest in Japan's constabulary force. These works deserve credit for drawing the attention to the important policing and broader constabulary work of the JCG, effectively complementing the navy's military potential. Nonetheless, this book's analysis of the JMSDF attention to a combat-oriented *esprit de corps* and outlook are explanatory of why these two organisations remain very different in nature. These differences had a direct impact on the way the navy shaped its force structure, capabilities and doctrines, and on the reasons why a degree of caution should be exerted in regarding the JCG as a 'second navy'.

Outside the literature on the JMSDF, one book dealt with one of the core issues addressed in this book, that is, Japan's post-war military identity. Sabine Frühstück's *Uneasy Warriors: Gender, Memory, and Popular Culture in the Japanese Army* remains to date the only monograph focusing on this question, though in the past, book chapters or short articles treated the subject.[47] Frühstück's research drew upon views that emerged in the early post-war era arguing that the imperial military and naval pasts were no longer regarded as suitable models for a modern armed force, and that the spectre of any connection with the past raises deep-rooted fears for the resurgence of forms of militarism.[48] Indeed, the JSDF defined their aspiration to be a 'normal military' in the absence of professional traits from their imperial ancestors.[49] This was particularly evident in places of public display, in ceremonies, vocabulary, and discipline, where the JSDF deployed strategies to 'break with the past' to 'shed the legacy of the IJA (Imperial Japanese Army)'.[50] In examining the post-war military institutions, Frühstück's research proposed an innovative way to study their professional makeup based on an ethnographic methodology to develop an understanding of the ethos of individual soldiers. The emphasis put on this methodology came at the cost of an underestimation of the crucial role that hierarchy and organisational structures play in the development of military institutions. As a result, in the case of her study of the Japanese military, core questions pertaining to the educational system and professional socialisation process remained unexplored.

More significantly, this lack of engagement with organisational issues prevented her book from factoring in the specificities of the Japanese imperial military and naval experiences. By her own admission, the core of her research materials rested on interactions with personnel almost exclusively from the Japan Ground Self-Defence Force (JGSDF) because it 'is the largest branch of the JSDF (Japan Self-Defence Forces, ndr) and allocated the largest share of the defence budget'.[51] In fact, whereas the post-war army openly sought to distance itself from its imperial ancestor (as her investigation shows), the navy did the opposite, and sought to embrace its imperial past. Her study's general unawareness of Japanese military history and historiography prevented it from fully assessing how the past relates to the present, and how the modern Japanese armed forces are defined by distinctive services' subcultures. In this book, I focus on the naval experience, seeking to trace how such different perceptions about the imperial past were developed and how they informed the navy's organisational outlook.

None of these works has enjoyed the degree of access to official document records and other primary sources for the entire post-war period that underscored the making of this book. More importantly, the research questions set out in these works either uncritically assumed a rejection of the past (Frühstück) or did not investigate the extent of its impact on the organisation (Auer, Woolley, Graham). As a result, the Japanese post-war military appears in the literature as an organisation without a past and with a narrow professional focus on technical matters like equipment and platforms. This, in turn, diminishes its importance in terms of how it thinks about its profession and how it contributes to the defence policy process, articulating why it matters to Japanese security. This book takes a different path, looking at how the navy faced its imperial past to shape its professional outlook. In so doing, this book does not shy away from exploring the crucial issue of the imperial military traditions. It places them at the heart of the narrative in investigating how a key state institution engaged with the past to address the concerns of the present, and, in turn, how this past informed and continues to inform military change.

The useful history: The three themes of the book

In the landmark essay 'The Useful History', historian John Dower argued that the success of core post-war economic reforms had its origins in the dark years of the Showa era, for the Japanese of the post-war era 'may have undertaken to reinvent themselves; but they necessarily did so with the materials at hand'.[52] The year 1945 was not a 'zero hour' in the political and economic history of Japan. This rupture with the past still allowed for significant continuity to the point that the experience of post-war Japan could not be understood without addressing the role of the past in it. Indeed, as another leading historian of Japan remarked, national history in the country was a composed, evolving picture, one in which different groups of people, from politicians to intellectuals to the media and private companies, endeavoured to reconstitute the past for different purposes.[53] Surprisingly, within the historiography, the question of the imperial legacy on Japan's post-war military institutions remained relatively under-explored. Historians engaged with issues pertaining to how soldiers and veteran associations kept the past alive in the post-war period. But what about the military itself as an organisation? How did the military reconstruct its past – if at all – and to meet what ends?

Military organisations do not discard the 'materials at hand', for the relationship with the past has two core functional reasons. The first pertains to the realms of strategy and policy. In the face of the lack of experience in war, the study of past experience – one's own, or that of others – offers an invaluable source of professional understanding; 'what happened in the last war' helps to 'prepare for the next war' and meet the challenges of national defence. This is particularly true in the case of navies, where some authors argued that 'study, understanding, and experience' are core feature of their strategic culture, intended here as meaning their shared beliefs, values, and habits with regard to the use of force.[54] Napoleon is said to have well summarised this view, noting that 'an admiral commanding a fleet and a general commanding an army are men who need different qualities. One is born with qualities proper to command an army, while the necessary qualities to command a fleet are acquired only by experience.'[55]

The leaders of the JMSDF were no exception to this rule. As they set out to create a new navy and argue the navy's case in national defence they had a rich experience to explore – full of victories – but, crucially, distinguished by a terrible defeat in the last conflict. Understanding what had happened and engaging with it was essential for the success of the new organisation in the realms of policy and strategy. This is the first theme of this book. In the aftermath of the shock of complete defeat, Japanese naval authorities were faced with some fundamental issues like What were the causes of the defeat? Where did the navy fail and how could they seek to address these causes and failure? The answers to these questions differed depending on the particular aspect of the organisation. In terms of strategy, the first generation of JMSDF leaders came to believe that the causes of the defeat rested on a pre-war lack of appreciation of how war at sea could destroy the economic foundations of the Japanese state. This inability to foresee and adapt to the type of war the Imperial Navy came to fight, in turn, was considered to be a policy failure resulting from the bureaucratic competition with the army over budgetary resources. Indeed, pre-war naval policy failed to articulate a strategic view that looked beyond the service interests to preserve the fleet in the face of military expansion on continental Asia.

The leadership of the JMSDF endeavoured to change this. Domestic constraints on the use of force as a legitimate means to solve international disputes provided the framework within which the navy reviewed its case. Connecting naval policy and strategy to the protection of the economic foundations of the country's export-oriented economy, to the defence of its shipping routes and, in more recent times, its interests overseas, became a vital factor in the JMSDF strategic calculation. The examination of the strategy and policy failures of the pre-war and wartime organisation, therefore, shaped the way the JMSDF sought to articulate its role in the context of defence policy and the development of its fleet and capabilities.

The question of understanding defeat to address matters of policy and strategy was not, however, the only issue the JMSDF leadership had to face. The second theme of this book focuses on the second reason why military organisations do not discard the 'materials at hand'. In creating a new navy, its leadership had to shape its professional identity. For an organisation born under sociopolitical conditions that gave little to no credit to military institutions – indeed the use of military forces to wage war was not to be allowed by the constitution – the navy needed strong 'traditions' to define its martial pedigree. Traditions – it has been argued – are a 'set of practices, normally governed by overtly or tacitly accepted rules and of a ritual or symbolic nature, which seek to inculcate certain values and norms of behaviour by repetition, which automatically implies continuity with the past'.[56] In a naval context, traditions 'constitute the essence of heroic enterprise, moral fiber, pride in the service, and correct deportment'.[57] Navies are technology-intensive organisations operating in a highly challenging geophysical environment.[58] The skills and commitment of their personnel is critical to their effectiveness. Traditions that captured the essence of 'heroic behaviour' are essential to inspire the members of a naval organisation 'to do likewise'; to commit to their profession to the best of their abilities.[59] In operations, the memories of organisational traditions nurture the ability to cope with stress and tension and maintain relevant professional standards. Traditions empower members of a naval organisation with an ethos, an *esprit de corps*, that powers their ability to carry out the ultimate task: defending a nation.[60]

For the JMSDF, the Imperial Navy offered a deep reservoir of traditions. The defeat in the last war did not mean that the ethos of the Imperial Navy had nothing to offer to the new navy. The JMSDF did not merely reintroduced imperial traditions. It carefully selected ideas, ceremonies and practices that its leadership considered quintessential to the emergence of the Imperial navy as one of 'the' top navies worldwide. In terms of traditions, the Imperial Navy that entered the genetic code of the JMSDF was closer, as a model, to the organisation crafted during the Meiji and Taishō eras than to the one that had fought the last war. In daily routines, practices of imperial connotation were reintroduced on board ships. They encompassed vocabulary, names, drills, and the very organisation of the working day. Education and training followed the pre-war practice of combining intense physical exercise with 'spiritual education'. The development of doctrinal ideas was presented by naval leadership as following 'operational concepts' used by the Imperial Navy, while platform designs were informed by imperial notions pertaining to the maximisation of firepower and the homogeneity of speed. Equally significant, the JMSDF connected with the Imperial Navy's pre-war practice of introducing foreign technology, educational and doctrinal ideas – especially from the Royal Navy and its own working relationship with the US Navy. The JMSDF made sure that all its members knew how the choices underscoring its professional makeup connected to the pre-war force.

While it is understandable from an organisational perspective that the JMSDF wished to look at its imperial history to give credibility and substance to its identity, this does not explain how it was allowed to do it. After all, since the early stages of the occupation, the Japanese military had been largely discredited as a credible professional model. How was this, therefore, possible? The answer concerns the third theme of this book, the role of the forerunners of the JMSDF in contributing to the shaping of post-war public narratives of the Imperial Navy and of the JMSDF leadership in consolidating them. By the early 1950s, military men, either as individuals or through organisations, had started sharing their personal experiences with the wider public, some lobbying to support veterans and their families. In different guises, all these groups kept the war experience alive in the Japanese political and social debates of the time.[61] In the literature, a feeling of rejection of the imperial military past – expressed especially by Japanese intellectuals and those soldiers who had lived traumatic experiences while serving in the army – coexisted together with successful examples of reintegration of former personnel in Japanese politics and the JSDF.[62] In a context where the publication of the recollections and memories of former imperial army soldiers, particularly the army 'stragglers', had brought to public attention issues of bad leadership within the army, the narrative that emerged of the Imperial Navy provided a contrasting picture.[63]

The forerunners of the JMSDF and its leadership afterwards combined strong ties with key journalists and intellectuals that had either served in the navy or had been close to its top brass throughout their professional career, with consistent public relations campaigns. This allowed the emergence of a relatively homogeneous public memory of the Imperial Navy as a symbol of Japanese 'tradition and progress', one that played to the needs of the service. The JMSDF reintroduced elements of the Imperial Navy's propaganda and pageantry machinery in its public relations, projecting a self-image that spoke of the imperial connection. Mastering advanced technology by virtue of the upholding of 'traditional' values became a major component of how the JMSDF presented itself to the Japanese public. The JMSDF, working in tandem with retired imperial naval officers, embraced symbols of the imperial naval tradition like the battleship *Mikasa* and offered them to the wider public as physical evidence of the connection. Official museums and core events like the fleet reviews displayed the nature of strong link between the two institutions. These initiatives were designed to attain legitimacy within and outside the navy. They served to strengthen the JMSDF's own ethos and public acceptance and support of the navy and of its role in national defence. In a fashion not too dissimilar to the process that Aaron O'Connell described in the US Marine Corps, the JMSDF's involvement in the way the Imperial Navy was remembered and what it said about the JMSDF was an asset, 'supporting its internal cohesion and its institutional expansion'.[64]

These three themes are instrumental to comprehend why and how the JMSDF developed its representation and comprehension of the past. What is crucial about this process is that regardless of whether they have actively (by seeking an understanding or previous experience) or passively (by rejecting it to various degrees) engaged it, the choice and the motivations behind it are an indicator of a specific response. The imperial factor offset the negative impact of the loss of social status and reduced military functions and it helped to address past issues of organisational factionalism and strategic inflexibility. For these reasons though, while the legacy of the Imperial Navy is crucial to understand the JMSDF, the latter progressively developed into a very different force from the former. The story of this transformation is one of particular significance. From its modest beginning, the JMSDF fields today a fleet with a surface force more than twice the size of the Royal Navy's and a submarine component twice that of the French Navy. Structural circumstances including the different evolution of the regional security landscape and the bilateral ties with the United States naturally mattered. Yet, this book explains how past experience guided the navy's organisational response to the national and regional environments and contributed to its ability to secure a prominent role in the country's national defence.

The layers of the cake: The book's structure

If one compares national history to a cake, with its different political, social, cultural and economic layers, naval history represents a slice of it. The study of navies requires an engagement with the various layers to comprehend their inner workings. This book is no exception and the rest of the text is structured accordingly. In terms of timeline, the narrative pre-eminently focuses on the period from the establishment of the Maritime Safety Force (MSF) in 1952–2004, though evidence presented in the different chapters highlights how reflections upon the imperial experience have been contextual, selective and in some cases entered Japanese professional debate well before 1952. As such, some of the chapters integrate earlier debates in the narrative. In a way, the objective of this book is to demonstrate the existence of a process of analysis, rather than to determine its boundaries.

The next chapter sets out the broader context of the book by exploring the nature and purpose of the imperial naval traditions. An observation of how the Imperial Navy set out its own traditions offers a remarkable similarity with the challenges that the JMSDF faced a little less than a century later. The chapter highlights how the Imperial Navy was marked throughout its history by the constant necessity to reconcile structural deficiencies and limited resources with ambitious strategic objectives. The fighting skills of its men and the quality of its assets became factors of paramount importance in the navy's quest for combat effectiveness. The chapter shows what factors underpinned the ethical glue which cemented the navy's *esprit de corps* and critically inspired its members to pursue excellence and secure operational successes 'against heavy odds'. Iconic symbols of Japan's regional seafaring heritage, samurai martial legacy and imperial ideology as well as British practices and approaches to seamanship were all eventually instrumental to the development of a modern professional force. *Mutatis mutandis*, when faced with similar dilemmas, the JMSDF had an important foundation upon which it could address them.

Yet, before exploring how the JMSDF recovered past traditions, Chapter 3 takes the narrative into the world of public memory. One factor that facilitated the JMSDF's process of selection and maintenance of past traditions was the existence of a public narrative that presented the positive aspects of the imperial naval experience. Against a general post-war context in which the armed forces lost all credibility, narratives highlighting the qualities of the Imperial Navy as a military organisation created a divide between the way the army and the navy were remembered. The chapter examines this naval narrative as it was popularised in the categories of journalism, literature and non-fiction novels by three authors: Itou Masanori, Agawa Hiroyuki and Agawa Naoyuki. The chapter shows how their personal and professional backgrounds gave them unique access and knowledge of both the Imperial Navy and the JMSDF. It also demonstrates that by cooperating with authors they respected professionally and trusted at the human level, Imperial Navy and JMSDF senior officers had the opportunity to benefit from these representations of the navy.

In light of the findings of Chapter 3, Chapter 4 examines the role of imperial traditions in the development of the JMSDF's educational system. It argues that internally, imperial traditions offered the raw materials against which the JMSDF defined its values and beliefs as a military organisation, its assumptions about the navy's function in national defence, and set the benchmark for its professional standards. In particular, like their counterparts in the imperial service, the JMSDF's top echelons used traditions from Japan's pre-war naval experience to maintain a sense of inner cohesiveness in the face of the adoption of American practices and technology. Imperial traditions allowed the JMSDF to remain 'a Japanese navy' in its spirit. Similarly, as major structural reforms were introduced in the post-war military system, especially the creation of a 'joint' academy training all future officers regardless of their service affiliation, the Imperial Navy enabled the JMSDF to give its officer corps a distinctive sense of self.

The distinctive character of the Japanese navy is further examined in the image the JMSDF projected outwardly. Chapter five focuses on the relationship between imperial traditions and the JMSDF's public image. In a country that for the majority of the post-war period gave little attention to its armed forces, the JMSDF actively engaged in embracing rituals and practices from the Imperial Navy in its public relations activities to build up its professional image. It enlisted memories of the naval past, as explored in previous chapters, as a strategic resource to introduce a wider Japanese audience to its professional qualities and corporate spirit. The JMSDF initially focused on ceremonies that emphasised professional and ethical categories like technological sophistication and traditional Japanese values. This choice enabled the navy to project a positive image without touching upon the more controversial aspects of the imperial tradition. Fleet reviews or short cruises became the service's main public relation currency. After the end of the Cold War, greater attention of the Japanese public required the navy to widen its public relations. The chapter reviews the representations of the service's professional identity in the *lieus de la mémoire*, the JMSDF's three service's museums.

The single most crucial area where the imperial experience had to be reviewed concerned matters of policy and strategy. Chapter 6 reassesses the circumstances informing the JMSDF analysis of the wartime experience, initially distinguished by direct ties between the leadership of the two services. Both domestic and systemic circumstances informed the post-war navy. The chapter details how pre-war service priorities limited the navy's wider understanding of the relationship between naval policy and national strategy. This, in turn, became an issue of which the JMSDF became painfully aware. This awareness in part came from the existence of severe legal and political constraints imposed upon the defence policy-making process. The need to articulate a case for the navy that met the requirements of these new circumstances was central to the JMSDF's ability to look beyond immediate concerns on matters of capabilities and doctrines. Eventually, the service took a different path, learning from the mistakes of the imperial past how to make a case for a naval service that could serve Japanese post-war security in the widest possible sense.

Chapter 7 takes the broader considerations on politics and strategy of the previous chapter into the realm of the difficulties of developing a fleet. The chapter investigates the evolution of doctrines, capabilities and force structure in the post-war period. It shows that the JMSDF initially applied doctrinal notions that had made the Imperial Navy an exceptional fighting force to rebuild its basic professional standards. In seamanship and fleet handling, the Imperial Navy set an aspirational benchmark. Accordingly, such an approach informed procurement policies and designs. Progressively, the leadership of the JMSDF modified the content of its doctrine to address evolving mission requirements, though it maintained imperial formulas to deliver them seeking to promote change within an established tradition. The chapter analyses the extent to which this approach required compromises in certain areas of capabilities, while the priority of matters of firepower inherent to the design process of the Imperial Navy persisted in the post-war era as well.

The book's conclusions draw together the ideas developed in the previous chapters offering a brief look at the developments of the past decade. The period from 2004 to 2014 witnessed a number of changes in Japanese defence policy. For the JMSDF, this period was characterised by a much-increased operational tempo compared to the Cold War. From the patrol and surveillance in the East China Sea to the contribution to international missions and diplomacy, the Japanese navy has become – if anything else – a much more crucial tool of statecraft. The ability to adapt to the new circumstances and deliver security had a lot to do with the experience of the previous sixty years. Its ethos rich in imperial traditions provided its members with a strong sense of purpose. The re-examination of wartime failures had prompted a better understanding of the symbiotic relationship linking the navy to the pursuit of national interests. Hence, the ultimate question: Has today's JMSDF succeeded in taking the legacy of the Imperial Navy forward?

2

Ethos and Traditions: The Navy of Imperial Japan

We must provide, first, a determination that no matter how grim a situation might become, one must never give up, and second, a strong bond of fellowship with one's brother officers. Imperial Navy traditions are maintained day-to-day at Etajima not for their own sake, but to foster these qualities.[1]

Vice Admiral Tamura Yūtaka, JMSDF
(Superintendent, Officer Candidate School)

The drive for 'a strong bond of fellowship'

Admiral Yūtaka's words well capture the essence of the task that the forerunners of the JMSDF faced when they set out to establish a new navy, one similar to that of their Meiji ancestors. In both cases, a small group of individuals aimed to create a modern military organisation. In both cases, they believed that an effective, professional navy needed more than just powerful assets. It needed a soul, an *esprit de corps*. Neither group was doing something unexpected. The core business of a navy is the application of military force within the given legal and operational boundaries set by political authorities. A navy entrusted with the defence of a country has to physically and psychologically prepare its members to man a fleet to fight and, if necessary, risk injuries or worse to fulfil their task. Its officer corps has to lead crews during both war and peace. For the leaders of both organisations, an ethos and a set of traditions were, therefore, quintessential to create, sustain and enhance a modern navy.

This chapter explores how the Imperial Navy created the country's first naval ethos and traditions. These were forged in the wake of the 1868 Meiji restoration[2] under the aegis of the slogan 'Japanese spirit, Western knowledge'.[3] The slogan was not created with the navy in mind, but it could not be more appropriate for an organisation that placed at the heart of its profession the mastering of technology that mid-nineteenth century Japan did not possess.[4] For the samurai elites of Meiji Japan this was no trifling challenge. Yet, like other Meiji oligarchs engaged in the establishment of modern state institutions, the first generation of naval leaders demonstrated 'an extraordinary sense of self-reliance, a fierce determination to maintain independence, and an almost religious belief in (their) distinctive identity'.[5] For them, the establishment of a new navy required the creation of an ethos and traditions that could perform two crucial functions. On the one hand, they were meant to validate the value of the country's martial past and reconcile it with the adoption of Western techniques in order to empower the nation with an adequate means of defence. The implicit logic was that Western technology and practices produced best results if they sublimated Japan's martial spirit. On the other hand, ethos and traditions provided the spiritual glue to inspire in Japanese naval personnel the pursuit of excellence and operational success 'against heavy odds'.[6] The latter aspect was particularly relevant for the Japanese navy, an organisation that remained marked, throughout its history, by the constant need to balance structural deficiencies and limited resources with ambitious strategic objectives.[7]

Reinventing the regional maritime heritage

In the opening lines of a 1945 study of early modern Japanese sea power, Arthur J. Marder took note of an old popular belief which set the origins of the Japanese naval tradition in mythological terms, noting how 'the life blood of Japan is the water of the sea'.[8] In fact, the popularisation of the notion of a manifest Japanese destiny at sea[9] started in the second half of the 1880s. This was largely the product of the Imperial Navy's comprehensive effort in the early stages of its existence to construct a national maritime consciousness, mobilising press and publications to build up its internal cohesion, public prestige, and to maintain political and budgetary capital.[10] As an authoritative study recently pointed out, 'Through pageantry, pomp, propaganda, and commemoration, the navy cultivated interest in and support for the navy at the rice-roots level'.[11] Propaganda activities took on a new level after the navy's victorious performance in the Russo-Japanese War, and similar ideas were still widely spread in the early 1930s. In the words of what Marder regarded as a popular naval history of the time:

> The archipelago of emerald isles which stretches a thousand ri[12] north and south in the Pacific is our native land, and the vast blue sea is the eternal cradle of our race. We live on the sea, we die on the sea. Since the foundation of the State, no, since the birth of the nation, our country and our people have placed their faith in the impossibility of being separated from the sea. A maritime country! A maritime people![13]

Mythological references and propaganda notwithstanding, the emergence of the modern Japanese navy in the second half of the nineteenth century was not connected to a 'natural vocation' based on a longstanding national maritime tradition. Rather, the contrary was true. In early modern Japanese history, the sea had operated pre-eminently as a defensive shield from invasions, not as a platform for national naval affirmation. The archipelago stood relatively isolated from continental affairs and, crucially, its rulers had little need for a standing naval force.[14] The self-sufficiency of local economies across the archipelago further reduced incentives for the creation of such a force.[15] No events epitomised the virtues of Japan's maritime isolation like the two failed attempts of invasion by Kublai Khan in 1274 and 1281. In particular, the 'divine' intervention of a tremendous typhoon on 15–16 August 1281, celebrated later as a 'divine wind of Ise',[16] proved the 'stopping power' of the sea and the challenge for any invading armada to reach Japan. Paraphrasing a comment on the failed invasion of England by King Philip II of Spain in 1588, maritime isolation allowed Japanese rulers to think that a divine wind was a sufficient option to defend the archipelago. 'God blew and they were scattered.'[17]

As a tool of foreign policy too, Japanese feudal rulers came to experience the difficulties of overcoming the maritime confines surrounding Japan to project national power. The ill-fated 1592 and 1597 expeditions against Korea organised by the feudal supreme warlord, or *Shōgun*, Toyotomi Hideyoshi, represented the only two naval campaigns of the period before a series of seclusion policies[18] were enacted in 1636.[19] For some 300 years, overseas navigation fell into oblivion and no real naval force existed beyond the borders of a few local dominions.[20] Indeed, the naval traditions that had previously flourished at the hands of regional families and sea lords[21] in the Inland Sea of Japan and in the Hizen (northwest) and Satsuma (southwest) provinces of Kyūshu slowly went into decay (Figure 2.1).[22] During the *sakoku*, only the Shimazu family of Satsuma (present Kagoshima) retained a degree of naval traditions and capabilities by virtue of its trade connections overseas, especially with mainland China through the Ryūkyū Islands.[23]

In light of this, it should come as no surprise that with the process of military modernisation implemented throughout the Meiji restoration, Japan's seafaring regions positioned themselves in the driving seat in the construction of a 'national naval vision'. In practical terms, the leading domains from Kyūshu, notably those in Satsuma, Fukuoka and Saga, were among the few to possess naval forces and therefore could contribute to the bulk of the eighty-three warships that came to constitute the new navy.[24] More importantly, a handful of samurai oligarchs associated with what had *de facto* represented Japan's most advanced maritime dominion, Satsuma, were among the first to realise that Japan needed to acquire a degree of naval capabilities as a way to defend its sovereignty against the encroachment of Western powers.[25] As a leading faction of the group of reformers who contributed to ending the Tokugawa shogunate, they subsequently manoeuvred in order to promote naval expansion in the context of the newly established political authority.[26]

Pragmatism motivated their approach to Japan's military problem. They saw in the adoption of foreign organisational models an essential step towards achieving 'equality' with Western military powers.[27] Such an approach stemmed from a series of three events that, in the final years of the Tokugawa's rule, critically exposed the country's maritime vulnerability, enabling Satsuma reformers to measure the importance of a modern naval force. The first was the arrival in 1853 of an American flotilla of 'black ships'[28] under the command of Commodore Matthew C. Perry, US Navy. The second concerned the 1861 Russian naval attempt to take control of the island of Tsushima frustrated only by the intervention of two British warships. The third consisted of the British bombardment and burning of the port of Kagoshima in 1863, highlighted the renewed potential of the foreign challenge from the sea.[29]

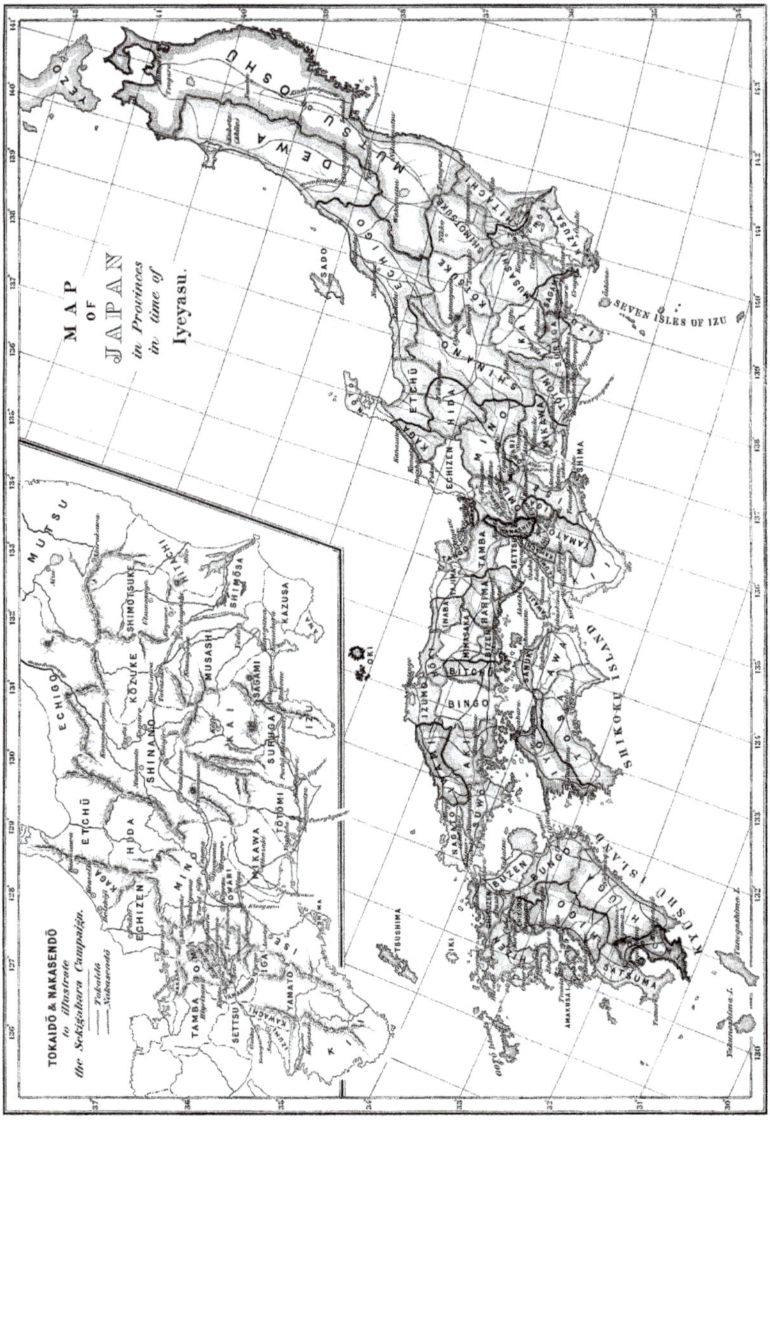

Map 1 Tokugawa Japan.

Source: http://www.fas.harvard.edu/~chgis/japan/images/japan_1573_1583.gif

Among those who realised the capability of Western naval technology during the bombardment was a very young Tōgō Heihachirō. According to one biography, it was also on that occasion that the future admiral came to the conclusion that 'the defence of a coast line begins at sea'.[30]

In the following decades, influential men from the former dominion of Satsuma like Kawamura Sumiyoshi, Saigō Tsugumichi and Yamamoto Gombei, or Gonnohyōe (no relation to Admiral Yamamoto Isoroku), took the lead in national naval affairs.[31] Even though those who governed the service at the beginning were pre-eminently samurais with limited or no professional naval background, they were all determined to succeed in transforming Japan into a naval power capable of safeguarding its independence and interests.[32] From the gestational stage, Admiral Kawamura laid the foundations of the logistical infrastructure and capabilities of the new navy as an efficient and dynamic administrator. In turn, under his leadership and that of other members of the faction, until the beginning of the twentieth century, Satsuma men uninterruptedly held key operational and administrative positions in the Imperial Navy. From 1881 to 1906, members of the 'Satsuma faction' continuously headed the Navy Ministry, moulding Japan's ascendancy in the business of naval warfare.[33]

The presence of a seemingly homogenous and pragmatic group of individuals orchestrating the development of the navy proved to be a relevant factor insofar as the service was able to cohesively lobby for naval expansion. Similarly, they could prioritise and effectively implement investments and reforms instrumental to the creation of a modern fighting force in an era of major changes in naval technology.[34] This was even more significant since the Japanese navy was part of a military system in which the army was considered the senior service.[35] In the early Meiji period, the navy's ancillary role was in fact formalised in two ways. First, in wartime, the navy was operationally subordinated to the army general staff. Second, in terms of missions, the army was responsible for the overall national defence,[36] while the navy was more narrowly tasked with maritime security.[37] With the progressive expansion of the naval service, the internal cohesion provided by the Satsuma leadership was a major reason for the relative improvement of status vis-à-vis the army, culminating with the eventual establishment in 1893 of an independent naval staff.[38]

In the process of constructing the navy's fighting pedigree, the prominence of leading figures from Kyūshū, and from the area of Kagoshima in particular, resulted in the imposition of a distinctive 'Satsuma character' on the service's traditions and identity. The region's longstanding military seafaring heritage combined with its active role in the military campaigns of the Meiji restoration offered a suitable combination. Initially, this stemmed from a patronage system that favoured representatives from within the faction leading to a capillary presence of Satsuma men throughout the entire organisation.[39] When, in the first decades of the twentieth century the original Satsuma powerbase lost its influence in the service's internal politics, the regional appeal of the naval service among young Japanese aspiring to a military career remained high. In the late 1920s, the navy was still composed of volunteers coming from the coastal regions of Hokkaidō or Kyūshu, most likely because they could adapt more easily to the harsh requirements of life at sea.[40] The region of Kyūshū, headed by the provinces of Kagoshima, Saga and Ōita continued to constitute a recruitment area of considerable significance for the navy's officer corps and manpower. As late as 1936, 30 per cent of the total of intake of the naval academy was from Kyūshū, a proportion higher than any other area of Japan. While data varied throughout the years, an analysis of the number of applicants and actual intakes at the naval academy suggests that young Japanese from the region of Kyūshū maintained a constant motivation, often providing up to a third of the navy's officer corps new recruits (Figure 2.1).

More broadly, the 'Satsuma spirit' stood as an example of the numerous important pre-unification seafaring traditions and, in that respect, it became an inclusive rather than an exclusive factor. Indeed, pride in pre-unification seafaring military traditions was a primary motivation among young applicants from other maritime regions too. In the 1960s, a senior captain veteran from all major surface engagements of the Pacific War who enrolled in the academy in 1918 recalled that though he had submitted applications to both the military and naval academies, he harboured a clear preference for the navy, because his 'spirit was simply responding to the tradition of (his) ancestral region (i.e. Takamatsu, in the Inland Sea)'.[41] A recent biography of another officer known for his exploits in the Pearl Harbour raid and against the British Eastern Fleet in 1941, and again at Midway in 1942, pointed out that the connection between the inland coasts of the Hiroshima prefecture and the famous Murakami's family of sea lords had reinforced his dream of becoming a naval officer.[42]

Traces of the navy's 'regional' character permeated its most elementary daily practices and official lexicon. On board Japanese warships, formal communications were passed on by speaking fast and using simple, direct words in a fashion typical of the inhabitants from the area of Kagoshima. In principle, this would seem an obvious choice for a naval organisation as it favoured the required levels of functionality and efficiency. Yet, in the Japanese case, this gave the service a very distinctive character. Satsuma was 'a proud, pugnacious province, noted for its beautifully rugged nature – a province whose relation to Japan is not unlike that of Ireland to Great

	1910		1930		1936	
	Applicants	Intakes	Applicants	Intakes	Applicants	Intakes
Fukuoka	101	2	292	1	352	12
Ōita	64	6	111	9	148	6
Saga	101	5	209	5	292	6
Kumamoto	100	4	220	7	300	8
Miyazaki	31	-	66	3	99	7
Nagasaki	NA*	NA*	123	3	181	1
Kagoshima	112	3	304	9	461	32
Total National	2,958	120	4,199	130	6,847	240
Kyūshū(%)	(17.2%)**	(16.6%)**	(31.5%)	(28.4%)	(26.7%)	(30%)

*NA: Data Not Available
**Data from Nagasaki area are not included

Figure 2.1 Number of students from Kyūshū at the Japanese Naval Academy.

Source: Bōei Kensyūjo Senshishitsu [presently Bōei Kenkyūjo Senshibu], *Kaigunshō Nenpō* (海軍省年俸 – Yearbook of the Navy Ministry, Various Years, Tokyo: Bōei Kensyūjo, 1983).

Britain'. In particular, while 'its inhabitants constituted no separate race like the Celts, they clung proudly to their native dialect, which was virtually incomprehensible to other Japanese'.[43]

Hence, in light of the sophistication of Japanese formal language, the decision to introduce a vocabulary and a method of delivery which reflected clear linguistic ties with the birthplace of the navy's founding fathers and of one of the nation's celebrated regional seafaring traditions helped to define the organisation's heritage. It is significant that today the same language continues to be used onboard JMSDF units. An informed guest is struck by how the elemental operational needs requiring clear and precise communications create, in such a context, a resilient, underlying connection to the regional origins of the navy.[44] In the words of novelist Shiba Ryōtarō, on land, Japan's national character was largely associated with the personal ties that the army core leadership had with the former dominion of Chōshū.[45] At sea, the nation's tradition reflected the image of the 'Satsuma of the sea'.[46]

Shaping the Wakon (Japanese) spirit

The Satsuma character was significant for another important contribution to the construction of Japan's modern naval ethos. It connected the service with the system of values embraced by the samurai leaders from that region who helped shape the process of transformation of the Meiji era. Among them, Saigō Takamori was certainly one of the most emblematic, embodying in both physical appearance and spirit the ideal of the Japanese martial figure *par excellence*.[47] Saigō, an imposing, broad-shouldered man more than six feet tall, was born into a samurai family of modest social ranking in which he was educated to honour the ancient Satsuma military values combining dignified frugality with valour and independence.[48] Saigō's star rose to prominence during the victorious Satsuma-led anti-shogunate military campaign and reached its momentum when he was nominated Commander of the armed forces in 1872 and appointed the unique rank of Field Marshal in 1873. In the following months, he grew dissatisfied with the anti-samurai laws of the new government and its policies towards Korea. He went into exile, before starting a movement that almost brought the country to the verge of civil war as a result of a major uprising in 1877.[49]

Saigō's astonishing rise in the ranks of the new ruling elite and dramatic fall fighting against it culminated with his death after a crushing defeat in the Battle of Shiroyama (24 September 1877). His lifestyle reflected a philosophy encapsulated in the expression 'revere heaven, love mankind',[50] one centred on the Confucian principles of respect for (imperial) authority and those demanding from the warrior a sense of justice and compassion vis-à-vis the weak and less fortunate members of society.[51] He was a traditional samurai figure for he lived to set an example by upholding the values of compassion, frugality, independence and unyielding commitment even in the face of death. He was also a 'pragmatic' patriot, one who had initially rejected Western ideas and eventually understood, in the aftermath of the 1863 bombardment of his hometown Kagoshima, the importance of modern industrial technology to combat the West.[52]

After his demise, he was officially listed as a traitor by governmental authorities. This decision was reversed in 1889 as Saigō's charisma and ethical line of conduct had a powerful grip on popular imagination, transforming him into one of Japan's most loved national heroes. While not without faults or misgivings (he was an ardent xenophobe and staunch supporter of the military conquest of Korea), Saigō Takamori well summarised the dilemma of a changing nation, striving to blend together elements of the 'old' and 'new' systems. More importantly, he was a public icon. His respect for the rightful power of the Emperor as a unifying national figure, his active support for peasants and the poor and his loyalty towards the Japanese nation as a whole defined his stature. In this regard, the drama of his ultimate failure assumed a heroic and 'noble' dimension with attributes that continued to inspire the devotion of the nation's military men well into the twentieth century. As Ivan Morris noted, 'During the Pacific War the kamikaze suicide pilots were given the name *kikusui*,[53] and these men revered the "death-defying Saigō" as their spiritual ancestor'.[54]

As an influential samurai from Satsuma and prominent reformer of the early Meiji era, Saigō became a source of inspiration for the members of the emerging armed forces, and though he was never directly involved with the navy, the first generation of its top echelons shared his Satsuma experience and samurai background. Admiral Kawamura, who was born in the same area of Kagoshima, knew him personally and was in fact sent by the government to persuade him to surrender before the outbreak of the hostilities in early 1877. Saigō's brother, Tsugumichi, was an influential Navy Minister and, for many years, a key figure within the service, physically impressive and with the character of 'the hero in the traditional mould' like Saigō.[55] These individuals impressed on the navy a similar ethos, though they made it a point to show their disagreement with Saigō's ways. Thus, unlike in the army, where a number of midlevel Satsuma men volunteered to serve in Saigō's ranks, no naval officer resigned to join his cause in 1877.[56] Saigō's legacy rested primarily on the values he embodied as a samurai, and as one head of the JSDF's recruitment centre for the Kagoshima Prefecture – usually a naval officer – recently noted, resonance of the appreciation for Saigō's persona and ideals still permeates today's profound connection between the navy and the people of Kagoshima.[57]

A major point of disagreement with Saigō's actions derived from the fact that the navy's fabric might have been regional in its origin, but it was created to embody a national institution. The values of the former leading samurai class were extended to the whole nation to strengthen its fighting ethos and unity, not to subvert the system.[58] In the words of Edward Drea, the mobilisation of a mythical warrior ethos represented 'government and army devices to promote the morale of a conscript force that neither the civil nor military leaders held in much regard'.[59] Yamagata Aritomo, the Chōsū army leader and Meiji statesman who chiefly manoeuvred to engineer Japan's modern military ethos, found in an Emperor-centred armed force the key catalyst for this process. This would prevent – in his view – the break-up of the national polity 'into independent units or its partition among foreign powers'.[60] In 1882, he formalised this idea in a document containing five cardinal tenets governing the conduct of the members of Japan's imperial armed forces in what became known as the Emperor's Rescript.[61] These were based on the Confucian notions of loyalty,[62] courtesy,[63] valour,[64] fidelity[65] and simplicity.[66] In this way, the army and navy came to be the custodians of the spirit laying at the foundations of the old martial tradition in a new 'imperial' sense, and as agents of the Emperor they defended the entire nation.[67]

In the Rescript, loyalty to the supreme national authority, the Emperor, was of paramount importance for the imperial armed forces. Without loyalty, even the best-trained crews with access to the most modern warships would still be 'no better than a rabble'. Loyalty was a serviceman's supreme duty and ultimate source of strength. Both were essential to carry out the extremely delicate task that the imperial armed forces were entrusted with, namely the 'protection of the nation'.[68] Loyalty nurtured a sense of duty that outweighed death in the same way a 'mountain' was weightier than a 'feather'. It was through an unyielding loyalty towards the Emperor that the men of the imperial armed forces were to find the necessary strength to act.[69]

Accordingly, in the Imperial Navy, the very imperial loyalty Saigō had fought and died for became a central feature of the service's traditions. Each ship in the fleet had a portrait of the Emperor. All crewmembers would pay homage to it on national holidays, and even put their lives at risk rescuing it in case the ship was to be abandoned.[70] Capital ships were systematically named after ancient Japanese provinces related to places of unique Japanese symbolism such as Ise or Hyūga (where there are two temples dedicated to the Goddess Amaterasu – a central figure in Japan's national religion, *Shintō*), or elements of nature. Both were tributes to the 'animistic' nature of *Shintō*, and to its connection with the Imperial family (Figure 2.2).[71] The Japanese metaphorically sailed under Imperial aegis as the naval ensign itself was designed featuring a rising sun positioned on the left side emanating sixteen beacons, a number equal to that of the leaves of the chrysanthemum symbol of the Emperor. A Japanese warship was an extension of the Imperial authority.

Class of Warships	Description
Aircraft Carriers	Named after mythical flying objects, animals, or large birds.* Ex.: Hiryū (飛龍–Flying Dragon), Shōkaku (翔鶴-Flying Crane)
Battleships	Named after ancient provinces.** Ex.: Yamato (大和), Ise (伊勢)
Heavy Cruisers	Named after mountains. Ex.: Mogami (最上), Myōkō(妙高)
Light Cruisers	Named after rivers. Ex.: Agano (阿賀野), Isuzu (五十鈴).
Destroyers (First Class)	Named after meteorological phenomena. Ex.: Hatsuyuki (初雪–First Snow), Shimakaze (島風–Island Wind)
Destroyers (Second Class)	Named after trees, flowers, fruits. Ex.: Sanae (早苗–Rice Seedling), Sakura (桜-Cherry)

*Kaga and Akagi were named after a province and a mountain, respectively, and represented an exception. The explanation is that they were initially converted from a battleship and a crusier.
**The battleships Haruna, Kongō, Kirishima and Hiei had mountain names as they were originally designed as battle cruisers.

Figure 2.2 Name classification of warships in the Imperial Navy.

Source: Paul S. Dull, *A Battle History of the Imperial Japanese Navy, 1941–1945* (Annapolis, MD: Naval Institute Press, 1978), 369; Hara, *Japanese Destroyer Captain*, 18–19.

Hector Bywater, one of the leading naval analysts of the first decades of the twentieth century, remarked that in the Japanese navy, patriotism and loyalty to the Emperor took the 'form of a religion and their devotion to duty' was very marked.[72] These values were celebrated in the more informal aspects of the naval profession. For instance, the song young cadets learnt throughout their formative years in Etajima and generally sung while performing sports, in summer camps and excursions, or in ceremonies, invited them to reflect on expressing their loyalty as follows:

Our hearts throb more and more with the hot blood
Of the sons of the Sacred Land.
We shall never stop scarifying ourselves
To defend the glorious foundations of our country.[73]

The words of the navy's official song struck a similar tone, conveying what was regarded as the standard ethical attitude of each serviceman vis-à-vis the purpose of his profession:

Across the sea, corpses in the water;
Across the mountain, corpses in the field;
I shall die only for the Emperor,
I shall never look back.[74]

From an organisational perspective, loyalty was a key component of the navy fighting spirit (and of the army's) because it was the source of military authority. As formalised in the 1889 Japanese constitution – itself inspired by Imperial Germany – the Emperor was the supreme commander of the nation's military apparatus. Through his mandate, the chiefs of staff of the two services held the 'right of supreme command' in the daily routine of the services, and their actions were carried out in the name of Emperor. Loyalty was the glue upon which the relationship between the throne and the military institutions rested and indeed, the Imperial armed forces as state organisations did not depend on civilian authority.[75] Apart from budgetary matters they were accountable only to the Emperor and he directly nominated their top representatives (Figure 2.3).[76] When the new armed forces were set up, such an organisational choice reflected the need for an apparatus that was meant to have in the imperial authority its highest (and only) source of legitimisation.[77]

While the notion of loyalty embraced the unifying reasons behind the purpose of the modern Japanese military, the remaining four tenets focused on the characteristics members of the imperial armed forces were to cultivate to succeed in their profession. Courtesy addressed a key feature of Japanese culture, namely that of vertical and horizontal relationships, in the specific context of military hierarchies.[78] On the backdrop of an 'animistic' description of Japanese military institutions,[79] the navy was to be one 'harmonious body' in which those 'inferior in rank and juniors must pay respect to their superiors and seniors even though not under their immediate control'. Consistent with this principle, superiors had to 'treat their inferiors with as much kindness and consideration as possible'.[80] As the third tenet listed in the Rescript, valour in the accomplishment of one's duty, without 'despising small numbers of the enemy

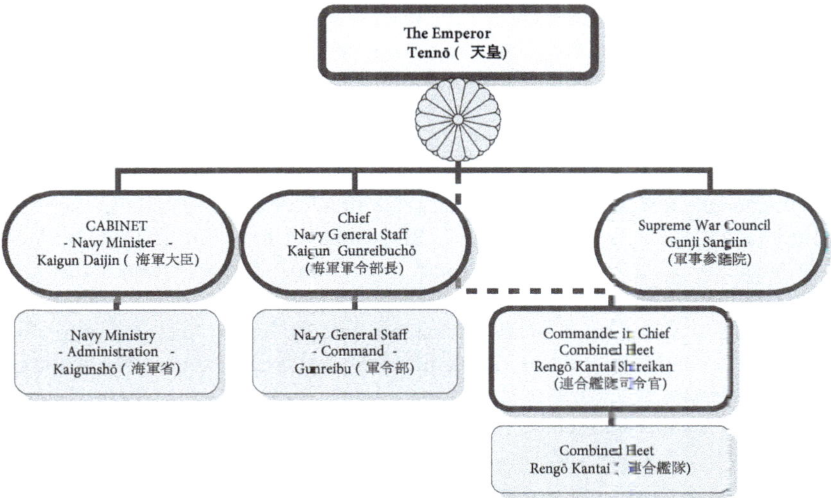

Figure 2.3 Command structure (1889 Japanese constitution).

Source: Adapted from Evans and Peattie, *Kaigun*, 27.

nor fearing large numbers' had its main *raison d'être*. Such a form of courage dismissed 'mere impetuosity to violent action' which only attracted wider social disapproval. Fidelity highlighted the requirement for all members of the armed forces to show faithfulness, or 'the keeping of one's word', and conscientiousness, 'the true performance of one's duty'. Finally, simplicity referred to the ability of uniformed men to endure a Spartan lifestyle, made up of simple and frugal endeavours. This was instrumental to avoid fondness for 'luxurious and extravagant ways' that would privilege selfishness, eventually preventing loyalty and valour from being fully pursued.[81]

In the navy, harsh discipline, intense training and spiritual education[82] became the main ingredients for achieving such high aims. Rear Admiral Tomioka Sadatoshi, who served as Operations Section Chief at the Naval General Staff from 1940 to 1943, recalled that at the Academy, cadets had 'a forcefully disciplined life with no leeway whatsoever'.[83] At the academy, for the majority of the year, cadets would wake up at 5.30 am and go to bed at 9.30 pm, after a long day of 'very strenuous' exercise, comprising Spartan early morning cutter rowing at 6.00 am martial arts, swimming, battery work, signalling, just to mention a few activities, and a 'heavily loaded' course timetable.[84] This helped cadets to 'steel their minds' and master the navy's demanding requirements for training and discipline, something of a professional trademark. In the fleet, such a tradition inspired expressions familiar, even today, to any Japanese seaman, such as *Getsu-getsu-ka-sui-moku-kin-kin*,[85] literally meaning that in the navy, the week had no weekend and was composed of just 'Monday, Monday, Tuesday, Wednesday, Thursday, Friday, Friday'.[86]

At the academy, and throughout the fleet, martial arts like *kendō* (Japanese fencing),[87] *judō*,[88] *jukenjutsu* (Japanese bayonet practice)[89] and *kyūdō* (Japanese archery)[90] were regularly practised. The attention of these practices to samurai-like methods of training instilling self-discipline and self-effacing dedication defined their main character-building functions.[91] Another peculiar practice at the academy to develop endurance and courage was the mid-summer swim of over 10 km from the island of Miyajima to Etajima, which saw the entire body of cadets swimming in group formation for almost twelve hours.[92] Rigorous practice and devotion contributed to build up in service members a 'will to fight' rooted in the tradition popularised by the actions of characters like Saigō Takamori, a tradition which rewarded daring actions to achieve fatal blows at great personal risk. The employment of the 'five minutes before code'[93] and of catchphrases like 'outward-bound ship',[94] further stressed this point, reminding sailors and officers alike that they had to be psychologically prepared to 'clear for action' at any moment, that 'readiness' entailed for a ship at anchor to always have its bow pointing to the sea. As one informed observer concluded, the willingness of young Japanese to submit 'to such a Spartan life lies in the seriousness of purpose with which the cadet is taught to regard his calling'.[95]

A strong sense of camaraderie unfolded from this approach to the naval profession. In the recollections of a Naval Academy graduate, 59th class of 1931, the bond among the members of each class was underscored by an 'oath of trust' animating the activities of the Class Association.[96] Each association was a socially cohesive group, not merely a milieu in which students shared opinions on military and professional matters with other fellow cadets; rather, it represented a family-like environment that comforted the cadet who had entrusted his life to the navy. The cadet was in fact reassured by the knowledge, the wishful thought, or *negaimasu*,[97] that under any circumstances, even when the utmost sacrifice for the country was demanded of them, his classmates would look after his personal affairs, his relatives and family permanently.[98]

The battle history of the Imperial Navy offers a considerable number of instances in which sailors and officers alike behaved along these ethical lines. In this ethos, the Emperor represented the legitimising source of authority and samurais like Saigō nourished its aggressive, death-defying fighting spirit. The will to fight derived from a constructed tradition the navy sought to honour until its very end. Upon the completion of the tragic suicide mission of the task force led by the battleship *Yamato*, Admiral Toyoda Soemu, Commander in Chief (CinC), Combined Fleet, sent the following note:

> This action greatly enhanced the traditions of the Imperial navy and the glory of our surface units. Many brave men, the commander in chief of the task force in the fore, laid down their lives in the noble cause of defending the Empire. Their utter sincerity in serving the country goes straight to our hearts, and their unswerving loyalty will shine through the ages.[99]

At Tsushima and Pearl Harbor, Admiral Tōgō Heihachiro and Admiral Yamamoto Isoroku (the latter following the example of the former) both sailed into battle flying a 'Z' flag signal from the masts of their flagships that well captured this attitude. The signal conveyed the message: 'The fate of the Empire rests upon this battle, let every man do his utmost.'[100] Yet, Admiral Tōgō, a Satsuma man who conceived the message, was honouring Japan's naval traditions in another sense too. His message echoed in style and delivery Lord Nelson's flag signals at the Battle of Trafalgar:

'England expects that every man will do his duty.' This was no coincidence, as he was not merely seeking to honour Japan's indigenous dedication and fighting skills. With that message, the admiral sought to celebrate the foreign origins of the style of seamanship that had allowed the Imperial Navy to successfully develop into a professional force. He was linking Japan's success to the model the navy had adopted, that of the Royal Navy.

Integrating the effectiveness of Yōsai (Western knowledge)

In the second half of the nineteenth century, Japan lacked the basic technical knowledge to create a modern naval organisation. Hence, the elite heading the modernisation process deemed it essential to rely on foreign assistance to develop the new armed forces. Already in the late years of the Tokugawa shogunate, both the Japanese central authorities in Tokyo and the regional domains headed by Satsuma had ventured into such a quest, benefiting from Dutch, French and British mentoring and instruction in various areas of naval science.[101] After the Meiji restoration, however, the reputation of the Royal Navy, combined with the closer ties that the British had established in the 1860s with the domain of Satsuma, made Great Britain the most obvious choice as tutor for the infant navy.[102] For the following two decades, the British offered continuous support to set up the educational structures necessary to build up the Japanese standard of seamanship, representing an invaluable source of information. Until the early 1890s, British officers were regularly hired, either individually or as part of larger foreign assistance missions to teach in Japan (Figure 2.4).

The hiring of foreign personnel was complemented with foreign education and temporary work placement programmes. The Japanese navy sent a number of

Period	Name	Function	No. of Personnel
1870-1873	Lt. Albert G.S. Hawes, RM Lt. Frank Brinkley, BA	-Instructors, Academy (e.g. Gunnery, Mathematics, English) -Discipline/Order Afloat	2
1873-1879*	British Naval Mission Cmdr. Archibald L. Douglas, RN	Instructors, Academy (e.g. Curriculum, General Organisation)	34
1879-1885	Lt. Cmdr. L.P. Willan, RN	Instructor, Academy (e.g. Tactics, Gunnery)	1
1887-1893	Capt. John Ingles, RN	Instructor, Higher Education (e.g. Mathematics, Tactics) General Advisor	1
1921-1924**	British Aviation Mission Col. William F. Forbes-Sempill, RAF	Instructors, Naval Aviation (e.g. Flying, Armament, Photography)	28

*In July 1875, Cmdr. Douglas returned to England and Lt. C. W. Jones was promoted and replaced him as Director of the Naval College.

**In October 1922, Colonel Sempill and some members of the mission returned to England, as their contract was not renewed, while the remaining skeleton mission was assimilated into the IJN's organisation.

Figure 2.4 Post-1868 main British naval education activities in Japan.

Source: Evans and Peattie, *Kaigun*, 11–13; Kennedy, *Some Aspects of Japan and her Defences*, 35; Ferris, 'A British "Unofficial" Aviation Mission and Japanese Naval Developments', 416–39.

young officers to England (and, to a lesser extent, to the United States) to increase the intellectual exposure of its future leaders to the latest trends and debates on naval affairs.[103] Until the termination of the Anglo–Japanese alliance in 1923, Japanese naval architects were regularly admitted to the Royal Naval College; engineers experienced periods of work and study in Sheffield (where high-grade steel for armour plates was produced), Glasgow, and port cities with shipyards like Barrow-in-Furness and Newcastle-upon-Tyne.[104] It is indicative that two of Japan's foremost naval thinkers and naval planners, Satō Tetsutarō and Akiyama Saneyuki, studied abroad, spending periods of research in England and in the United States.[105] Naval assistance was not limited merely to education; it encompassed also the industrial sector, with British manufacturers Armstrong and Vickers acting as leading contractors in Japan.[106] Indeed, at the Battle of Tsushima, Tōgō's flagship, *Mikasa*, was a true naval gem of the age, combining British cutting-edge technology with Japanese manpower, a visually impressive statement of the Anglo–Japanese relations in the field.

As the Japanese navy consolidated its professionalism through operational experience in the First Sino-Japanese War, the practice of relying on foreign assistance progressively faded away. Nonetheless, the professional bond established with the Royal Navy and the privileged exchange of information between the two navies continued for several years.[107] The signing of the Anglo–Japanese alliance in 1902, and its renewal in 1905 and 1911, ensured a degree of continuity in the naval partnership until the end of the First World War.[108] Early in the 1920s, against the backdrop of innovations in the field of naval aviation and limitations on naval armaments as set by the Washington Naval Treaty (1921–22), the Japanese navy turned one last time to its old mentor to acquire a more systematic understanding of maritime air power.[109] By the end of the decade, concerns within Japanese naval circles in regard to an ABCD (American–British–Chinese–Dutch) strategic encirclement, domestic political quarrels with the army, increasing economic ambitions in Southeast Asia to counter a serious shortage of primary resources, all coupled with British growing suspicions vis-à-vis Japan, set the two navies adrift. From maritime partners the Japanese and British navies became fully fledged peer competitors.[110]

In Meiji Japan, foreign military assistance programmes, known as the *oyatoi gaikokujin*[111] system, were a rather common practice, but one of particular importance for a technology-intensive organisation like the navy. This might contribute to explain both the more extensive use of foreigners by the navy as well as the consistency in relying upon one main provider. Throughout the period, the navy requested the services of a total of 182 foreign-commissioned and non-commissioned officers against the 166 uniformed men from different foreign army establishments employed by the army. In the navy, the *oyatoi* came pre-eminently from England (130 men, equal to 71.4 per cent of the total), whereas in the army, the bulk of the assistance was divided between France (78 men, or 46.9 per cent) and Germany (48 men, or 28.9 per cent).[112] This is not to say that British influence was exclusive. In the latter half of the 1880s, the Imperial Navy did contract the design of a class of warships to a distinguished French naval architect, Emile Bertin, which marked the penetration of strategic ideas from the *Jeune Ecole* into the service.[113] Yet, the British maintained a clear position of primacy, influencing the moulding of the entire naval organisation at the different levels of the educational system.

By contrast, the Japanese army's progressive shift to German assistance in the aftermath of the Franco–Prussian War (1870–71), had the result of bearing considerable influence only in specific areas of military science, most notably the army's staff college curricula.[114]

As a former naval officer put it after the Pacific War, in the Japanese navy an officer was a 'patriot, a seaman, and a gentleman', and the Royal Navy contributed in a decisive fashion in shaping the last two aspects.[115] Among the different British initiatives to improve Japanese naval education, the Douglas Mission is widely regarded as the most influential in that it introduced at the academy (which at the time of the Mission was still in Tsukiji, Tokyo) the core practices and principles at the foundation of the Royal Navy's traditions.[116] The transmission of British naval traditions was facilitated by the strong personality and character of the leader of the mission, Commander Archibald Douglas. He was described in the literature as highly competent although perhaps not 'particularly imaginative or farsighted' by the changing standards of the day.[117] He was a man who emphasised routine and 'always liked to do the same thing at the same hour'.[118] He was a patriot who endeavoured to foster 'the passionate love and pride felt by every son of Nippon towards his country' and a good sportsman 'who encouraged games among the students at the college'.[119] With such a spirit, it is not a stretch of the imagination to consider why the Japanese felt comfortable with his methods and gave him 'almost complete freedom to change the system'.[120]

Commander Douglas aimed at making of each cadet a 'gentleman' with a broad general education, knowledgeable in English manners and social customs as much as a professional in naval science, a member of an elite corps to be modelled according to the canons of British public schools.[121] Such ideas well outlasted the duration of the mission and throughout the history of the Japanese navy, the curriculum of the academy continued to reflect such a philosophy, creating an underlying similarity between the instruction provided at the Royal Navy's college in Dartmouth and Etajima.[122]

In Etajima, a broad general education soon became a tool that favoured the engineering of a certain 'aristocratic' spirit in naval officers. Unlike their British colleagues, Japanese cadets came from different social and economic backgrounds, but while the Royal Navy's officer corps 'was never divorced from the nation', the Etajima product was considered to be in a class of his own.[123] Differences in the background of the cadets did not matter as the academy offered them an instruction in a variety of subjects such as mathematics, physics, foreign languages (English, French and German), Japanese literature, Chinese classics, philosophy, leadership and even 'hygiene'.[124] The difference rested in that naval officers, as direct executioners of the Emperor's will, had a privileged status in Japanese society, one demanding of them to inspire the respect of the Japanese people with their actions, and to set a positive 'model' for the entire nation.[125] Indeed, cadets were naturally accustomed to thinking of themselves as belonging to a uniquely prestigious group and the selection process for the academy was such that it further reinforced such perceptions. Only the best and most physically fit applicants would be successful and on average, less than 4 per cent of the applicants succeeded, a factor that made the academy the subject of the aspirations of many young Japanese. Young Japanese who failed the first examination would usually try again in the next year or two depending on the financial situation of their family.[126]

In that respect, a broad academic curriculum stemmed from the service's need to strike a balance between the ability of future officers to possess a broader understanding of the world beyond the technical borders of the naval profession and the nation's expectations from its naval elite.[127] In the case of the education of Japanese naval officers this was no secondary challenge. British instructors emphasised that the quality of a navy was marked by the seamanship of its manpower and this could be achieved only with constant dedication. In Japan, such an emphasis was even more important given the relatively limited knowledge that many young cadets had of modern technologies. As late as 1923, Colonel Sempill remarked that contrary to the average British boy, who had in his motor-bicycle and mechanical toys valuable sources of primary training, the Japanese pilot 'never comes into contact with any kind of machinery until he has left school, and sometimes even later than this'.[128]

It is therefore understandable that the primary focus of instruction was on core subjects like navigation, gunnery, torpedo instruction, tactics, aeronautics and communications, with a consequent detrimental effect on the young officer's variety of interests. In particular, to some foreign observers, the tendency to concentrate on technical subjects was rather pronounced in Japanese naval officers. Already at the beginning of the twentieth century, British naval expert Frederick Jane noted that Japanese officers were as 'philistine' as their British colleagues, defying stereotypes of the age regarding the natural Japanese 'art instinct'.[129] The Japanese officer was dedicated to his profession to the point of 'ignoring of everything else'. The very idea of holiday (when in England) seemed to consist of a day-long visit to Portsmouth dockyard, followed by a moment of relaxation playing naval war games at Jane's house.[130]

Against this backdrop, cadets were educated in order to maintain a certain cosmopolitan *savoir faire*, an ability to interact at the international level to fulfil their double role of seamen on the one hand and agents of the Japanese Empire on the other. In this respect, particularly important was the overseas training cruise, a formative experience with no equal in any other Japanese educational institution, military or civilian.[131] For all these reasons, the study of the English language, which was compulsory for all cadets, was equally highly valued. It comprised three hours of study per week, including one of conversation; it encompassed grammar as well as social manners and customs. From 1888 to 1938, this part of the education was under the responsibility of two Englishmen, integrated into the teaching staff at the academy.[132] Language teaching was kept in high esteem, to the point that it was never stopped, even after 1938. Etajima remained the only university in Japan that continued to teach English throughout the Pacific War.[133]

The overall impression is that the British tradition of the 'gentleman officer', while fulfilling the educational profile of an elite organisation, was eventually adopted emphasising more its function as a method of empowering servicemen to increase national prestige and naval power than as a means for the cadet's individual development. Loyalty, patriotism and *esprit de corps* were in fact given greater importance than leadership.[134] This dilemma was reflected in the different interpretations of the system expressed by the representatives of what historian Asada Sadao called the 'fleet' and 'treaty' factions of the Japanese navy.[135] Vice Admiral Katō Kanji, a key player in the demise of the navy's moderate treaty faction in the 1930s and commandant of the academy from 1920 to 1922, held a view charged with shrewd national pragmatism. As he pointed out, a broad education empowered the service with the necessary knowledge of the enemy mentality and ideas and thus allowed his weaknesses to be exploited.[136] By contrast, Vice Admiral Inoue Shigeyoshi, a well-known associate of the navy's treaty faction who served in the same position from 1942 to 1944, invited cadets to study hard and take full advantage of the school's academic courses for their own personal improvement. The knowledge learnt at the academy was just the initial step in a lifelong path to learn how to differentiate between carrying 'a fine sword' and knowing 'how to use it'.[137] As he summarised it in a manual he issued for the academy's instructors,[138] students were to be encouraged to master contemporary culture and to look at the most advanced civilisations worldwide as a gateway to pursue constant improvement.[139]

This also explains why becoming a 'Japanese gentleman' was closely connected to 'spiritual education'. While spiritual education was not given priority over the study of technical subjects, especially at the beginning – when the navy had to develop a broader technical know-how – it was intrinsic to the process. It disciplined each cadet to the values praised in the Imperial Rescript, relying on a series of activities that could favour their practice and their inner assimilation.[140] The emphasis of martial arts on self-discipline certainly offered an important contribution to the 'spiritual awakening' of the cadet, but also visits to temples for the purpose of meditation were not uncommon. In 1935, Vice Admiral Oikawa Koshirō, another officer who opposed the Pacific War and led the academy from 1932 to 1935, took the entire college (staff and cadets) to spend a weekend at a famous Buddhist temple in the nearby area of Hiroshima to meditate.[141]

As the navy developed into a battle-hardened organisation, other practices were introduced, including cadet visits to the area of the academy dedicated to its war-heroes and traditions. By 1936, a white marble mausoleum-like educational reference hall[142] was built to accommodate the increased number of exhibits. Inside the building, cadets could draw inspiration from the exploits of Admiral Tōgō Heihachirō, and from the sacrifice and utmost dedication of young officers like Lieutenant Sakuma Tsutomu, who, in 1910, died together with fourteen crewmembers during a dive exercise onboard submarine No. 6. As stressed in the museum, once the submarine was recovered, Sakuma and his men were found still sitting at their assigned posts. A copy of his last note explaining the causes of the accident and apologising for failing the Emperor was also displayed to convey to the cadets the 'shining example' of the Japanese brand of officership.[143] Similar emphasis on self-sacrifice, duty and spirit of comradeship unfolded from the space dedicated to Commander Hirose Takeo. In Saigō's death-defying fashion, Hirose commanded an extremely dangerous mission during the second attempt to blockade Port Arthur on 27 March 1905 and lost his life while searching for a missing subordinate. As former JMSDF Chief of Staff Admiral Sakuma Makoto pointed out, the reference hall aimed at detailing the example of 'seniors' to guide the cadet through the nature and the significance of the navy martial spirit.[144]

In 1932, as a way to commemorate the first fifty years of the Rescript, and probably alarmed by signs of 'hyper nationalism' among young naval officers in the wake of the assassination of Prime Minister Inukai Tsuyoshi (15 May 1932), the then superintendent of the academy, Rear Admiral Matsushita Hajime, presented the 'five reflections'.[145] These were five questions that each cadet had to recite five minutes before the end of the daily lessons as a form of self-assessment of his personal behaviour.[146] They addressed both physical and spiritual commitment and were phrased using a grammar style that put each point on equal terms. The five reflections were:

> Hast thou not gone against sincerity?
> Hast thou not felt ashamed of thy words and deeds?
> Hast thou not lacked vigour?
> Hast thou exerted all possible efforts?
> Hast thou not become slothful?[147]

The five reflections are still in use today, and as two former chiefs of staff pointed out, the reflections' inherent pedagogic value did not and does not just rest on the answers that each cadet provides during the time spent at the academy. Both remembered that at the academy they were extremely focused on the delivery, reciting them without making mistakes. As a result, they could give little thought to their content. Throughout the years, however, this practice led them to develop a mental attitude that helped them to assess and develop their personalities. Over time, the 'reflections' favoured a morally responsible, forceful and loyal endeavour, one in which the understanding of their limits was instrumental to improve their personal qualities.[148]

Thus, the adoption of British traditions, while widely celebrated by the navy as a way to validate its status and develop its professional standards (both in terms of seamanship and in terms of technical knowledge), did not eventually produce the same breed of gentlemen. The Japanese officer differed from his British colleague because he was educated to think of himself as belonging to a distinct group, one in which knowledge and skills demonstrated his right to be part of this elite, but personal performance was not necessarily a gateway to success. Rather, performance was considered as an indicator of his superior spiritual commitment to serving the navy, the Emperor and the nation. He was not any gentleman; he was a Japanese gentleman.

Conclusions: The navy of Imperial Japan

As one study of the battle of Midway put it, the Imperial Navy had at its core 'a group of fighting men who feared the shame of ignoble failure more than death itself'.[149] The traditions created throughout the Meiji period rested at the foundations of the ethos of such an organisation. They were originally devised to address a critical professional issue. They had to promote inner cohesiveness and fighting spirit against the background of a broader nation-building process with no prior reference model. Hence, imperial ideology, samurai values and spiritual education became the cornerstones of a system of practices bearing the responsibility of transforming a young person into a resolute naval officer or seaman. Duty and loyalty, principles familiar to military establishments worldwide, assumed paramount importance in the Japanese naval ethos, reaching 'standards few navies have seen'.[150] In this respect, scholars widely agree on the fact that such attributes played a significant role in the effectiveness of the Japanese imperial military machine, particularly in terms of the popularity of the armed forces within the Japanese society, and motivation to kill and to die on the battlefield.[151]

In the Japanese navy, traditions had an additional function. As a 'technical' service, the navy endeavoured to adopt a foreign model to establish professional and technical standards adequate for a modern naval organisation. The Royal Navy – and in particular its century-long history as the world's foremost naval power – offered such a source of professionalism. At the beginning of their journey into the business of naval warfare, the Japanese turned largely to British assistance to create the grassroots conditions for the development of a modern force. Traditions, especially those pertaining to Japan's medieval naval heritage, helped give a specific connotation to this process by setting its borders. The Japanese navy would learn to build and man warships according to the best standards. Its officer corps would display the traits and the manners most suitable for the naval officer of the day. Yet, this gentleman-officer was to remain at heart wholly Japanese. His traditions, most of them rooted in regional customs and imperial mythology, enabled him to maintain his distinctive identity.

Naval traditions and military ethos gauged the complexity of the Japanese modernisation process. The requirements to preserve Japan's 'national spirit' made the pursuit of foreign technology and know-how a function of the goal of securing international power and status. Traditions contained an inherent tension with the result that the Japanese navy 'was both ferocious and sentimental', and 'extreme loyalty and discipline were matched by an equal aptitude for brutal behaviour towards the rank and file, and a callous disregard for the lives of its men'.[152] It was the progressive erosion in the 1930s and early 1940s of the delicate balance between the two sources of the service's traditions that eventually led to its downfall in the Pacific War. The navy had adopted features of Japan's martial past to qualify its imperial status; these, on the other hand, provided a framework for an understanding of military prowess centred on discipline, training, readiness and lethality in combat as the pillars of effectiveness. Its failures, therefore, reflected the anxiety of what Richard Samuels regarded as Japan's struggle as a latecomer to the modernisation process of the second half of the nineteenth century to ' "catch-up and surpass"[153] the West to become a "first class nation" '.[154]

By the end of the Pacific War, Japan's naval traditions had brought both glory and tragedy to the country through national heroes like Admiral Tōgō and Admiral Yamamoto; defining victories like Tsushima; and terrible defeats like the sinking of the battleship *Yamato*. As the early post-war Japanese naval leaders ventured into the setting up of the new organisation, therefore, they found themselves in a situation that was both similar and different to that of the Meiji oligarchs of mid-nineteenth century. Like their predecessors, the post-war leadership was faced with the task of selectively looking at the past to validate and inspire those who were to meet the challenge of the present in dedicating their lives to the purpose of national defence. In contrast, in the post-war era, the naval traditions underscoring the rise of the Imperial Navy offered a national model unavailable to Meiji reformers. These traditions could help rebuild a shattered pride by inspiring and motivating the will to fight of post-war sailors and officers. Similarly, these traditions could enable the introduction of foreign procedures, tactics and technology while preserving a distinct 'Japanese' identity. In this respect, imperial traditions and ethos would pave the way for post-war naval recovery. Yet, was the post-war Japanese society ready to accept such an organisational tie? Public perceptions of the Imperial Navy were crucial to the matter.

3

History and Memory: The Imperial Navy of the Post-war Era

> *While we can only make educated guesses, however, there are certain factors which, as popular defence attitudes congeal, would seem likely to assert themselves. Foremost among these are Japan's long and revered naval tradition and its continuing dependence on the sea. Over the long run, we believe that this combination of emotional and pragmatic considerations will give the Maritime Self Defence Force a distinct edge over the other services in public acceptance and, ultimately, in respect and popularity.*[1]
>
> Richard W. Petree
> (US Embassy, Tokyo)

Japan's 'long and revered naval tradition'

In the early days of the occupation, the notion of a 'good navy' as opposed to a 'bad army' made its first appearance.[2] It gained momentum after the conclusion of the proceedings of the International Military Tribunal for the Far East (also known as the Tokyo Tribunal), the legal body tasked with the investigation of the Japanese wartime responsibilities.[3] In the words of Sir Arthur S. Comyns Carr, the chief British prosecutor, until the last months before the hostilities broke out the Japanese navy acted as 'a restraining force on the impetuosity of the army'.[4] These assessments were not isolated and were shared at the domestic political level too. Prime Minister Yoshida Shigeru (1946–47, 1948–54) wrote in his memoirs that the navy was never favourable to the war for it 'had been modeled on British lines and well knew what such a war would mean'.[5] The different attitudes of the two services seemed to also concern their professional conduct. As army stragglers and veteran associations started narrating their wartime experiences, the army gained an image distinguished by harsh behaviour and brutality. In the early phases of the post-war era, the narrative of the wartime military was being crafted; generals seemed more to blame than the admirals, and soldiers less professional than sailors.[6]

This chapter examines the development of this naval narrative and how it became linked to the JMSDF in the realm of public memory. The emergence of the notion of a 'good navy' was not necessarily gauging the military reality in the run-up to the war – and it has in fact recently come under scrutiny.[7] Yet, in the fields of journalism, literature and non-fiction novels, two authors, Itō Masanori and Agawa Hiroyuki, were instrumental in popularising it, and a third author, Agawa's own son Naoyuki, tied the concept to the JMSDF. Itō and the two Agawas were not alone in writing about the Imperial Navy, but they were among the first to explain its role as a military organisation in the inter-war and wartime eras.[8] They articulated its traditions and contextualised its limits throughout these controversial periods, presenting a narrative that explained failures and rehabilitated the navy's professional ethos. Crucially, the authoritativeness of their voices rested on the fact that they were not merely academics. They entertained privileged contacts within both navies. Indeed, Agawa had been a wartime naval officer and, as a veteran, he kept close ties with retired officers. Their work was symptomatic of a process that took place in the public sphere consolidating a narrative of Japanese naval tradition that eventually played to the strengths of the JMSDF's willingness to entertain an open connection with it.

'Mr Ito', the reporter of naval affairs

When Itō Masanori started writing about the navy in the early post-war years, he was already Japan's most respected naval reporter.[9] He was born in 1887 in the former domain of Mito (Ibaraki Prefecture), birthplace of the influential philosophical and political neo-Confucian movement 'revere the Emperor, expel the barbarians'.[10] According to later characterisations of his personality, Itō fully embraced his region's history and traditions. He was a taciturn person, possessed of the same energy and patriotic dedication that distinguished many well-educated men of his cultural background.[11] He grew up in the decade that witnessed Japan winning its first two tests of strength of international power and status against China and Russia. War accounts in national newspapers and governmental propaganda on the staggering victories on the battlefields of Korea and Manchuria and in naval encounters in the East China Sea and the Sea of Japan nurtured his pride and patriotism.[12] Later accounts asserted it was the sense of duty unfolding from his patriotism that led him to develop an inquisitive mind and great discipline in his intellectual quests.[13]

The experiences of his childhood had a profound impact, informing Itō's professional style throughout the rest of his life. In December 1913, he was able to secure a position at *Jiji Shinpō*. One of Japan's most progressive newspapers of the time, *Jiji Shinpō* had been founded in 1882 by influential Meiji thinker Fukuzawa Yukichi, and was renowned for its balanced assessment of current affairs, crediting Western innovation and techniques for much of Japan's national success without discarding the country's own traditions, values and distinctive culture.[14] The intellectual environment of a newspaper room matched Itō's Mito upbringing, Meiji experience and character inclinations. There he started specialising in military and naval affairs, developing a preference for naval affairs and the issue of how technology was transforming war at sea. In fact, the struggle for moral rectitude and technological mastery had been key attributes – in his perception – in the Japanese Meiji experience. In this respect, Itō fully embraced the emergence of the Imperial Navy on the world stage as a synecdoche for the success of modern Japan.[15] Itō became a regular contributor to newspaper and magazine columns and his analysis of military topics earned him a sound reputation in Japan as well as abroad as one of the country's outstanding and most prolific naval correspondents.[16]

In Japan, the main strength of Itō's 'powerful pen'[17] lay in his ability to convey a genuine passion for the navy through an appealing writing style. He used sophisticated language and was attentive to details. He enjoyed technical matters and kept himself constantly updated on the latest developments in the field of naval technology and tactics. He was also a traditionalist and demonstrated it by employing 'old' Chinese characters in his articles. When writing the term *rengō kantai* (Combined Fleet), for example, he used an elegant and ancient ideogram that was unfamiliar even to some of Itō's editors of the time.[18] Literally with a single stroke, Itō's pen gave a traditional connotation to Japan's modern and powerful fleet. He was old-fashioned in his style, but modern in his choice of topics, sophisticated in content but very engaging in his delivery. He was a perfect example of a man of his time, a figure displaying a measure of what some Western specialists have labelled Japan's 'romantic nationalism'.[19]

A workaholic, he dedicated most of his free time to reading and writing on history and strategy, learning by heart the particulars of foreign classes of warships and pennant lists.[20] His dedication to technical knowledge stunned editors and colleagues, who often exhorted him to work less only to be told that writing about navies was a form of relaxation.[21] By the time the First World War broke out, he had already established himself within Japanese press circles as an expert with a mastery and an understanding of naval matters comparable to that of a scholar. This was of particular advantage in that he could channel his expertise in a clear, informative prose that made naval matters easily understood by a wide readership.[22] One reported example conveys both his dedication and the effectiveness of his approach. When in June 1916 news reached Japan of the Battle of Jutland, Itō had just set off for a vacation in Hokkaido. After receiving a telegram on what clearly looked to be the most significant naval encounter since the Battle of Tsushima (the main naval battle of the Russo-Japanese War), Itō returned to his newspaper's headquarters to prepare an analysis of the battle. He had no direct source on which to base an in-depth examination of the events. Nonetheless, in the following days, using the information available to the press and his professional judgement, he wrote seven well-informed articles for different national and regional newspaper editions.[23]

A man with Itō's dedication to naval affairs could not go unnoticed by senior Japanese naval officers. By the end of the First World War, he had already established a network of acquaintances within the group of promising naval officers clustered around Admiral Katō Tomosaburō, influential Navy Minister (1915–21), and Japanese mastermind of the arms control system devised at the Washington Naval Conference (1921–22). Indeed, it was while reporting on this conference that Itō came into closer contact with some of the key figures of the three international naval agreements of the 1920s, including Captains Yamanashi Katsunoshin and Nomura Kichisaburō, both later to become admirals.[24] The relationships he established with senior officers in the navy would prove to be of mutual benefit. Itō was a knowledgeable man, willing to articulate a navy perspective, and he was in the right position to reach out to a large readership.[25] In turn, naval connections guaranteed him first-hand information for his work as a reporter. This often set him a step ahead of his colleagues, and enabled him to secure sensational scoops; he would be the first to report the imminent shift in Japan's alliance system with the dissolution of the Anglo–Japanese alliance in favour of the Four-Power Treaty (United States, Great Britain, Japan and France).[26]

In particular, the international naval conferences of the 1920s and 1930s had a threefold impact on Itō's professional career. First, the conferences represented major media events, setting the stage for continuous interviews, private conversations and meetings with members of the delegations. These circumstances strengthened his naval network among the officers of what became subsequently known as the navy's 'treaty faction'; he would become a good acquaintance of rising stars such as Admiral Yamamoto Isoroku. Second, the trust he established with many of them did not diminish over time, and the books he published in the 1950s and early 1960s were filled with the personal reflections of the numerous wartime naval protagonists who had found in him an 'old friend' and a professional with whom to discuss controversial issues. Naval contacts also facilitated his access to archival material.[27] Third, the news coverage of the conferences gave Itō great exposure, enhancing his reputation at home as well as abroad as a top commentator on the subject of the arms control process. As some informed Japanese observers later put it, 'Mr Itō' was a respected name familiar to many inter-war analysts of international relations in the Pacific.[28]

Reviewing the wartime experience

Itō Masanori's files at the archives of the *Sankei Shinbun* – the Japanese newspaper where he worked for the majority of his post-war career – contain very little concerning his activity as a journalist during the war. This makes it difficult to compile a comprehensive picture of his wartime reporting. In this context, however, what is relevant is that in the aftermath of the war, Itō's reputation, professional pedigree, direct contacts and respect for what the rise of the navy had represented in Japan's modern history, put him in an ideal position to investigate it. Prior to the conflict, he had provided informed views of the Japanese position vis-à-vis arms limitations. Now, against an increasing public sense of disapproval of the military, his quest was to focus on 'what had gone wrong'.

In the two decades that followed the end of hostilities, numerous multi-volume wartime operational histories, of variable scholarly value, were published in Japan. Those authored by the journalist were among the first to present an insightful, though at time narrowly focused, operational narrative.[29] Of particular note was the dramatised and powerful style of delivery that denoted Itō's personal connection to the topic and clear willingness to reach out to a wide readership.[30] His publications penetrated the psyche of pre-war Japanese military leaders, focusing on the roots of decision-making failures and tactical and strategic misjudgements. In so doing, they reflected the personal journey of an informed insider who had come to question the patriotism the imperial armed forces had inspired in him during his adolescence. Now, like many of his fellow countrymen, he wished to understand why those forces had failed to meet his expectations with their conduct in war. His books possessed an almost cathartic value as he explored the reasons for defeat.

Itō's post-war works often crossed the subtle line dividing his professional agenda from personal emotions, making them unusual products. They are authoritative, but also dramatic and emphatic. It is said, for example, that the death of his second wife prompted the decision to write *The End of the Imperial Japanese Navy*, one of his most successful publications. He seemed to identify his personal loss with the downfall of the service and the heavy human cost it entailed.[31] Itō set the tone in the book's introduction, explaining that the nostalgia for the Combined Fleet in many Japanese hearts and the deep respect for the memories of many friends who had perished in the heat of battle, pressed him to reconsider his initial reluctance to write on such a difficult topic as Japan's military defeat.[32] These were feelings he shared with thousands of Japanese who had fought in the war or counted family members among Japan's over three million dead. With them, he wished to share the findings of his quest as a way to pay homage to the memory of the many who perished. The book's opening lines underscored the character of the narrative:

> Movements to Romanise our language may some day succeed, but the ideographs for *rengō kantai* will always stir Japanese hearts, just as do some of Admiral Heihachirō Tōgō's famous words. Quotes known to all are his dispatch as battle was about to be joined in Tsushima Strait – 'The enemy has been sighted; the Combined Fleet is moving to annihilate him. The waves are high but the day is clear' – and his famous Z-signal: 'The rise or fall of the nation is at stake in this battle; all hands exhorted to do their utmost.'[33]

The mix of drama and technical information in his books impressed foreign scholars too. In a 1963 review of the English translation of *The End of the Imperial Japanese Navy*, the official Royal Navy historian of the Second World War and Cambridge research fellow, Captain Stephen W. Roskill, remarked how the strengths of the book lay in its interesting and vivid portrayal of the war 'through Japanese eyes' and on 'the candid comments on the errors made by his countrymen'. Roskill, a line officer with years of service at sea who fought the Imperial Navy off the Solomon Islands in July 1943, approved of Itō's 'well-deserved tribute to the courage and endurance of the ordinary Japanese sailor, whose fighting spirit never failed in spite of the terrible losses suffered'.[34] In his main criticisms of the publication, Roskill acknowledged indirectly Itō's core agenda. He maintained one critical issue had passed virtually unnoticed, namely the navy's substantial failure to adopt adequate convoy escort measures throughout the majority of the conflict.[35]

Yet, naval strategy was not as central to the book's theme as the life and struggle of the individuals and assets that had made the Japanese navy an internationally renowned national totem. Itō's literary achievements and publishing activity on wartime military events reached its zenith in December 1960, when he became the ninth recipient of the prestigious Kikuchi Kan Prize, awarded by the Japanese leading monthly magazine *Bungei Shunjū* (where he had started publishing the findings of his research activity in 1946) to individuals making outstanding contributions to Japanese society.[36]

Itō had professional credibility, but he was not a 'dry' observer, particularly in the eyes of the disillusioned Japanese post-war readership of the late 1940s and of the 1950s. His views possessed a public appeal and were well received because they sought to give depth to the mechanics of the military 'betrayal' of the Japanese people. For Itō, the navy was not without sins.[37] He criticised the fact that the navy's intention to implement the disarmament treaties had lost momentum well before its delegation withdrew from the negotiations for the Second London Naval Treaty in January 1936. Preliminary studies for the behemoth *Yamato* that was laid down in Kure only a few months after the failing of the negotiations were emblematic of 'Japan's intention to vitiate the treaty'.[38]

With equal clarity, Itō made no excuse for what he regarded as the two main political responsibilities of the navy. First, the navy's high command had failed to present serious opposition to General Tōjō and his militarist clique as the country embarked on a warpath. Second, the navy had downplayed Japanese material weaknesses and failed to articulate more clearly its limited confidence in the ability to wage a protracted confrontation with Western powers.[39] Itō's informed assessment gave voice to the visceral sense of betrayal felt by Japanese people who, like him, had been accustomed by previous successes and propaganda to place the utmost confidence in their military leaders. In one particularly poignant passage, he admitted that:

> The Navy, knowing that Japan would lose any war with the United States, should have shown the courage expected of leaders, and accepted humiliation in order to preserve the nation from defeat. Such a sacrifice would have proven that the Navy was worthy of the people's high regard and confidence.[40]

These critiques are important, but they still fell short of addressing other controversial aspects of the militarism of the 1930s, and the more brutal aspects of Japan's war conduct. In this respect, Itō remained more focused on the policy dimension of the country's military failure, arguing that the burden of Japan's decision to engage in an all-out war weighed more heavily upon the shoulders of the Imperial Army. This was no doubt because the individuals who had acted to prevent the escalation towards war were those naval officers who to him represented the prime expressions of the navy that had brought respect and prestige to Japan.[41] Itō seemed to clearly 'root for the navy' in the inter-service rivalry that existed between the imperial armed services. For him there was one fundamental difference that set the two organisations in different classes of professionalism, and it was that the army seemed to be considerably more self-destructive and reckless. As he explained it:

> Death in war is inevitable, but it should not be pointlessly courted. It was a basic tenet of the Japanese navy to avoid any operation which offered no chance of survival. … This tradition was not violated until the adoption of the tactics which called for the Kamikaze Special Attack Force [the suicide pilots] and the human torpedoes [*kaiten*], at a time when Japan realised that the war was lost.[42]

In Itō's book, the differences between the two services were summarised by one of the foremost naval figures of his narrative, Admiral Yamamoto, a close acquaintance of his. Yamamoto was a 'stubborn man', a gambler and a womaniser, as much as a warrior loyal to the emperor and a product of the Japanese martial code. He was certainly not one to fear taking risks. Yamamoto was both knowledgeable in technical matters and meticulous in his appraisal of tactical problems. He disagreed with more conservative doctrinal views on the tactical dominance of battleships in naval warfare and was one of those who voiced fears 'that Japan had no chance of victory in a war lasting more than one year'.[43] Until 1939, from his position at the Navy Ministry, together with the acting Minister Admiral Yōnai Mitsumasa and Rear Admiral Inoue Shigeyoshi, he systematically opposed Japan's alignment with Germany and Italy. Itō charted with details and anecdotes the admiral's difficult journey into the increasingly tense atmosphere of late 1930s Japanese politics, almost in an effort to legitimise his subsequent actions. First and foremost an officer of the imperial navy, Yamamoto remained at his post (as Commander in Chief, Combined Fleet) once the decision to wage war had been taken, and channelled his energies into the preparation of operations capable of giving Japan the upper hand in the conflict. Faced with the dilemma of whether to accept humiliation, admit the lack of capabilities to face a protracted confrontation with the US navy, or seek victory in an all-out test, he chose this last course.

For Itō, Admiral Yamamoto was the embodiment of the Imperial navy ethos. He was a professional trained to plan and fight campaigns for his country, a loyal servant of the Emperor, a daring warrior. His later actions in the war and those of many other front-line commanders demonstrated such qualities, and even when it became clear that the Japanese were 'the pitchers for the losing team' he and many of his colleagues did not fail in their duty.[44] Yamamoto lived, fought and died standing by a martial code connecting the actions at the Yalu (1895), Tsushima (1905), Pearl Harbor (1941) and Midway (1942). The combination of his demise in 1943 and his overall characterisation as a capable and resolute officer imbued with samurai values, fluent in English and knowledgeable of the impact of naval aviation and other new technologies, naturally conferred on him the status of the ultimate Japanese hero.

Itō's war narrative sought to provide an even more controversial conclusion. The Imperial Navy had not failed to honour the traditions traced by its Meiji forerunners, opposing the war first, but eventually sparing no resources to fight it. Japan had made a grave mistake, and millions of men had paid for it. Who was to be made responsible for this dramatic downfall? In the author's estimation the answer could not rest solely on the shoulders of the armed services. As Itō put it, 'The Combined Fleet will never return. Its existence and achievements are now but a page in history which will show that blame for the loss of the Combined Fleet must rest, not on the enemy who destroyed it, but on Japan itself.'[45] Concurrently, by highlighting the positive attributes of the navy, Itō sought to rescue part of Japan's martial ethos from a broader collective post-war rejection. The victories of the Imperial Navy and the men who achieved them were to be treasured as a precious heritage of Japan's national identity.

Debating military identity and traditions

For Itō, this heritage had to find its way into the post-war society and its appreciation of the role of the armed forces. He endeavoured to plant the seeds for such an appreciation in two ways. In his role as journalist and military analyst he sought to inject the question of the legacy of the imperial naval traditions into the controversial debate around the professional ethos of the JSDF.[46] In particular, in January and July 1954, as the debate over their establishment was unfolding, he authored two series of newspaper articles.[47] These comprised seven instalments each and appeared in the conservative newspaper *Sankei Shinbun*. They dealt with what he perceived to be a central issue concerning the future of any Japanese military apparatus. Both moments were carefully chosen, providing timely opportunity for public debate. The January series appeared as political negotiations on the laws to define the nature of the new military forces were entering their final phase. The July instalments were intended to offer in-depth comments on the establishment of the Defence Agency and the JSDF.[48] By that time, Itō was 'the' authoritative Japanese military analyst of his generation, a position in many ways comparable to that of Sir Basil Liddell Hart in Britain in the years between the wars.

In both series, he did not seek to directly engage in the ongoing debate between conservative forces led by controversial figures like ex-foreign minister Shigemitsu Mamoru (1943–45, 1954–56), Hatoyama Ichirō (soon to be prime minister 1954–56) and Kishi Nobusuke (prime minister 1957–60) and more liberal pragmatists headed by Prime Minister Yoshida Shigeru (1948–54). The Byzantine legal schemes envisioned for the status of the new forces were at the centre of their exchange.[49] Itō, by contrast, sought to shift the focus of public attention to the fundamental relationship between a nation and its armed forces. He felt this was a core question, one he feared would remain unaddressed due to the social and educational reforms conducted during the Allied occupation and the military sensitivity generated by the trauma of defeat.[50] His approach seemed to well capture anxieties later expressed by former Imperial naval officers like Admiral Hasegawa Kiyoshi, commander of the Navy Air Squadron at the time of the 1937 bombing of the USS Panay, who pointed out that:

> Under our Constitution it is impossible for the armed forces to have proper military spirit. The men today are treated like civilians. They can't act like soldiers and sailors. No one wants to die. But soldiers and sailors must die for their country in an emergency.[51]

His argument was twofold. On the one hand, he strongly disagreed with many of his contemporaries who insisted on an uncritical and absolute break with the past. Militarism had blinded Japan's pre-war strategic calculus, but Japan's military had not always been pervaded by the extremism of the late 1930s.[52] Nor was the existence and maintenance of armed forces to be considered a manifestation of aggressive nationalism, an increasingly common assumption among Japanese people and politicians.[53] Indeed, a more in-depth assessment of Japan's modern past demonstrated that at the turn of the twentieth century the country had been able to strike the right balance between the natural requirements of national defence and the creation of an appropriate military apparatus. Itō therefore refuted what seemed to be a mainstream idea according to which the only way for Japan to re-establish armed forces was by dismissing the pre-war system.[54] For him, public amnesia was no solution.

This consideration led to a second and – in his perception – more fundamental issue. Itō regarded military forces as a product of the societies that created and maintained them. Japan was no exception, and the identity crisis he perceived in his fellow countrymen on the importance of national defence could be, he feared, a fatal weakness capable of undermining the ethos of the new forces.[55] For this reason, in the July instalments he subscribed to the conservative tendency to speak of 'Jieigun' rather than 'Jieitai',[56] using the character *gun*[57] that was generally employed in the Japanese language to define a military organisation.[58] Providing numerous examples from Japanese, American and British history, Itō argued that the effectiveness of military forces did not rest on their equipment and on their strength levels alone.[59]

Reviewing the past and the part played by the imperial armed forces in the rise of Japan as an international state actor was an essential step for post-war Japan to regenerate the sense of trust, respect and perceived social value attributed by a society to its armed forces.[60] In turn, these attributes were essential to nourish the JSDF's fighting spirit and efficacy. Japan needed to turn to its national heroes and draw inspiration and guidance from their actions in order to reconstitute the ethos of its military. In Itō's view, the performance of the Japanese imperial military in the Meiji and Taishō eras had delivered heroes who deserved greater consideration than the current state of oblivion.[61]

Itō's second main contribution to the development of a Japanese post-war attunement to its martial past was entwined with this last argument and he actively lobbied for its realisation. In the last years of his career, and his life, he put his pen and energies at the service of a campaign to re-contextualise Japan's modern naval experience and rebuild national pride. He joined an effort to bring back into the public consciousness what he believed to be Japan's defining military success and an iconic moment in its modern nation-building process: the Battle of Tsushima. He campaigned for the restoration of the battleship *Mikasa*.[62]

Originally, it would appear it was a letter sent on 24 September 1955 to the editor of another newspaper, the *Nippon Times* (presently *Japan Times*) that ignited the process to revitalise and preserve Admiral Tōgō's flagship. The letter had been written by a British man named John S. Rubin, native of Barrow-in-Furness in the north of England, who had recently returned from a visit to Japan where he had visited Yokosuka, and observed the state of abandonment of the pre-dreadnought battleship. In the letter, Rubin explained that from 1900 to 1902 he had observed the ship being completed and launched at the Vickers Sons and Maxim's Shipbuilding Works dockyards in his home town and felt deeply moved by the condition of the relict that – to his eyes – was to the Japanese what HMS *Victory* represented to the British.[63] The newspaper, following the publication of the letter, received numerous requests for information on the ship. This gave an old acquaintance of Itō's, Admiral Yamanashi – who had explained the circumstances to Mr Rubin in his new capacity as president of the Japan Naval Association (the veterans association of the Imperial Navy) – a suitable opportunity to gather momentum for the ship's restoration.

Admiral Yamanashi knew Itō from the hectic days of the naval limitation conferences. The admiral belonged to the group of senior retired uniformed men of the pre-war treaty faction who, in mid-September 1952, at the facilities of the former naval museum in Yoyogi (central Tokyo), had established the association together with 200 other former naval officers. Other founding fathers of the association were Admiral Nomura Kichisaburō, Vice Admiral Sakonji Masazo (acting as vice-presidents), and Admiral Sawamoto Yorio, reportedly a leading promoter of the organisation.[64] For all of them, Itō was more than a familiar name. His personal inclinations, writings and professional status made his involvement in the operation decisive, if not essential.

Their expectations were not disappointed. Itō took the campaign to heart and set about raising funds privately for the restoration. Meanwhile, in the pages of the *Sankei*, he sought to stoke attention for the project by publishing a commemorative article on 27 May 1956 (the anniversary of the battle) about the significance of the battleship.[65] Throughout this process, local Japanese dignitaries from the city of Yokosuka were involved. Also extremely important was the participation and support of influential retired American naval officers, who had come to appreciate the valour of the Imperial Navy as a foe during the war and contributed to the formation of the JMSDF in its aftermath, most notably Fleet Admiral Chester Nimitz and Admiral Arleigh Burke. They went to great lengths in the fund-raising mission. Admiral Nimitz wrote an article on Admiral Tōgō for the magazine *Bungei Shunjū* and donated the 20,000 yen he received for it to encourage other Japanese to contribute to the restoration cause.[66] By the spring of 1959, representatives of American naval forces in Yokosuka presented an additional 91,000 yen to the mayor of Yokosuka as a token of their support. The amount was soon to be matched by an equivalent sum that Itō and other naval enthusiasts and former officers had raised.[67]

Itō's 1956 article on the *Mikasa* was constructed along intellectual lines similar to those of the series on the JSDF. He wrote of the most important reason for the *Mikasa* to be preserved. It was a symbol of the achievements of the Japanese modernisation process, achievements that met the highest international standards of the day. He highlighted the universal character of the achievements of the Imperial Navy in the Russo-Japanese War, presenting evidence of how the leaders and assets deployed in the Battle of Tsushima were celebrated worldwide as textbook examples of tactical brilliance and impeccable execution.[68] Itō was playing to the 'modernity' of this ship and of the crew that manned it.

In another commemorative article appearing in 1959, just as the collection of funds was coming to its conclusion, Itō sought to expand on the idea of the importance of the *Mikasa* and of the navy to the Japanese nation. He did so by emphasising the contribution of the Combined Fleet in shielding Japan from the Russian threat.[69] In a period of increasing popular concerns over the intensifying Cold War and its consequences for Japan, the image of the navy's victory over the Baltic Fleet indirectly served as a source of security and inspiration. To elevate the navy's role in the defence of Japan, Itō further compared Tōgō's *Mikasa* to HMS *Victory* and USS *Constitution*. Like its British and American counterparts, the *Mikasa* too defined the success of the country's military tradition. For this reason – he pointed out – this battleship too deserved to become a site of proud public memory. His words did not fall on deaf ears, and to the present day, the attributes he stressed are still central to the exhibition on board the ship, where scale reconstructions of these three vessels and the portraits of their respective commanders occupy a central space.[70] Itō passed away shortly after the *Mikasa* regained its place in national history, but by then, he was no longer alone in exploring the world of the Imperial Navy, its traditions, and their significance to post-war Japan. A young novelist, Agawa Hiroyuki, was to carry on some of Itō's ideas.

War writing as a 'personal affair'

Agawa Hiroyuki's experience with the Japanese navy was different from Itō's. Unlike the journalist scholar, Agawa did not familiarise himself with the world of the navy in the heyday of the powerful battle fleet of the beginning of the twentieth century. Nor did he experience the bureaucratic tensions unfolding from the naval arms control system through a network of influential friendships. Yet, for over fifty years, Agawa's novels and publications shaped the mainstream image of the country's navy and its traditions.

Agawa Hiroyuki was born on 24 December 1920 in Hiroshima. The son of a local businessman, he possessed a natural talent for humanities and Asian classical literature which he cultivated by attending reputable local schools before moving to the capital to study Japanese literature at the prestigious Tokyo Imperial University (present Tokyo University). He graduated in 1942 with a dissertation on the famous novelist and short-story writer Shiga Naoya, immediately before he was conscripted into the navy at the rank of lieutenant through the Temporary Active Duty Officer System.[71] He served for the remainder of the war. As a 'man of letters' with a knowledge of Chinese and Japanese literature, the naval personnel department assigned him to the communications intelligence division of the Naval General Staff before posting him to China in a similar capacity.[72] The years spent in the navy left a lasting mark on Agawa, one that inspired his production and personal life. The fictional characters of some of his most renowned novels were made real and human by the numerous personal memories cultivated while conscripted in the service. Naval themes regularly recurred in his publications, while elements of the Japanese naval tradition and spiritual education such as songs, or the 'five minutes before code', featured in his children's education.[73]

Agawa's debut as a novelist came only a few months after his repatriation to Japan in 1946. His work appeared at a moment of feverish transformation throughout the domestic intellectual and publishing landscape. When the war ended, the censorship system of the 1930s collapsed. A 'hunger for words in print', combined with a genuine wish to find refuge in written works from the harshness of the daily routines, led to an impressive increase in the publishing activity.[74] Editors started considering manuscripts that had been previously censored. Writers poured into the capital. Allied authorities imposed restrictions on a number of topics, chiefly among them those implying criticism of their reforms or praising values they considered anti-democratic and jingoistic. Yet, 'the efflorescence of the publishing industry represented a triumph of intellectual and entrepreneurial spirit'.[75] As one scholar later remarked, public desire for literature and printed word showed that a phase of renewed 'literary renaissance' had dawned.[76]

By the end of 1945, more than 200 different magazines were printed, and this number doubled during the following year.[77] By 1949, occupation authorities surveyed for censorship reasons some 13,000 periodicals and a stunning 45,000 books and pamphlets.[78] Magazines of wide circulation featured in many cases literature sections. Throughout the same period, some 110 weekly and monthly publications, including leading titles such as *Bungei Shunjū*, *Chūō Kōron*, *Sekai*, *Ningen* and *Kindai Bungaku*, regularly published literary work. For the year 1946, approximately 28 per cent of all new books and 22.5 per cent of reprints were related to the field of literature.[79] Early in the 1950s, their circulation had reached remarkable levels, with prime magazines like *Sekai* having an average circulation of some 70,000 copies and, according to a contemporary source, a readership of well over 200,000.[80]

The literature of this period had two characteristics. The first concerned the rejection of what some had perceived as a form of 'intellectual slavery'. The 'wholesome literature' typical of pre-war Japan, celebrating neo-Confucian values and the organic vision of an Emperor-centric society permeated by the ethical values of the former samurai class, was abandoned in favour of a minimalist approach to morality, one with the needs of the individual at its heart. Decadence replaced wholesomeness in the literature of early post-war Japan; eroticism and self-indulgence became the themes that writers used to portray authenticity and individuality.[81] Novelist Sakaguchi Ango was one of the main icons of the bohemian intellectual spirit of the period. His April 1946 short essay titled 'On Decadence'[82] represented a manifesto of these writers' deeply felt contrast between the wartime illusion of grandeur and the decadent reality of post-war Japan. Sakaguchi considered the pre-war process of social engineering aimed at creating a homogeneous national identity based on the code of the samurai as an attempt to impose inhuman prohibitions on individuals.[83] He regarded wartime expressions of this orthodoxy such as the 'kamikaze hero' little more than 'a mere illusion'. In his view, 'The Emperor too is no more than illusion,' and his real history 'begins from the point where he becomes an ordinary human'. Sakaguchi's conclusion was that Japan's downfall represented a true moral watershed, since 'Japan was defeated, and the samurai ethics has perished, but humanity has been born from the womb of decadence's truth'.[84]

The second factor underpinning early post-war literary production was entwined with the first. The preference to focus on the individual and on the material demands of human nature reflected a rejection of the past with fundamental political ramifications. Writers and editors alike associated the darkness of the past with the intellectual and social tyranny imposed by the nation's military elites. Against this atmosphere, the vilification of the Japanese militarist leadership and the *j'accuse* launched against their deception of the nation throughout the years of the war became inherent components of the message of the literature of this era. Writers, editors and intellectuals tended to align their views with left-wing – often Marxist – political ideas. Democracy, respect for individual freedom of speech and religion, along with the idea of world peace, entered the basic vocabulary of the 'man of letters'. The flagship magazine of this new progressive intellectual expression was the monthly publication *Sekai*. Published by the highly reputed publisher Iwanami, the journal acknowledged the wartime 'unreasonableness, fraud, bluff and injustice'. It rejected armaments and empire to stimulate in Japan 'broad and bright morality and culture'.[85] By the end of the occupation, *Sekai* was an established journal wherein intellectuals and writers debated Japan's political choices in defence and security, championing a socialist neutrality vis-à-vis the East–West confrontation.[86]

Agawa's first short story appeared in the September 1946 issue of *Sekai*.[87] It dealt with a rather sensitive topic, one that was particularly problematic for the Allied forces and regularly subject to their control. The story revolved around the experience of a young survivor of the A-bomb in Hiroshima, and succeeded in passing official censorship almost unaltered, apart from one passage on rumoured genetic side effects of radiation.[88] This first story displayed all the attributes that became trademarks of Agawa's prose. His style was terse and aligned with the 'I-novels' (a literary genre which was first developed in the Taishō era), placing the protagonist's personal recollections at the centre of the story. These allowed the author to emphasise individuality and to enrich the character with his personal experience and thoughts.

The result was a product with a powerful human dimension that was key to the story's ability to appeal to its potential readership. In this regard, the influence of the old *maestro* Shiga Naoya on Agawa's works was clearly detectable.[89] In addition to specific stylistic solutions, Agawa's prose was appealing because of a dose of subtle irony and positivism that underpinned his approach to a topic as sensitive as the A-bomb experience. It was an attitude he often maintained when conversing about this subject. For instance, during an interview he gave a few years later, he recounted how he was amused by a joke often reported in Japanese magazines according to which in the case of another war, poison would be an item that everyone should keep never too far away.[90]

His first story was very well received and in just a few months, Agawa started other collaborations with leading Japanese literary periodicals such as *Shinchō*, *Kokoro*, *Bungakukai*, while maintaining his commitment with *Sekai*. These opportunities represented a valuable testing ground before he embarked on his first novels, published between 1952 and 1956. *Citadel in Spring*[91] and *Burial in the Clouds*[92] became Agawa's gateways to national fame. Both novels possessed an ideal appeal for a Japanese popular audience of the 1950s. They had relatively simple structures since they fell into the category of the I-novel genre he had tested in his shorter fictions. Equally significant, in both works the main character was a young Japanese student who had to abandon his civilian life and was drawn into the drama of war. In *Citadel in Spring*, the main character could very well be Agawa's alter ego. He was from Hiroshima, posted to serve in the navy in China and while there, he experienced the loss of friends and relatives who succumbed to the nuclear holocaust. In *Burial in the Clouds*, the protagonist was a suicide pilot trainee who died in July 1945, during the last days of the war.[93]

Both stories are filled with recollections, details and experiences from Agawa's personal life. The two novels dealt with the theme of the war as presented through the contradictory feelings of young Japanese conscripts, torn between loyalty and duty on the one hand, and concerns for their families, frustration for the difficulties of their tasks and a genuine desire to survive, on the other. In both novels, the individual stories created a portrayal of the navy as an institution that gave the conscripts' lives a sense of purpose and meaning on a daily basis, but that also required of them their ultimate commitment and sacrifice. In a world full of contradictions, the traditions of the navy seemed to offer a measure of comfort. In 1953, for the cultural contribution to post-war Japanese literature in the field of fiction, *Citadel in Spring* was awarded the prestigious Yomiuri Literary Prize (which Agawa won a second time in 2002).[94]

A navy with a human face

The style and topics of Agawa's books were in line with the literary trends of the time. Yet, their underlying ambitions stemmed from very different motivations. As a young man who had served in the war, he felt uncomfortable with the atmosphere of post-war Japan. The intelligentsia's backlash against wartime state institutions and the indiscriminate condemnation of those who had worn a uniform was to his eyes deeply unfair.[95] Agawa remembered that like many other young men of his generation, he had not cherished the idea of being drafted into the armed forces. Through that experience he had learnt first-hand that not all Japanese military officers were members of warlike factions and indeed, many of them did question the meaning of the war, as much as the attitudes of the ultra-militarist cliques. They all fought, however, for their country, a point of fundamental importance which contemporary writers and intellectuals alike too often tended to forget. Paraphrasing Maruyama Masao, Agawa regarded many of the 'progressive intellectuals' of this period and their attempt to de-humanise the imperial military as the hypocrite members of a 'community of remorse'[96] in which

> Many writers who had apparently been doing all right for themselves by cooperating with the militarists during the war had suddenly shifted their positions after the defeat and the beginning of the occupation. Many of them were busy explaining that they had always been peace-lovers and that they had also foreseen the defeat of Japan. I was angered by their conduct and actually hated them for their opportunism. So I decided that what I had to do as a writer was to set down the truth about the war as my fellow students and I had seen and experienced.[97]

Thus, war and atomic devastation became the primary tools Agawa's novels employed to bring the human dimension of the Japanese naval experience back into the realm of public memory. Through the pages of the protagonists' journals, readers were acquainted with naval customs and traditions, smart and incompetent officers, experienced and inexperienced non-commissioned officers. Through the informed and sensitive accounts of these *Tangen* officers, readers were projected into the complexities of the experience of war at the various levels of the commander, the instructor, the trainee. These scenarios enabled the audience to sympathise with the young Japanese officers at the heart of the stories and more importantly, to comprehend that the navy of the culminating phases of the war was not an evil aimless organisation. Rather, it was a handicapped military institution, with a rich combat tradition that lacked resources and, increasingly, well trained manpower. It had a duty to carry on the fight but it was not in the condition to do it properly.

Agawa's work shared one common factor with Itō's. It did not seek to simply justify naval authorities. On the contrary, in several passages his characters manifested disapproval of the senior naval leadership, even though each decision or order corresponded in his stories to the face of an individual wearing a uniform. The men who constituted its fabric were fallible. Contrary to the dark, monochromatic picture that progressive writers were giving of the wartime armed forces and of the futility of the war, Agawa used a wider canvas to portray the organisations and its members. Thus, abstract concepts such as militarism and ultra-nationalism were replaced by the dilemmas the protagonists faced in their daily duties. This was particularly the case for the young Tokkotai pilot in *Burial in the Clouds*. The protagonist harboured doubts about the spiritual rhetoric of the 'beautiful death' of the superior Japanese soul. He rationalised it by presenting this sacrifice as the only way for the service to atone for its earlier mistakes and continue to fight, while at the personal level, it demonstrated the young man's unaltered commitment to fulfil his duty. Agawa captures the contrasting feelings of the young educated man as follows:

> It's not that we must prepare ourselves to die by summer. No, he is telling us simply *to die*. What, in the name of heaven, is their goal? Is it to carry the war through to completion, or merely to kill us all. If we really can save our country by dying, then by all means let us do precisely that.[98]

Commenting on a prose poem written by another former student of Tokyo's Imperial University who served on the last voyage of the battleship *Yamato*, a leading American scholar noted that the author wished 'to expunge the impression of meaningless death from the memory of his comrades, liberate them from shame, memorialise their sincerity and bravery, and mourn those who perished'.[99] Similar reflections applied to Agawa. As a former *Tangen*, Agawa had a personal sympathy for the navy rooted in his war experience, and he wanted to share it with his readership.[100] In this respect, Agawa's perception of the navy stood in sharp contrast with that of other *Tangen* officers who had served in the army. Compared to the navy, graduate students conscripted in the army received a harsh treatment and were chiefly used as foot soldiers.[101] These different management policies weighted heavily on the emotional ties that many entertained with the two armed services and the way they expressed them. Former Prime Minister Nakasone Yasuhiro (1982–87) proudly acknowledged his service in the navy's *Tangen* programme and often attended veteran meetings. By contrast, political or business figures who had been drafted in the army tended to remain silent about it.[102]

Agawa too had remained in contact with naval comrades through the activities of the Japan Naval Association.[103] Through that link, he came to know former junior imperial naval officers who were now serving in the mid-upper ranks of the JMSDF. In the 1960s, as a famous novelist, a naval aficionado and above all, a former fellow officer, Agawa had become a welcome celebrity guest on board JMSDF warships at festivals and naval parades. His son Naoyuki recalled how during one of those events held in the summer of 1969, he had the opportunity to meet for the first time the then Chief of Maritime Staff, Admiral Uchida Kazuomi (1969–72).[104] Agawa held the men who served in the navy in high esteem, and they certainly respected him. In the initial months of the occupation, Admiral Uchida had commanded units repatriating soldiers and nationals overseas, worked in the Second Demobilisation Ministry, and eventually lived the drama of the sudden and fierce resentment of the Japanese people towards the uniformed men of the armed forces.[105] For young officers of Uchida's calibre, Agawa's novels had given voice to the human experience of the sailors who had served the country with dignity.

In the two decades from 1965 to 1986, Agawa took his initial activity as a naval novelist to a new level. He used his exploration of the individuals that made up its human fabric to explore the organisation and its professional identity. In the process, he went on to complete four naval books, including three biographies that consecrated his reputation as the chronicler of the navy treaty faction. In the early 1960s, Agawa was approached by the editors of the *Asahi Shimbun* who were preparing a special issue aimed at re-examining the attempted *coup d'état* of 26 February 1936 led by an ultra-nationalist faction of the Imperial Army.[106] Agawa initially declined the offer, as he had no real interest in writing about the army. In subsequent conversations with the editors, however, he reconsidered his position and started exploring issues related to the pre-war military leadership. This was a question of central significance in the 1930s' shift towards militarism, and he suggested that a study of the life of Admiral Yamamoto Isoroku – a key protagonist – was ideal to explore the matter.[107]

Agawa took the new task to heart and conducted extensive research on Yamamoto, consulting military documents and interviewing veterans and former naval officers who had either known him or served under his command. Part of his enthusiasm came from the fact that the navy he was examining was different from the armed force he had known as a junior officer in China. Reflections on individual leadership, human networks, strategy, politics, and bureaucratic tensions all blended together to define the admiral's life. Agawa found his research rewarding, especially insofar as the analysis of the causes of the war were concerned, and the role that key senior naval officers like Yamamoto played in opposing the Tripartite Pact with Germany and Italy (27 September 1940).[108] In the book, Agawa sided with the admiral and his moderate colleagues (the members of the so-called treaty faction), emphasising the army's responsibilities for the bellicose path of the late 1930s. Agawa used one of Yamamoto's closest associates and protégé, Rear Admiral Inoue Shigeyoshi, to fully convey this idea:

> From his position as Chief of Staff (in Yokosuka), Inoue could clearly see the increasingly sinister turn that events were taking both inside and outside the navy. Even among naval officers themselves, people were so busy sounding each other out to find whether they belonged to the 'fleet faction' or the 'treaty faction' that it was impossible to talk frankly to any but one's closest acquaintances. Inoue began to feel the need to take precautions so that, should something happen, enough men could be sent from Yokosuka to guard the Navy Ministry. What ever course the Army chose to take, it had plenty of troops at its disposal in Tokyo, but the navy had no active units there at all.[109]

For Agawa, Yamamoto summed up the virtues and limits of the naval leadership. At the conference of September 1940 where the navy top brass had to decide its position on the Tripartite Pact, Yamamoto showed his disapproval not on a question of principle;

rather, he did so on the basis of what the novelist biographer considered the admiral's sphere of competence:

> I haven't the slightest intention of raising any objections to steps on which the minister has already decided. However, there is one point that worries me greatly and on which I would like to ask your opinion. According to the cabinet Planning Board's blueprint for the mobilisation of the material resources – as it was until August last year when I was vice-minister – eighty per cent of all materials were due to be supplied from areas under the control of Britain or America. The signing of the tripartite Pact will inevitably mean losing these, and I would like you to tell us quite clearly – since I wish to be able to carry out my duties as commander in chief of the Combined Fleet with an easy mind – what switches have been made in the materials programme in order to make up for the resulting inadequacies.[110]

Agawa's final assessment of Yamamoto's position, while not acquitting the navy from its incapacity to obstruct the new political and military alignment, was animated by the sympathy for the dilemma it revealed:

> If Yamamoto had carried opposition to the Tripartite Pact to the point of threatening to resign his post as commander in chief, the result might well have been a domestic upheaval more serious, even, than the celebrated February 26 Incident. It was Yamamoto's oft-stated opinion that domestic revolution would not itself ruin the country, and would be better at least than a war against America. But he might well be killed. Or his threat to resign might have been welcomed in some quarters and accepted without demur, in which case he could have been put on the reserve list and obliged to remain inactive while the storm swept over his head, Either way, such questions can never leave the realm of speculation.
>
> In practice, Yamamoto remained in his post as commander in chief of the Combined Fleet and thus found himself obliged to consider how the navy should wage the war with America that was now so fast becoming a real threat. If such a war came, there would be little hope of victory, or even a favourable and early peace, unless some quite extraordinary measures were resorted to.[111]

For Agawa, there seemed to be no ideal solution to the situation. Agawa seemed to marry the line that the navy tried to prevent the war on a technical basis with the line that it eventually, on the same basis, was prepared to fight the war. Once the Yamamoto biography was finished, Agawa felt that the navy's internal struggle deserved further attention and he continued to study the anti-axis, administrative faction. Eventually, he produced the biographies of its two other core representatives: Admiral Yonai Mitsumasa (published in 1978) and Admiral Inoue Shigeyoshi (published in 1986). Both books contributed to strengthen the notion that the navy had been divided over the question of the war, and that those belonging to the treaty faction had acted in line with the country's naval traditions in opposing the war politically, but had still fought it with no hesitation once the war course was set in motion. In a fashion not too dissimilar from Itō, Agawa too gave the navy a human face to explain the controversial aspects of its role in the decision to go to war and, in so doing, sought to highlight the value of its professional ethos in the decision to fight to the bitter end when no other alternative was left.

Humanising the Japanese naval experience and allowing the Japanese public to identify themselves with the country's naval traditions became a theme he further explored in another major publication. In addition to the biographies of the two admirals, in 1975 Agawa published a dense two-volume non-fiction on the history of the battleship *Nagato* (Yamamoto's flagship before the battleship *Yamato* joined the fleet). In it, he deployed the captivating style of his previous I-novels to explore the career of the vessel marking the rise and fall of the Japanese influence in East Asia.[112] The approach used in the book aimed at presenting a period of Japanese history from the perspective of the crew, almost as a way 'to mourn and speak well of the dead'. This stylistic solution was reminiscent of Yoshida Mitsuru's extremely popular *Requiem for Battleship Yamato*.[113] Like Agawa's prior and subsequent works, the volumes were a staggering success. As the 1980s dawned and the public grew nostalgic for a past of quintessential Japanese values, Agawa became the ambassador of the ideals of respect for traditions, smartness and cosmopolitan sophistication associated with the navy.[114]

In the late 1960s and in the 1970s, Agawa's naval stories, with their accessible prose and not overly moralistic tone, had a great appeal to an increasingly consumer-oriented society. The 'Agawa style' nicely matched the preferences of a readership that enjoyed quality products but had less interest in in-depth critical views of the fundamental issues connected to Japan's past military experience.[115] More crucially, by focusing on the actions of the component of the naval leadership (the Yamamoto, Yonai, Inoue 'trio') that fought to prevent the war, Agawa constructed a positive narrative of the past. In it, he created a continuum of 'tradition' and 'modernity', highlighting the liberal, anti-militarist attitudes of inter-war Japan.[116] His books were ideal mass consumer products of the day: they were well researched, well written, charged with drama, dealt with interesting themes and presented to the nation heroes with human faces and real dilemmas from an age previously portrayed as plainly dark. Agawa's publications also created an intellectual continuum with the production of other contemporary maestros like Shiba, who wrote expressing similar views on the navy, but focusing on earlier events of the Meiji era.

In 1967, for his *Yamamoto Isoroku*, Agawa became the recipient of another prestigious literary award, the 13th Shinchōsha Literary Prize. His portrayal of the admiral inspired Akira Kurosawa's initial contribution to Yamamoto's dramatised characterisation in the 1970 American–Japanese fiction film *Tora! Tora! Tora!* In 1979, Kodansha International translated the book into English with excellent sales. Reportedly, editors at Kodansha 'proudly' listed the book among the company's best sellers marketed in the 1970s.[117] Since its publication, *Yamamoto Isoroku* remained the standard bibliographical reference on the Japanese admiral and a mass consumption novel, even though later scholarship put in perspective some of Agawa's conclusions on Yamamoto's intellectual affiliation to the treaty faction as well as his sympathies for the admiral's strategic choices.[118] Long-term specialists on the Battle of Midway, Jonathan Parshall and Anthony Tully, fully captured the virtues of this work noting that *The Reluctant Admiral* was the piece to read 'if you want to get a feel for Admiral Isoroku Yamamoto'.[119]

General interest and literary recognitions for Agawa's naval works continued well into the 1980s and 1990s. In 1987, he was awarded the Japan Prize in Literature for his *Inoue Seibi* and, in 2007, he became the 55th recipient of the Kikuchi Kan Prize. Eventually, the greatest recognition of his lifelong contribution to Japanese contemporary culture and literature arrived in 1999, when he received the Order of Culture,[120] the single most prestigious official Japanese decoration in the field of humanities, directly conferred each year by the Emperor of Japan on 'culture day' (3 November).[121] Agawa, the naval chronicler, had officially entered the Olympus of the Japanese post-war intellectual landscape.

As a former junior naval officer, Agawa strove to portray the navy as an organisation with a human dimension, and the preparation of the biographies of renowned admirals and of crew activities kept him in contact with former fellow officers and naval aficionados. These interactions allowed him to enrich the narratives with personal stories and recollections from real experience. Indeed, for the volumes on Admiral Inoue, Agawa had the unique privilege to spend a considerable amount of time with the late admiral himself, hearing his accounts first-hand. This was remarkable given that, after the war, Admiral Inoue had withdrawn from public life and had little inclination to speak of the wartime years.[122] Agawa was the exception to the rule and shared many conversations with him.[123] As Agawa's acquaintances included pre-eminently veterans associated with the pro-Anglophone faction, and these officers mentored many first generation leaders of the JMSDF, Agawa became relatively close to them too.[124]

Agawa Noyuki and the navies of past and present

By the second half of the 1980s, retired chiefs of staff like Admiral Uchida and Admiral Nakamura Teiji would be in the habit of meeting with Agawa for an evening out in central Tokyo. Among the occasions for such social events were the periodical meetings of the *Tan Tan Kai*, an informal gathering organised by people like Agawa and the two JMSDF admirals to celebrate the visits of American friend and Pentagon representative, Dr James Auer.[125] Agawa used his literary talent, irony and *naval esprit* to come up with the name for the meetings. The Chinese character 'awa' was pronounced in Japanese with a sound similar to Auer's surname but when doubled it also meant 'to be philosophical about life', an expression describing a typical attitude of Japanese naval officers who 'did their job and did not show it off'. Given the nature and the background of the majority of the members of this informal group, the name seemed particularly appropriate.[126] Other attendees to the meetings included Captain (later Rear Admiral) Kawamura Sumihiko, *Asahi Shimbun* correspondent Sasaki Yoshitaka and, later on, US navy Lt. Commander Torkel Lloyd Patterson, who in 1988 replaced Dr Auer as Japan desk officer at the Pentagon.[127]

Over the years, however, Agawa became less regular in his attendance to the events, but he made sure that this family tradition was passed on to his son. Agawa Naoyuki had lived in the United States until early in the 1990s, first graduating in law from Georgetown University in 1984 and subsequently working for an American law firm. It was shortly after his return to Japan in 1991 that he took over from his father in attending the *Tan Tan Kai* events. Nauyuki had known Auer in the United States and as a result, he invited the young Agawa to these events when he visited Japan.

As someone who had learnt about the navy through his father's work and personal stories, Naoyuki was struck by the intellectual stature of the JMSDF admirals whose names, compared to those of their imperial forerunners, were unknown to the majority of the Japanese people,[128] an impression that was confirmed when the young Agawa attended some of the JMSDF's public relations events. In particular, in 1992, Naoyuki was invited to the graduation ceremony at the Naval Academy in Etajima.[129] On that occasion, he was introduced to Captain (later Admiral) Furushō Kōichi,[130] an officer possessing the politeness and composure typical of the senior naval heroes of Agawa's novels, with whom Naoyuki established a friendly relationship. Over the years, Furushō continued to mentor the younger Agawa whenever they met in social events, introducing him to the world of the JMSDF, eventually becoming one of Naoyuki's closest contacts within the navy.[131]

Mutatis mutandis, in the 1990s Agawa Naoyuki took on his father's mantle by entering the world of Japanese naval traditions as they were maintained by the JMSDF.[132] Naoyuki did not have to wait long to share his knowledge of the navy with a broader audience. In the United States, he had already started publishing for the Japanese *Chūō Kōronsha* general audience books on his experience with the American legal system.[133] In the mid-1990s, the first feature articles on the JSDF started appearing in weekly and monthly publications as a consequence of their first international overseas operations. Naoyuki was asked by one of his editors to write on this subject for the magazine *Chūō Kōron* and his thoughts went to his personal encounters with the JMSDF. Little was known of the post-war admirals. Yet, the navy of the 1990s was 'the direct result of what some of those officers had done back in the 1950s and the 1960s'.[134] His argument was convincing especially since he had met many of them and could comment meaningfully on their actions.

Shortly thereafter, Naoyuki started conducting interviews and wrote for the magazine on some of the JMSDF's key figures, chiefly among them Admiral Uchida and Nakamura. He described their experience in war and defeat with the Imperial Navy, the impact on their lives of the change of status of the armed forces in the post-war period, and their willingness to react to an environment unfavourable to defence and military affairs. Throughout their careers in the JMSDF, they had not fought in battles, but that did not mean that their effort was of less importance. They had fought a different fight, one not newsworthy, but equally critical. Agawa later employed Admiral Uchida's words to emphasise that the JMSDF's daily routine resembled to that of a rehearsal for a play since

> For soldiers and sailors, it can be said that everyday life is nothing but a rehearsal. Everything – training, discipline, education, exercise, and inspection – is a rehearsal for an emergency. Yet, this rehearsal is decisively different from actual combat, however hard it is conducted. First of all, you are not under fire. Opponents, weapons, battlefields, and friends can change every time. ... No matter how hard you rehearse, no victory in actual combat is guaranteed – it is completely different from a play in this way.[135]

They had fought hard to reconstitute Japan's 'shattered' naval spirit and capabilities, drawing inspiration and guidance from retired imperial officers and comrades like Admiral Yamanashi.[136] Learning from the shortcomings of wartime operations, they knew their mission was vital, namely the defence of the country's economic interests at sea. To that end, the JMSDF cultivated close ties with the American forces in the Pacific. In turn, the reciprocal respect underpinning the partnership between the American and Japanese navies throughout the Cold War proved – in Agawa's view – the JMSDF's professionalism and the indispensable character of their missions.[137]

Public response to the articles was good, and the magazine received numerous letters from retired sailors and officers – some of them inevitably providing feedback on the facts reported – as well as non-professional readers, who had simply found the stories unusual and thus, stimulating.[138] These were small forgotten stories of post-war Japan. Eventually, in 1997, *Chūō Kōron* gave Agawa two more years to complete his research and transform what had been a part-time endeavour into a book-length manuscript. The end product appeared in 2001, and – for a book on a rather niche topic – it yielded a positive market response. As of Spring 2010, it had sold some 27,000 copies, remaining to that date a major success in the *Chūō Kōron* wide circulation series.[139] The JMSDF too was pleased with the book, adopting it as one of the 'required' readings for midshipmen studying at the academy. The young Agawa had carried on his father's legacy giving a human face to the Japanese navy, connecting the imperial force to its post-war successor. As the late Admiral Uchida later wrote to Agawa, he lived as a 'nobody' when he was an admiral and a chief of staff, to become 'someone' after people read his book. With a touch of irony, he was pleased to note that he 'was given the honour of being recognised as a professional from amateurs'.[140]

Conclusions

In retrospect, these three authors' work focused on a niche topic, that of the navy and in that guise had no secondary significance. In their different professional endeavours, they joined contemporary trends and debates and provided informed views of remarkable public appeal. Itō was the military correspondent of his age, working for Japan's top media agencies for half a century. Agawa Hiroyuki remains an acclaimed novelist whose work appeared in the most reputable magazines and was distributed by prime labels of the publishing business. His son Naoyuki drew upon his father's contacts and experience and contributed to connect the JMSDF to the public image of a 'good navy' explaining how the essence of the Imperial Navy lived on in the post-war era. Taken altogether, their work fit into the literary genre defined elsewhere as the 'Kōdansha culture' (in reference to the publisher Kodansha who championed such an approach to publishing). Their books sought to create a 'new culture tied to a radiant past' bringing it into the realm of Japanese everyday life.[141]

This radiant past blended traditional Japanese values such as commitment, loyalty, sense of duty and modern Western attributes such as open-mindedness and mastery of technology. The navy was, in this sense, traditional and modern, and this professional ethos delivered a stark contrast with the militaristic spiritual emphasis put forward in post-war army accounts. Crucially, Itō and Agawa offered narratives encompassing all aspects of the navy, from senior leaders like Tōgō, Yamamoto, Yonai and Inoue to life on iconic battleships like *Mikasa* and *Nagato*, to individual *Tokkotai* conscripts. They described the navy as an organisation made up of core professional tenets and human dilemmas, allowing the readership to emphasise with its actions and understand its mistakes.[142] In so doing, they managed to steer clear of an uncritical apologetic argument, not sparing irony and criticisms for some of the navy's activities. A passage from one of Agawa's novels is particularly indicative in this regard. Facing harsh training, the young pilot protagonist of *Burial in the Clouds* remarked that:

> I don't know what will ultimately be written about the Imperial Navy, or about the education men received at the Naval Academy, with its (supposed) spirit of patriotic self-sacrifice. I have no idea what the future will say about any of this. But how often the precept 'A superior officer's order is implicitly the order of the Emperor himself' is used, conveniently, to provide cover for essentially selfish acts![143]

Agawa Naoyuki built on this narrative and, in telling the story of the first generation of JMSDF senior officers (all former imperial war veterans), portrayed how it lived on in the post-war navy. In the 1990s, against an expanding market for information on the JSDF, Agawa's novel looked at the relationship between Japan's two navies to validate its professional pedigree. In this process, retired top echelons from both services offered crucial assistance, giving access to source materials otherwise inaccessible to civilian researchers. Long interviews, reunions at the Japan Naval Association, attendance to pageantry events or informal meetings, all served as gateways into the more intimate sphere of the two navies' *esprit the corps*. Within the safety of these spaces, officers from both navies told 'their' story, one that tended to focus pre-eminently on the navy's moderate faction. Their narrative was not about all the facets of the navy; it was about the 'good navy', the one that seemed to capture its real professional essence.

The wider significance of these representations of the Imperial Navy was to be found in one very influential defence-related document of the early 2000s. In the foreword to the report of the civilian body tasked by Prime Minister Koizumi with drafting policy recommendations to reform Japan's defence posture in the post-9/11 security milieu, Chairman Araki Hiroshi, advisor to Tokyo Electric Company, wrote:

> According to Hiroyuki Agawa, Shigeyoshi Inoue, a Japanese Imperial Navy Admiral widely known as the 'last navy admiral', strongly objected to the navy headquarters' gigantic budget request calling for the construction of large battleships, contending that the navy was attempting to 'fight war in the Showa period with the equipment of the Meiji era'. Inoue insisted on incorporating air power into the navy. I kept this anecdote in mind in moderating the sessions of this Council. There is no way of knowing what Admiral Inoue would have recommended had he lived in this era, but I would note the increased importance of soft power in dealing with

> security and defence issues in the twenty-first century. Hard power is necessary. But it works effectively only when combined with reliable intelligence and good managerial skills.[144]

In this passage, the Imperial Navy was no longer history. It had become public memory. The question is this: How did the JMSDF internalise its own history?

Photo 3.1 Shattered sword: The *Mikasa* in 1954.

Photo 3.2 A new beginning: The *Mikasa* in 1959.

Photo 3.3 Emperor Shōwa visiting the Mikasa Museum.

Photo 3.4 Royal Prince Akihito visiting the Mikasa Museum.

4

Experience and Legacy: The Education of a New Navy

I expect the crews of the units deployed overseas to avoid becoming overexcited and concentrate on each one's duty. I believe they are able to accomplish their given duties without fail, by demonstrating the capabilities of the JMSDF, which have been developed through years of training, and the unbroken tradition and culture of the former Imperial Navy. Their success will be an asset to Japan.[1]

Admiral Kōichi Furushō, JMSDF
(26th Chief of Maritime Staff, 2003–5)

In your opinion, what is the major difference between the Imperial Japanese Navy and the JMSDF?

The name.[2]

Anonymous Lieutenant Commander, JMSDF
(Command and Staff Course, Maritime Staff College)

Japan's self-righteous and traditional sailors

In 2003, the *Nippon Hōsō Kyōkai* (NHK) published a ground-breaking volume covering little-known events preceding the establishment of the JSDF. The book was based on a television documentary in which the JMSDF had been involved in a consultancy role. The book, like the documentary, sought to explore the historical circumstances around the creation of the post-war military and how these had affected the organisational cultures of the three services. In it, Japanese soldiers were colloquially known as those who 'prepare carefully'[3] in an organisation that suffered from chronic 'arteriosclerosis',[4] reflecting the self-defence role enshrined in the constitution. Airmen were awarded epithets such as 'brave and daring'[5] designed to tease an organisation 'disjointed'[6] from its peers as it lacked a pre-war tradition and shared missions.[7] Crucially, sailors were the only military group of the three armed services to be professionally defined by their link with the pre-war forerunners. In the JMSDF, sailors possessed a 'self-righteous'[8] attitude for they 'defended traditions'[9] of imperial memory – a point of view shared by Admiral Furushō. In supporting the project, the JMSDF seemed keen to make the point that this connection defined its members' sense of pride and belonging, and the way they wished to present themselves to a broader public.

This chapter investigates this concept and details how the JMSDF processed the experience of the Imperial Navy to create a legacy that functioned to shape its own professional identity. In education and training, the JMSDF turned to the Imperial Navy that had won the first tests of strengths at the turn of the century to set values and standards, and to qualify assumptions on the navy's role in national defence. In the microcosm of educational establishments and ships, its leadership introduced terminology and consistent practices that put a premium on teamwork and seamanship in a fashion not dissimilar to the Imperial Navy. The importance of the imperial legacy rested not merely on the need to define a brand of naval professionalism; it served to distinguish naval personnel – especially officers – from colleagues in the other branches of the military. At the higher level of military education, the reintegration of imperial traditions was complemented by a more critical analysis of the experience of the Pacific War as 'an indication of the pitfalls that lie in the path'.[10]

The past as prologue: An academy for gentlemen-officers

When in 1952 it started to become clear that Japan would re-establish some form of military organisation, the layout of the educational system for the officer corps of the National Safety Force,[11] the paramilitary precursor of the JSDF, emerged as one of the top priorities of governmental officials. In the pre-war era, officers' education was firmly under the control of the Imperial Army and Navy, and Japanese political authorities regarded this as an issue that needed to be addressed. For Prime Minister Yoshida himself, the imperial military academies – particularly the army's – had produced officers who were elitist imperial devotees with a narrow professional focus, inclined to support military policies based on their respective services' budgetary interests rather than a wider strategic vision.[12] Admiral Yonai Mitsumasa, a respected officer and former navy minister (1937–39 and 1944–45) and prime minister (January–July 1940) shared this view; he pointed out that inter-service frictions in the 1930s and 1940s had stemmed from substantial differences in officers' education. The army taught its members 'nothing but war' to empower its officers with the ability to face the tactical and operational challenges of the front line. In turn, officers had 'a narrower vision' on matters of national strategy and international affairs in comparison to their colleagues wearing a navy uniform.[13] Recent scholarship proved that the Admiral's views downplayed the navy's own problems with the 'radicalisation' of its middle echelons in the second half of the 1930s.[14] Yet, the constructive behaviour of former senior naval officers like Nomura Kichisaburō, Hoshina Zenshiro and Yamanashi Katsutoshin in the early post-war years implicitly seemed to confirm Yonai's assessment of the differences between the two educational systems.

The elitist imperial character of the pre-war officer corps, the lack of inter-service dialogue, and a narrow interpretation of the military profession underscored the set of issues that post-war military education had to address.[15] Prime Minister Yoshida felt strongly about the subject. In this area, he enjoyed a considerable degree of autonomy from occupation authorities. As such, he worked to devise a system that would produce 'highly educated, well trained, strongly motivated' officers, but officers that would also perceive themselves as an integral part of the national social fabric.[16] He wished them to digest the notion that in the contemporary world, the meaning of defence transcended the protection of one's country from conventional threats to include the creation of the conditions to secure the freedom, prosperity and well-being of its people. Yoshida wanted to pave the way for a national armed force, geared to defend the Japanese people and their well-being rather than merely executing imperial orders expressed by military leaders.[17] Civilian instructors and managers were to make sure that this idea governed the spirit of the new officers' school.

These premises set the stage for the single most crucial difference introduced in the Japanese post-war military education system. In 1952, the creation of the National Defence Academy[18] marked the dawn of civilian control over the primary institute for the education of the post-war officer corps. Yoshida's input informed ideational as well as practical aspects. Concerning the school's location, for instance, the initial idea was to establish it in the former facilities of the Naval Academy in Etajima. Yoshida found the option unsound on the grounds that it would be difficult to have qualified academic staff working at such a distance from Tokyo. He also felt that a place in the vicinity of the capital would facilitate students' understanding 'of values through contact with the present-day world at home and abroad'.[19] Yokosuka was eventually selected as host city since it met all the above criteria. It was well suited for training on land and at sea, and it provided a quiet environment to favour the students' focus on their professional socialisation.[20]

The Defence Academy's formative philosophy was modelled on the liberal lines of Japan's top civilian universities. No man possessed better credentials to carry out the job at hand than the institute's first president, Maki Tomō, professor of political science from Keio University. Maki had studied at Oxford before the war, was a charismatic teacher and an inspiring orator with some managerial experience.[21] He shared Yoshida's view that the new officers were to be educated not as war technicians, but as 'first-class human beings who can present themselves anywhere in society'.[22] This also had a practical reason in that academy graduates were not obliged to join the JSDF and therefore, the standard of education had to compete with that provided by other civilian institutions.[23] For the Defence Academy, it was important to prove the value of its methods in a context where approximately 5 per cent of the graduates choose civilian life or other branches of public administration as career paths.[24] Spiritual education as it was instilled by pre-war military academies was to find little space in a curriculum embracing science and engineering at its core. The goal was to develop the students' rational thinking capabilities and to that end, the academic departments applied standards comparable to those of the Tokyo Institute of Technology. Indeed, in the early years of the academy, the teaching of scientific subjects was to occupy just a little less than half of the entire duration of the four-year programme.[25]

Physical training, the study of military affairs and the learning of discipline and good manners complemented the science-based curriculum.[26] Reportedly, Maki sought the advice of Vice Admiral Inoue Shigeyoshi, the former commandant of the Naval Academy who had advocated that cadets had to be educated first as 'gentlemen'.[27] The admiral's considerations matched Maki's ideas, and one controversial practice he introduced was designed to foster this spirit. He introduced a formal ball dance to celebrate the end of the academic year. In Maki's understanding, this was to oblige students to practise their social skills in a civilian context. Regarded with profound contempt by former Imperial Army officers like Tsuji Masanobu when first introduced, the annual ball still takes place and continues to represent a formative experience for the young cadets.[28] Maki's vision was one imbued with a flavour of *noblesse oblige*, where the sense of responsibility would grow in students as a result of their knowledge and individual sophistication.[29] Maki's long tenure as president of the Defence Academy (1952–65) ensured his legacy. In fact, though not without detractors, almost all of the subsequent seven presidents, including leading liberal political scientist Inoki Masamichi (1970–78) and more recently, Nishihara Masashi (2000–6), sought to follow in his footsteps.[30]

The military identity of the JSDF, as it became formalised in the ethos[31] adopted in June 1961, further echoed the democratic spirit embraced by the academy. The text *de facto* replaced the Imperial Rescript in providing the basic tenets underpinning the meaning of the military profession.[32] The core concern of the researchers who drafted the document was the removal of all references to the imperial ideology, placing the peace and independence of the nation at the core of its message.[33] Democratic ideals and martial values were to blend together in a formula that required service members to identify themselves with the 'Japanese people' and to take 'pride in serving the public without thinking of their personal interest'.[34] In pursuing their line of duty, service members had to follow criteria that stressed individual development through discipline. This, in turn, was to serve teamwork and enhance an 'awareness of the core mission' of national defence.[35]

Over the decades, the application of the Defence Academy spirit[36] entailed regular upgrading of the curriculum to maintain adequate academic standards. In 1960, at the request of the defence agency, the initial emphasis on science-based subjects was reconsidered to introduce the study of humanities.[37] Such requests were characteristic of the dilemma over the balance between academic learning and military education, an 'Athenian intellectual spirit' and a 'Spartan military culture', as academics teaching at the academy summarised it.[38] In this respect, for many years the requirement to instil a martial spirit into future officers was counterbalanced by public concerns over an excessive emphasis that could lead to a militaristic drift.[39] Eventually, in 1974, a degree in humanities and social sciences was established. Progressively, the number of hours allocated to military training over the four years decreased from 1,428 to the current 1,005, giving academic activities the lead role in the educational process.[40]

By the end of the twentieth century, the National Defence Academy possessed six academic departments,[41] and an array of undergraduate and postgraduate programmes (including PhD degrees since 2001). Taught subjects varied from avionics, chemistry and engineering to languages, defence studies, military sociology and international development.[42] The result is a demanding daily schedule, starting at 6.30 am and ending at 22.30 with the 'lights-off', where even free time is allocated at specific moments of the day.[43] In numerous personal conversations, academy graduates proved to be well spoken and thoughtful, showing a good understanding of the subject areas they studied.[44] This does not mean that the knowledge of a secured job at the end of the programme, the intense curriculum, and the regimented life have not at times had a negative effect on the students' attitude to learning.[45] Yet, when exposed to a social context, the cadets' educational background and manners seemed to meet the ambitious standards originally set by president Maki.

In a second critical area education at the Defence Academy aimed at instilling different values from pre-war institutions, namely inter-service cooperation. From the moment cadets enrolled, they joined one of the platoons[46] of the four battalions[47] into which the entire student body was organised. As the selection for the students' future service branch was performed at the end of the sophomore year, all platoons eventually included students from the ground, air and maritime services. There is wide agreement among senior uniformed and civilian personnel about the benefits of this system, which for many of them set out the long-term foundations for the relatively smooth nature of the recent transformation towards a higher degree of cooperation within the Japanese military.[48]

The platoon was central to the cadets' life. There, students learnt to share pain, difficulties, to compete against other platoons and battalions regardless of their future service. All cadets underwent joint-programmes, practising sea training and the use of firearms and taking part in combined military exercises such as maritime transportation of ground forces.[49] This, coupled with various club associations encompassing sports or other intellectual activities, ensured that by the end of the four years, camaraderie was created on the basis of the students' unit and individual interests beyond the division of services.[50] At the dawn of the twenty-first century, the fruits of this longstanding approach are being harvested, especially at the higher organisational and operational levels, where more than fifty years of shared history among former graduates seems to be compensating for lack of joint operational experience.[51] One retired vice admiral who was among the first to promote the strengthening of joint functions at the operational level summarised this point, noting that:

> If we conduct some joint operations and I, as naval officer, am on the bridge of a ship and someone else in the army is responsible for his part of the operation, we can reach each other easily and talk each other because we were at the National Defence Academy together. That is a very beneficial aspect for us.[52]

The making of a naval officer: Education, training and the spirit of Etajima

Within the wider context of post-war reforms addressing the shortcomings of the pre-war system, for the forerunners of the JMSDF too, the issue of quality naval education was a top priority. As early as autumn 1951, the consultative body tasked to investigate initial naval rearmament, the 'Y' Committee,[53] devoted a series of sessions to establish the requirements for education in naval matters and seamanship.[54] The former naval officers who joined the committee perceived the modernisation of the education system as a pressing necessity. They all seemed to agree that the limits in technical knowledge and innovation of the Japanese military machine had been a key factor in the country's naval downfall.[55] In the early 1950s, such an understanding was coupled with the awareness that further technical and tactical changes were characterising the transformation of air, surface and submarine operations.[56] In addition, the setting of guidelines for the new Defence Academy also meant that a solid service-oriented education was indispensable to complete the basic naval instruction received by the new breed of cadets.[57]

A modern educational system that could take account of all these factors was crucial to rebuild the professionalism of the Japanese naval service (Figure 4.1). In August 1952, with the support of American naval authorities who closely monitored Japanese naval rearmament plans, formal training started in Yokosuka with a programme fulfilling the parameters indicated by the 'Y' Committee. It included courses on navigation, communications, ship maintenance and logistics, naval aviation, together with modules on combat systems for surface engagements, anti-submarine warfare and mine counter-measures and detection systems such as radar.[58]

A little less than a century after the founding fathers of the Imperial Navy had adopted the Royal Navy's system of training, the leadership of the post-war naval service looked at the world's leading naval power of the day to model the curricula of its schools. The establishment of an educational system enriched by elements of the American experience served to reconstitute, in a post-war age, a fine brand of professionalism.[59] This was certainly the idea of Admiral Nagasawa Kō, the first JMSDF Chief of Maritime Staff (1954–58). In November 1955, accompanied by Rear Admiral Nakayama Sadayoshi (later Admiral and Chief of Staff, 1961–63), he visited the United States to discuss with American counterparts organisational procedures and structure to ensure that the infant JMSDF would set itself on the right path.[60] In areas like submarine warfare, where Japanese know-how was particularly outdated and facilities either non-existent or inadequate, Japanese crews were allowed to attend courses in the United States.[61] Further input on the instruction of Japanese officers and crews in the latest tactics and procedures was provided by short courses organised when American surface and subsurface units visited naval bases in Japan.[62]

In the following years, the JMSDF's plans for naval education took the shape of two institutions for basic and higher education: the Officers Candidate School in Etajima and the Maritime Staff College in Yokosuka. Additional service schools for basic, intermediate and advanced technical instruction were also set up.[63] In detail, the 1st and 2nd Service Schools,[64] established in 1953 and 1956 in Etajima and Taura (Yokosuka), respectively, were attended by officers destined to serve on the fleet's surface units and in logistics-related posts.[65] These were followed in 1960 by the opening of the 3rd Service School (located in Shimofusa, Chiba Prefecture), where courses focused on the training and preparation of the uniformed men of the fleet's air wing. In 1975, the establishment of the 4th Service School was authorised in the aftermath of the 4th Build-up Plan to accommodate the increased demands for the preparation of personnel in matters of administration, logistics and electronic systems.[66]

As technology-intensive organisations, navies have an essential interest in maintaining schools that can provide comprehensive and updated naval instruction. The JMSDF was no exception to this rule, and its top echelons regularly underlined the importance of ensuring the material conditions necessary to create a first-class naval force.[67] In 1969, Admiral Uchida noted that the JMSDF had the duty to give its best to the nation, and smartness and seamanship were two of the core parameters that measured its members' level of excellence.[68] In the second half of the 1970s, following the adoption of the first NDPO that set the navy's Cold War force levels, Admiral Ōga restated the JMSDF's attention to platforms and training (at sea and ashore) as critical enablers for performing its missions.[69] The unyielding commitment to offer top instruction did not diminish in the aftermath of the Cold War. From 1989 to 2005, the JMSDF dispatched fifty to sixty officers and non-commissioned officer personnel a year abroad (mainly to the United States) for postgraduate programmes in international relations, security or management, as well as *ad hoc* technical courses to refine the control of cutting-edge combat systems, helicopter and aircraft piloting and maintenance, computer technology and security.[70] These opportunities were in addition to other regular experiences overseas, notably the possibility for top academy graduates to attend an advanced staff course at the Naval War College in the United States, or an advanced and a senior staff course at the Joint Staff College and the Royal College of Defence Studies in the United Kingdom.

Technical instruction to enhance standards in seamanship was certainly essential to plant the seeds for an operationally capable force, but it was not sufficient to inspire inner cohesiveness and the will to serve at sea. As a former chief of staff who graduated from the first class of the Defence Academy pointed out, the navy was a victim of the combined effect of post-war changes on the perception of the armed forces and the natural challenges unfolding from a life in the navy, distinguished by periods of deployment away from the commodities of life ashore.[71] This made a career path as a JMSDF officer a less attractive option to young Japanese. Indeed, apart from those who came from Japan's seafaring regions and were attracted by the charm of the oceans, many cadets faced an initial 'mental block' in regard to their willingness to join the naval service.[72] In addition, the focus on democratic values and inter-service cooperation at the Defence Academy was only of limited benefit to the formative path of a naval officer.[73]

Thus, the role of naval education was to offer a 'spiritual' education that could enable the members of the naval organisation to nourish their pride and sense of belonging. For that reason, this aspect assumed a core position in the JMSDF's educational system, a privileged position it maintains to the present day. Imperial traditions offered a set of values and practices well suited to the spiritual requirements of the post-war navy. At sea, there was no functional distinction between the motivational requirements and the discipline needed by a crew to man a combat unit of a 'navy' or a 'self-defence' force.[74] Similar considerations applied to the spheres of leadership and command. The Imperial Navy, with its longstanding battle-hardened tradition of unyielding discipline, fine combat skills and refined *esprit de corps*, provided an ideal spiritual model. In a country where defeat in the recent war had shattered the nation's pride, the glorious past of the navy – especially when associated with its performance in the Meiji and early Taishō eras – was an invaluable resource because it referred not to a foreign tradition, but to a Japanese one. In this regard, the respect accorded to the history of the Imperial Navy by the Japanese public and American naval authorities, and the simple fact that the core of the new maritime establishment came from the Imperial Navy, made this model a natural choice.

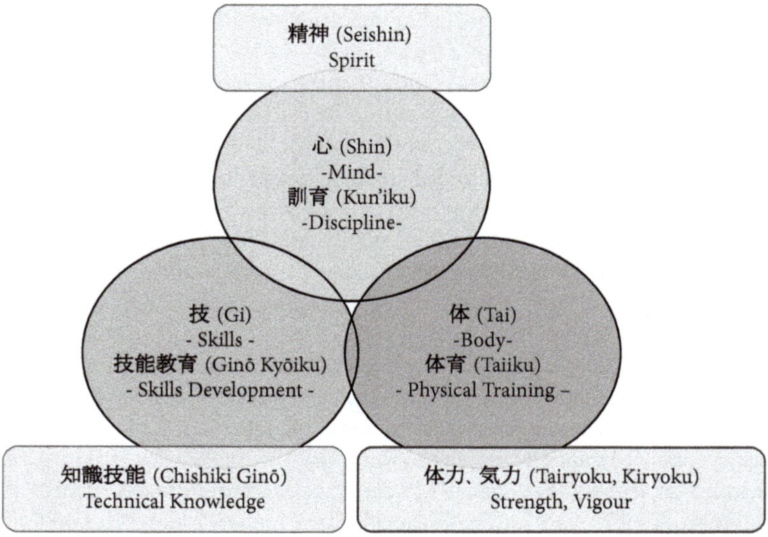

Figure 4.1 The JMSDF educational system.

Source: Captain Ōtsuka Umio, JMSDF, interview with the author, 14 March 2005.

The injection of the Imperial Navy's 'spiritual genes' into the new service did not aim to undermine the fundamental principles of the new armed forces' ethical core. On the contrary, generations of chiefs of staff regularly sought to explain the characteristics of the naval service using a vocabulary that conformed to the language and the principles of the ethos of the JSDF's personnel and the Defence Academy. In 1961, only weeks after the ethos had been adopted, Admiral Nakayama reminded the JMSDF that the well-being of the Japanese population was at the centre of the service's *raison d'être*.[75] In the 1960s, the limited capabilities of the fleet severely constrained its operational radius. Yet, its leaders had no doubt that the JMSDF was essential to the economic survival of the country, especially in the long run, and that this idea had to motivate officers and crews in fulfilling their daily tasks.[76] This forecast was realised in the second half of the 1970s when the national political debate that culminated in the adoption of the NDPO envisaged greater responsibilities for the navy in terms of sea lane defence. By definition, the defence of sea lanes was about the defence of Japan's economic survival and independence as a nation. It was, at heart, about the people's well-being. In 1976, Admiral Nakamura summarised the symbolic tie between the democratic values intrinsic to the post-war military system and the navy's evolving core mission, pointing out that the JMSDF had to be aware that its very existence protected Japan's economic 'lifeline'.[77]

Imperial traditions made officers and crews act according to the brand of discipline, teamwork and leadership needed by the JMSDF to carry out its missions. The responsibility unfolding from representing Japan's first line of defence demanded that naval personnel follow the old imperial naval slogan of 'devotion to silence'.[78] This was instrumental to focus on the inner strength needed to endure harsh discipline and training essential to become an 'elite force'[79] of imperial flavour and to possess a strong sense of camaraderie and identification with the service.[80] The traditions and practices of the Imperial Navy were the avenues where officers were to understand that the effectiveness of the navy rested on its readiness, a concept that will be explored in greater detail in the later chapters. Indeed, in the view of its leadership, decades of preparation following the imperial naval formula were eventually a major component in the JMSDF's first operational successes of the early 1990s. In the wake of the overseas missions to the Persian Gulf (1991), Cambodia (1994) and Mozambique (1993), Admiral Hayashizaki remarked with a note of pride that positive results reflected a more important long-term achievement in fielding true 'sea warriors'.[81]

The Naval Academy in Etajima and the ships of the fleet became the prime battlegrounds where the campaign for the navy's soul was to be fought. In 1956, the Naval Academy reopened its doors to the first class of graduates from the Defence Academy and other civilian universities.[82] While the curriculum of its one-year programme had been adapted to the standards of the day, its delivery was deeply steeped in a routine of familiar imperial character.[83] Upon their arrival, midshipmen went through the 'Etajima typhoon',[84] a practice that saw personal possessions dispersed in the dormitory's corridors by an unexpected 'strong wind', symbolically marking their initiation to the life of the Japanese naval officer.[85] This symbolic watershed served to introduce midshipmen to a daily schedule in many areas similar to the pre-war era. At 6.00 am, activities started with one hour of outdoor calisthenics and continued with an intense agenda including the study of navigation, ship-handling, international law, English, naval training and infantry tactics. Throughout the day, midshipmen learnt to live according to imperial traditions: to put team interests before their own. Similar to the Imperial Navy, teamwork and discipline received the highest attention.[86] Midshipmen sung classic imperial naval songs while running, practised at least one martial art, took part in rowing competitions in 1.5-ton cutters and reenacted customs such as the 12 km endurance swim in formation through Etajima bay.[87] Fostering a shared naval ethos was the main goal of these practices.

At the individual level too, naval education resembled that of the Imperial Navy, as attention to traits favouring leadership was less dominant at Etajima than in equivalent institutions in countries like the United Sates.[88] Midshipmen were taught to recite by heart the 'five reflections' and to be 'ready five minutes before' as methods of self-assessment and character building. The aim was to create an understanding of the ultimate purpose of the profession, an identification with the service and a perceptive attitude to perform any given task with diligence and commitment. The significance of imperial traditions in the character-building process of officers who were to feel proud to be 'Japanese' was also evident in the maintenance of specific Japanese practices and instruments. Midshipmen learnt to master the use of the two triangles to plot positions, the unusual single-wire pelorus to navigate, and to conduct damage control drills efficiently and silently. The final product was a brand of seamanship that conjugated Western technology and Japanese naval practices and experience, one that would not fail to impress visiting foreign midshipmen and exchange instructors with the elegance of its sophistication and the quality of its manifestations.[89]

At sea, imperial naval practices were restored to recreate the conditions necessary for crews and officers to perform at the best of their capabilities. First among these practices was the overseas training cruise. As of January 1957, the JMSDF reintroduced this activity at the end of the year in Etajima as a compulsory part of its officers' education aimed at enhancing their awareness of the cosmopolitan and diplomatic character of navies. Given that at the time the JMSDF had severe budgetary limitations and possessed only a modest fleet, the training cruise was a remarkable sign of the service's long-term ambitions to create skilled and open-minded personnel. Admiral Nakayama was appointed commander of the training squadron for its first cruise, which lasted forty-six days and reached Hawaii. The visit had a practical training value but was also highly symbolic, marking the first visit of a Japanese fleet to Pearl Harbor since December 1941 in a mission that underlined the changed nature of US–Japan naval relations.[90] In this respect, the JMSDF wished the overseas cruise to represent an opportunity for young midshipmen to open their eyes to the value of the navy as a diplomatic tool. This fact became apparent in 1963 when, at the initial suggestion of Prime Minister Ikeda (1960–64), who wished to further capitalise on his late 1962 visit to Europe, the training fleet visited the old continent and remained at sea for 130 consecutive days.[91] The fleet returned again to Europe eleven years later and by that time, the number of days had been raised to 155. Since then, like their pre-war imperial colleagues, JMSDF midshipmen have had the opportunity to experience first-hand the direct connection between the navy and the country's political interests, by visiting ports scattered over the most remote corners of the five continents.[92]

On board JMSDF units, imperial practices and vocabulary were present in all aspects of the ships' life. Officers' cabins maintained pre-war characters that conventionally designated a military officer, rather than those adopted in the post-war era for self-defence officials.[93] Ships' canteens, though they no longer served alcohol to crew members (a custom the JMSDF introduced from the US Navy), maintained the IJN's designation 'room for the consumption of alcohol'[94] – a term the Imperial Navy had adopted from the Royal Navy.[95] Ship names were assigned according to pre-war practices, and the linguistic tie with the dialect from Kagoshima for onboard communications was restored. This *de facto* transformed the confined spaces of each unit of the fleet into a floating microcosm of symbolism that served not to destabilise post-war democratic values, but to nourish the fighting spirit of those who were tasked to defend the maritime interests of the Japanese nation. At sea and ashore, members of the JMSDF relived the experience of the Imperial Navy on a daily basis as a way to improve education and training. That functional experience aimed at creating naval professionalism and thus represented the most important component of the post-war imperial naval legacy.

The past as prologue – part 2: Thinking critically about the Imperial Navy

At the middle-rank level of the JMSDF's educational system, the experience of the Imperial Navy has had a different role to play. From an organisational perspective, plans for a staff college and its programmes were informed by the wealth of information that its first president, Rear Admiral Nakayama (1954–56), had gathered during his

1955 visit to the United States.[95] As the admiral remarked in the guidelines he set for the school, Japan had to follow in the footsteps of the United States and the United Kingdom and create an institution that could equip middle-ranking officers with the intellectual tools needed to formulate sound judgement on matters of strategy. Analytical skills represented the quintessence of the type of leadership and command expected from future senior officers. Instructors had to promote attitudes leading towards a 'Mahan type of officer', rewarding students with inquisitive attitudes and favouring class debates.[97] Students were to be given free time to deepen their study of specific themes of personal interest and were required to work on an individual research project which was assessed as part of the final grade. In the intellectual grammar of the staff college, 'academic freedom'[98] was a pivotal element in developing officers' individual skills.[99]

At this level, ties with the imperial past operated in two ways. On one hand, the introduction of a modern curriculum enriched by the experience of leading Western navies did not mean the rejection of the qualities of Japanese naval higher education.[100] The scientifically rigorous analysis of campaigns and battles that had distinguished the work of one of the Imperial Navy's master tacticians, Lieutenant Commander Akiyama Saneyuki (later Vice Admiral), was a legacy of undiminished significance for the post-war JMSDF officer corps.[101] More importantly, modern naval history represented in itself an invaluable source of understanding of the profession. Since the college's inception, former imperial naval officers and the JMSDF top echelons made sure that the new generations would be aware of this. Elements of Japanese military and naval history were integrated into the courses on strategy, tactics and doctrine.[102] Particular emphasis was given to events from the navy's battle history, from the First Sino-Japanese to the Pacific War, on the basis of their relevance to post-war operational requirements. Civil–military relations, military policy and inter-service rivalry were some of the other main subject areas in which the imperial experience was debated.[103] In particular, from 1959 to 1966, senior naval figures with wartime and pre-war experience like Admiral Yamanashi, a key member of the inter-war treaty faction, lectured at the staff college on history, setting the tone of the new re-examination of Japan's past naval experience.[104]

Since the first class of fifteen students who attended the college in 1955, between thirty and thirty-five mid-career officers destined, to various degrees, to occupy positions of responsibility within the JMSDF have invested twelve months of their career path in thinking critically about their profession. There, the study of imperial experience and methods of analysis helped them learn of the relevance of the sea to Japan's economic survival and independence. They engaged with the past to debate the navy's role in securing the country's maritime interests. In so doing, they became the thinking elite of the service. By the beginning of the twentieth century, history was still not part of triumphal celebrations of glorious victories at sea. Instead, a methodical re-examination of naval campaigns planned and conducted by imperial naval commanders in the Sea of Japan and the South Pacific remained intrinsic to the intellectual endeavours pursued at the staff college.[105]

In more recent years, the facilities accommodating the college in Meguro (Tokyo) further emphasised the way the institution had been carrying out its mission. Positioned just a few metro stops from Tokyo's political heart, Ichigaya and Kasumigaseki, the white concrete building towers over its surroundings as a gem of functionality and modern architectural engineering.[106] It is a structural embodiment of the higher education requirements of a first-rate military organisation striving to remain abreast of the business of war in the contemporary world.[107] Inside the building, where all three JSDF staff colleges are allocated one floor each, a peculiar decoration outside the maritime college entrance characterises the unique place of the Imperial Navy in the post-war identity.[108] The college entrance is guarded by an Italian-made bust of the late Vice Admiral Akiyama, a powerful reminder to all mid-career officers of the roots of the post-war navy's intellectual pedigree.

In August 2005, as a way to gauge the extent to which the past informs the navy's professional identity, this author conducted a survey followed by a series of group discussions among the students of the staff college. All the participants volunteered to take the survey and join the discussion. The group included one female JMSDF officer, one foreign student from India and one from the Republic of Korea.[109] The youngest officer was thirty-four years old, the oldest thirty-eight. Approximately 60 per cent of the officers who took part in the activity were aged between thirty-five and thirty-six. More than 66 per cent had graduated from the Defence Academy, the others having either attended civilian universities or risen through the JMSDF's ranks. All branches of the naval service were represented, with a prevalence of officers from surface specialties and logistical corps.[110] They had all joined the navy in the 1990s, and they represented the next generation of the navy's leadership.

Employing descriptions reminiscent of a Robert Louis Stevenson novel, an elemental passion for the sea, the chance to travel abroad and attraction for a working activity that entailed technical skills had originally influenced the decision of half of the officers to join the JMSDF.[111] In several cases, a family heritage or a willingness to serve and defend the country completed the canvas of their motivation. Only five respondents had initially entered the navy for reasons completely unrelated to the nature of the profession, two of them following indications they received from instructors at the Defence Academy. They all agreed that, in comparing the Defence Academy with Etajima, the latter was different in that it represented a testing ground for their transformation from students into military officers. They explained that the programme at the Defence Academy had planted the seeds for their growth as individuals, offering good education, lessons on the decorum required by a future officer and continuous physical training. By contrast, in Etajima, they had learnt of the place that the two core features of their profession, namely seamanship and *esprit de corps*, held in Japan's naval tradition. They treasured both features as essential, not merely to man a modern piece of military hardware, but to develop a sense of loyalty to a team, courage in adversity 'to never give up' and determination to fight. There, they felt they had entered the world of military professionals.

In the process, all of them had visited Etajima's Educational Reference Hall, as it is expected of all midshipmen, and five of them had visited it several times. In the reference hall, which 'commemorates heroes who fought for their country in battle' and therefore has no space dedicated to the JMSDF,[112] they reflected for the first time on the experience of their predecessors in the Imperial Navy, of the meaning of ideals like patriotism[113] and sacrifice.[114] They recognised the spiritual commitment required of officers in order to succeed in case of war, where mistakes and misjudgements can entail the ultimate human cost. In retrospect, while there was general consensus over the pedagogic value of the hall, a minority of officers added that they considered such an aspect of their education as of fundamental importance in a country like Japan where, by avoiding a critical study of the country's wartime history in the Shōwa era, school education leaves students unprepared on the demanding standards of a life in the service.

As students heading towards graduation from the staff college, this middle echelon firmly identified qualities related to the spheres of command, commitment to the defence of the country and discipline as the cornerstones of the naval officer's identity.[115] Their foreign colleagues shared the same impressions about JMSDF officers' core priorities. For some JMSDF officers at the college, the value attributed to such qualities was a confirmation of an initial personal drive. For others, it was a consciousness matured throughout years of work in the field, one that the programme at the college had helped them understand more deeply. It is also worth noting that a large majority of them envisaged two additional traits of crucial importance, namely, the willingness to take risks and technical knowledge.[116] These elements, combined with personal characteristics such as courtesy, flexible thinking and proficiency in foreign languages, completed their officer's Decalogue, a code of conduct pointing to a resolute officer-gentleman of a strong imperial flavour.[117]

They maintained similar views when they were asked to comment on three top admirals who embodied different types of leadership in the history of the Imperial Navy.[118] Admiral Tōōgō Heihachirō, the 'Nelson of the Far East', is celebrated in Japan as the naval hero *par excellence* for his complete victory at the Battle of Tsushima. Admiral Inoue Shigeyoshi, the navy's unorthodox thinker of the late 1930s, distinguished himself by challenging some of the navy's ossified doctrinal assumptions. Admiral Yamamoto Isoroku was the navy's most controversial commander and strategic planner, seizing command of the sea in the opening stages of the Pacific War but suffering also a staggering defeat in the Battle of Midway (4–7 June 1942).

Traces of the intellectual sophistication Admiral Nakayama wished the future elites of the JMSDF to demonstrate marked their assessments of the three figures. Admiral Tōgō, for instance, was respected for his command skills, determination, charisma and situational awareness of the battle space, to borrow a modern expression, and of the broader strategic issues related to a campaign. Respect for his role as a symbol of national achievement in a delicate moment of Japanese modern history notwithstanding, a few officers underlined that in the inter-war period, the personal cult of the fleet admiral worked to the detriment of the navy as an effective organisation. Almost a deity-like figure, in his late years, Tōgō's interventions in matters of naval policy had great influence, an Aristotelian *ipse dixit*, which was used by reactionary middle echelons to strengthen their anti-naval limitation treaty position.[119] In the view of JMSDF officers, his scintillating performance as a naval commander was clouded by a later dose of arrogance and limited interest in innovation, features explaining his endorsement of the dogmatic views of the navy's anti-treaty group.

In one of the reference studies of the Imperial Navy, historians David Evans and Mark Peattie, expanding on the 1970s research conducted by JMSDF Commander (and former imperial officer) Senō Sadao, brought the visionary ideas of Vice Admiral Inoue Shigeyoshi to the full attention of a Western readership.[120] Admiral Inoue was one of the navy's few intellectually outstanding pre-war moderates. In 1940, he headed the Navy Aviation Department at the Navy Ministry and fought alongside Admirals Yonai and Yamamoto to keep Japan from forging stronger military ties with Germany and Italy. In 1941, he submitted a memorandum to the Navy Minister exposing the navy's 'blind, unthinking response to American building programmes' which focused on massive battleships rather than a wider array of forces capable of operating at all three dimensions of modern naval warfare.[121] He subsequently commanded the Fourth Fleet based at Truk (Micronesia), before being assigned to the direction of the Naval Academy in 1942. In the literature, Admiral Inoue is portrayed as a Cassandra-like figure. He was the man who foresaw many of the difficulties that progressively hindered the navy's operational capabilities, who analysed the forthcoming conflict in strategic terms not as a function of a single decisive victory, but whose words fell on deaf ears.[122]

A similar image emerged from the responses of the officers studying at the staff college. They pointed to Inoue's human stature as an educator committed to broadening the intellectual horizon of young officers, to his acumen and realism – which according to one of them made him too smart for the navy. Yet, for many of the mid-career JMSDF officers responding to the questionnaire, Admiral Inoue was a good educator but not an example of a commanding officer. He was a man of letters, not a combat leader, a fact he demonstrated while in command of the Fourth Fleet. In particular, Inoue's 'excessive' caution was fully exposed when his orders to Admiral Takagi's carrier force to break off action in the battle of the Coral Sea in May 1942 were countered by Admiral Yamamoto himself.[123] In this respect, the officers' responses were consistent with the views of other senior JMSDF officers who underlined that Inoue was more of a 'philosopher' than a 'warrior'. Though every navy is in need of such men to innovate and advance, the crucial personal attributes required to win in battle cannot be underestimated.[124]

It is in Admiral Yamamoto that the JMSDF officers identified the right blend of commitment, open-mindedness and determination at the heart of the fabric of the professional naval officer. Apart from one negative assessment of the admiral's command skills based on his defeat at Midway, and two unenthusiastic views regarding his planning of the Pearl Harbor raid, qualities like charisma, creativity and compassion defined the impression that the officers had of the admiral. His committed and human character (for instance, the students who took part in the group discussion expressed sympathetic feelings for his gambling vice) gave him a natural talent for communication, enabling him to empathise with his men and inspire their respect and that of common Japanese people.[125] For today's JMSDF officers these qualities seem to be invaluable assets, attributes that awarded him the legacy of a leader of the highest order. In their view, Yamamoto was more than an inspiring figure. His frontline dedication to the development of naval aviation throughout the 1930s, his opposition to radical, warlike arguments in the run-up to the conflict in the Pacific and his resolve as a military commander demonstrated the right brand of leadership. For these officers, he was a balanced figure, and, more importantly, a person that reminded them that a hero is a human being. He was emotional and fallible, thoughtful and knowledgeable, decisive and bold.

Are these admirals of the past suitable models for the complexities of today's naval profession? For all the students, apart from one who preferred not to respond, the answer was inescapably yes. Half of them considered the example set by these figures as completely relevant, as the fundamental requirements for command have not changed. The remaining part of the group maintained, on the other hand, that the admirals' actions had to be properly contextualised in order to extrapolate guiding principles for a modern officer's behaviour. Rather than simply idolising the individuals, they preferred to study their actions and single out their positive achievements. Among those who argued for a selective, contextual approach, Admiral Yamamoto appeared frequently as a controversial a case in point. At the personal level, they praised his moral standards and they valued his tactical skills, key to a leader's fabric. However, from an organisational perspective, they felt that the shadow of the Imperial Navy's downfall and of Japan's defeat paved the way for broader questions on the drawbacks of the navy's war-planning and on the inadequacies of figures like Yamamoto who supervised it.

Elements of this dilemma were evident in the students' responses on the primary causes of the nation's defeat in the Pacific War. Their answers were informed and detailed, highlighting three main weaknesses, namely Japan's limited natural resources and an industrial depth that was inadequate to undertake a protracted war effort, the lack of clearly defined national political objectives, and the navy's lack of strategic and tactical flexibility. Many of them further argued that the Imperial Navy's limited understanding of the evolving nature of naval warfare stemmed from an underestimation of the role of intelligence and information gathering.[126] This, in turn, led to serious miscalculations during the inter-war period of the navy's potential adversary (i.e. the US Navy) and prevented tactical changes during the conflict necessary to secure vital primary resources. For all these reasons, the qualities of the individuals in terms of command skills and intellectual acumen did not excuse the limits of their actions on war preparation and the conduct of operations.

The officers' understanding of the virtues and limitations of naval leadership and of the negative repercussions at the strategic level of the Pacific War clearly informed the way they perceived the role of the JMSDF in national security. The underlying idea that the Imperial Navy had failed to secure the maritime arteries vital to Japan's war machine had echoes in the students' almost unanimous tendency to list sea lane defence as the single most important mission of the modern JMSDF. In the group discussion, normative constraints and alliance commitments with the United States further enriched the canvas of reasons for their opinions.[127] An underlying perception of the intrinsic defensive nature of JSDF missions consistent with the content of the 'members ethos' seemed to be primarily responsible for their tendency to establish a direct link between the very existence of the JMSDF and the protection of the country's economic wealth and society.

Their image of the imperial experience, therefore, was one in which the navy sought to shield Japan by luring the enemy into a major decisive duel on the high seas, annihilate it and secure as a result the country's core maritime perimeter. It was primarily a Mahanian fighting force, an instrument to wage and win naval campaigns. By contrast, in the students' perception, the JMSDF was not simply an instrument to win battles by means of firepower. They seemed to value the JMSDF as a versatile tool at the service of Japan's national interests with a wide range of potential applications to achieve security. In listing other core functions, they emphasised the JMSDF's central role in deterrence, sea control, good order at sea and strategic lift. This perception was translated in missions like defence against ballistic missiles, defence from maritime terrorism and piracy, military operations other than war, and naval diplomacy (including activities such as visit exchanges, joint training, seminars and conferences).

In this respect, the portrait emerging from the students' responses was one where elite middle echelons had a fundamentally Corbettian vision of naval warfare. In their understanding of duty, national security cannot be attained by means of military victories alone. The ability to control maritime communications, to freely access the seas, seemed to be a central focus of their concerns. The navy's *raison d'être* was not only to eliminate military threats, but to protect the whole of the national lifestyle. For them, the legacy of the Imperial Navy was one that had enabled the JMSDF to inculcate a 'maritime' rather than a 'naval' approach to strategic thinking, one that better suited the requirements of a maritime country like Japan.[128] It is for this reason that all officers, apart from two, considered themselves 'naval officers' insofar as the purpose of their profession was concerned.[129] As military professionals, the requirements of national security and of naval warfare defined their profession and, in that sense, they felt themselves no different from naval officers worldwide. The difference they felt was legal, not functional, or as one officer remarked:

> I regard myself not as a navy officer, but as a maritime self-defence official. I am patiently waiting for the day to come when the Japanese government and the people of Japan recognise JMSDF as Japan's Navy.[130]

Conclusions

At a first glance, the JMSDF would appear to be an organisation made up of self-righteous personnel looking back at the past to inform their professional outlook, just as the NHK book suggested. Elements of the navy's educational system are designed to keep the link between the two navies alive. Yet, this link should not lead to the conclusion that the two are the same.

The adoption of vocabulary, practices and procedures that defined the education, training and life on board Imperial Navy warships enabled the JMSDF leadership to create an important psychological connection between the initially modest fleet and the powerful force of the past.[131] The JMSDF shared with the Imperial Navy modest beginnings and a model that had eventually risen to international professional prominence, one that served to motivate officers and crews, nourishing their will to fight and sense of belonging. This had particular significance at the early stages of the rearmament process, when the JMSDF heavily relied on American technology to reconstitute its arsenal. Today, corporate spirit, training and seamanship remain crucial, as the JMSDF strives to retain a force capable of manning cutting-edge technologies.[132] In this respect, the notion of *wakon-yōsai* served very well in post-war circumstances. It offered a model of development with a strong spiritual appeal, where the technical means for modernisation were absorbed and digested while maintaining a strong 'Japanese' identity.

Equally important, the legacy of the Imperial Navy served the purpose of reinforcing the JMSDF's organisational subculture in the different post-war military setup. This was particularly true at the officer corps educational level. The establishment of the civilian-run Defence Academy ensured that the new military elites were socialised with a strong 'civic-oriented' outlook. Loyalty and commitment to defend the Emperor were replaced by the protection of the Japanese people and their well-being as the supreme missions. Changes in military education reflected the effort of Japanese authorities to address critical drawbacks of the imperial armed forces, most notably their elitist character, the lack of inter-service cooperation and their narrow, interest-based policies. The new system, though successful in these areas, did little to prepare officers for the difficulties of their future career path. Against this backdrop, the JMSDF used Etajima as the testing ground where cadets would be transformed into naval officers. The hardship of the training and the emphasis on spiritual values and practices fulfilled the Janowitzian notion of introducing every midshipman to the specificities of life at sea:

> To the particular style of life of military existence and indoctrinate him in the importance of the heroic leadership. They must seek to weaken regional ties and develop a sense of broader national identity. Once the potential officer gains admittance and survives the ordeals of initiation, the purpose of an academy education is to transform him into a member of a professional fraternity.[133]

The use of the pre-war navy as a model to attain high professional standards, to complement the requirements of a different education system and to instil a strong sense of organisational identity did not mean a lack of re-assessment of the mistakes of the Imperial Navy. At the level of higher education, the imperial experience became an invaluable resource for examining and understanding the requirements of Japan's maritime defence. The study of the characters of the foremost Japanese commanders and their actions as leaders provided the raw materials needed to reflect upon the qualities required in the art of command. Concurrently, the processing of battle experience was essential to expose the catastrophic consequences of the decisions made in the 1930s. Methods of analysis in studying campaigns and operations designed by imperial officers like Akiyama Saneyuki were retained as signs of the qualities of the pre-war higher education. Concurrently, the curricula of the staff college were enriched with activities to stimulate relevant debates on grand strategy. The staff college used the past to widen the 'intellectual horizons' of the JMSDF's elite, to discipline them to think in terms of 'maritime' rather than merely 'naval' strategy, thus connecting the existence of the navy to the wider sea-based economic interests of Japan. In this respect, the legacy of the Imperial Navy had contributed to the making of a new organisation in the post-war era.

5

Ethos and Propaganda: Ships, Men and the Image of the Naval Profession

The image (of the Imperial Navy and the JMSDF) is totally the same. The audience, however, is not. Fans of the Imperial Navy are primarily elder citizens, so we needed to appeal to new generations of fans.

Politicians did not consider the JSDF at all; the alternative was a completely different sort of character, the so-called 'Otaku', i.e. people with a passion for ships, aircraft, and subs. I didn't want people to think of us just for our ships. I wanted them to think about the people. In dramas and movies, I wanted the audience to focus on the personnel in the JMSDF. The key point was to show the complexity of the lives of the men in white uniform.[1]

Captain Toshiyuki Itō, JMSDF
(Chief, Public Affairs Office)

The image of a navy made of ships and men

On a brisk autumn morning in 1957, Prime Minister Kishi Nobusuke was standing next to Admiral Nagasawa Kō on the deck of the brand new destroyer *Yukikaze* (DD 102). The ship was named after the most successful of the nineteen *Kagero* class destroyers built by the Imperial Navy before 1941, and had survived the war after taking part in battles like Midway, the Leyte Gulf, and the Philippine Sea. Sailing across Tokyo bay, *Yukikaze* reviewed thirty-two naval vessels and forty-nine aircraft gathered for the JSDF 'Commemoration Day'.[2] On that 2 October, the navy held its first post-war fleet review. Visually, the parading fleet was a shadow of the Combined Fleet.[3] The Imperial Navy had been a statement of power of the tallest order. In the case of the JMSDF, the total tonnage of the fleet on display, some 38,500t, was just a little more than half that of the single battleship *Yamato*. Yet, ship names, vocabulary and manoeuvres all had an imperial flavour. The date for the event itself created a line of continuity with the last imperial fleet review, which was held in October 1940.[4] The aim was clear. In its first major post-war public display of seamanship, the JMSDF wanted to show that the professionalism of the Imperial Navy lived on, if not in size, at least in spirit in the new navy.

This chapter engages with the way the JMSDF deployed the imperial naval past, including notable public affairs techniques, to develop its public image and self-representation strategies. Fleet reviews and short cruises, a core tool of the pre-war navy propaganda machinery, were combined with visits to bases and, as the decades progressed, museum projects. These activities were designed to appeal to existing public perceptions about the importance of navies as modern and technologically advanced forces. Initially, the modernity of the fleet served to counter the controversial nature of the JSDF and its lack of capabilities and social recognition.[5] In particular, the JMSDF held pageant events to nurture ties with selected groups of people, including politicians and intellectuals (like Itō and Agawa) as well as to appeal to a public of naval aficionados. By the end of the Cold War, however, Japanese public interest in the JSDF started to increase and so did the public affairs machinery intent on evolving the navy's message beyond the focus on its assets. New displays in larger official museums were developed to detail the meaning of life at sea, the character of the men in white uniform, and how the naval tradition they embraced could assist in meeting the requirements of national defence.

In which we serve: Ships, fleet reviews and the navy's public appeal

From the halls of Etajima to the classrooms of the staff college, and across the ships of the fleet, Japan's naval past had consistently informed the JMSDF's fighting spirit and professional character. In public affairs, the JMSDF's approach was no different. It never sought to deny its organisational connection with the Imperial Navy; in fact, it used it systematically and selectively – just like in other aspects of its activities. Yet, the adoption of imperial practices and images did not mean that they had the same purpose. Before the war, the Imperial Navy employed pageantry and propaganda to consolidate and increase its political influence as well as to appeal to a wider audience. In the JMSDF, the order was reversed with a stronger emphasis on public appeal. Public affairs aimed to foster 'mutual reliance between the J(M)SDF and the public, promoting cooperation and a feeling of connection, and consequently enhancing and strengthening the foundations for defence'.[6] The core aim was to guarantee a steady stream of recruits.

One of the primary prerequisites of military institutions is their ability to recruit, train, discipline and maintain forces capable of engaging in combat. For the leaders of an all-volunteer force like the JMSDF, this was no simple undertaking, especially as they faced a society that had become allergic to military affairs and cared little about the new military.[7] The first generation of JMSDF top echelons, through a web of civilian contacts like Itō Masanori and illustrious veterans like Agawa Hiroyuki, were aware that the Japanese people still respected the country's naval tradition. They also knew, on the other hand, that this did not automatically translate into an appreciation for the new naval service. At the outset of rearmament in the early 1950s, the few ships in the JMSDF inventory, including several that were loaned from America, qualified the service only as a distant offspring of the powerful force that had roamed across the Pacific. Indeed, as of June 1956, the JMSDF main surface fleet included a mere four Destroyers (DD), five Escort Vessels (DE), eighteen Patrol Frigates (PF), and forty anti-submarine patrol planes. The Patrol Frigates had been made available by American authorities, while Japanese shipbuilding plans included twelve DDs (two funded by the United Sates) and three DEs.[8] This was not a strong visual statement for public consumption, but the existence of emotional ties and perceptions of the imperial past meant that the new navy was at an important starting point.

Hence, the JMSDF made use of the Imperial Navy to plant the seeds for wider public support. To that end, one of Admiral Nagasawa's first actions as chief of staff was to reinstate the prime delivery tool of pre-war naval propaganda, the Fleet Review.[9] Since 1957, fleet reviews have systematically featured in the JMSDF public relations calendar, except for an eight-year gap (1973–81) dictated by the austere budgetary conditions created by the oil shock of the early 1970s.[10] Over the decades, the reviews grew in complexity and retained a major public appeal to the point that the official parading day was complemented with a number of rehearsals to accommodate more visitors. The fleet reviews came to include features such as live fire exercises from destroyers and ASW units, submarine-synchronised emergency surface manoeuvres, music performances by ships' bands, and 'educational moments', where crew members explained the functioning of the combat systems as well as basic elements of seamanship, like tying knots and semaphore signals.[11] They became a visually engaging display of modernity and technology that attracted thousands of people, representing one of the most popular public events organised by the Japanese military. Above all, compared to the annual live fire exercise of the ground forces and the JSDF acrobatic air exhibition, the JMSDF fleet review was the only one to draw its roots in a longstanding pre-war tradition (Figure 5.1).[12]

Until the end of the 1980s, the JMSDF public relations strategy remained aligned with the fundamental idea of attracting the Japanese audience by displaying the evolving capabilities acquired by the service. The fleet's build-up in the late 1970s with cutting-edge hardware and the enhancement of the technical skills of officers and crews played to the strengths of this strategy. Public relations were an opportunity to gain the respect of the civilian society by advertising images of the navy's material qualities. In turn, public references to the Imperial Navy underscored the institutional *esprit de corps* and professional outlook that made the effective manning of such advanced capabilities possible. This was certainly the impression of a key contributor to the development of the JMSDF public image. In his thirty-year-long collaboration with the JMSDF, photographer Shibata Mitsuo remarked that until the end of the 1980s, ships and imperial naval traditions were central to the message delivered by the navy.[13] Indeed, the JMSDF invested in 'open days' for visiting naval bases, short cruises, small in-base museums, concerts featuring classic imperial songs like 'The Battle of the Sea of Japan'[14] and 'Battleship',[15] calendars and posters – all designed to secure public approval by displaying seamanship and modernity *à la* Imperial Navy.

Public relations remained crucially important to the JMSDF throughout the entire Cold War, precisely because they allowed the service to nurture the relationship with the Japanese public and craft a consistent message about its professionalism. By

No.	Location	Date	Fleet Composition	No. Attendees
1	Tokyo Bay	02 October 1957	32 Units, 49 Aircraft	---*
2	Tokyo Bay	02 November 1960	43 Units, 47 Aircraft	---*
3	Tokyo Bay	02 November 1961	32 Units, 29 Aircraft	1,021
4	ŌsakaBay	03 November 1962	48 Units, 31 Aircraft	3,829
5	Tokyo Bay	02 November 1964	52 Units, 36 Aircraft	775
6	ŌsakaBay	03 November 1965	49 Units, 51 Aircraft	4,248
7	Hakata Bay	03 November 1966	37 Units, 50 Aircraft	5,033
8	Ise Bay	05 November 1967	43 Units, 75 Aircraft	6,369
9	Tokyo Bay	03 November 1968	44 Units, 47 Aircraft	6,216
10	Ōsaka Bay	03 November 1969	50 Units, 51 Aircraft	6,838
11	Sagami Bay	03 November 1970	45 Units, 48 Aircraft	4,606
12	Sasebo Bay	03 November 1971	45 Units, 59Aircraft	8,393
13	Sagami Bay	05 November 1972	51 Units, 63 Aircraft	9,091
14	Wakasa Bay	16 September 1973	39 Units, 48 Aircraft	17,467
15	Sagami Bay	03 November 1981	45 Units, 55 Aircraft	---*
16	Sagami Bay	04 November 1984	53 Units, 51 Aircraft	---*
17	Sagami Bay	03 November 1987	54 Units, 49 Aircraft	29,586
18	Sagami Bay	05 November 1989	55 Units, 51 Aircraft	33,971
19	Sagami Bay	11 October 1992	52 Units, 54 Aircraft	40,966
20	Sagami Bay	16 October 1994	45 Units, 52 Aircraft	33,464
21	Sagami Bay	26 October 1997	46 Units, 43 Aircraft	42,012
22	Sagami Bay	29 October 2000	62 Units, 61 Aircraft	55,516
23	SagamiBay	13 October 2002	24 Units (Japan) 17 Units (11 Countries)	---*
24	Sagami Bay	26 October 2003	45 Units, 40 Aircraft	---*
25	Sagami Bay	29 October 2006	40 Units, 28 Aircraft	---*

*Detailed Data Not Available

Figure 5.1 Main fleet reviews of the post-war era.

Source: JMSDF, *Kaijōjieitai Gojū Nenshi – Shiryōhen*, 252; author's attendance 2006 Fleet Review.

the early 1980s, these activities were well practised, integrating fleet reviews with a variety of other activities. In 1983, for example, the navy organised over one thousand visits to various vessels, for a total of approximately 33,000 visitors.[16] Ships were open to visits to show off the JMSDF's commitment to manning a fleet with technical and moral traits comparable to that of the Imperial Navy. In 2002, the chief of staff himself, Admiral Ishikawa Tōru (CMS 2001–3), illustrated the function fleet reviews played in the navy's public affairs strategy. On the occasion of the first International Fleet Review ever hosted by Japan, he stressed that the event helped 'a greater number of people to see today's JMSDF and our renewed resolve for the future'.[17]

Beyond the ship: The Public Affairs Office

Imperial traditions took on a different role in the JMSDF public relations strategy after the Cold War. In the early 1990s, the considerable and unexpected increase of media attention on the armed forces put great pressure on the machinery of service information.[18] As a former chief of the Public Affairs Office[19] remarked, for forty years, the JMSDF had sought to widen public understanding of its roles and missions, but in many cases its initiatives fell on deaf ears. In the 1990s, the tide changed radically and the public affairs section was flooded with requests for information.[20] A defence correspondent captured this shift, noting that 'the end of the Cold War … has been [for Japan] a turbulent period, one in which many people and organizations – politicians, bureaucrats, diplomats, banks and big businesses – fell from power. However, the JSDF … are an exception.' In his view, throughout the 1990s and the early 2000s, increased public awareness of security issues 'pushed the JSDF to the fore'.[21]

In little more than a decade, the Japanese people came to display an interest in the military apparatus of national defence; equally, they grew confident in the deployment of the JSDF in overseas operations, albeit only for emergency relief, humanitarian assistance and reconstruction missions.[22] The perception of the military in Japan improved significantly compared to the first two decades after the end of the occupation, when the profession was given either little consideration or regarded as 'a necessary evil'.[23] The JSDF social status experienced a revaluation even when compared to newspapers headlines in 1990, which pointed out how 'young Japanese [were] unwilling to be soldiers' and that uniformed men received 'no respect' in the archipelago.[24] One of the most evident indicators of this accomplished transformation was the January 2007 official 'upgrade' of the Defence Agency to a fully fledged Ministry of Defence.

In this shift of public attention and appreciation, the armed forces were expected to justify more than just their material resources. This was perhaps most true for the JMSDF, which had focused primarily on displaying the modernity of its assets. *Mutatis mutandis*, the JMSDF seized the initiative and took advantage of the existing emphasis on the material connection with the Imperial Navy to articulate its message. With different nuances, videos, pamphlets and gadgets stressed the notion that 'by upholding the seventy seven year-long history and tradition of the Imperial Navy', the JMSDF could succeed in meeting the challenges to national security.[25] On this particular point, it has been argued elsewhere that in sites of communication such as recruitment posters, informational pamphlets and promotional pictorial books, the nature of the Japanese military profession was consistently downplayed, emasculated and removed of its martial component, which was replaced by 'cute' attractive cartoon characters like the JSDF's mascot Prince Pickles. This was not the case for the navy, where characters like Prince Pickles never received strong internal support.[26] In fact, media products were developed with different audiences in mind, and only a small fraction included 'cute' images, like pop group dances, specifically conceived to engage children and youngsters.[27]

The Public Affairs Office became the engine where the different expressions of the navy's message were developed and implemented. Strengthened in the early 1990s to meet new demands, the office, by the early 2000s, had become an industrious centre for the public dissemination of JMSDF-related information.[28] It fed public curiosity on the roles, missions and other aspects of more social interest of the Japanese naval service and, in turn, contributed to create, manage and control the JMSDF's image. For instance, the office had responsibility – in a fashion not dissimilar to its homologues in the sister services or indeed other militaries worldwide – for the release of information on delicate matters such as incidents involving JMSDF personnel, including accidents, suicides or episodes of corruption or major insubordination.[29] Similarly, the office coordinated the preparation, advertisement and news coverage of major events including parades, base festivals and naval reviews. If these events were the tools that delivered the JMSDF image, the Public Affairs Office was the engine room behind the operation.

At its offices in Tokyo, planning was entrusted to some nine uniformed staff, including officers and NCOs, coordinated by a senior Captain who was assisted in his functions by an officer of Commander rank.[30] Officers assigned to the office rotated every two or three years; by contrast, NCO personnel were likely to be attached to the office for longer periods as they usually received more in-depth training in public relations. In many ways, they constituted the backbone of the structure and compared well in terms of expertise with professionals from broadcasting and marketing companies. They mastered the techniques and state-of-the-art technologies used in publishing, advertisement and mass communication. Reportedly, specific training programmes on newspaper textual analysis were introduced by the Defence Agency as of 1993 for that purpose.[31] Formal instruction provided to personnel was usually complemented by feedback and experience passed on by mentors (often personnel previously occupying a similar position in the public relations system) through *sempai/kōhai* forms of interactions, a common practice at all levels of Japanese society.[32]

By the early 2000s, an average of four staff members handled relations with reporters from newspapers and TV networks. Three staff members acted as liaisons with television networks and producers, providing professional consultancy for increasing requests to support TV dramas and movies. The remaining two staff members were responsible for the updating and management of the website and photographic archive.[33] In regard to the latter, the JMSDF approach to public relations seemed to have achieved positive results. Committing to a major restructuring of its website in November 2004, in the early months of the following year, the office scored a major result in surpassing the number of net users of the JASDF website. By the end of the year, the JMSDF had totalled 183 million 'hits' against 181 million of the JASDF and a more distant 134 million of the JGSDF.[34] The average monthly number of hits in the case of the JMSDF ranged from 370,000 to 420,000 virtual visitors.[35]

Admiral Furushō and the navy of traditions

In the 1990s, as a new and more articulated message became necessary, the mastermind capable of engineering it belonged to the elite of the JMSDF officer corps. Between the 1990s and early 2000s, Admiral Furushō Kōichi was the real drive behind connecting imperial naval traditions to the public representation of the JMSDF. Admiral Furushō was committed to public information and was strongly convinced of the potential of memories from the imperial past to power the JMSDF public image. These beliefs were the outcome of an unconventional career path for an officer who eventually became the navy's 26th chief of staff (2003–5).[36] Born in 1946 in the Ōita Prefecture, in the northeast of the island of Kyushu in western Japan, the Admiral did not develop any particular sympathy for the Japanese navy in his youth. The island of Kyushu is known for being the main guardian of the archipelago's modern naval tradition. Yet, seafaring and naval customs were not part of the cultural heritage of the inhabitants of the Ōita Prefecture. This was true for the admiral's own family and his father had even served in the Imperial Army.[37]

The military heritage of his family led him to develop a curiosity for the country's military past, and to study heroic samurai-like characters of the Russo-Japanese War such as General Nogi and, more importantly, Commander Hirose, one of the war's great naval heroes and a fellow countryman from his prefecture.[38] Respect for his country's military tradition and admiration for the values this naval icon of the Meiji era represented were some of the key ingredients that motivated his final decision to apply to the academy in 1965. In the following four years, he dedicated his energy and passion to the cadet training, graduating among the top students of the 13th Class of the Defence Academy before finishing with similar results the year after in Etajima.[39] In 1970, the young Furushō was commissioned and started specialising in an essential, if unusual, expertise: mine warfare.

For a young talented officer, becoming a pilot of fixed-wing aircraft or a warfare officer serving on a front-line destroyer represented the most natural pathways to distinction, increasing the likelihood of a good career in the service, not to mention an exciting opportunity to become a 'warrior of the sea'.[40] Mine warfare was (and is) a complex, time-consuming and particularly dangerous activity conducted primarily to deny access to potential enemies to littoral areas. As a consequence, it usually offered fewer chances for rapid career advancement. In the JMSDF, however, specialising in mine warfare had a unique meaning. Mine warfare had a longstanding tradition dating back to the early stages of the Allied occupation of Japan in 1945. The forerunners of the JMSDF mine warfare force had worn the imperial uniform and fought for Japan in the Pacific War before crucially contributing to its survival by clearing access routes to main ports.[41] Subsequently, they had participated in operations during the Korean War in 1950 and had continued sweeping mines across the archipelago well into the 1960s.[42] By the time Ensign Furushō joined this component, the skills of its force and the quality of its platforms represented one of the most evident professional legacies of the Imperial Navy.[43]

Promoted to the rank of commander in 1984 and to captain in 1989, Furushō alternated assignments at sea with duties ashore at the staff office, primarily in the departments responsible for Administration or Personnel and Education. When he assumed the direction of the Public Affairs Office in August 1990, Captain Furushō was already an experienced and respected officer. Attention to Japanese naval traditions and an ability for mentoring junior officers and creating a brotherly bond with personnel under his command had distinguished the professional life of an exceptionally perceptive personality.[44] In the new task of delivering the image of the service to the public, his approachability and strong views on the value of the cultural heritage linking the Imperial Navy to the JMSDF became invaluable assets. In retrospect, it seems more than a timely coincidence that an officer with expertise on mine warfare was assigned to public affairs right at the moment when a series of events gave this force an opportunity to redefine national media perceptions of the country's military professionalism.

On 2 August 1990, the Iraqi invasion of Kuwait and the subsequent military response by the American-led, UN-sponsored multinational coalition exposed the limits of Japan's post-war low profile in security affairs and crisis management systems.[45] International expectations on Japan's responsibility to offer some form of military support to the coalition paved the way for a tedious political negotiation, eventually culminating in the government's decision for a post-bellum dispatch, in April 1991, of a flotilla of five minesweepers accompanied by the refuelling ship *Tokiwa* (AOE-423) to the Persian Gulf.[46]

As one authoritative study pointed out, since the early stages of the crisis, the eventuality of a military deployment in the Persian Gulf had not caught the JMSDF unaware.[47] As early as 1987, the United States had unsuccessfully sought to involve Japan's navy in western European escort duties and minesweeping in the area. At that time, the maritime staff office in parallel with a private think tank directly connected to the JMSDF and the ruling party drafted a series of studies of the operational implications of the deployment of minesweepers in the region. When regional events escalated again in 1990, staff members at the JMSDF Plans and Programmes Division knew that a deployment of minesweepers could be a real option: it represented an appropriate relatively low-risk mission for which the JMSDF possessed the necessary legal, operational and risk-assessment insights.[48] Fully aware of the sociopolitical complications that a first engagement overseas would entail, the JMSDF needed a reassuring figure to orchestrate the dissemination of information. Captain Furushō's aptitude, resulting from a blend of primary knowledge of mine warfare and views on the nature of the professional attributes of the service, defined his reputation.[49] He was the right person for the right task at the right time.

For the JMSDF, the 1991 dispatch to the Persian Gulf constituted a key test because for the first time since its establishment in 1952, units of the fleet were officially engaged in an operationally delicate and politically controversial mission overseas. In Japan, beyond the polemics over the constitutionality of the armed forces, little was known about the JMSDF and its mine warfare force.[50] The success of the mission acted as a major catalyst, fostering public confidence in the potential peacekeeping role of the archipelago's military and paving the way for participation in other peacekeeping and relief missions throughout the 1990s.[51] Captain Furushō contributed to the initial stages of the process by writing a technical article on the future requirements of the mine warfare force which appeared together with a first assessment of the mission in the Persian Gulf in the July 1991 issue of Japan's leading journal on maritime affairs.[52]

In the following months, he elaborated on the causes of the navy's success. He identified one of the customary JMSDF public relations initiatives, the invitation of civilian elites to the graduation ceremony at the academy in Etajima, as the ideal platform to deliver the message. His idea was to acquaint this audience with a crucial ceremony in the navy's most sacred space where memories of the naval past were fused together with the reality of the JMSDF. There, he could convey the inherent relevance of past traditions to the service's operational success.[53] As one of his 1992 guests noted, Captain Furushō 'found time to teach us many traditions of the navy'; he explained their functions and how they contributed to the midshipman's professional socialisation. As he put it, 'Furushō's deep pride in the naval tradition permeated his words.'[54] The Captain's pedagogic instinct and heartfelt passion were met, in one authoritative case, with deep appreciation for what was perceived as his unmatched capacity to explain in simple, convincing words the significance of the navy to Japan's security.[55] A new chapter of the JMSDF public affairs history had started.

Explaining men and traditions: Museums and more

In the subsequent four to five years, the presence of officers like Furushō allowed the JMSDF to focus on specific initiatives to further its image. In particular, the navy's two main museums were heavily refurbished to perform this task.[56] The first to be adapted was the Naval Air Museum in Kanoya, in the Kagoshima Prefecture, dealing – as the name suggests – with the history of Japanese naval aviation. Though the museum was first established in 1972, it was substantially restructured and enlarged in 1993. The refurbishment of the early 1990s brought the museum to its present shape. When it reopened to the public, the museum occupied a 27,000 square metre surface adjacent to the naval air base, receiving visits from a little more than 7,000 people each month, including foreign tourists, notably from Taiwan and different parts of Southeast Asia.[57] The large Japanese garden of the museum was enriched by the presence of different kinds of aircraft and helicopters used by the JMSDF. Inside, the centrepiece attraction consisted of an original Zero carrier fighter found off the nearby coast and completely restored by the base technicians using original spare parts. The majority of the items on display focused on the Imperial Navy, though two galleries sought to show how the skills that produced the fine fighting force of the past continued in the post-war era, and defined the Japanese approach to maritime patrol, ASW, and to search and rescue.

At first sight, the gardens provided the museum with a calm and extra-temporal atmosphere. The structural features of the building and the richness of the exhibitions enabled Kanoya to deliver visual information on the technological achievements of the Japanese navies in a spiritually charged environment. This seemed to be deliberate since the museum specifically engaged with Japan's pre-war 'military culture', also treating one of its most controversial aspects.[58] A museum dealing with Japanese naval aviation could not shy away from addressing the problem of the wartime suicide Special Attack Force.[59]

The curators of the museum – working in collaboration with authorities at the nearby base – did not. According to one inscription, 'complete altruism' and 'unfaltering commitment to the greater good' dominated the culture of Japanese military sailors and officers. This explained the different types of behaviour that had distinguished the actions of the men wearing the white uniform. Across the galleries, examples of naval commanders such as Vice Admiral Ota Minoru, author of a letter to the Navy Ministry in which he praised the heroic contribution of the population of Okinawa to the defence of the island, were displayed to substantiate a genuine sense of dedication and respect for the Japanese people.[60] On the other hand, the culminating point of the exhibition, the main gallery featuring the Zero fighter, illustrated the ultimate subordination of the individual to the requirements of the organisation. There, little ambiguity existed concerning the message the museum intended to deliver. The sacrifice of the members of the Special Attack Force was a consistent – if extreme – expression of the same military culture of dedication. A romantic interpretation of Saigō Takamori's death-defying spirit underscored the intended message. The Japanese 'military culture' of dedication and selflessness bonded the navy together, determined past naval successes, explained hard choices and failures and animated today the *esprit de corps* of the JMSDF.[61] Since the post-war era had heralded different air missions for the JMSDF, the message seemed to suggest that today the imperial spirit lives on, though without its wartime excesses.

If naval aviation was required to address the complexity of naval culture, the JMSDF Naval Historical Museum in Sasebo, also known as Sail Tower, focused on a different message altogether. Opened in March 1997, it engaged with the history of the surface force and Japan's two navies.[62] The link between the two services was literally 'set in stone'. The building used for the museum had previously hosted the Imperial Navy's local officers' club.[63] Requisitioned after the war to serve as a 'town club' for American naval officers, local authorities reacquired it in the 1990s and proposed that the JMSDF turn the building into a museum.[64] The former early twentieth-century club was given a massive architectural makeover. A modern glass six-storey building was added on top of the original structure. The new component was designed to exploit sunlight to reduce energy waste. The contrast between the new and the old could not be greater, as was the effort to blend the two styles. The new Sail Tower was meant to speak of what the JMSDF was all about, 'traditions and progress'.

Inside the structure, white marble, carpet, large LCD flat-screens and well-disposed hi-fi speakers were arranged to create a welcoming atmosphere of understated elegance produced by modern technology. The observation lobby on the top floor commanded a panoramic view of the harbour, further enhancing these impressions. The navy itself was on display, and similar to Kanoya, past and present blended together in every corner of the building. Unlike Kanoya though, Sasebo was designed to use the past to charm young generations rather than to impress their spirit. Scale models of past and present warships, weapons and piloting simulators, interactive computer-based tests, videos, lights, even the simple disposition of the objects in the exhibition rooms were meant to detail information on the two navies and to present in a positive light the choice of a life at sea. In a city like Sasebo with strong seafaring traditions, this was not a difficult message to deliver.

The eventful history of the Imperial Navy was presented across three floors, while the JMSDF's was on display on two floors. The main idea behind the entire exhibition seemed to be to attract the attention of the visitor to the complexity of the business of naval warfare and to the countless skills and tasks that need performing for a ship to operate successfully. This, in turn, seemed designed to suggest that naval personnel had to be extremely skilled, dedicated and willing to perform at the utmost of their personal capabilities in order to operate, maintain and improve the fleet. In this museum, the message focused less on the spiritual credentials of an individual joining the navy and more on the practical skills that the profession required. Indeed, the history of the successes of the Imperial Navy was displayed to reinforce this idea. Constant training and drills represented the foundations of well-executed manoeuvres, precise gunnery and combat proficiency. The history of the Imperial Navy seemed to also set the stage to present how the JMSDF retained the quest for proficiency and technology from its imperial forerunner, and how this, in turn, required the service to seek the brightest and most skilled individuals for the purpose of national defence.

In two respects Sasebo and Kanoya were very similar. In both museums, key naval figures like Admirals Tōgō and Yamamoto were mobilised together with more specific figures – like Admiral Ota – to embody the essence of the Japanese naval figure. In both museums, the imperial military past, tested and refined in the hardship of war, served to empower the present's martial pedigree.

It is no coincidence that both museums mobilised images of assets and capabilities to explain the relationship between the navy and its manpower. According to Shibata Mitsuo, what separated Furushō's formula for the JMSDF self-representation strategy from previous organisational efforts was his stronger emphasis on the 'people'.[65] In the post-war period, the trend had been to advertise capabilities and effectiveness, emphasising the cutting-edge technology of naval assets in both pictorial representations and parades. When Furushō was first handed the duties of a public relations officer, the country was on the cusp of a major change in the way it looked at its military. As he witnessed this new trend consolidating, the admiral was the first to propose a shift in focus; his reference to the imperial legacy was not pursued through the association of present technological assets with icons of past military prowess like battleships or fighters. It condensed around the qualities of the men who operated the ships, and revered war heroes like Tōgō, Yamamoto or Hirose, who had set the standards of Japanese officership.

Commenting on the principles the Public Affairs Office followed in providing consultancy for TV dramas and fiction films during Admiral Furushō's tenure as chief of staff, the section chief pointed out that the JMSDF wanted the people 'to focus on the personnel in the JMSDF'.[66] They sought to appeal to existing popular perceptions of the pre-war navy that presented officers and sailors as possessing a balanced mix of traditional values and technological ability; patriots with a cosmopolitan outlook, capable of individual initiative and rigorous discipline. In turn, the values embedded within the figures of the past sought to suggest that the capabilities of today's JMSDF rested on the qualities of its personnel who were instructed in line with that tradition. For this reason, in 2004, Admiral Furushō strongly supported a documentary on the life of the JMSDF cadets in Etajima. Significantly, the video featured an interview with the admiral in which he explained the essence of the 'navy's culture' with a small statue of Admiral Tōgō clearly visible behind him, as support and example.[67]

Promoted to rear admiral in 1997 and to admiral in 2001, Furushō was appointed commander in chief of the Self-Defence Fleet, to return to the maritime staff office as vice chief of staff in 2002, becoming chief of staff in January 2003. Thirteen years after his assignment at the Public Affairs Office, Japan was in a renewed phase of intense public debate on the use of its armed forces. Core issues concerned the participation of the JSDF in multinational military operations on the one hand, and their ability to address regional sources of security concern, most notably North Korea's nuclear arsenal and China's military modernisation, on the other.[68] More specifically, controversies surrounding an initial September 2001 governmental plan to dispatch JMSDF's P3-C maritime patrol aircraft and an *Aegis* destroyer in the Indian Ocean to offer logistical support to coalition forces had drawn the nation's attention to the navy.[69] In this context, Admiral Furushō's position at the apex of the service's hierarchy combined with his prior experience enabled him to retain a firm grasp of the communication strategy.

Several circumstances facilitated the use of public events to further the connection between the Japanese navies. In October 2002, the celebrations for the 50th anniversary of the establishment of the JMSDF offered such an opportunity as Japan hosted the International Fleet Review for the first time in its history. This represented a 'landmark event' which projected the 'dignified appearance of the JMSDF' onto the world stage, one that the Japanese Postal service decided to celebrate by issuing a stamp featuring the destroyers *Shirane* (DDH-143) and *Chōkai* (DDG-176), the first stamps in the post-war period dedicated to the then Defence Agency and the JSDF.[70] Concurrently, the navy organised a week-long series of promotional activities in the cities of Tokyo, Yokosuka, and Yokohama, including a parade, a concert, and a 'night illumination' of the ships at anchor while hosting the 8th Western Pacific Naval Symposium (WPNS) and a multilateral search and rescue exercise (SAREX).[71] In terms of image, this undertaking was designed to give the service the highest possible public exposure and to strengthen its reputation by displaying the organisational, operational and diplomatic skills of the imperial period. As a way to subtly underline this notion, the fleet review DVD, produced by a well-known Japanese company specialising in war-related documentary series, featured extra tracks with original video footage from pre-war imperial fleet reviews.[72]

In 2005, the 100th anniversary of Japan's victory in the Russo-Japanese War and the 60th anniversary of the end of the Pacific War presented two more opportunities for a set of diversified and wide-reaching initiatives for naval advertisement. The Russo-Japanese War had exceptional significance for the JMSDF as this conflict had generated Japan's most celebrated naval heroes. In both men and operational conduct, it encapsulated an ethos the post-war service considered inherent to its image. Thus, numerous celebrations were held, culminating on 28 May (the day of the victory at Tsushima) with two official ceremonies, one ashore on board the battleship museum *Mikasa*, and one at sea, where a small flotilla headed by the veteran destroyer *Hiei* (DDH-142) sailed in the area where the actual battle took place.[73] As 2005 also corresponded with the 200th anniversary of the British victory in the Battle of Trafalgar, the JMSDF sent its training squadron to Europe to attend the Fleet Review held in Portsmouth, creating a symbolic connection between Nelson and Tōgō, Trafalgar and Tsushima, the Royal Navy's longstanding history and heritage and Japan's naval tradition. These events received prime media coverage, supported by the release throughout the year of documentaries, promotional videos and fictional films produced either by the service or with its support, all playing to the strength of the JMSDF's longstanding message regarding the cultural and professional ties between the Imperial Navy and the JMSDF.[74]

Conclusions

By the time Admiral Furushō retired, his confidence in a navy that entertained a strong bond with the past went beyond the realm of public affairs.[75] His contribution to the

JMSDF post-Cold War communication strategy rested on the idea that only taking the Japanese people into the navy's confidence could enhance social trust in a fashion consistent with the evolving public exposure of the organisation. By fostering public understanding of the men, their assets and their mission, Admiral Furushō argued that the JMSDF could reinforce its bond with the Japanese people, enhancing the perception of the social utility of the navy.[76] For this reason, he encouraged the JMSDF to invest in public relations.[77] He noted that the need for a renewed effort to widen this scope was prompted by the post-Cold War transformation of both the domestic and international milieus. The navy's operational tempo had increased, and with it, the visibility of its conduct and the 'scrutiny of the nation's eye'.[78] As the admiral put it, the JMSDF had to adapt to this new environment to nourish the social foundations of its fabric.[79]

The Imperial Navy played a double role in public relations. As the new navy was set up, past practices offered both an idea for the content of the main message – the navy as a modern and smart organisation – and a method of delivery, including fleet reviews and base visits. Public nostalgia and emotional ties that connected the Imperial Navy to the rise of the modern Japanese state offered a relevant option for a navy that faced a society committed to economic recovery and largely uninterested in military affairs. Pageantry and public relations reminded the Japanese society that the pillars of the imperial naval success – seamanship and powerful platforms – were at the heart of the new force. Modernity and progress continued to drive Japan's post-war recovery and naval re-emergence. Until the end of the 1970s, public visual displays focusing on the equipment and the professionalism of the force had an important function; they highlighted virtues and ethos, and diverted attention away from budgetary, structural and normative limitations. They bridged the gap between the navy and the civilian society during a time of limited public interest in defence policy, a time the JMSDF used to construct of public image as post-war guarantors of the imperial professional legacy.

The groundwork conducted during the Cold War was a preliminary condition of significant importance in its aftermath. Decades of targeted public relations activities and the controlled environment of ships and bases where they were delivered had allowed the JMSDF to present a clear message. As such, when in the 1990s public attention increased, the JMSDF had personnel with the vision and confidence to strengthen its public relations machinery, the PAO, accordingly. The contribution of individuals like Admiral Furushō in particular was essential to diversify the framework and the delivery methods. In this respect, the main shift concerned the greater emphasis given to the navy's manpower – emphasising more the moral fabric of the navy than its equipment. In this, the legacy of the Imperial Navy remained firmly in the background of the main public relations initiatives as the source of the JMSDF's success as an organisation. Seamanship and professionalism were explained as based on the same traditions that had secured Japan's emergence at the turn of the century. This, in turn, constituted a guarantee of the service's ability to meet the growing challenges to Japanese security. Contrary to its sister services, the JMSDF had been able to use its imperial past to create and maintain its public outlook and seek social support for it.

Photo 5.1 Reinstating old traditions: The first post-war fleet review.

Photo 5.2 An established event: The contemporary fleet review (2006). Photo by the author.

Photo 5.3 Connecting with the people: The JSDF concert in Yokosuka.

Photo 5.4 Tradition and modernity: The 'Sail Tower' in Sasebo. Photo by the author.

Photo 5.5 Japan's military culture: The naval air museum in Kanoya. Photo by the author.

6

Strategy and Policy: The 'Sea Power' of the Pacific

How a war is fought will, in the end rest upon the leader's perspective and personality. … What is important is not to force the matter into a single answer.[1]

Admiral Uchida Kazuomi, JMSDF
(8th Chief of Maritime Staff, 1969–72)

In drawing up new National Defense Program Guidelines to take effect in fiscal (year) 2010, it is vital for Japan as a maritime nation to increase its defense budgets, strengthen its maritime defenses within constitutional limits, and buttress the alliance with the United States. A stronger Japanese Maritime Self-Defense Force can gain more respect from its Chinese counterpart and build more credible mutual confidence.[2]

Masashi Nishihara
(President, Research Institute for Peace and Security)

Naval strategy, the Corbett way

Early in the morning of 6 October 1950, Japanese maritime authorities in Yokosuka had reason to feel apprehensive. A squadron of twenty-four minesweepers and one mother ship were about to join the Wonsan landing operations as part of the international task group CT 95.6 under the command of Captain Richard T. Spofford, US Navy.[3] For the following two months, a total of forty-six minesweepers flying UN colours would sweep 327 km of channels and anchorages around Korean ports, including Wonsan, Chinnampo and Inchon.[4] This was a dangerous job for any navy, but especially for one that formally did not really exist and, more crucially, was not supposed to be there. Two ships were lost; one of them – the MS14 – after striking a mine that caused the death of a young crewmember, Nakatani Sakatarō, Japan's only known 'killed in action' of the post-war era.[5] As the war for Korea continued to unfold, the American requests for minesweepers made Japanese authorities fully realise that their country stood on the frontline of the evolving Soviet–American confrontation in East Asia. In that context, naval rearmament was to be a core part of the wider political debate on defence and security. As Admiral Nomura Kichisaburō pointed out, Japan needed a navy 'strong enough to absolutely check Communist invasion from either Russia or China' to protect the Japanese seaboard and maritime air space, including the main sea lanes directed to Japan, and to control the Straits of Sōya, Tsugaru and Tsushima.[6] Naval rearmament was to be a crucial part of national strategy.

This chapter explores how the experience of the Imperial Navy contributed to the JMSDF's development of a coherent strategic vision and to champion relevant naval policies. For the JMSDF leadership, an understanding of the past was not a matter of 'if'; it was a question of 'which past' and 'how'. It was, as Admiral Uchida put it, seeking relevant answers. Reassessments had to be functional to define new roles and missions in national defence, seeking 'not to point out lessons, but to isolate things that need thinking about'.[7] Crucially, the investigation of the past focused on strategy and policy failures from the last war to address relevant concerns on bureaucratic politics to secure adequate capabilities and on operational concerns on anti-submarine warfare (ASW). In so doing, the JMSDF became a different organisation from its imperial forerunner. It pursued organisational interests as an inherent part of national defence policy, rather than employing the latter to secure the former. Compared to the Mahanian endeavours of the Imperial Navy, the JMSDF developed as a very Corbettian organisation. Corbett argued that the 'paramount concern' of maritime strategy is 'to determine the mutual relations of your army and navy in a plan of war'.[8] In formulating a maritime strategy, the key question to address is 'What will the war be about?' and how the navy fits into it.[9] As the JMSDF argued the case for naval defence, their strategic approach sought to build on the imperial experience to answer that very same question.

Shattered trident

Institutional memory is an invaluable commodity for strategic planners. In the Japanese case, the foundations of post-war strategy and naval policy trace their roots to the *ex post* understanding of the annihilating defeat suffered by the Imperial Navy in the Pacific War. Assessments formulated by top echelons identified specific aspects of pre-war planning and wartime conduct as central to explaining the defeat. In terms of planning, at the grand strategy level, 'there was a mistake at the top from the very beginning as to the nature of modern warfare' based on the belief that the war would be of short duration. This, in turn, led naval leadership to serious miscalculations on the consumption of matériel and resources such as oil and steel.[10] Similarly, plans to seize control of the Pacific were not complemented by adequate assessments of the operational requirements to maintain it. Admiral Nomura observed that:

> When they (Japanese naval strategists) plan an operation they should be prepared to take the defensive; that is, to maintain and support what they acquired offensively, and this must be calculated carefully. But they only thought of pushing forward; they were little concerned with the defensive. They did not calculate shipping losses or materials to supply and maintain in their positions acquired.[11]

Nomura's reflections on the shortcomings of Japanese strategy in matters of logistics should be examined in context. Nomura was in the United Sates in the months subsequent to Pearl Harbor, and he witnessed first-hand the potential of the American economy fully mobilised for 'total war'. Throughout the first half of 1942, Nomura was particularly troubled by reports on American naval construction programmes, set to exponentially increase the number of fast cruisers, aircraft carriers and submarines in the fleet. Nomura feared especially the doubling of the number of submarines, which were ideal platforms to 'threaten Japan's lines of communication'.[12] This experience is likely to have informed his post-war views of the Japanese failures in the planning and conduct of the naval war. Far from being isolated, his remarks found further support in subsequent scholarship.[13]

According to another retired admiral, this problem stemmed from the fact that, since 1907, Japanese naval planning had been heavily affected by budget politics.[14] Concerns about procurement were dictated domestically by competition for financial resources with the army and internationally, especially later on in the 1920s and 1930s, by the ratios imposed on the number and displacement of warships by the Washington and London naval agreements.[15] The desire to compensate material and numerical deficiencies led much of the navy's leadership to obsessively focus on technical matters concerning speed, armour protection and firepower to produce qualitatively 'superior' platforms. Questions concerning the 'who', the 'why' and the 'what for' were slowly being set aside in the service's inner debate. Further, after 1937, the Japanese increased military involvement in China exacerbated tensions with the army and inter-service competition for material resources assumed a prominent role in discussions on national defence. By the end of the 1930s, the issue of 'how to' build up a fleet that could successfully engage in one culminating blow against its main peer competitor in the Pacific, the US Navy, slowly became the overarching concern.[16] A 'hypothetical' enemy was essential to justify requests for funds; in turn, this mechanism constrained the naval debate on strategy, limiting it to a series of tactical and technological problems aimed at perfecting warships that could overwhelm a numerically superior adversary. As a result, 'there was little correlation between national defence theory and the strategic plans of the army and navy'.[17]

Post-war re-examinations by former imperial officers highlighted a second problem with the Imperial Navy's conduct – its inability to adapt strategy and operations to the evolving wartime circumstances.[18] Throughout the conflict, the preparation for the decisive surface engagement with the United States drove the navy's attention away from the crucial aspect of the protection of shipping. The defence of Japanese maritime routes that transported core natural resources and raw materials was vital to the Japanese war-fighting machine.[19] Maritime communications were the lifeline of the Japanese Empire and, at the same time, its Achilles heel. The Allied forces set out to exploit this weakness and the Japanese failed to recognise this shift in focus, persisting in their quest to target the enemy's combat fleet. By the end of 1943, Japan had already lost over two million tons of shipping, suffering a three million-ton shortfall in bulk commodities compared to the previous year. The situation worsened dramatically in 1944 and 1945, when Japanese oil imports fell from a 1943 peak of 740,000 tons to a meagre 178,000 tons (third quarter of 1944), with just 9 per cent of oil shipments from Southeast Asia reaching their final destination in Japan in 1945.[20]

As the war progressed, the Allied forces engaged in a ruthless offensive campaign against Japanese merchants. Submarine operations had a devastating impact. In the South China Sea, as of June–July 1944, patrols by American subsurface assets were sinking some twenty ships a month, approximately 60,000 tons.[21] The tonnage of Japanese shipping sent to the bottom of the ocean doubled in the period September–October 1944 (a little less than 130,000 tons) and reached its pinnacle in the months from November 1944 to August 1945, when fifty-eight ships, including naval and merchant vessels, totalling 178,230 tons, were sunk.[22] Inherent doctrinal deficiencies in the Japanese approach to ASW combined with the failure to reassign sufficient assets to escort duties and to refocus the Japanese submarine effort on harassing American ships doomed the Japanese war at sea.[23] A comparative analysis would confirm this assertion. In the Atlantic, German U-boats sunk 60 per cent of total Allied shipping, equal to 14.57 million tons, with losses amounting to 781 submarines and 39,000 men. In the Pacific, American submarines sunk 55 per cent of the total of Japanese shipping (equal to 4.8 million tons), at the cost of fifty submarines and 3,500 men lost.[24] The war of the *Maru*, as the campaign against shipping came to be known after the generic designation for Japanese merchant vessels, was later considered by the United States Strategic Bombing Survey as 'perhaps the most decisive single factor in the collapse of the Japanese economy and logistic support of Japanese military and naval power'.[25]

From the perspective of the senior officers who survived the war, the shortcomings of the late inter-war and wartime policy and strategy were the result of a narrow interpretation of the role of navies as tools of statecraft. The navy's increasing diplomatic isolation in the 1930s and its constant fights with the army over budget shares affected its ability to think about its roles in a wider national security context. This approach affected the ability of Japanese naval planners to develop a strategy that could be relevant to national policies in the late 1930s and adjust to the circumstances of the battlefield as the war unfolded in the 1940s.[26] Eventually, the Japanese trident was shattered.

Naval policy and national security

These 'lessons' were not going to be lost on the first post-war generation of naval officers. Since the closing days of the Navy Ministry and, throughout the demobilisation, a strong bond was created between pre-war senior personnel and what became the first generations of JMSDF top echelons. In November 1945, just days before the ministry was disbanded, Navy Minister Yonai Mitsumasa asked Admiral Nomura to be involved in the future reconstruction of the Japanese navy.[27] Yonai knew that during the occupation any decision about a Japanese rearmament would be taken in Washington rather than in Tokyo and therefore, his wish to have senior retired officers like Nomura involved seemed to be motivated by both professional and practical motivations.[28] In practical terms, individuals like Nomura, Yonai and Yamanashi were regarded in the United States as moderate, professional individuals belonging to the more pro-Anglophone group of the Imperial Navy.[29] They all had personal friends in the United States, especially Nomura – who had served as Ambassador in Washington just before the war. After the war, Nomura corresponded regularly with American contacts in key positions of the US political and military establishments and regularly discussed and lobbied for naval rearmament.[30]

From this vantage point, retired officers like Nomura engaged with the officers who were in the driving seat of the demobilisation process, and ensured that assessments of the failures in the 'last war' filtered through as these younger officers became involved in the preliminary planning of the post-war navy. In particular, the setting up in the autumn of 1951 of the 'Y Committee', a group tasked to study the use of a set of vessels that the United States had offered to Japan, proved just how intertwined the professional paths of the two navies were throughout this transition.[31] In this respect, one scholar that led the uncovering of new evidence regarding Nomura's impact on this period noted that the Admiral was not a formal member of the committee. He nonetheless 'remained in the background, offering his advice, encouragement, and support'.[32] The value of the imperial experience was exactly where it was supposed to be, in the background of the process.

From 1952 to 1954, the forerunners of the JMSDF set out to understand the imperial experience, especially the reasons behind the defeat, and make use of this understanding to develop better policies to meet the challenge of the present. One of the service's premises was that the dynamics of the Cold War would likely require the navy to be a crucial player in the national military position. The geographic location of the Japanese archipelago gave it a strategic advantage in limiting a Soviet naval expansion in East Asia. Its islands were home to naval bases vital to a strategy of containment, its straits crucial access points to the ocean. Soviet planners too seemingly feared the strategic advantages of Japanese geography, as they proved when the Japanese Peace Treaty was signed in San Francisco. On that occasion, the Soviet representative reportedly suggested limiting the Japanese straits for the use of Soviet naval ships only with a prohibition to keep Japan from fortifying the coastline surrounding them.[33] Considerations on Japan's strategic geography became even more relevant as Cold War politics evolved. By 1949, the Chinese civil war had ended with the establishment of the communist regime in China, and the seriousness of the Communist threat from the Eurasian continent was reaffirmed during the Korean War.[34]

The domestic political outlook had an equally significant share of influence on the ways in which military planners reconsidered pre-war assumptions on the defence of the nation. Article 9 of the 1947 'Peace' Constitution prohibited Japan from using war as a means to settle international disputes and to that end, no army, navy or air force was to be maintained.[35] The constitution had several consequences that naval planners had to factor into their calculations as they discussed rearmament. From an operational perspective, this meant that Japanese naval thinkers could no longer consider offensive operations to seize command of the sea as a viable foundation for naval strategy. Politically, civilian oversight on military affairs meant that the post-war military could not use direct political access to the Emperor as a way to force its own procurement plans. Strategically, the political consensus emerging in Japan under the aegis of Prime Minister Yoshida aimed at privileging economic recovery and therefore favoured a security alignment with the United States as a way to keep a low profile in military matters.[36] In particular, insofar as naval affairs were concerned, the cooperation with the United States was regarded by the Prime Minister as the most suitable option for Japan to develop its maritime economy, access the world markets and resources and guarantee the safeguarding of her sea routes without embarking upon a substantial naval build-up.[37]

Against this overall framework, the lessons from the Imperial Navy were to find initial application shortly after the creation of the Safety Agency. In September 1952, the Safety Agency set up a consultative body composed of three subcommittees (defence, economics and organisation), known as the Systems Investigative Committee,[38] to conduct preliminary research on the future requirements of Japanese defence.[39] Uniformed officers from the newly established Maritime Safety Force[40] contributed to the definition of the force level for maritime security.

In drafting their recommendations, naval experts focused on the wartime problem of securing the continued flow of vital primary resources to the archipelago, a concern that matched the country's emerging new security framework. The subcommittee's proposal pointed to a thirteen-year build-up, with a force level goal of 475,000 tons. The protection of maritime transportation[41] was one of the core objectives of national security, while maritime convoying and anti-submarine warfare were to constitute the guiding principles for procurement.[42] A second set of priorities identified in the document concerned the acquisition of the necessary capabilities to prevent foreign aggression against Japanese territory.[43] The roles identified for the new navy were well in line with the views that former officers like Nomura had expressed on previous occasions.[44]

These views continued to underpin naval policy planning for the following two years after the formal establishment of the JMSDF in 1954. Naval planners in Tokyo as well as in Washington insisted on the strategic imperative to learn from past mistakes. As a 1956 official study commissioned by the newly established Japan Defence Agency pointed out, the susceptibility of the Japanese territory and main sea-trade arteries to eventual Soviet hostile military actions underlined the need to reconstitute and maintain a modern fleet.[45] The policy options for Japanese naval capabilities focused on defensive roles, pointing to escort missions instead of the projection of power. They were, however, rather ambitious especially given the fragile state of Japan's post-war economy.

Indeed, the ambitious figures outlined in the original Committee's report did not meet with favour in the influential Ministry of Finance. The ministry dismissed the plan as putting unnecessary economic pressure on the government's austere annual expenditures at the time.[46] Naval rearmament could count on a small, but influential group of political supporters within Japan's ruling party, most notably the chairman of the party's Security Policy Study Committee, Vice Admiral Hoshina Zenshiro, a retired imperial naval officer. Nonetheless, a naval build-up did not rank high in the Japanese government's agenda of the time. Apart from obvious considerations about the country's limited economic and shipbuilding potential of the early 1950s, in the short-term, naval policy was a less pressing issue compared to the strengthening of ground forces.[47]

Two main reasons underpinned the government's position. Domestically, the strengthening of a ground force showed the Japanese people the government's political commitment to accelerate the withdrawal of the core of American troops stationed in Japan. Diplomatically, it represented a tangible sign of Japan's pledge to the security partnership with the United States while having no real strategic role beyond national borders.[48] Though the circumstances of the time did little to favour the JMSDF's ambitions, the significance of these early plans should not be underestimated. They highlighted an early attempt to process the past to meet the challenges of a fast-evolving present, one in which Japan's economic dependence on maritime trade was likely to grow.[49] These plans were a sign of the navy's appreciation of the need to inscribe the role of naval power in the context of a national security strategy. Further, the navy's focus on maritime defence was in line with the new constitutional framework, though the quest for a force capable of protecting regional sea lanes was symptomatic of an ambition to pursue sea control, rather than sea denial and coastal defence.

In 1956, the final decision was to provide the JMSDF with a relatively modest force goal in the first Defence Build-up Plan.[50] This was set at approximately 124,000 tons, including some 20 major surface units (DDs and DEs) and 180 aircraft of various types, to be attained during the period 1958–60 (Figure 6.1).[51] The plan effectively relegated naval matters to a secondary role, with the JMSDF's sole mission consisting of strictly 'defence from direct aggression of the mainland'.[52] A similar rationale underpinned the drafting of the second Build-up Plan, though JMSDF planners continued to argue the case for naval defence vigorously.[53]

These decisions underlined the extent of the subordination of post-war military officers to their civilian counterparts in the policy decision-making process. Similarly, they proved that naval planners had identified a way to argue the case for a maritime-oriented military posture and that they had started to cut their teeth in the attempt to present it. Political inexperience did not prevent naval assessments and fleet target goals from aiming high. Initial plans were regarded as politically and economically disproportionate to the Japanese need of the time. In this respect, one senior planning

Plan	Period	DD	SS	MSC	**Tot.**	Aircraft	Helicopters	**Tot.**
---	1953–57	15*	1	14	**30**	156	13	**169**
1st Build-up	1958–60	5	4	8	**17**	78	15	**93**
2nd Build-up	1962–66	9	4	11	**24**	71	29	**100**
3rd Build-up	1967–71	13	5	12	**30**	56	43	**99**
4th Build-up	1972–76	8	3	14	**25**	81	40	**121**
Post-4th Build-up	1977–79	8	3	6	**17**	36	18	**54**
Mid-Term	1980–82	9	3	6	**18**	26	16	**42**
Mid-Term	1983–85	8	3	6	**17**	27	29	**56**
Mid-Term	1986–90	9	5	10	**24**	60	60	**120**
Mid-Term	1991–95	8	5	10	**23**	68	63	**131**
Mid-Term	1996–00	7	5	6	**15**	18	42	**60**

Figure 6.1 JMSDF's procurement programmes, 1953–2000.

Source: JMSDF, *Kaijōjieitai Gojū Nenshi – Shiryōhen* (海上自衛隊五十年史、資料編 – JMSDF's Fifty Year History – Data, Tokyo: Maritime Staff Office, 2003), 278–9, 302–3.

officer with in-depth knowledge of the JMSDF's draft studies of the time explained that in these early stages of rearmament, a latent anxiety to rebuild the fleet underscored the restless activity of naval planners at the Maritime Staff Office.[54] Naval planners had started their career in the Imperial Navy and wished the new service to grow beyond the limitations of a force made of a few patrol boats and minesweepers. What the JMSDF seemed to have realised was that in the relationship between the service's strategic views and national policy, the former defined the boundaries of the latter and that the imperial experience could offer the means to close the gap between the two.

The strategy of a 'trading nation'

Between the second half of the 1960s and the early 1970s, three factors were transforming the Japanese political debate in defence affairs. On the one hand, President Richard Nixon's 1969 announcement of the Guam doctrine was seen as casting a shadow over American commitment to East Asian security. This challenged one of the fundamental underpinnings of the security policies enacted by Yoshida and his successors.[55] Concurrently, the stunning economic revival of the 1950s, coupled with the expansion of the national maritime space deriving from the reversion of the Ogasawara and Ryūkyū Islands in 1968 and 1972, respectively, prompted the widening of the Japanese debate on the core priorities in national security and the best means to protect them.[56]

Addressing Japanese defence problems in the 'post-Okinawa reversion' era were a priority for the Diet member who had replaced Admiral Hoshina at the Liberal Democratic Party's Security Affairs Research Council, Funada Naka. He captured the problem of the era by expressing deep concerns about Japan's trade routes security 'in view of the bitter experience of American submarines operating as they liked in the Sea of Japan during the War'.[57] Confident of the experience that it had gained in the previous years, the JMSDF sought to capitalise on the changing political atmosphere. It tailored its requests for the third Build-up Plan by penning a proposal which was not ambitious in the increases it proposed, but that could lay the foundations for a larger, balanced force in the future.[58] The service proposed a financially feasible and politically acceptable increase in its total tonnage of 20,000 tons. This allowed the navy to shift the battle for its status in national defence away from 'the question of the numbers', in order to fight for a target of much greater long-term importance. In 1966, thanks to ever-growing trade numbers, the JMSDF managed to obtain the inclusion within its primary roles of the 'protection of maritime transportation' within territorial waters.[59]

As its duties expanded to include the surveillance and defence of Japan's main straits, the enhancement of the navy's effectiveness and the development of a relevant strategy became a top priority. In regard to the former, the JMSDF sought to profit from the relatively confined geography around its straits to conduct more sophisticated tactical training involving surface, subsurface and air assets.[60] In relation to the latter, contingency plans to protect Japanese sea trade routes were evaluated. According to an unpublished official document, the third Build-up Plan detailed an emergency scenario in which maritime transportation was to be organised along two main 'sea route zones',[61] heading southwest and southeast of Japan's principal maritime Pacific hubs.

The 'southwest route'[62] extended through the Ryūkyū Islands and the Nansei Shotō towards the Bashi Channel for 840 NM (1,555 km) and was 150 NM (277 km) wide; the 'southeast route'[63] moved across the Ogasawara/Bonin Islands to a point north of Guam for 1,000 NM (1,852 km) and was 240 NM (444 km) wide (Map 2).[64]

The usefulness of a fleet that could meet the economic requirements of national security became evident just a few years later, when the first serious threat to the Japanese economy materialised. The 1973 oil crisis shook 'Japan's economic and social systems at their very foundations', making defence policymakers more aware of the importance of 'maintaining the safety of maritime transportation'.[65] The 'oil shock' highlighted one of the fundamental vulnerabilities of the maritime-oriented nature of Japanese post-war economic power. University of Kyōto Professor Kōsaka Masataka, advisor to Prime Minister Ōhira Masayoshi (1978–80), was the first to adopt in the 1960s and 1970s the terms 'maritime nation'[66] and 'trading nation'[67] to explain the distinctive features of Japan's successful industrial recovery.[68]

As an island nation poor in natural resources, the archipelago's dependence on foreign markets and raw materials was a direct consequence of its export-oriented development. This increased 'both the vulnerability and the influence of Japan' worldwide. As he pointed out:

> Japan could live anonymously twenty, or even ten years ago; but now her exports, because of their volume, create problems in other countries. And if raw materials should become less easy to obtain Japan would suffer more because she now needs them in larger quantities.[69]

Maritime trade had been the source of the country's rise as an economic power, and for the same reasons it was also fast becoming a potential Achilles' heel – in a way already demonstrated by the wartime experience. Kōsaka's views embodied the evolving consciousness of an influential part of Japanese academia vis-à-vis Japan's future economic security challenges.[70] His writings did not directly address the role of military and naval forces in the realm of security. Yet, his input on the nature of the Japanese economy likely informed the policy-making process of the time as he joined the consultative body drafting the pilot study for what became the main Cold War defence policy document, the 1976 National Defence Programme Outline (NDPO).[71] Other informed observers noted the economic connection with the debate on the Japanese naval problem. Defence analyst Maeda Tetsuo stressed that the question of the movement of maritime imports from food supplies to energy was central to the way sea lane defence was debated in the country. As he put it, 'The main questions were how to carry industrial resources and the necessities of life to Japanese ports, how to protect the routes, and how to compose the convoys.' He further concluded that from his perspective, the 'defence of sea lanes seemed appropriately commercial for an economic giant'.[72]

Other naval advocates in the civilian sector, notably former imperial navy officer and retired JMSDF Commander Sekino Hideo, shared the strategic implications of Kōsaka's view.[73] Naval advocates like Sekino envisaged a much enlarged Japanese navy that could be capable in wartime of establishing a 'maritime safety zone' to escort Japanese shipping from Japanese shores to Indonesia, through the East and the South China Seas. Sekino estimated a fleet of 500,000 tons with 570 aircraft was necessary to defend convoys against Soviet naval and land-based air power.[74] However, a strategy based on the protection of maritime traffic was not without detractors within the civilian circles of the Defence Agency.[75] Kaihara Osamu, a senior civilian defence official, led the group of those who dismissed the protection of the vast areas comprising the sea lanes as impracticable and financially unsound. Instead, he suggested a more passive defence position based on the countering of a Soviet invasion.[76] A fundamental intellectual difference existed between these two views in their approach to the role of the military in national security. Navalists put a premium on the use of military power to secure wider national security interests, along with the country's trade and economic lifelines. The main assumption was that the sea control necessary to achieve this would also prevent a potential invasion. Civilians like Kaihara, on the other hand, attributed to military power a more 'minimalist function', one that confined its use to the defence of the Japanese coastline, air and land spaces against the prospect of an amphibious Soviet operation.

By the time the NDPO was officially adopted, an expanding consensus existed on the critical contribution of a maritime strategy to Japan's national security. Support from political figures like Nakasone Yasuhiro, head of the Defence Agency from 1970 to 1972, helped the naval case, as he endorsed the idea of enhancing a sea-based defence posture for Japan in order to increase the country's 'autonomy' in security affairs.[77] In the mid-1970s, a Japanese maritime strategy of defending the archipelago against limited, direct attempts to cut the country's economic lifelines at sea was finding its place within the country's defence and security policy. As one author put it, the defence of maritime trade became 'an elegant and useful device towards overcoming the controversy surrounding all aspects of Japan's post-war maritime rearmament'. In terms of popular resonance too, it was 'matched by few other potential justifications for the JSDF'.[78] On the other hand, this did not mean that Japanese politicians fully supported a substantially expanded maritime commitment to protect the sea lanes on the high seas. In 1972, the government set the boundaries of Japanese policy action when it expressed the position that the exercise of the right of collective self-defence was not permitted by the constitution.[79]

The challenges ahead: Evolving fleet, evolving enemy

In this context, the NDPO did not revolutionise post-war defence policy. It did not propose plans for open-ended military expansions. It did, however, create the conditions for the Japanese maritime strategy to be implemented. How? The document focused on a qualitative improvement of the Japanese armed forces, shifting the attention for the first time away from the question of numbers. The procurement of enhanced assets to improve the quality of Japan's military apparatus sought to maximise, within the existing legal boundaries, its deterrent effect in the waters of the Sea of Japan and of the East China Sea. The maritime strategy that had emerged from the 1970s political debate about the country's defence posture was well within reach, due to this emphasis on quality. Indeed, a fleet with enhanced capabilities – rather than just a larger fleet – was precisely what was needed. In supporting this, political elites in Tokyo could also seek to achieve a degree of autonomy in the realm of defence policy vis-à-vis Washington's Pacific strategy.[80]

From a naval perspective, the document's core notion, the 'basic defence force' concept,[81] reflected this new quest for quality. It sought to strengthen the navy to guarantee an effective force for sea control in the Sea of Japan (especially around the country's three main straits) to deter Soviet naval adventurism and harassment of Japanese shipping. In a narrow sea like the Sea of Japan, chokepoint control in peacetime was crucial to guarantee the blocking of the Soviet fleet based in Vladivostok. For similar reasons, it was an essential prerequisite for gaining control of the adjacent sea areas in case of escalation of military tensions. This was to be a primary mission of the navy. Surface, air and subsurface patrol operations along routes in the East China Sea were to complement chokepoint control and were to be conducted within 500 NM from Japanese shores.[82] In cases of military crises, these peacetime operations would likely constitute the basis for the organisation of escorted convoys. To meet the requirements for these missions, the Japanese were to aim for a more balanced fleet, one that could perform peacetime surveillance and deter aggression in narrow seas, while retaining a degree of blue-water capabilities to perform ASW in open waters to preserve the flow of goods to and from the archipelago.[83] In this respect, the new national policy rewarded two decades of efforts by the naval authorities to secure the navy's place at the heart of Japanese national strategy by directly linking its existence with the country's vital maritime interests.[84]

Internal debates on naval policy since the second half of the 1960s had prepared the ground for the JMSDF to engage with the challenges of the 1970s and 1980s. Discussions and assessments continued to benefit from the service's engagement with the imperial past. One example of this process is particularly relevant. In 1973 the JMSDF assigned one of its experienced officers, Commander Senō Sadao, to the historical branch of the National Institute for Defence Studies. His task was to undertake a research project on the 1941 memorandum written by the then chief of the Navy Ministry's Naval Aviation Department, Admiral Inoue Shigeyoshi. In 'On Modern Weapons Procurement Planning',[85] Admiral Inoue had been the first flag officer to warn the navy of the need to drastically redirect its procurement policy in order to provide the fleet with assets designed to secure transportation routes. Equally, he denounced the potentially disastrous consequences of the fixation on a fighting force conceived to seize sea control by means of a decisive battle without complementing this endeavour with considerations concerning how to maintain it.[86] Commander Senō, a 1944 Naval Academy graduate, had studied under Admiral Inoue at the academy, was trained to serve on midget submarines and was reassigned to a minesweeper operating in home waters after the end of the war.[87] He was the ideal candidate for the task, having both the professional skills necessary to analyse the subject and a personal knowledge of the officer who had conceived the original text.[88]

Rising oil prices were menacing the energy supply policies of Western democracies, while technological innovations in combat and detection systems were forcing navies to reconsider procurement and tactics, particularly in relation to the balance of naval, submarine and air assets. The internal support made it clear that Commander Senō was a timely choice. This opinion was largely shared by then Vice Admiral Stanfield Turner,

President of the US Naval War College, who offered Commander Senō the opportunity to publish the results of his work in the college journal. In a letter to Senō, whom he had met during a tour of duty in Japan, Admiral Turner recognised the merits of his work:

> The lessons from the rejection of Admiral Inoue's forward thinking are very applicable today. The Admiral pointed out that the battleship was no longer the principal naval weapon. Are we looking seriously today at whether the carrier is still the principal naval weapon? The Admiral rejected the idea that major fleet engagements would be the way the next war would be fought. Are we looking at whether our current concepts of naval warfare fit the likely shape of things to come? I particularly liked his comment that 'the control of the sea is not as absolute in the days of submarines as it was in the old days'. That thought was way ahead of his time. I do not believe we have fully absorbed it even today.[89]

In an age where dominance of the sea was not absolute, as it had been in the past, the JMSDF knew that its quest for sea control would have greatly benefited from an injection of new assets. Based on Soviet estimates of 1974, naval planners considered the ASW capabilities of the fleet to be half the level required to secure sea areas around Japan. Exercises conducted off Ōshima the following year further confirmed deficiencies in this area.[90] To fulfil its missions, the NDPO set the JMSDF's fleet target goal at approximately 60 major surface vessels, some 220 aircraft to patrol Japan's maritime space and 16 submarines to hunt potentially hostile naval assets.[91] These levels were short of what in some naval circles was considered necessary for sea lane defence, and they were not alone in having these fears. As late as 1981, during a senior-level meeting with their American counterparts, United States navy officials recommended that the Japanese boost their fleet up to 70 surface ships, 25 submarines and 125 P-3C (as opposed to the NDPO's 100).[92] Observers later noted that these figures were very similar to those the JMSDF was considering in the preparations for the NDPO.

The evolving nature of the Soviet military in East Asia, regarded by Japanese experts as the archipelago's primary security challenge, complicated Japanese calculations as to how to best implement their strategy.[93] From the second half of the 1960s, the Soviet navy had been acquiring 'blue-water'[94] capabilities that were eroding the margins of Western supremacy in the control of the oceans. The Soviet Pacific Fleet had the largest operating area of all Soviet fleets and in the 1970s it started conducting more frequent forays and temporary deployments in the South China Sea and in the Indian Ocean.[95] It had also started operating in Southeast Asia as it observed operations in the Vietnam War, deploying surface and submarine assets, and flying patrol aircraft in reconnaissance missions from Da Nang over the South China Sea. Throughout the 1970s, the unsettled political situation in Southeast Asia as well as continued unrest along the eastern coast of Africa prompted more modernisation and expansion. Front-line units were added to the fleet and regular visits were conducted well beyond the borders of Northeast Asia with access to naval logistics in places like Cam Ranh Bay in Vietnam.[96] The iconic moment of this escalation occurred in June 1979 with the transfer to Vladivostok of the carrier *Minsk* and the *Ivan Rogov*, the largest amphibious ship in the Soviet Navy, along with four guided missile cruisers and several submarines.[97]

By the beginning of the 1980s, land-based air power was similarly being enhanced to the point that, in 1982, American Admiral Robert L. J. Long, Commander in Chief Pacific Command, voiced his concerns for the threat Soviet bombers posed to carrier strike groups.[98] In Japan too, scrambles to intercept Soviet aircraft flying in the vicinity of Japanese air space increased from 281 in 1975 to 939 in 1981.

All in all, evidence clearly suggested an increase in Soviet naval and air activities around Japan. In 1976, more than twenty Soviet warships were observed operating in areas used by Japanese oil tankers, while more than 300 warships of various kinds were sighted passing through Japan's major straits.[99] Paraphrasing another authoritative estimate of the time, the Soviet Pacific Fleet was growing at a steady pace and included between one-half and one-third of the entire Soviet surface and subsurface assets.[100] This rate of growth continued well into the 1980s, and by 1984, the Pacific Fleet could count on another carrier, the *Novorossiysk*, a nuclear-propelled battle cruiser, 28 per cent of the total of major surface vessels, and the largest air arm with 32 per cent of the total naval aircraft.[101] Numerical increases were coupled by more regular training, including the *Okean* exercises – held twice in the 1970s simultaneously by the entire Soviet navy across different theatres. In *Okean* 1975, the Soviet Pacific Fleet was reported to have four operational task groups while 126 aircraft were detected approaching the Japanese air space.[102] These large exercises were constrained to the Sea of Japan and the Sea of Okhotsk, though smaller task forces conducted other extended manoeuvres in the Pacific. These included many different types of operations, including long-range air strike operations.[103]

Insofar as Japan was concerned, sea control in the Sea of Japan and along the southwest shipping route was aimed at countering a Soviet *guerre de course*. By raiding Japanese shipping, Soviet forces could severely endanger the flow of goods to and from Japan without provoking, under article five of the US–Japan Security Treaty, any American action.[104] A Japanese direct commitment to minimise such an eventuality was essential. Hence, operations encompassing surveillance, gathering of information, straits control and sea lane defence in the East China Sea to deter 'hostile submarines from being deployed in the outer seas and oceans' were to become the trademarks of the JMSDF's defensive matrix in peacetime. Mines, submarines and patrol aircraft were central to block the straits of the Sea of Japan. The ASW-centred hunting group was the key asset in securing the sea lanes. Had deterrence failed and conflict broken out, the aim of the fleet was to bottle up the Soviet Pacific Fleet, and the ASW force was regarded as essential to hunt any Soviet assets that managed to pass through the straits guarded by the Japanese (Map 2). In implementing this strategy, the JMSDF amounted *de facto* to a 'shield' of the western Pacific (a metaphor often used in subsequent years in which the United States Navy – with its carrier-centred battle groups – was depicted as the 'spear').[105] In 1980, Admiral Uchida, a retired Chief of Maritime Staff who remained quite influential in the 1970s, explained the Japanese naval strategy in this period as follows:

> An anti-submarine capability must be the first charge on the resources of any nation precipitately faced with the possibility of starvation and exhaustion by hostile blockade. A force structure based upon the overall striking force of the United States and the regional defence forces of various nations must be the basic military concept in East Asia.[106]

Map 2 Cold War strategy.

Sea control and alliance requirements

This passage highlights a second important feature of how the JMSDF approached the implementation of its strategy. Close coordination with the United States Navy was a firm premise in its operational planning. In implementing naval strategy, senior personnel in the JMSDF knew that while a fleet capable of performing ASW operations was within the service's grasp, capabilities for maritime power projection were not. The signing of the 1978 Guidelines for US–Japan Defence Cooperation made this point by creating a legal framework for the division of labour. Japanese missions to secure sea control in the Sea of Japan and in the East China Sea were formalised and included the requirement to 'conduct maritime operations for the defence of the surrounding waters and sea lines of communication' in coordination with the United States Navy.[107] The document emphasised the complementary nature of the two navies, pointing out that the United States were 'to supplement functions that the Self-Defense Forces do not have', including 'mobile striking power'.[108] It is equally worth stressing that in regard to the command structure in case of conflict, the Japanese navy was not subordinate to its powerful ally. The document stated that both navies were to operate in combat 'as ordered by their respective command systems' though it also described adequate mechanisms of coordination as a sensitive question to address.[109]

As a result, the JMSDF had in the Guidelines a legal framework that empowered it with a specific context to implement its strategy with the additional guarantee of the American navy supplementing functions it could not perform. Indeed, one experienced Japanese defence analyst remarked that the Guidelines prompted the establishment of research and liaison institutions with the responsibility for looking after joint operations, planning and exercises. From a naval perspective, the Guidelines allowed the security treaty to be implemented as 'though it were a two-nation version of NATO'.[110]

A closer working partnership with the United States under the Guidelines offered another important advantage in the view of the Japanese naval leadership. Qualitative improvement did not depend solely on the possibility of having a framework to implement strategy. More complex training to test platforms and doctrines was required for any strategy to be effective, and this became a priority for the JMSDF. As early as March 1975, while the service was still battling over the drafts of the NDPO, naval planners envisaged using the alliance to this end.[111] One main target was the possibility of joining the Rim of the Pacific Exercise (RIMPAC), a multilateral exercise held since 1971 that involved the US Navy, the Royal Navy, the Royal Canadian Navy and the Royal Australian Navy. This was a major training opportunity for the Japanese navy and the Guidelines offered an essential condition to favour Japan's participation.[112] When the Guidelines finally materialised, Japanese naval strategy and policy had scored an important success. By supporting American naval forces in the western Pacific, the service could now implement, within the geographical spaces of the Sea of Japan and the East China Sea, its own naval strategy.[113]

The Japanese approach was met favourably in American naval circles too. Indeed, it provided breathing space in what George Baer called the 'disarray' of the 1970s. Then, 'bloc obsolescence' – the need to replace a sizeable component of the entire navy – combined with the impact of the high costs of the war in Vietnam and of the development of new naval systems on procurement were fast reducing the size of the United Sates Navy and putting pressure on its worldwide commitments.[114] From 976 ships in 1968, the fleet dropped to 477 in early 1976 and by 1982, Secretary of Defence Caspar Weinberger was reporting to Congress that force level in the Pacific had fallen to half of the 1965 level.[115] In addition, by 1979, the joint chiefs of staff had expanded the operational area of the Seventh Fleet, the United States main force in the western Pacific, to include the entire Indian Ocean, further stretching American capabilities.[116] At the strategic level, this meant that throughout this period, sea control was becoming an increasingly more relative concept and the navy was to accept an understanding of it that pointed to 'the use of a limited area for a limited time'.[117]

Against this background, the presence of a strong naval ally with a clear operational sphere, both in terms of missions and area, offered a real contribution in aiding the western Pacific to remain firmly within American maritime control – a fact recently acknowledged in the first complete history of the Seventh Fleet.[118] In 1979, Chief of Naval Operations Admiral Thomas Hayward emphasised the Japanese contribution to American operations in the Pacific, pointing out that

> The United States Navy and the Maritime Self-Defense Force coordinate so that they do not duplicate each other's efforts. This enables American warships to operate independently. The Maritime SDF's submarine P-3Cs are deployed so as to fulfil this duty.[119]

In a force planning study published in 1978 as *Sea Plan 2000*, Admiral Hayward argued that in the Pacific, the United States Navy was to take an offensive posture, taking advantage of the fact that Soviet fleets and bases were exposed to prompt action – isolated as they were logistically. This offensive posture had significant global implications, as it would have tied down Soviet forces that could be otherwise used against NATO flanks.[120] The 'Pacific model' represented an important stepping stone towards what became in the 1980s the American 'Maritime Strategy'. This argued for a 600-ship navy, with an emphasis on American offensive missions.[121] In the Pacific, its implementation *de facto* rested upon the Japanese pursuit of regional sea control. By the beginning of the 1990s, the United States Navy was on the path to renewed global superiority, but in the western Pacific, the main capabilities remained centred on a striking force, a carrier battle group home-ported in Yokosuka, and limited maritime patrol capabilities. The Japanese fleet with its sixty-four main surface combatants had main responsibility for the Sea of Japan, a task it pursued with thirteen submarines and an air arm of 66 P-3C and 10 P-2J.[122]

The Japanese bid to secure a more capable fleet did not come without sacrifices. The ability to devise a strategy that could meet national security priorities masked one of the main limitations of naval policy in this period: the ability to secure adequate capabilities for fleet air defence to conduct operations on the high sea. Beyond the range of land-based air power, the JMSDF would have to rely on the United States for over-the-horizon air cover. As a way to limit criticism on the content of the NDPO, the government made it clear that the new policy did not leave an open door to massive rearmament and that 'offensive capabilities' like 'attack' aircraft carriers were not allowed by the constitution, an interpretation that remains unaltered today.[123] By 1978, 'attack' aircraft carriers were carriers similar to those of the United States Navy, which left Japan the only option of pursuing smaller platforms designed for ASW.[124] This interpretation was further emphasised by the imposition of a ceiling of 1 per cent of the gross national product (GNP) on defence spending.[125]

The apparent limitations and gaps in capabilities created by these decisions left the Japanese maritime strategy exposed to constant domestic criticism over the remaining duration of the Cold War. Some defence analysts and officials took the position that sea lane defence and regional sea control were aimed more at managing the alliance with the United States than as key pieces of an actual strategy.[126] Nor did the idea of a defence posture with a strong naval–air balance eliminate the need to address ground operations in defence of northern Japan. Throughout the 1980s, Soviet amphibious capabilities continued to expand – indeed, by the mid-1980s, the only Soviet Naval Infantry Division was deployed in East Asia. The logic that fuelled Japanese concerns pertained to the assumption that in case of war, Soviet forces would seek to occupy Hokkaido to neutralise the Japanese control of the straits and facilitate Soviet naval operations.[127] Foreign assessments of the time shared Japanese concerns about such scenarios.[128]

These considerations notwithstanding, the ultimate political support of the cardinal role of the navy in guarding the nation's economic security was guaranteed in 1981, when Prime Minister Suzuki Zenko (1980–82) pledged to commit Japan to the protection of its sea lanes out to 1,000 NM. At the highest political level, the Japanese government had adopted a posture that defined geographic boundaries for the JMSDF to take action, boundaries that had been previously left ill defined. In his 1983 visit to Washington, Prime Minister Nakasone Yasuhiro (1982–87), who endeavoured to implement the 1,000 NM policy throughout the rest of the decade, remarked that one of Japan's chief objectives was 'to have complete and full control of the three straits that go through the Japanese islands so that there can be no passage of Soviet submarines or other naval activities'.[129] Japan's reliance on the sea, combined with the practical contribution that regional sea control, including the patrolling of the sea lanes in the East China Sea, provided to the management of the alliance with the United States, secured constant political support for naval policy.

Post-Cold War transition

The end of the bipolar confrontation left Japanese defence and military circles – as much as those in other nations of the Western bloc – disoriented on how best to go about guaranteeing future security.[130] The failure to provide some form of military support

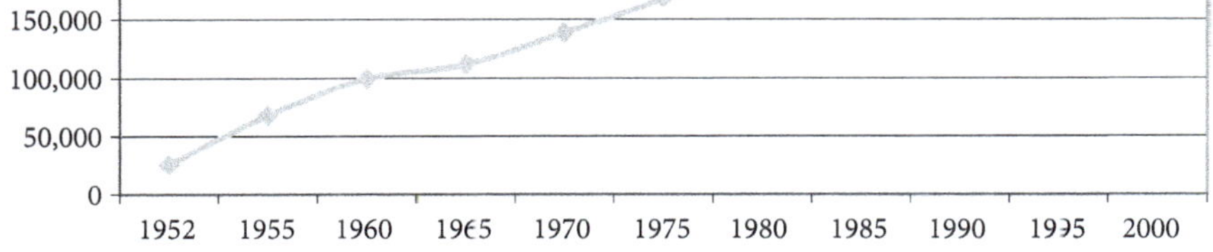

Figure 6.2 Growth of the JMSDF's fleet by tonnage, 1952–2000.

Source: JMSDF, *Kaijōjieitai Gojū Nenshi – Shiryōhen* (海上自衛隊五十年史、資料編 – JMSDF's Fifty Year History – Data, Tokyo: Maritime Staff Office, 2003), 272–3.

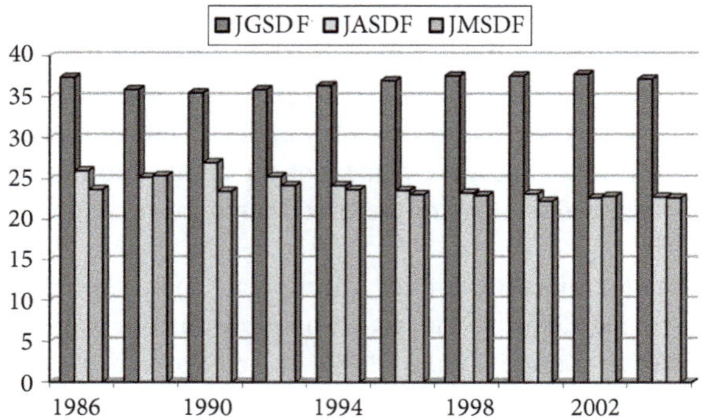

Figure 6.3 Defence expenditures by organisation, 1986–2006.

Source: Japan Defence Agency, *Defence of Japan* (Tokyo: Japan Times and Intergroup Corp., 1986–2006).

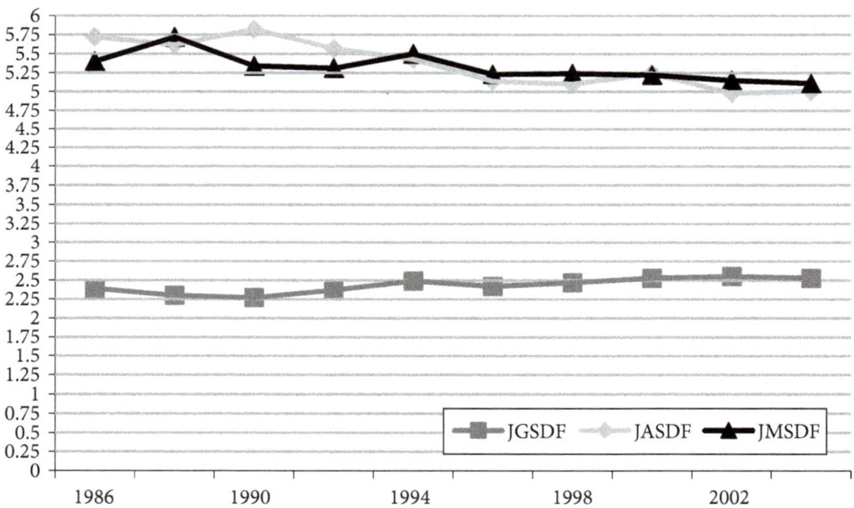

Figure 6.4 Defence expenditures by organisation per number of personnel.

Source: Japan Defence Agency, *Defence of Japan* (Tokyo: Japan Times and Intergroup Corp., 1986–2006).

in the first Gulf War left a deep mark on defence policy circles,[131] and had prompted many to question the merits of Japan's passive, Soviet-centric deterrence-oriented position.[132] Tokyo – they argued – had to address some of its constitutional constraints in order to be able to participate militarily in operations under international mandate, 'normalising' its behaviour as a state actor.[133]

Within the Japanese navy, the need to adjust to this phase of transition was felt less in terms of 'normalisation' of its functions and more in the form of 'where' naval capabilities would be deployed to perform them. In fact, when the Gulf War broke out, the JMSDF was not shocked, nor unprepared for the possibility of being deployed. There was a precedent in recent history that had prepared the service for this eventuality.

In 1987, the United States had explored with the Japanese government the possibility of the country's military contribution to the policing operations in the Persian Gulf.[134] The government eventually decided against a naval deployment, but the JMSDF completed a study of the options available – highlighting the use of minesweepers as an appropriate response that would offer a critical contribution to the operations while still meeting Japanese legal restrictions. In its evaluation of the operational requirements in the Gulf, the JMSDF benefited from the results of research conducted by two retired Japanese admirals that were working for a think tank in Tokyo.[135]

As a result, two years later, when President George Bush as well as other foreign officials including the Australian Prime Minister Robert Hawke and British Foreign Secretary Douglas Hurd, started suggesting both privately and publicly that a Japanese military contribution using minesweepers would be most welcomed, the navy already had contingency plans in place that needed just updating.[136] In April 1991, after the hostilities had ceased, the Japanese government agreed to deploy a flotilla of six ships, including five minesweepers accompanied by the refuelling ship *Tokiwa* (AOE-423).[137] From operational planning to public relations, the JMSDF carried out careful preparations. Preoccupations remained over the logistical difficulties of a mission involving the dispatch of 511 men, on relatively small ships (four of them were only 510 tons), on a 7,000 NM journey.[138] The JMSDF minesweepers arrived in the Persian Gulf by the end of May and for the following four months worked with American forces in the Mine Danger Area 10 (MDA-10), alongside Belgian, Dutch, French, Italian and German forces assigned to the adjacent MDA-7.[139] Operations were completed on 10 September. The Japanese naval group destroyed 31 mines, a smaller number compared to other coalition forces, though it performed with unquestioned professionalism.[140] The main issue for the flotilla turned out to be of a logistical nature. Upon arrival in the theatre, the Japanese were – as one Japanese admiral put it – 'in desperate need' of a magnetic field calibration in order to conduct the mine clearance. Notwithstanding the absence of diplomatic arrangements, the Royal Navy agreed to offer support at its mine counter measures support range in Dubai.[141]

The Japanese decision to send minesweepers to the Gulf was described by the *Wall Street Journal* as a 'cautious but significant step in an effort to define an international role beyond that of banker and trader'.[142] In the navy, the likely impact of systemic changes on the Japanese maritime strategy was assessed differently. The defence of national maritime interests stood at the heart of the navy's approach. In the Cold War, this had meant regional sea control in the Sea of Japan and ASW hunting groups employed to escort maritime traffic along the main sea lanes in the East China Sea. Outside regional borders, the defence of maritime trade and shipping rested pre-eminently on the shoulders of its more powerful, global ally.

Operations in the Gulf had proved the limits of the JMSDF operational reach and highlighted the need to consider contributions beyond East Asian waters.[143] As early as July 1991, the JMSDF Chief of Staff, Admiral Okabe Fumio, remarked that the future would see the emergence of new forms of localised conflicts that would question core assumptions about the game of deterrence between the superpowers. The First Gulf War was an example of these new forms of wars. For Japan this entailed two questions, the first concerning the extent to which the country would and could be drawn into such new forms of conflicts, the second pertaining to the role that the eventual military forces deployed in the area would have. While it was too early for clear answers, he expected the JMSDF to become more active than in the past and that, more generally, Japanese forces would be likely called upon to share the burden of international security.[144] In this context, one dimension of naval capabilities was completely missing: amphibious and transport vessels. The navy's first adjustment to its Cold War policy was swift and benefited from the difficulties experienced in deploying one engineering battalion to Cambodia under UNTAC (UN Transitional Authority in Cambodia).[145] In 1993, shortly after new legislation was passed to allow Japanese participation in peacekeeping operations, the navy secured the procurement of a first amphibious ship to plant the seeds for future commitments overseas.[146]

In November 1995, the adoption of a new NDPO gauged in a wider sense the impact of the post-Cold War environment on Japanese defence policy.[147] The document stressed that cooperative patterns of security represented the likely *leitmotifs* of future international relations and suggested a defence agenda aiming at a more 'active and constructive security policy'.[148] Attention to international stability and to the ways in which Japan could contribute militarily represented a departure from the Cold War defence posture, but it was not the only priority for Japanese strategic planners. This was an opinion shared by influential senior officers within the JMSDF.[149] In Northeast Asia, the power vacuum created by the disappearance of one of the superpowers had made the situation more volatile, with unresolved and potentially escalating tensions in the Korean Peninsula and across the Taiwanese strait. Equally testing for regional stability were the actions of state actors such as China seemingly profiting from the post-Cold War transition to achieve greater influence, engaging to that end in a comprehensive scheme of economic and military modernisation.[150]

The NDPO constituted a first attempt to integrate the requirements of a higher international military profile with those necessary to deal with closer regional sources of military (and naval) apprehension.[151] The document did not envisage the need to abandon the 'basic defence force' concept. It proposed a series of measures to increase the mobility and overseas 'deployability' of the Japanese armed forces. In the official defence establishment jargon, the Japanese armed forces had to become 'streamlined, effective and flexible'.[152] Systemic changes were not, however, the only factor guiding reforms in defence. More crucial domestic factors, notably a period of severe economic recession and political transition with the end of the dominance of the Liberal Democratic Party, were also affecting the country from the beginning of the decade.

The JMSDF's involvement in the events of the Gulf War gave the service a degree of perspective on the subject of defence policy transition. Accordingly, adjustments in naval policy and strategy did not entail a radical departure from the principles the service had followed during the Cold War. In the NDPO, this notion was captured in the fact that 'the defence of adjacent seas and the securing the safety of maritime traffic are essential in order to secure the foundations of national survival'. Security at sea still constituted a 'matter of life or death' whether in peacetime or in cases of emergency.[153] A mix of capabilities aimed at implementing regional sea control, guaranteeing extended mobility to secure Japanese shipping in East Asian waters, and contributing to the coalition away from regional shores were still central to a viable maritime strategy.[154]

In addition to investing in a balanced, ASW-oriented fleet, the top brass sought to enhance the navy's ability to offer agile[155] and accurate[156] responses to operations away from regional shores. At-sea logistical support, amphibious lift, and fleet air defence were the areas to prioritise, in principle. New programmes were to be pursued, however, examining the extent to which the service could guarantee sufficient funding to retain sea control in Northeast Asian waters.[157] Regional deterrence gained momentum especially in the aftermath of the 'Taepo-dong shock', North Korea's 1998 missile tests, with the Japanese government committing to joint research with the United States on Ballistic Missile Defence (BMD).[158] In that context, the navy was to be heavily involved since the weapons systems and sensors of its AEGIS-equipped destroyers were a central component of BMD.[159] At the normative level, the reaffirmation of the US–Japan Alliance in April 1996, and the revision of the Guidelines in 1997 offered, in a fashion similar to the late 1970s, an opportunity for the Japanese to formally codify some forty items for cooperation, ranging from intelligence gathering to surveillance to peacekeeping and disaster relief, to meet expanded security requirements.[160] This was also why the controversial expression 'cooperation in areas surrounding Japan' included in the Guidelines was later clarified to be understood as a 'situational', rather than a 'geographic' notion. The key point concerned the activities that were included in the cooperation.[161]

Those involved in the naval debate were weary of the tighter budgetary requirements of the Post-Cold War transition, and the identification of key areas to strengthen did not prevent the downsizing of the fleet's inventory and a slow-down of the shipbuilding programmes. In the Pacific, the naval core of Japan's most apparent Cold War threat had been reduced and while China's expanding 'scope of activities in the high seas' was observed with a keen eye, its force modernisation was 'expected to gradually proceed at a moderate rate'.[162] The result was that, compared to the force level established by the 1976 NDPO, the new document called for a reduction of approximately 16 per cent of the surface fleet and of almost 23 per cent of the air component. These restrictions were partly rebalanced by the continuous growth in terms of tonnage (Figures 6.2, 6.3, 6.4).[163] In specific areas of modern naval warfare, assets vital to the fleet's capability to retain sea control in the straits and along Japan's island chains and in the East China Sea, most notably the submarine force, were not affected by budget cuts.[164]

By the end of the 1980s, the JMSDF had achieved the primary goal of adding at least one large amphibious ship to its pennant list. Similarly, the service had succeeded in maintaining a high expenditure relative to personnel strength, symptomatic of the costs associated with the procurement of technology-intensive equipment. In the uncertain and austere atmosphere of the 1990s, the strategy developed in the 1970s and 1980s was still sound. Adjustments were made to fit new circumstances, with an attempt to introduce new platforms and consolidate the range of operations within existing political, legal and economic boundaries. The navy could not prevent reductions in the arsenal, but it made sure to complement its ASW-centred force with a minimum of capabilities to organise *ad hoc* task forces for escort and expeditionary missions to meet the international objectives of Japan's transforming security agenda.

In 1999, the policy adjustments of the previous years were actually implemented when the new amphibious ship saw action a mere year after its commissioning in the international disaster relief mission to Turkey. The ship was instrumental in delivering materials such as temporary dwellings, necessary for the relief of the Turkish population, who had been affected by a major earthquake. The mission lasted three months (23 September to 22 November) and involved 426 personnel.[165] As had happened in the past, decisions again came at the cost of extended capabilities for fleet air defence, which remained the JMSDF's main weakness in operations where land-based assets or international partners could not provide air cover. On the other hand, in the navy's calculations, it was highly unlikely that Japanese overseas deployments would happen outside the scope of some form of bilateral or multilateral agreement. Equally unlikely were scenarios of deployments overseas in combat zones. With the Soviet threat rapidly disappearing, sea control in East Asia and the use of the navy as a tool for regional security remained the central tenets of the Japanese maritime strategy and, in that respect, the capabilities procured in the 1980s were still up to the task.

Conclusions

In 2004, while the structural changes initiated in the 1990s were being implemented, strategic planners at the Defence Agency decided to embark upon a revision of the NDPO. The main goal was to account for the systemic transformations brought about by the 9/11 attacks on the United States, North Korea's political brinkmanship and nuclear programme, and China's double-digit investments in military modernisation. The new document, which was approved in December 2004 as the National Defence Programme Guideline (NDPG), partly reviewed previous emphases on multilateral cooperation, though it sought to maintain an overall balanced approach. The archipelago's military apparatus was to retain state-of-the-art defensive capabilities and an expeditionary-oriented, versatile posture, completing its transition towards a 'multi-functional flexible defence force'.[166] Japanese forces were to continue recalibrating their internal organisational and procurement policies to maximise the prevention of threats to the nation and, in case of emergencies, to determine 'where and how' to employ of the country's military might 'to maximum effect'. In particular, the reorganisation of the Joint Staff Council from an advisory-only role into a Joint Staff Office with operational responsibilities in regard to joint operations like missile defence and disaster relief represented one key step in this direction.[167]

For the JMSDF, the development of a new strategy presented a familiar dilemma under different geographic circumstances. In the Cold War, sea control in the Sea of Japan – especially the control of key chokepoints – had offered an effective response to the Soviet challenge. In a new security environment emphasising the potential of a Chinese security challenge, sea control had to be pursued in a much wider area – that of the East China Sea – and opened up the question of maritime security in the adjacent South China Sea, where China had bases and capabilities. In addition to traditional functions in operational theatres close to Japanese shores, the Japanese navy was transforming from a Cold War force for regional sea control and defence against maritime power projection to one capable of exploiting sea control and performing international missions. On the other hand, changes to the nature of the security threats and the expansion of missions had still left naval leaders with a sense of anxiety vis-à-vis the material resources available to them.[168] In this respect JMSDF Chief of Staff Admiral Ishikawa Tōru (2001–3) remarked that the challenge 'of modernising its inventory is real for the JMSDF given the considerable budget restraints it faces' and that the navy had to overcome these problems 'if the JMSDF is to maintain effective defence capabilities in the future'.[169]

This consideration notwithstanding, fifty years after its establishment, the JMSDF was no longer a pale shadow of its imperial ancestor, and in policy and strategy it had succeeded where the Imperial Navy had failed. It investigated the past not to confirm preconceived ideas, nor to find guidance solely in narrow technical matters such as tactics and procurement. The history of naval policy in the 1950s and 1960s is the history of a service displaying a deductive logic by studying the experience of the pre-war service to address fundamental questions about the role of the navy as a tool of national policy. As Japan's post-war welfare rested on the maritime nature of its economy, the JMSDF's endorsement of policies and doctrines enabling the fleet to safeguard the country's main sea lanes pointed to a professional force aware of its main missions. In turn, such a position played to the strengths of American strategic goals to contain Soviet naval power in the Pacific, a fact that further strengthens the notion of a rational strategic calculus balancing limited means with wider political ends. Learning from the wartime mistakes of its imperial forerunner, the JMSDF had developed a strategy that matched the requirements of national security.

While the Imperial Navy was less at the forefront of the debates in the post-Cold war era, the process of re-examination of the past that distinguished the understanding of its legacy at the policy level continued to inform Japan's naval posture. The disappearance of the Soviet threat coincided with the emergence of new international missions beyond regional shores and the possibility of another potential naval competitor from the nearby continental landmass, China. In this transitional phase, Japanese strategy did not radically change, though naval policy was adjusted to meet the expanding geographic scope of intervention. As Japan's international profile expanded, the service re-evaluated existing studies to pursue new capabilities to increase its strategic lift and give its fleet wider operational 'flexibility'. As in previous decades, the navy was seeking again to adjust the role of maritime strategy in national security, learning from the past to inform the present.

7

Doctrine and Capabilities: The Quest for a Balanced Fleet

My policy as Chief of Maritime Staff is to maintain 'prowess' and 'readiness' at the heart of the JMSDF's ethos. There are two reasons for this. Firstly, it creates a line of continuity with the policies of my predecessors; secondly, it is in line with the culture and tradition of the navy, which has been developed by our ancestors since the times of the Imperial Japanese Navy.[1]

Admiral Kōichi Furushō, JMSDF
(26th Chief of Maritime Staff, 2003–5)

In your opinion, what is the major difference between the Imperial Japanese Navy and the JMSDF?

The size.[2]

Lieutenant Commander Keizo Kitagawa, JMSDF
(National Defence Academy)

Smaller navy, similar grammar

Since 1954, JMSDF and defence publications alike have fallen short of presenting contents that could amount to a cohesive maritime doctrine. The 1957 Basic Policy for National Defence, the 1976 and 1995 NDPO, and the subsequent NDPGs all outlined principles of military policy, not how the individual services doctrinally approached their implementation.[3] This should not come as a surprise, for the JMSDF followed the practice – not uncommon among navies – of avoiding the formal publication of its doctrine in dedicated volumes.[4] Its leadership wished to limit the risks of dogmatism unfolding from a strictly defined set of all-encompassing directives and procedures, and to leave room for judgement in the application of core doctrinal notions.[5] Concurrently, the nature of the JMSDF main missions did not require the service to produce documents to facilitate inter-service cooperation or participate in multinational operations.[6] This, however, did not mean that the JMSDF did not possess a doctrine, because it did – and the legacy of the Imperial Japanese Navy rested at its very heart.

This chapter ventures inside the navy's professional grammar, looking at how policy choices were matched by the development of a doctrine to build-up and operate a capable fleet. For the JMSDF, the imperial past offered battle-tested principles to develop a coherent fighting force. In the initial stages of the rearmament, operational concepts like prowess (intended as fighting power) and battle readiness were pursued to aspire to set high standards. As professional competence increased, concepts of imperial flavour evolved and were complemented to allow the navy to further develop and operate alongside the US Navy. Doctrine informed design and procurement, and the JMSDF referred to the tradition of the Imperial Navy to justify capabilities maximising firepower to compensate for limited numbers. Yet, in these areas too, the making of the new navy did not result in the same fleet as the old. This was no longer the maritime shield of an Empire engaging an opposing enemy in fatal battles on the high seas. In the realms of fleet structure and design, the imperial wartime experience served as an example of the risks of a fleet that, in seeking to maximise firepower, lost the ability to adapt to perform a variety of missions. This experience illustrated that doctrine, procurement and strategy had to be connected to each other. Thus, the imperial naval experience was not deployed to recreate the glory days of the past. It helped to highlight the virtues of possessing a balanced fleet, and provided the doctrinal building blocks to realise it.

'Big ships, big guns'

On the eve of the war, Japanese naval authorities had come to the conclusion that due to the limits of the national resource base, the navy had to plan for the only war it could win, one that would preferably be of short duration and aimed at the rapid annihilation of the enemy. On 24 July 1941, Admiral Nagano Osami, chief of the Imperial Navy General Staff, summarised the advantages and risks of Japanese naval plans as follow:

> Although there is now a chance of achieving victory, the chances will diminish as time goes on. By the latter half of next year [1942] it will already be difficult for us to cope with the United States; after that the situation will become increasingly worse. … If we could settle things without war, there would be nothing better. But if we conclude that conflict cannot ultimately be avoided then I would like you to understand that as time goes by we will be in a disadvantageous position.[7]

In fact, during the previous decade, naval planners had set doctrine, capabilities and procurement priorities in a way that would allow them to be ready to implement this plan. The main Japanese fighting force, the Combined Fleet, was the tool designated to prevent the conflict from lasting beyond what the navy could afford. The accepted idea had long been that if the navy's powerful sword had to be drawn to inflict a fatal blow, it had to be sharpened accordingly. Thus, in the 1930s, from the design and procurement of platforms to the training of crews, front-line equipment for the execution of surface engagements – in daylight and especially at night – was prioritised.[8] Indeed, one scholarly study noted that the Japanese navy entered the war in 1941 with a fleet of 'superb night fighters' that in ship-to-ship engagements won ten out of the thirteen surface battles that occurred until October 1943.[9] Yet, the same fleet was 'ill-suited to the kind of extended naval conflict that Japan was obliged to wage'.[10] Crucially, assets to cover other vital wartime functions, such as tankers for fleet logistics and escort vessels for convoys, were never built in sufficient numbers, nor were they fully integrated in the navy's operational grammar.[11] In the words of a retired Japanese admiral, the wartime fleet was the intellectual child of a 'shock and awe' naval doctrine.[12]

To those former officers who reflected upon the defeat, assessments of doctrine and procurement policies featured critiques consistent with those on matters of strategy. Naval doctrine too was regarded as exceedingly inflexible and too exclusively focused on the pursuit of the decisive battle. In principle, the centrality of the decisive battle to doctrine was not unique to Japan.[13] In the Japanese case, however, the Imperial Navy's fixation on the decisive battle was rooted in a longstanding 'poverty complex', or a 'psychology of material inferiority' vis-à-vis its enemies. Already in the conflicts against Imperial China and Russia, Japanese naval tacticians had planned operations on the basis of an 'offensive-defence' approach. Painfully aware of the qualitative and quantitative limitations of their fleet, imperial naval officers planned both conflicts with the intent to wage offensive campaigns that would allow them to quickly achieve control of the main maritime theatres. Failing this, their plans rested on operations against enemy forces anchored in ports, seeking to lure them into battle.[14] Until 1907, the quest for a strong combat fleet was encapsulated in formulas to build a 'six-six' fleet: six battleships and six armoured cruisers.[15] From 1907 to 1922, this original plan was upgraded to an 'eight-eight' fleet, consolidating what became known as the 'big ships, big guns ideology'.[16]

In the inter-war era, the naval arms control agreements did much to consolidate existing Japanese fears on the limits of their fleet in coping with the British and American equivalents in case of war. By the time the Japanese delegation withdrew from the negotiations for the Second London Naval Treaty in January 1936, it was clear that its planners had found the solution to their numerical inferiority in a more powerful battle line capable of outranging its enemies.[17] A few months later, the authorisation to build the *Yamato* class became the most iconic symbol of the Japanese quest for a qualitative superiority designed to offset the disadvantages of numerical inferiority. Similarly, the Imperial Navy's 'battle instructions',[18] one of its key doctrinal documents, left no doubt about this approach. In the 1934 edition, they clearly stated the point that 'the battleship divisions are the main weapon in a fleet and their task is to engage the main force of the enemy'.[19]

Nor had the situation changed once the limitations imposed by the treaties were removed. In fact, the build-up plans drawn up in 1934, 1937 and 1939, as well as the supplementary programmes drafted between 1939 and 1941, were still restricted by the limits of national financial, material and industrial power. Admiral Toyoda Soemu, Director of the Naval Shipbuilding Command from 1939 to 1941, pointed out that even if the navy was no longer under treaty restrictions as to tonnage, 'the same idea of improving quality remained in the minds of our shipbuilding experts.

and we used to receive orders from different sections of the Navy for ships of higher efficiency'.[20] If the country could not afford to out-build its enemies, the navy would develop superior platforms to over-power them. Again, the battle instructions were quite clear about the reasons for this since 'war once declared must be waged offensively, aggressively'.[21]

This meant that other combat platforms like cruisers and destroyers as well as 'new technologies' like submarines and aircraft were enlisted primarily to serve the main battle force. Until 1939, the navy's 'interception-attrition' approach to operations aimed at reducing the strength of the larger American fleet before luring it into a duel with a line of battleships headed by the gargantuan *Yamato*.[22] Long-range submarines were to ambush American units crossing the Pacific to recover the possessions lost in initial Japanese operations, while repeated night torpedo actions conducted by heavy cruisers and destroyers of the 'night combat group'[23] were to prepare the ground for aircraft carriers and above all, battleships.[24] In 1936, as night actions came to be considered an important prelude to the 'decisive battle' strategy, the navy formed the Night Battle Force.[25] Air power too was eventually developed with the aim of improving the odds of the Japanese fleet annihilating its main American adversary.[26] As Vice Admiral Ōnishi Takijirō (the father of the Special Attack Units – then a captain) wrote in 1937, superior land-based air power would make it possible to prevent an enemy fleet from gaining naval superiority within 1,000 miles of its base. In his view, both the navy's interception and attrition principles were to benefit from this tactical application of air power.[27]

Doctrinal choices had an impact on command and force structures too, with naval assets distributed between the 'external line' fleet, and the 'internal line' fleet.[28] The former included all front-line surface, submarine and air units under the command of the Combined Fleet. These constituted the cutting edge of the Japanese naval sword and were supported by the majority of investments, resources and capabilities. The internal line fleet served 'secondary functions' and included platforms – usually more obsolete and less capable warships – for the defence of the country's littoral areas, remote islands, and of the merchant shipping approaching them.[29]

The Japanese secondary attention to the defence of shipping, in particular, differed from that of other navies, notably the Royal Navy. Throughout the 1930s, the British Admiralty had in fact started developing escort vessels integrating combat systems like the anti-submarine detection system ASDIC and the high-angle/low-angle (HA/LA) anti-aircraft guns to reflect submarine and air threats.[30] In the Imperial Navy, on the other hand, prior to 1943, no major procurement of assets for the protection of shipping occurred, and the coastal defence vessels[31] designated for these tasks were far from being well suited to anti-submarine warfare (ASW).[32] In part, the reason for this was that the war the Japanese expected to fight was very different from the one the British Admiralty envisaged against Germany.[33] Yet, the real difference in the two approaches rested on the flexibility of the two doctrines. The doctrinal grammar, procurement policy and fleet structure developed by the Japanese to implement their strategy focused so much on fleet-to-fleet engagements that little room existed for different operations, failing the sinking of the enemy fleet in one blow.

Commenting on pre-war preparations and wartime operations, Admiral Nomura concluded that Japanese naval authorities had 'made the mistake of thinking an attack is the best defence'.[34] The imperial naval doctrine had been instrumental in the design of combat systems that compared well and in many cases surpassed their equivalents in other navies. The *Yamato* itself was the largest and most heavily armed battleship ever to set sail. In 1941, the Mitsubishi 'Zero' fighter was unmatched in speed and manoeuvrability, and few bombers surpassed the Mitsubishi G3M in terms of range and speed. Similarly, the *Type 93* long-lance torpedo was, with 40,000 metres range at 36 knots, superior to all other weapons of the same kind until the war was well underway.[35]

These achievements came at a very high cost. Other technologies less fundamental to the navy's doctrinal assumptions such as for anti-air and anti-submarine warfare were sacrificed or could receive only limited attention. The deficiencies of the Japanese resource base imposed such choices. As a result, before the war, the Japanese technological base provided an edge in 'first stage' technologies like torpedoes, optics and ordnance. As the war progressed, however, the navy was unable to sustain that lead and, equally crucial, unable to compete with the United States in the development of 'second stage' technologies like radar, VT (proximity) fuse and ASW weapons.[36] As one leading scholar noted, 'In the Japanese navy perhaps more than any other, it was doctrine – particularly the concept that quality could always overcome quantity – that drove technology'.[37] In this respect, the longstanding Japanese dilemma of how to address material limitations led different generations of naval leaders to become increasingly more dogmatic about the fleet, proving *a contrari* that 'strategic flexibility flows not only from sound doctrine and an open but educated mind but also from numbers; and inflexibility flows from the absence of numbers'.[38]

By 1950, former naval officers had dissected pre-war strategy and doctrine and debated their strengths and weaknesses. Japan was a now different country, one with a constitution that prevented any future naval organisation from adopting the Imperial Navy's 'offensive' position. How was past experience to help the post-war doctrinal journey? With a fleet that needed to be entirely rebuilt, were there any elements of the Imperial Navy that could be salvaged to help the creation of the new naval organisation?

New name, same people, different anatomy

From an organisational perspective, key individuals like Admirals Nomura and Yamanashi knew that crucial past structural deficiencies had to be addressed. In order to comprehensively address issues of doctrine and capabilities, two preliminary conditions had to be secured. Internally, the new navy had to make sure to feature a different chain of command. In the pre-war era, the management of the navy and its fleet was entrusted to two bodies, the Navy Ministry[39] (responsible for matters of administration and policy) and the Navy General Staff[40] (in charge of operational and tactical affairs). The Navy Minister 'controlled the naval establishment in peacetime, an arrangement that ensured internal harmony and a fraternal spirit among officers and men'.[41] In 1933, this system was challenged when the responsibility for decisions concerning the 'size of armaments' and peacetime fleet command was moved to the Navy General Staff. This, combined with the 1934 purge of key senior officers who had supported the naval treaties, heralded the ascendancy of a group of aggressive officers to key policy and military positions.[42] Admirals Nomura and Yamanashi had both been members of the 'treaty faction'[43] and experienced first-hand this internal struggle, as Admiral Yamanashi had been forced to retire during the 1934 purge.[44]

Before 1952, however, these concerns remained in the background of a more pressing issue: the establishment of an independent naval organisation in the first place. In 1947, the demobilisation had been completed but the creation of a new navy was far from being a reality. Operationally, a small number of vessels for minesweeping, coastal defence and transport had been continuously operating in home waters since 1945.[45] Structurally, as of 30 April 1948, these forces had been integrated into the newly established Maritime Safety Board (later Agency),[46] a civilian organisation part of the Ministry of Transportation. Assisted by personnel from the US Coast Guard and in consultation with American occupation authorities, the Japanese had *de facto* created their first coast guard, though the presence of minesweepers meant that it exceeded the normal functions of an organisation of this kind. More importantly, the men that manned this force were naval officers whose original appointment had been approved by Admiral Yōnai Mitsumasa himself as the Navy Ministry was being demobilised.[47] This force had been conceived as a civilian institution but operated in a military manner and was manned by former military personnel.

Allied operational requirements in the early stages of the Korean War did much to expose the functional contradictions of a coast guard operating military assets, keeping senior American military authorities in Japan alerted to the question of the establishment of a separate 'navy'. Indeed, the Japanese naval lobby headed by Admiral Nomura found in Rear Admiral Arleigh Burke a very influential ally.[48] At the outbreak of the Korean War, Admiral Burke was the Deputy Chief of Staff to the Commander Naval Forces Far East. In that capacity, he consulted with Ōkubo Takeo, the Head of the Maritime Safety Agency, and Prime Minister Yoshida to establish the terms of the deployment of the Japanese minesweeping force off the Korean peninsula as part of the amphibious landings in Wonsan.[49] As he explained to Okubo, the presence of minefields off the Korean coast and the scarcity of means available to American forces to sweep them meant that a Japanese contribution was of crucial importance – especially in light of the experience developed during the de-mining of the Japanese islands.[50] The Japanese were eventually deployed as 'integral elements' of the international naval task force, and '*deployed overseas in combat operations* (original emphasis)'.[51] The entire operation had proved that a coast guard was not the right organisation to control missions of this kind.

By July 1951, the Japanese debate about the functions of the National Police Reserve[52] (that had come into existence on 10 August 1950) and of the Maritime Safety Agency were now connected to questions regarding the future of the military defence of an independent Japan.[53] Prime Minister Yoshida, under the advice of Lt. General Tatsumi Eiichi, a former army officer whom he knew from his time as ambassador in London in 1936, had come to accept the idea that the National Police Reserve was to become a military organisation of sorts.[54] By contrast, the debate over whether the

Maritime Safety Agency was to remain the sole naval organisation in Japan continued. Yanagisawa Yonekichi, the civilian official who took over the agency in May 1951, wanted the organisation to develop into a fully fledged coast guard.[55] Naval officers disagreed. The situation took a decisive turn in the summer of 1951, when Admiral Nomura was informally made aware by Admiral Turner Joy, the Commander of the Naval Forces Far East, that eighteen frigates returned by the Soviet Union to the United States were currently in Yokosuka for refit, and that they could have made available to Japan.[56] Working in coordination with Admiral Burke, authorities in Washington submitted a formal offer of sixty-eight vessels, including the eighteen frigates, to the Japanese government on 19 October 1951. Prime Minister Yoshida accepted the offer and the 'Y' Committee was set up to study the integration of these platforms into the Maritime Safety Agency.[57] For this committee the end goal was a new and separate navy.[58] To that end, a key assumption was that the new platforms were to remain organisationally and functionally together, operationally separated from the command structure of the Maritime Safety Agency.[59] The Coastal Security Force[60] was the name proposed for the new force that would provide wider 'maritime security', something that Admiral Burke had summarised in a April 1951 memo to Washington as including the escort of shipping, the patrolling of the Japanese sea lanes, and minesweeping.[61] Director General Yanagisawa objected to this plan, but naval officers like Captain Nagasawa – reassured by the support of American naval counterparts – did not yield. In the meantime, in January 1952, a small group of thirty perspective officers had started training with American instructors on one of the frigates to be acquired by the force.[62]

The plan went ahead and the Coastal Security Force was to be activated on 26 April 1952, following the amendment of the Maritime Safety Agency Law. With it, the seeds for a future independent navy were planted. Just as these changes were implemented, however, one new obstacle emerged. Prime Minister Yoshida's commitment in the US–Japan Security Treaty to increase Japanese efforts in the defence of the archipelago had opened the way for the National Police Reserve to gradually expand its capabilities to fulfil this mission. Accordingly, the National Police Reserve was to expand to include land and maritime operations. Prime Minister Yoshida was aware that the addition of a naval dimension to the future defence forces would be met with reservations from other Asian nations, but he also considered a 'managed rearmament' necessary.[63] On this matter, both the civilian and uniformed chiefs of the Police Reserve, Masahura Keikichi and Hayashi Keizo, honestly felt that, in its new guise, the organisation had to feature a unified command and headquarters to prevent the rivalries that had damaged the imperial armed forces. Naval officers naturally objected to such an idea and Admiral Burke even spoke to Yoshida himself to explain the difficulties and dangers of such a solution. However, at the Maritime Safety Agency, Director General Yanagisawa saw this transformation as a personal opportunity to head the maritime side of the new structure and lobbied for his agency to be included in it. Bureaucratic tensions between civilian and uniformed actors increased, and only the intervention of Prime Minister Yoshida enabled a solution to emerge. His conclusion was that the Coastal Security Force was to be detached from the Maritime Safety Agency to partake into the new organisation, changing its name to the Maritime Safety Force.[64] This new force was what naval officers had wished, worked and lobbied for over the course of several years.

It was a naval force with a full command structure controlling a small fleet of frigates, minesweepers and landing ships placed under the civilian authority of what became on 1 August 1952 the National Safety Agency.[65]

Two years later, on 1 July 1954, the National Safety Agency was further expanded to give birth to the Japan Defence Agency and three independent air, ground and maritime services. A joint staff council with consultative functions was also created to coordinate their operation. The new navy was now an organisational reality and the concerns about the chain of command were immediately addressed. A Maritime Staff Office was established to sit at the top of the hierarchical structure as the navy's governing body.[66] Under the new organisation, the potential for bureaucratic competition between 'fleet' and 'administration' factions was minimised. All administrative, political and operational functions were firmly placed under the responsibility of the Chief of Maritime Staff. In 1954, this was not a very complex task as the fleet was relatively small. In 1961, when the role of commander in chief of the Self-Defence Fleet was established, he became responsible for the fleet's operational activities, but his position remained subordinate to the Chief of Maritime Staff.[67]

As these events suggest, such a structure was the result of former officers' concerns about internal bureaucratic conflicts as much as the historical circumstances that had surrounded the creation of the Coastal Security Force. The need to have all its functions centralised to keep it separated from the Maritime Safety Agency meant that fleet and administration had to be symbiotically connected, with the latter identifying and managing the operational requirements of the former. By the time the JMSDF was established in 1954, the centrality of the staff office to the new navy supported this initial approach. Internally, the staff office was composed by a series of departments. In 1954, five departments (Administration, Operations and Plans, Intelligence, Supply and Finance, Engineering) managed the navy and set its goals, while the fleet carried them out.[68] Over the decades the number of departments varied slightly, and by the mid-2000s, their number had been raised to six. Within this structure, one element had not changed throughout the entire post-war period. The Operations and Plans Department was (and still is) the most influential in developing and adopting the navy's core policy and doctrinal notions. From within this department, naval officers controlled and coordinated matters of policy, strategy, and doctrine and supervised their implementation throughout the fleet (Figure 7.1).

The emphasis on the central role of the Maritime Staff Office in the new navy also aligned with the views of the men who had been involved in rearmament plans since the days of the Demobilisation Ministry. Admiral Yōnai had handpicked mid-ranking officers like the Captain Nagasawa and Commander Nakayama Sadayoshi (who later became the first and the third chiefs of maritime staff), for their professional proximity to the 'administration' faction. Both Captain Nagasawa and Commander Nakayama were working together as section and subsection heads at the Military Affairs Bureau of the Navy Ministry at the time of surrender.[69] As they took on the task of ferrying the navy through demobilisation and slowly towards rearmament, they used their understanding of the inner workings of the Ministry to shape the JMSDF. In this respect, the new navy ended up being very different from its wartime ancestor. The imperial precedent this new leadership looked at was the one of the pre-1933 Imperial Navy, described by one scholar as the 'traditional navy', an organisation that

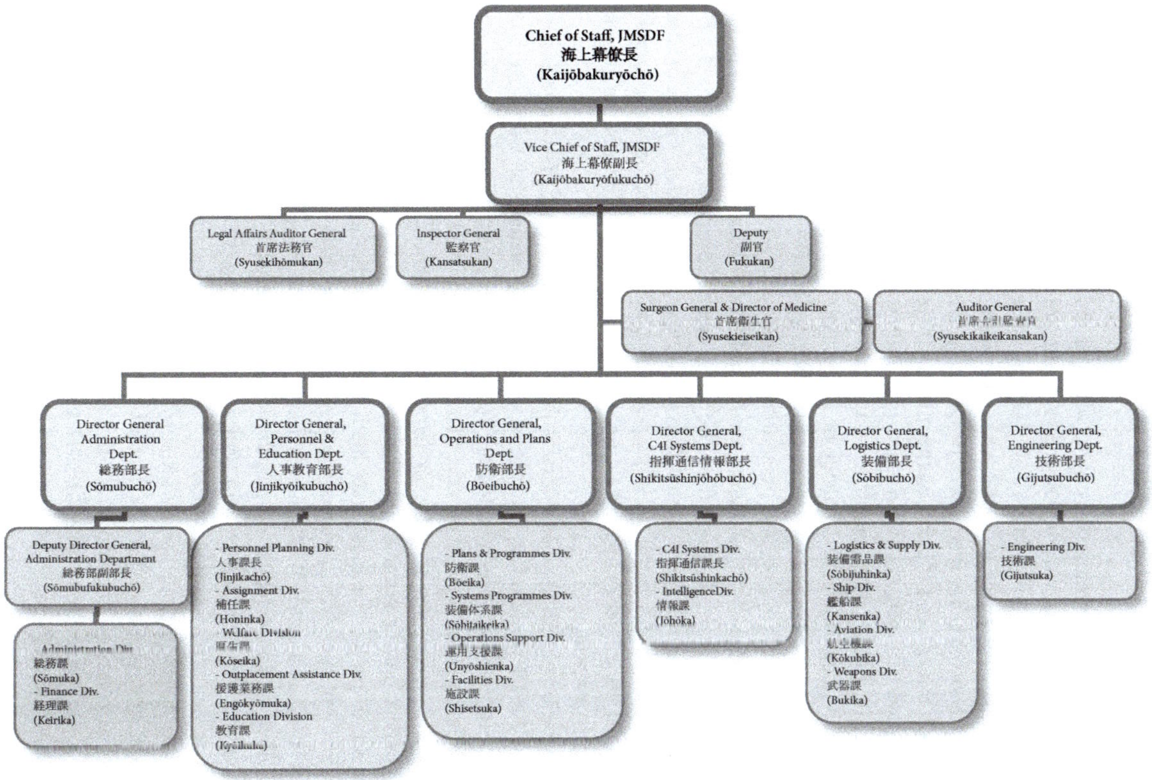

Figure 7.1 Structure of the Maritime Staff Office.

Source: Editorial Department, 'KaijYōjieitai 2008-2009' (海上自衛隊２００８－２００９ – Ships and Aircraft of the JMSDF), *Sekai no Kansen* 世界の艦船, 2008: 7, 161.

was 'well-ordered and unified' and that had produced respected and cosmopolitan flag officers like Nomura and Yōnai.[70]

The foundations of doctrine: A well-ordered and unified navy

One factor that further prompted the pursuit of a 'well-ordered and unified' organisation came from outside the navy itself. The return to the pre-1933 system was not really a return to the *status quo ante*. In post-war Japan, occupation authorities and Prime Minister Yoshida agreed that a strict civilian oversight on military matters should be introduced and Yoshida thus instructed the Cabinet Legislation Bureau to ensure that a layer of civilian bureaucrats supervised the military.[71] This principle was quite different to the one adopted during the Meiji era, where military affairs were the business of military men. By 1952, a first group of one hundred civilian staff – at the time mostly civil servants joining from the Ministry of Home Affairs with experience in police matters – assisted the Director General of the National Safety Agency in managing policy, budget, administration and personnel.[72] This nucleus evolved in 1954 into a body of civilian counsellors belonging to the Internal Bureau.[73] Former imperial officers and, later on, retired officers from the Self-Defence Forces would not be eligible to access positions in it.[74] The Internal Bureau worked with the staff offices of three services to allocate resources for debating policy and to control personnel promotion at the top level. Its influence applied to the confirmation of the chiefs of the ground, air and maritime staffs.

This separation of military and civilian affairs meant that a centralised organisation like the new JMSDF could retain a degree of autonomy in matters that were specific to the service. Since the service operated on the basis of securing relevant platforms to operate, the development of a strong core that could formulate clear requests to civilian authorities and could oversee their implementation became a crucial requirement. As one Japanese author pointed out, the creation of the Internal Bureau was more a mechanism to protect Japanese state institutions from the military by establishing the supremacy of the civilian bureaucracy in defence matters rather than a tool to implement civilian control.[75] With these arrangements, the JMSDF's governing body – the Staff Office, and especially the Operations and Plan Department – took the lead in the interactions and negotiations with civil servants, giving the JMSDF's top brass an additional reason to make sure that the service could develop one cohesive voice.

The career advancement of individual officers was one institutional mechanism that the first generation of JMSDF leaders reinstated from the Imperial Navy to enhance inner cohesion and cooperation. Criteria for assignment at the Staff Office, especially at the Operations and Plans Department, were (and still are) based on an officer's standing at the academy in Etajima and his overall performance and attitude.[76] In turn, these factors determined how fast an officer would rise within the hierarchy and the category of positions he would likely be assigned to. Throughout their career, officers with pronounced seaman-like attitudes spent proportionally more time at sea – as was the case in the Imperial Navy. Those with stronger managerial skills had their time equally divided between duties ashore and at sea. In the case of fast-track officers, the decision to seek a balanced career path, creating regular alternations between assignments at sea and ashore, was a direct result of the study of the human resources management system of the Imperial Navy.[77] Figure 7.2 provides an example of the differences in career paths in the JMSDF officer corps. It shows the profiles of the commanding officers of the units of the Japanese flotilla participating in the 2006 RIMPAC exercise. The extensive command experience of the commanding officers mirrored the value of the assets deployed, and stood in contrast with the profile of the admiral assigned to serve with the staff. In that case, the JMSDF had sent first-class captains, modern destroyers and one of its most qualified staff officers. This was no accident. It was the result of a system rooted in a century-long tradition.

At the staff level, this system had other implications. Officers assigned to the different branches of administration possessed similar backgrounds and career profiles, and had academy classmates with similar standing serving in equivalent posts in other sections of the Staff Office. The case of Captain Nagasawa and Commander Nakayama was not isolated. On the contrary, it captured the essence of a particular brand of patronage. Officers serving at the Staff Office, especially at the Operations and Plans Department, were selected among top-class naval academy graduates to serve at the various levels of the department as they advanced in their careers.[78] This method of human resources management singled out promising young officers in the interests of the organisation. It nurtured them to learn the complexities of naval politics and administration and bound them together by

	JDS Kirishima (DDG-174)	**JDS Samidare (DD-106)**
Rear Ad. X (1955)	Capt. Y (1955)	Cmdr. Z (1956)
1978: OCS 1992: Cmdr. 1994: CO, JDS *Sendai* 1995: PPD, MSO 1997: Capt. 1998: Pers. Div., MSO 2000: Com., 3rd Escort Div. 2001: Pers. Div., M SO 2003: CS, Esc. Flot. 1 2004: Rear Adm. 2004: Com. Esc. Flot. 1	1978: OCS 1989: Lt Cmdr. 1989: Recr. Off., Yamanashi Pref. 1990: WO, JDS *Yamayuki* 1992: Edu. DIV., MSO 1994: EO, JDS *Sawakaze* 1995: Instr., OCS 1996: Cmdr. 1997: EO, JDS *Kongō* 1998: CO, JDS *Yoshino* 1999: CO, JDS *Asagiri* 2000: Instr., 1ST SC 2001: Staff, JDS *Ōnami* 2003: CO, JDS *Ōnami* 2004: CO JDS *Kirishima*	1979: OCS 1992: Lt Cmdr. 1993: Yokosuka Test Stat 1995: CPO, JDS *Yamagiri* 1997: CPD, MSO 1999: CPO, JDS *Kurama* 2000: Staff HQ Kure 2002: CO, JDS *Yūbetsu* 2003: OPD, Maizuru Tr. Group 2004: Cmdr. 2005: CO, JDS *Samidare*
JDS Ariake (DD-109)	**JDS Hiei (DDH-142)**	
Cmdr. B (1960)	Cmdr. A (1956)	
1982: OCS 1993: Lt Cmdr. 1993: EO, JDS *Makigumo* 1995: OPO, JDS *Yūgiri* 1997: Staff, HQ Ōminato 1999: Staff, HQ, Esc. Flot. 4 2001: Cmdr. 2001: Edu. Div., MSO 2003: CO, JDS *Mineyuki* 2004 Staff, JSDF Fleet 2005: CO, JDS *Ariake*	1979: Tōkai University 1990: Lt. Cmdr. 1997: Cmdr. 1997: EO, TS *Kashima* 1998: CO, JDS *Noshiro* 1999: CPO, Prog. Centre 2001: Pros. CO, JDS *Takanami* 2003 CO, JDS *Takanami* 2004: Staff, Esc. Fleet 2005: CO, JDS *Hiei*	CO: Commanding Officer Pers. Div.: Personnel Division Com.: Commander CS: Chief of Staff Recr. Off.: Recruitment Office WO: Weapons Officer EO: Executive Officer Intr.: Instructor OPO: Operations Officer OPD: Head of Operations Pros. CO: Prospective CO

Figure 7.2 Biographies of the senior JMSDF officers to RIMPAC 2006.

the Japanese 'senior-junior' mentorship system.[79] Noting this form of patronage is critical to comprehend the extent to which the navy had returned to the 'traditional' outlook of the Imperial Navy. This system enabled the officers who reached the apex of the organisation to serve as section chief and director general of the Operations and Plans Department as they rose through the ranks, while their mentors occupied similar positions higher on the hierarchical ladder. As Figure 7.3 shows, during the tenure of Admiral Nakayama as Chief of Staff, Rear Admirals Nishimura Tomoharu and Itaya Ryūichi, the sixth and seventh Chiefs of Staff, respectively, directed the Operations and Plans Department. This type of situation persisted throughout the decades that followed. For half a century, homogeneity, group interests and patronage all contributed to shape the nature of the JMSDF.

The symbiotic network linking the different chiefs of staff to a skilled group of subordinates in key posts within the department was at the heart of the JMSDF machinery, and set the tone for the 'Japanese way' to produce higher-level doctrine. In the JMSDF, maritime doctrine has been developed and disseminated through the *New Instructions* of the chiefs of staff. These documents consist of written texts delivered orally during the inauguration ceremony on the day of appointment of a new chief. The formality of the occurrence has a particular value in that it grants these few pages a highly authoritative character, while the ritual nature of the ceremony and the oral delivery emphasise the informal purpose of the 'instructions'. Senior JMSDF staff officers explained that all service members (and especially officers in positions of responsibility) are well aware of the fundamental concepts set forth in the *New Instructions*. They are part of their professional grammar.[80] These key notions could be rendered in English as 'operational concepts'. The Staff Office is heavily involved in their development and their aim is to provide a coherent intellectual basis for policy, command and fighting spirit. Within its departments, the fast-track junior and mid-career officers in the Plans and Programmes Division (as per Figure 7.1 of this chapter) of Operations and Plans Department lead the process. This mechanism took advantage of the personnel system to foster a wider sense of intellectual ownership, while promoting 'prudence, competence, and steady evolution'.[81] Indeed, over the years, the progressive character of the changes articulated through the operational concepts has led some senior officers to jokingly remark that the *Instructions* have hardly ever changed.[82]

Their development was and is a function of a bottom-up decision-making process common to other bodies of Japanese administration, in which section chiefs[83] form the main working-level officers.[84] Throughout the decades, the main practice has been for the *New Instructions* to be initially assessed and debated within the Plans and Policy section. When an agreement was reached on a proposal, it was subsequently discussed in meetings with other sections and divisions. Thereafter, feedback was integrated into the initial draft, before receiving final approval by the Operations and Plans Department's director. Within this process, the role of the chief of staff, especially in the drafting of the *New Instructions*, is significant in that he decided at what level of the organisation the discussion on the development of the operational concepts should be started. Chiefs of staff with substantial experience in the inner mechanics of the system relied less on junior officers and involved more senior and flag officers at the departmental level. Others with less exposure to the service's planning activities tended

Year:	**Functions:**	**Graduation Class:**
1962	4th CMS: Adm. Nakayama	IJN (NA)
	DG, OPD: Rear Admiral Itaya (7th CMS)	IJN (60th Class)
1963:	4th CMS: Adm. Nakayama	IJN (NA)
	DG, OPD: Rear Adm. Nishimura (6th CMS)	IJN (59th Class)
1964–1965:	5th CMS: Adm. Sugie	IJN (NA)
	Chief, PPS: Captain Ishida (9th CMS)	IJN (64th Class)
1966:	6th CMS: Adm. Nishimura	IJN (59th Class)
	Chief, PPS: Captain Samejima (10th CMS)	IJN (66th Class)
1967–1968:	7th CMS: Adm. Itaya	IJN (60th Class)
	DG, OPD: Rear Admiral Uchida (8th CMS)	IJN (63rd Class)
1967:	Chief, PPS: Captain Samejima (10th CMS)	IJN (66th Class)
1969–1971:	8th CMS: Adm. Uchida	IJN (63rd Class)
	DG, OPD: Rear Admiral Samejima (1th CMS0	IJN (66th Class)
1972:	DG, OPD: Vice Admiral Nakamura (11th CMS)	IJN (71st Class)
1973:	9th CMS: Adm. Ishida	IJN (64th Class)
	Chief, PPS: Captain Yada (13th CMS)	IJN (72nd Class)
1974–1976:	10th CMS: Adm. Samejima	IJN (66th Class)
	DG, OPD: Rear Admiral Ōga (12th CMS)	IJN (71st Class)
1977:	11th CMS: Ad. Nakamura	IJN (67th Class)
	DG, OPD: Vice Admiral Yada (13th CMS)	IJN (72nd Class)
	Chief, PPS: Captain Nagata (16th CMS)	IJN (76th Class)
1978:	12th CMS: Adm. Ōga	IJN (71st Class)
	Chief, PPS: Captain Nagata (16th CMS)	IJN (76th Class)
1979:	12th CMS: Adm. Ōga	IJN (71st Class)
	DG, OPD: Rear Admiral Yoshida (15th CMS)	IJN (75th Class)
	Chief, PPS: Captain Higashiyama (17th CMS)	
1980:	13th CMS: Adm. Yada	IJN (72nd Class)
	DG, OPD: Vice Admiral Yoshida (15th CMS)	IJN (75th Class)
1981:	14th CMS: Adm. Maeda	IJN (73rd Class)
	DG, OPD: Vice Admiral Nagata (16th CMS)	IJN (76th Class)
1982:	14th CMS: Adm. Maeda	IJN (73rd Class)
	DG, OPD: Rear Admiral Higashiyama (17th CMS)	
1986:	16th CMS: Admiral Nagata	IJN (76th Class)
	DG, OPD: Rear Admiral Sakuma (18th CMS)	NDU (1st Class)
	Chief, PPS: Captain Hayashizaki (20th CMS)	NDU (4th Class)
1987:	16th CMS: Adm. Nagata	IJN (76th Class)
	DG, OPD: Rear Admiral Okabe (19th CMS)	NDU (2nd Class)
1989:	17th CMS: Adm. Higashiyama	
	DG, OPD: Rear Admiral Hayashizaki (20th CMS)	NDU (4th Class)
1990–1991:	18th CMS: Adm. Sakuma	NDU (1th Class)
	Chief, PPS: Rear Admiral Fujita (13th CMS)	NDU (9th Class)
1995:	21st CMS: Adm. Fukuchi	NDU (5th Class)
	DG, OPD: Rear Admiral Ishikawa (25th CMS)	NDU (11th Class)
	Chief, PPS: Captain Saitō (27th CMS)	NDU (14th Class)
1996:	22nd CMS: Adm. Natsukawa	NDU (5th Class)
	DG, OPD: Rear Admiral Ishikawa (25th CMS)	NDU (11th Class)
1997:	23rd CMS: Adm. Yamamoto	NDU (7th Class)
	DG, OPD: Rear Admiral Saitō (27th CMS)	NDU (14th Class)

Key: CMS: Chief of Maritime Staff; DG: Director General; OPD: Operations and Plans Department; IJN: Imperial Japanese Navy; NDU: National Defence University.

The area in grey highlights periods when both the OPD and the PPS are directed by officers who have later been appointed chiefs of staff.

Figure 7.3 The 'symbiotic network' of the Maritime Staff Office.

Source: Japan Defence Agency, *Jieitai Nenkan* (自衛隊年鑑 – Yearbook of the JSDF, Tokyo, 1961–1998).

to rely more on the bottom-up approach.[85] To a large extent, the functioning of the Staff Office mirrored that of private Japanese companies, in which cooperation and reciprocity among officers was regarded as a key enabler to achieve wider consensus on matters of priority to the organisation.[86]

Setting the navy on course: Fighting power and readiness with a strong spirit

The evolution of the JMSDF doctrine can be divided into three main phases. The first concerns the initial period of naval rearmament, from the establishment of the service to the adoption of the 1976 NDPO. During this phase, doctrine aimed to set out the service's basic professional standards. As the JMSDF strove to build up its capabilities, the security envelope provided by the American naval presence in the western Pacific allowed the Japanese to prioritise issues related to its technical skills. At the end of the 1970s, new concepts were introduced, gauging increasing operational responsibilities, notably the commitment to sea lane defence up to 1,000 NM. This second phase lasted throughout the remaining years of the Cold War and drew to a close in the first half of the 1990s. By the end of the decade, the JMSDF had entered the current phase and introduced new operational concepts in response to the security challenges of the post-Cold War era.

By the first half of the 1960s, two concepts emerged as the basis of JMSDF doctrine. The operational concepts were prowess[87], also rendered in English as 'fighting power', and readiness (Figure 7.4).[88] In 1969, Admiral Uchida was the first chief to publicly remind service members that these concepts had been introduced to allow the JMSDF to strive to achieve the professional standards of the Imperial Navy. Irrespective of limited capabilities and limited missions, he was convinced that the service should

Chiefs of Maritime Staff, JMSDF	**Operational Concepts:**			
	Kyōkona Seishin (強固な精神)	**Sōikufū (創意工夫)**	**Seikyō (精強)**	**Sokuou (即応)**
Nakayama Sadayoshi 4th CMS, 1961–1963	✵		✵	
Sugie Kazumi 5th CMS, 1963–1964			✵	
Nishimura Tomoharu 6th CMS, 1964–1966			✵	✵
Itaya Takakazu 7th CMS, 1966–1969	✵	✵	✵	✵
Uchida Kazuomi 8th CMS, 1969–1972	✵		✵	✵
Ishida Suteo 9th CMS, 1972–1973	✵	✵	✵	
Samejima Hirokazu 10th CMS, 1973–1976		✵	✵	
Nakamura Teiji 11th CMS, 1976–1977	✵	✵	✵	✵

Kyōkona Seishin (強固な精神): Strong Spirit/Mind; Sōikufū (創意工夫): Originality/Creativity (Literally: Original Device); Seikyō(精強): Prowess (Literally: Toughness); Sokuou (即応): Readiness.

Figure 7.4 The JMSDF's operational concepts, 1961–1977.

Source: Chief of Maritime Staff, JMSDF, *Chakuninni Saishi Kunji* (着任に際し訓示 – Official Instructions, Tokyo: Maritime Staff Office, Japan Defence Agency, 1961–1976).

uphold the imperial slogan 'devotion to silence',[89] and develop skills in training and seamanship of imperial connotation.[90] The aim of the first generation of chiefs of staff was the improvement of the service's material and spiritual fabric. In this respect, the association of these concepts with the imperial legacy offered a well-tested, battle-hardened model. More significantly, it helped addressing constraints on personnel strength offering a narrative (the so-called 'policy of small numbers, but a high state of readiness'),[91] that nicely matched JMSDF requirements.[92] Indeed, this was the primary interpretation given to the pursuit of 'fighting power'. The concept indicated a method centred on intensive training at sea that aspired to the procurement and maintenance of cutting-edge equipment. In the 1960s, these improvements primarily concerned the navy's ASW capabilities.[93] Over time, this concept emerged as a cornerstone of the JMSDF doctrine that lasted well beyond the formative years. As a former commander of the Escort Fleet pointed out, 'sailors need to train hard, to learn discipline, because only in this way they can be prepared for the heat of the battle, and the stress that it entails'.[94]

In 1976, at a time when the navy already fielded four escort flotillas (for a total of forty-four major surface combatants), two submarine flotillas (including fifteen submarines), two minesweeper flotillas (comprising thirty-five units) and an air wing of approximately 180 aircraft (rotary and fixed-wing), Admiral Nakamura reconsidered the question of maintaining military fighting power in peacetime. Whereas some argued that 'the business of the military man lays in the battles',[95] Admiral Nakamura stressed that peacetime missions such as surveillance and control were crucial to national security and should not be underestimated. Soviet naval power in the Pacific was a serious threat to Japan and prowess – intended to mean intense preparation, a high level of readiness, and a sustained investment in manning a modern fleet – was a prerequisite for victory in war and had to be meticulously pursued in peacetime.[96] Prowess made Japanese naval power a credible means of deterring the Soviet naval presence in the northeast Asian region. In 1981, Admiral Maeda further added that service men had to view fighting power as the most eloquent evidence of the navy's unyielding responsibility to meet public expectations vis-à-vis its role in national defence. To that extent, the professionalism unfolding from the pursuit of fighting power was the navy's primary tool to win the trust of the Japanese people.[97]

For these reasons, naval officers had to possess a 'strong spirit' – an additional concept employed in the first phase of the JMSDF's evolution.[98] In the formative years, the internal battle for the 'hearts and minds' of navy personnel was linked to the controversial status enjoyed by the JSDF. In 1966, Admiral Itaya used the expression 'cultivation of the individual'[99] to highlight the necessity of paying particular care in managing personnel development.[100] Admiral Uchida was clear on this subject: officers had to be 'tough-minded' and fully aware of the seriousness of the naval profession and its critical role in Japan's security. Discipline, a sense of responsibility and an open-minded approach to problems were paramount to the officer's spiritual fabric.[101] As an operational concept, 'strong spirit' was no longer systematically included in the *Official Instructions* from the early 1980s onwards, with one main exception. In 1983, Admiral Yoshida made reference to the bond existing between the requirement for tough-minded service men and the nature of naval operations in Japan's strategic environment, one demanding resolute action and quick responses.[102]

In the second half of the 1960s, a strong spirit became a virtue that had to be cultivated together with a degree of 'creative thinking'.[103] Introduced for the first time by Admiral Itaya, this concept addressed the growing need to develop a strategy that could meet the requirements of the navy's new role in maritime trade defence. In the view of the chief of staff, creativity prevented complacency and lack of innovation in the spheres of tactics and technology. Concurrently, such a mental attitude encouraged a flexible approach to strategy that was instrumental in a period of the JMSDF's history in which the structure of the fleet and its capabilities were rapidly evolving.[104] It is worth noting that this concept, after being abandoned in 1976, reappeared in *Official Instructions* that were delivered in perceived moments of transition or in times of major changes in defence policies and procurement programmes (1989, 1994, 1996). Admiral Sakuma explained the use of the concept, pointing out that creativity was essential to perpetuate the navy's traditions in that it enabled service men to re-contextualise the essence of their content. Hence, the JMSDF had to favour independent thinking and freedom of expression among its officers – without undermining the role of discipline. As the admiral warned, creativity was the key to the expression 'when you govern, don't forget to revolt'.[105]

The last of the operational concepts of this first period, like fighting power, defined the JMSDF throughout its entire history. 'Readiness', like 'prowess', was inherited from the Imperial Navy's genetic code. It addressed the fundamental issue of the navy's ethical and operational behaviour, soliciting its members to always be mentally alert and 'aware of the mission' (Figure 7.5).[106] In the words of Admiral Nagata, personnel had to be ready to 'vibrate at a sound'.[107] Training and education drew upon imperial traditions to promote a willingness to pay attention to the external environment. Midshipmen learnt in Etajima the inherent value of readiness through the 'five minutes before' code, the practice of sports activities and martial arts, and 'naval expressions' like 'outbound ship'. Across the fleet, readiness had a crucial operational implication. Geography favoured Japan in frustrating Soviet naval ambitions of accessing the open oceans from Vladivostok. Readiness was critical to take full advantage of regional geography in patrolling the archipelago's main straits and surrounding waters. The proximity of Japan's main security threats further entailed the JMSDF to maintain a high level of readiness, a necessity that became even more cogent after 1981, in the wake of the navy's increased responsibility in protecting the archipelago's sea lanes. Hence, as Admiral Yada put it, the JMSDF could not embrace an attitude 'of waiting until something happens';[108] it had always to endeavour to be 'prepared before hand'.[109]

Testing the navy: The US–Japan alliance and beyond

The 1976 NDPO and the 1978 Guidelines marked the JMSDF's entrance into a new phase of professional growth. The official doctrine registered the significance of closer bilateral naval interaction with the United States with the adoption in 1980 of the concept of 'cooperation'.[110] In that year, for the first time, Japan joined RIMPAC, a goal that had been an ambition of the JMSDF since Admiral Ōga was appointed as chief of staff, and one that the service had pursued with considerable conviction. Cooperation with the US Navy played a significant threefold role in strengthening

Chiefs of Maritime Staff, JMSDF	Operational Concepts:			
	Renkei (連係)	Danketsu (創意工夫)	Seikyō (精強)	Sokuou (即応)
Ōga Ryōhei 12th CMS, 1977–1980		●	●	●
Yada Tsuguo 13th CMS, 1980–1981	●	●	●	●
Maeda Masaru 14th CMS, 1981–1983	●		●	●
Yoshida Manabu 15th CMS, 1983–1985	●	●	●	
Nagata Hiroshi 16th CMS, 1985–1987	●	●	●	●
Higashiyama Shuichirō 17th CMS, 1987–1989	●	●	●	
Sakuma Makoto 18th CMS, 1989–1991	●		●	●
Okabe Fumio 19th CMS, 1991–1993	●		●	●
Hayashizaki Chiaki 20th CMS, 1993–1994	●	●	●	●
Fukuchi Takeo 21st CMS, 1994–1996	●	●	●	●

Renkei (連係): Teamwork/Coordination; Danketsu (団結): Union/Solidarity; Seikyō(精強): Prowess (Literally: Toughness); Sokuou (即応): Readiness.

Figure 7.5 The JMSDF's operational concepts, 1977–1996.

Source: Chief of Maritime Staff, JMSDF, *Chakuninni Saishi Kunji* (着任に際し訓示 – Official Instructions, Tokyo: Maritime Staff Office, Japan Defence Agency, 1977–1994).

the capabilities of Japan's post-war naval power. First, joint training and exercises allowed the JMSDF to test capabilities in conditions as close as possible to real combat scenarios.[111] Second, close ties with the US Navy enabled the service to be regularly exposed to the effects of innovation in the fields of tactics and operations. Third, the overcoming of technical problems unfolding from closer cooperation favoured interoperability, setting the preliminary conditions for the JMSDF to be able to operate at a broader international level.[112] For the remaining years of the Cold War, this concept represented a *passe-partout* to maximise the impact of JMSDF capabilities, improving the service's effectiveness and testing its potential as a contributor to multinational coalitions.

In 1985, Admiral Nagata refined the concept, adding to the 'strengthening of the partnership with the US Navy' the enhancement of cooperation with 'the JGSDF and JASDF'.[113] In the navy-to-navy relationship with the United States, the areas of equipment, tactics, language, and personnel exchange were regarded as of pivotal importance. In terms of inter-service cooperation, Admiral Nagata and his successors maintained a favourable position on the enhancement of mutual trust and understanding with the JGSDF and the JASDF, especially since the latter had primary responsibility in providing the fleet's air cap within the national maritime space.[114] Indeed, they argued that it was unthinkable in modern military operations to pursue an independent service-oriented approach. Eventually, in 1994, in light of the changes in Japanese defence policy set out in a pilot study to the 1995 NDPO, Admiral Fukuchi was the first to invert the order of priorities within the operational concepts, listing joint preparation[115] with the sister services first.[116]

In the 1980s and 1990s, as the navy's operational undertaking grew in scope and radius, the question of the navy's inner cohesiveness was perceived by the chiefs of staff as an issue requiring closer attention. As a result, a new concept made its appearance in the official doctrinal grammar. This could be adequately translated as *esprit de corps*, though literally in the *Official Instructions* is referred to as 'strong solidarity'.[117] The question of internal cohesion first appeared in the 1977 speech by Admiral Ōga. He argued that with the modernisation of the fleet, service men had to not forget mutual trust and a general sense of belonging. These, he believed, remained the bedrocks of seamanship. Striking a similar tone, Admiral Yada stressed that he expected his personnel to act like a single unit, one in which its members could 'all eat from the same iron bowl'.[118] In 1983, Admiral Yoshida reviewed the meaning of the concept. He argued that a shared understanding of the vital nature of the mission of naval defence rested at the heart of individual efforts in training. In turn, training strengthened cohesiveness further, recreating the ideal conditions for a forthright dialogue on issues concerning the naval profession. According to the admiral, such an approach was in line with the imperial naval ethos where 'frank talking' was a precious part of the decision-making process. Discipline[119] had a primary role in framing the debate on a topic, and together with 'strong cohesiveness', it enabled naval officers to make competent plans and decisions.[120]

As the century drew to a close, changes in the international system and Japan's regional security environment demanded that the navy recast some of the fundamental concepts of its doctrine. Greater 'flexibility'[121] was needed to deal with a plethora of security concerns. Admiral Furushō officially adopted the notion of flexibility in 2003, though Admirals Natsukawa and Yamamoto first raised the question of the JMSDF's tactical and operational 'flexibility' in 1997 and 1999, respectively. According to Admiral Furushō, growing demands on the contribution of the armed forces in securing the post-9/11 international arena, coupled with increasing budgetary constraints, entailed for the JMSDF a higher predisposition to quickly adjust its priorities.[122] Each task was not to be blindly carried out along pre-established lines or plans, but had to be adjusted to meet changing environmental conditions. As Japan's international landscape evolved, the chiefs of staff of the new century realised that a successful force had to be capable of 'challenging change' and sought to put in motion doctrinal changes that could capture these new needs.[123] In this process, across the entire post-war period, the imperial experience represented a constant reference source for content and methods of delivery. It offered a model to strengthen the navy's corporate spirit and shape its approach to matters of innovation and operation (Figure 7.6).

Admiral Ishikawa's concluding remarks well summarised more than half a century of doctrinal evolution, noting that 'for the JMSDF, the dawn of the 21st century led the way to an "era of [hard] work".[124] At once, learning the lessons of the more than 70-year long history of the Imperial Navy, the JMSDF has passed from a period of "infancy" to one of "maturity"'.[125]

Chiefs of Maritime Staff, JMSDF	Operational Concepts:			
	Sōikufū (創意工夫)	Jūnansei (柔軟性)	Seikyō (精強)	Sokuou (即応)
Natsukawa Katsuya 22nd CMS, 1996–1997	❁		❁	❁
Yamamoto Yasumasa 23rd CMS, 1997–1999		❁	❁	❁
Fujita Kōsei 24th CMS, 1999–2001	---	---	---	---
Ishikawa Tōru 25th CMS, 2001–2003			❁	❁
Furushō Kōichi 26th CMS, 2003–2005		❁	❁	❁

Jūnansei (柔軟性): Flexibility; Sōikufū (創意工夫): Originality/Creativity (Literally: Original Device); Seikyō (精強): Prowess (Literally: Toughness); Sokuou (即応): Readiness.

Figure 7.6 The JMSDF's operational concepts, 1996–2005.

Source: Chief of Maritime Staff, JMSDF, *Chakuninni Saishi Kunji* (着任に際し訓示 – Official Instructions, Tokyo: Maritime Staff Office, Japan Defence Agency, 1996–2005).

A new sword: Building a balanced fleet

The pre-war fleet was 'like the sword of the samurai', 'a weapon of immense precision, workmanship, and quality'.[126] It was a force designed to excel in a major surface engagement and was trained to outperform its enemy in such a culminating moment. Combat experience gained in the First Sino-Japanese and Russo-Japanese Wars had taught the Japanese the value of the decisive battle, with the staggering results obtained at Tsushima setting the benchmark of excellence. Indeed, the battle of Tsushima represented the Japanese 'Trafalgar' and the warships designed in the 1920s and 1930s were meant, in a way, to 'Tsushima' their opponent. The corollary to this view was an offensive approach to sea control, key to the command of the sea, requiring a homogeneous fleet of fast and powerful warships. Firepower came to be regarded as of paramount tactical importance in Japanese naval warfare. Speed and armaments were the core capabilities to be maximised in warship designs.[127]

The idea of a homogeneous fleet had its value, but this had been pursued at the cost of balance among the fleet's different functions and tactical and operational flexibility. The lessons identified from the disaster of the war were not lost in the development of the post-war fleet. In the early 1950s, achieving sea control in the form favoured by the Imperial Navy was simply no longer part of the new tasks. The JMSDF was therefore to focus its attention on the procurement of capabilities that would allow it to deny[128] hostile forces access to Japan's maritime space. In this respect, the JMSDF organised the fleet in a fashion different from the Imperial Navy. Naval forces were divided not according to the pre-war *Naisen-Gaisen* logic; they were placed under the command of the regional districts and under an 'escort' fleet.[129] The new fleet was not meant to be an offensive sword like the *Gaisen Kantai* of the past; it was a force designed to safeguard maritime movements within Japan's home waters. Eventually, the missions of the escort fleet expanded to encompass the defence of trade arteries

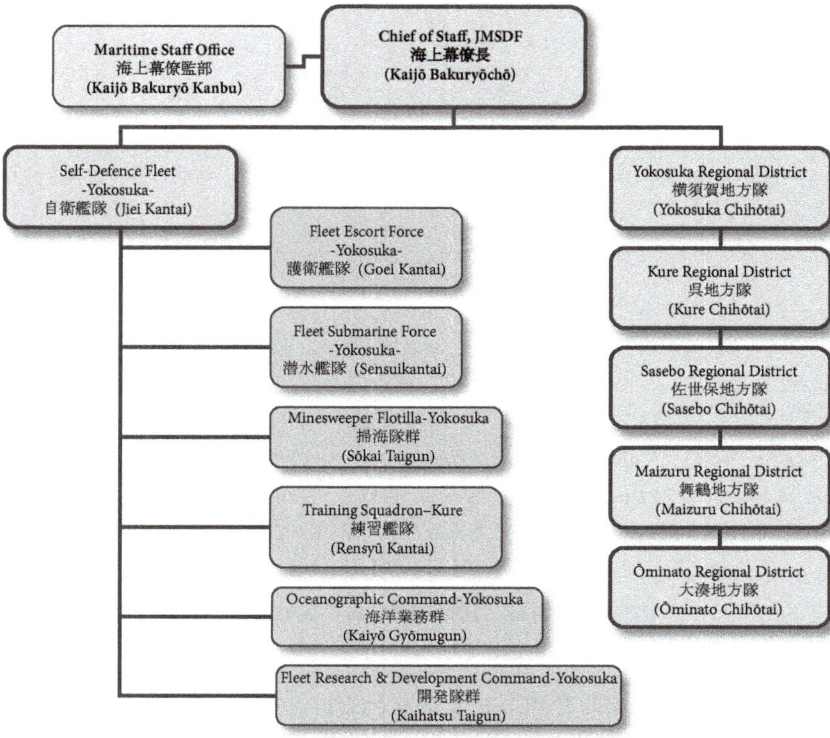

Figure 7.7 Current organisation of the JMSDF's fleet.

Source: Editorial Department, 'Kaijōjieitai 2008-2009' (海上自衛隊２００８－２００９ - Ships and Aircraft of the JMSDF), *Sekai no Kansen* 世界の艦船, 2008: 7, 162–3.

in the open ocean. In that capacity, the enhanced self-defence fleet moved away from sea denial and aspired to sea control in the conduct of its core sea lane defence mission.[130] The fundamental doctrinal shift from an offensive to an overall defensive naval posture was captured in the fleet's structure, which remained unaltered until the early 2000s.

In terms of main naval missions, geography enabled the JMSDF to opt for two different sets of operations against its principal Cold War adversary, the Soviet navy. Japan's three straits and chain of islands presented a formidable natural barrier to limit Soviet naval activities in the Pacific. The depth of the straits in the Sea of Japan, essential to gain access to the Ocean, was less than 100 metres, making these areas ideally suited for mine-laying.[131] Hence, the patrolling and, in a war scenario, the blockading of these focal points represented valuable options which offered both defence from an invasion and the protection of shipping.[132] The second category of operations concerned the defence of crucial areas of the sea highways that delivered Japan's economic lifeblood. In particular, according to an informed defence analyst, the numerous islands of the maritime space comprised between what became known within naval circles as the 'eastern route' and the 'western route' offered an advantage in the defence of shipping if a combined action of air patrol, sonar stations, hydrophones, and direct escort were to be pursued.[133]

The abandonment of the Imperial Navy's offensive posture did not entail a similar distance from 'offensive' tactical preferences. For this reason, as of the mid-1950s, when ASW capabilities were given top priority, the JMSDF started approaching the question of its escort duties in tactically offensive terms. The ASW force would hunt the enemy. To that end, the creation of a relevant air component was imperative, and this allowed the JMSDF to procure the first rotary and fixed-wing aircraft, including eight S-55As, forty-two P2V-7s and sixty S2F-1s. In 1959, the JMSDF went a step further and started studying the feasibility of procuring a domestically built 6,000–7,000-ton helicopter carrier, referred to as CVH.[134] The plan was not adopted in the 1959 revision of the first build-up programme. The following year though the navy inquired with the Military Assistance and Advisory Group – Japan (MAAG-J) to develop a joint project for an 11,000-ton CVH. This project would have allowed the JMSDF to strengthen its ASW core. The carrier would be equipped with HSS-2 anti-submarine helicopters and it would be built with American assistance.[135] Outside strict Japanese and American naval circles, the CVH project failed to gain any civilian support, but the JMSDF was like a child 'seeking to suck as much breast-milk as possible so to grow stronger'.[136]

In the late 1950s and early 1960s, naval technology and its application in ASW was undergoing major changes and the navy sought to address this issue by preserving a degree of flexibility in the design of its platforms and the selection of combat systems. This process was greatly facilitated by access to cutting-edge technology and up-to-date tactical procedures through the partnership with the United States. In no area was this more evident than in submarine warfare, another component that the JMSDF regarded as of critical significance to a multilayered ASW defensive matrix. The ten-year gap between the disbanding of the Imperial Navy and the commissioning in 1955 of Japan's first post-war submarine, *Kuroshio* (SS-501), had been a period of substantial technical and operational developments.[137] For the JMSDF, that had been, to borrow an expression from modern economics, a true 'lost decade'.

Their interaction with the fast evolving American submarine world proved to be extremely fruitful, especially since it forced the Japanese to grasp the major leaps that had occurred in the field. It also confirmed the questions surrounding the role of submarines in this early stage of Japanese post-war naval posture. Submarines could have a critical role in strait and sea lane defence, though the rather uncertain economic conditions of the archipelago precluded the possibility of the navy pursuing a clear-cut build-up of a submarine force designed with specific missions in mind. During one of the first technical missions to the United States, when asked what sort of submarines the Japanese were planning on building, the team leader answered that they were looking for a 'flexible option', one that could deal with both surface and underwater targets.[138] At that stage, flexible designs also served the idea that training was of paramount importance for the establishment of new professional standards while future options regarding the force's missions were evaluated.

Following the second build-up plan, naval defence gained higher priority and by 1966, the fleet was already in the process of achieving its primary goal of establishing an ASW core.[139] The inventory totalled some 209 units, and it included the first destroyers with displacements of over 2,000 tons, *Amatsukaze* (DD-163), *Yamagumo* (DD-113) and *Makigumo* (DD-114), all armed with variable depth sonar (VDS) and anti-submarine missile (ASROC) launchers.[140] The navy also fielded seven submarines, including four small hunter-killer boats (765 tons) of the *Hayashio* and *Natsuhsio* classes designed for sea denial operations in littoral waters, and a sizeable air wing of fifty-nine P2V-7 and fifty-six S2F-1.[141] The JMSDF's keen commitment to building up its muscles made inevitable sacrifices in other areas. Apart from one destroyer, *Amatsukaze* (DD-163), which was armed with a single-arm anti-air warfare (AAW) Tartar launcher, the JMSDF air defence capabilities rested solely on 40 mm anti-air gunfire and 76 mm guns.[142] Whereas this problem was assumed to have only a limited impact as operations were to be conducted within the range of land-based air cover, the tonnage increase in front-line equipment also left untouched the question of logistics and maintenance. As a contemporary observer put it, 'There was no effective, independent, sustained capability except for the minesweeping force, which was growing, becoming modernised, and still sweeping the World War II mines.'[143]

By the time the JMSDF had to argue a case for the third build-up, its leaders had digested the skills of budget politics and possessed the experience to set forth a plan that would gain civilian endorsement while fulfilling the navy's operational requirements. In such a context, the CVH proposal was no longer reiterated; instead, the plan called for a helicopter-carrying destroyer (DDH). The request was considered appropriate given the expanded set of missions (including by now the defence of maritime traffic), and thus the navy's inventory was strengthened with fourteen destroyers, including the first surface-to-air missile (SAM) units, and the first DDH, *Haruna* (DD-141). New ships were fitted with modern ASW detection systems like the Japanese-modified SQS-23 sonar.[144] The air wing introduced the P-2J maritime patrol aircraft, and by 1971 the new platform had already replaced approximately 28 per cent of the fleet's land-based air component.[145] In the same year, the JMSDF also commissioned *Tachikaze* (DD-168), its first destroyer with a computerised combat direction system (CDS).[146] In parallel, funds were approved to implement training and education, restructuring and upgrading of facilities and bases, and improvements in communication technologies.[147]

Between the end of the 1960s and the first half of the 1970s, the expansion of Japan's defensive maritime perimeter, now including a considerable number of offshore islands, demanded more adequate platforms for logistical transportation to cover the distances within the archipelago. These requirements were coupled with the duties in support of land operations in Hokkaido – one of the likely areas for a potential Soviet invasion.[148] Thus, in the context of the third and especially of the fourth build-up plans, the navy procured its first domestic-built tank landing ship, the 1,550-ton *Atsumi* (LST-4101) and her two sister ships, *Motobu* (LST-4102) and *Nemuro* (LST-4103), commissioned in 1972, 1973 and 1977, respectively.[149] These units were built along with another class of three larger landing ships of 2,000-ton displacement, *Miura* (LST-4151), *Ojika* (LST-4152) and *Satsuma* (LST-4153), the last entering service in 1977.[150] With the two small 590-ton utility landing crafts of the *Yura* (LCU-4171) class joining the fleet in 1981, the JMSDF attained a first small amphibious core. This was designed to support ground operations in case of Soviet invasion attempts while also assisting the Japanese population in cases of natural disaster during peacetime. This set of capabilities would have been insufficient in wartime, but it did provide the JMSDF with an opportunity to retain a minimum of expertise in basic maritime transport operations.

In the subsequent years, the completion of a fleet that could effectively perform ASW operations remained the primary focus of the JMSDF attention. This process reached its pinnacle in the aftermath of the adoption of the 1976 NDPO. In particular, the document underlined the necessity of maintaining a high level of readiness. At least one escort flotilla had to be 'on alert at all times' to counter eventual aggressions to maritime trade in areas surrounding Japan, and 'at least one ship division in operational readiness at all times in each assigned sea district' to protect home waters.[151] Given the fleet's requirements for training, repair, and patrol activities, four escort flotillas, each including one DDH, seven destroyers and eight helicopters (three carried by the DDH and the remaining five deployed on an equal number of destroyers), and ten divisions (two in each regional district) were deemed essential.[152]

The '8-8' flotilla concept – this was the name of the basic tactical formation of the ASW hunting group – was symptomatic of the navy's two decade-long commitment to developing a homogenous and effective force to carry out its duties (Figure 7.8). The first studies of this tactical formation had appeared in the mid-1960s, when technical limitations on helicopter operations on smaller destroyers forced the navy to focus on an '8-6' flotilla, comprising two DDHs carrying three helicopters each.[153] By the end of the decade, improved arresting gear systems, combined with test results obtained by fitting a helicopter deck on an old landing ship, had set the service on the right path towards solving these issues and improving its original scheme.[154] In the final version, two guided missile destroyers were tasked with the flotilla's air cover, five destroyers operated as escort to the group, defending it from both surface and submerged threats, while the helicopter component – composed of HSS-2B – would be deployed to actively hunt enemy submarines as the flotilla's search attack unit (SAU).[155]

In terms of design, Japan's numerical inferiority vis-à-vis its potential Soviet adversary made pre-war notions such as homogeneity, speed and firepower still very relevant. Units procured after *Haruna* were to follow what JMSDF naval architects dubbed the '6 S' principle, namely, they were to maximise 'speed, strength, stability, space, silence, and style'.[156] Speed, stability and space were functional for operations

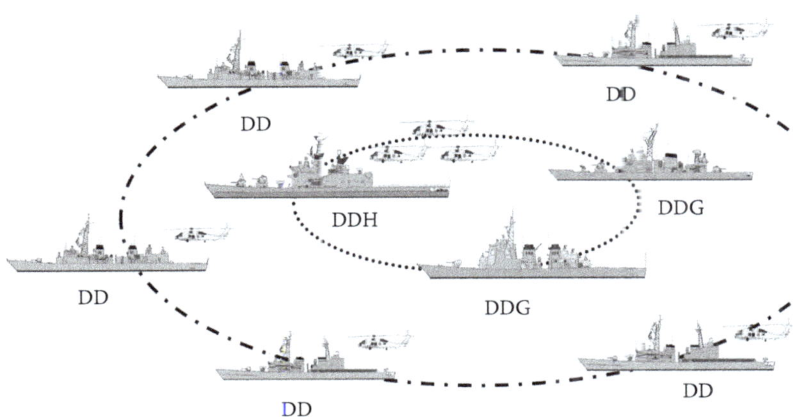

Figure 7.8 The JMSDF's '8-8' fleet formation.

Source: Public Affairs Office, MSO, JMSDF.

in the open ocean, while style referred to a degree of uniformity and compatibility in combat systems and performance among the different component of the flotilla. Strength and silence aimed at enhancing the ship's combat capability and survivability. From this period onwards, all new destroyers were designed to possess similar speed performance (maximum 30 knots) and propulsion systems. In 1977, the procurement of *Atsuyuki* (DD-122) marked the navy's passage from diesel to combined diesel or gas turbine engines (CODOG), the first of a series of progressive steps to improve both the fleet's 'speed and silence' in performing ASW functions.[157]

In terms of combat capabilities, the introduction of the naval tactical data system (NTDS) improved the coordination between data collected by the ships' sensors (like radar and sonar) and their application for tactical use.[158] Destroyers' firepower was consistently enhanced by fitting a range of capabilities encompassing close-in weapons systems (CIWS) for AA point defence, ASW Mk46 ASROC torpedoes, Sea Sparrow surface-to-air missiles (SAM), Harpoon surface-to-surface missiles (SSM) and 76 mm or 127 mm guns for naval gunfire support (NGS).[159] In 1986, the JMSDF solved the long-postponed question of fleet air defence by becoming the first navy to secure the procurement of the extremely advanced American AEGIS air defence system.[160] In particular, as Assistant Secretary for East Asian and Pacific Affairs Gaston Sigur remarked, the extended coverage provided by Aegis-equipped destroyers represented a 'keystone in Japan's effort to upgrade its anti-air warfare capability in each of four escort flotillas'.[161] In 1989, the JMSDF completed the balance of its fleet by commissioning the first of three replenishment vessels, *Towada* (AOE-422), which extended the fleet's operational endurance.

This philosophy continued to underpin the development of the fleet well into the 1990s. Sensors and weaponry continued to grow in sophistication, and by the time the destroyer *Murasame* (DD-101) was commissioned in 1996, the JMSDF had a completed fleet with staggering ASW capacities. The *Murasame* featured cutting-edge solutions in all required departments of the '6 S' design process, including Mk41 and Mk48 vertical missile launching systems (VLS), OQS-5-1 bow sonar, OPS 24B and OPS 28D radars, an advanced combat information centre (CIC), and tactical air navigation (TACAN) antenna.[162] The 1980s had witnessed a phase of substantial continuity in the nature of Japanese fleet operations; this, in turn, facilitated the shift from the quantitative expansion of the 1950s and 1960s to a qualitative refinement of Japan's ASW force. The *Murasame* class, and even more so its upgraded version, the *Takanami* (DD-110) class, were large, capable and, by means of intense training and joint exercises with the US Navy, effective.[163] They embodied an approach to ship design that had married post-war strategic circumstances with the strengths of the imperial tradition.

The pursuit of the most advanced systems on the market for this fleet of powerful and versatile platforms proved to be an asset in the changed security environment of the end of the century. The acquisition of the AEGIS air defence system gave naval platforms a leading role in the BMD programme.[164] In air surveillance, the JMSDF had introduced the EP-3, a variant of the P-3C maritime aircraft equipped with a reconnaissance system capable of detecting and exploiting tactically significant electronic signals and communication Signal Intelligence (SIGINT) information.[165] In submarine warfare, between 1991 and 1992, two research studies took place to identify new courses of action that could lead to the implementation of the hunter-killer and endurance capabilities of the next generation of submarines.[166] Subsequent to their recommendations, the JMSDF started eyeing the

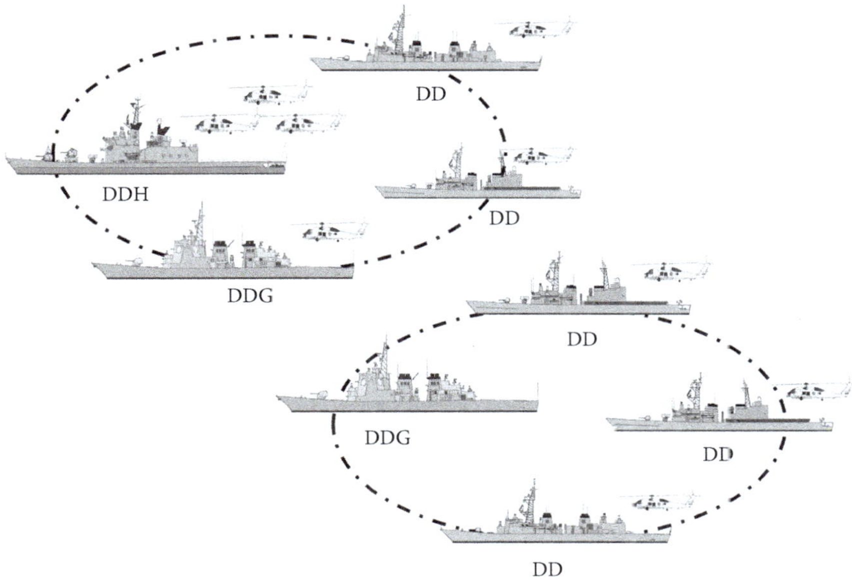

Figure 7.9 The Escort Division tactical formation.

Source: Public Affairs Office, MSO, JMSDF.

innovative Air Independent Propulsion (AIP).[167] In 1993, the JMSDF dusted off a mid-1980s study for a large amphibious unit originally conceived to redeploy ground forces from western to northern Japan in case of an invasion and used it to design and procure its first landing ship, *Ōsumi* (LST-4001).[168] With its flat upper deck (the front deck is used as vehicle loading space, the rear deck for helicopter landing) and internal landing platform dock equipped with landing crafts air cushion (LCAC), the *Ōsumi* soon became an iconic symbol of the JMSDF's response to Japan's revitalised international profile.[169] In all, the ASW core pursued throughout the Cold War had empowered the JMSDF with a strong experience that the service exploited in the 1990s to acquire new capabilities and consolidate existing results.

Japanese naval deployments during the first multinational operations of the 1990s and, more crucially, in the Indian Ocean in 2001, represented precious learning opportunities. They exposed weaknesses in JMSDF command and control capabilities and in its cooperation with its sister services.[170] In turn, this process spurred a debate within naval circles on how to reconsider the tactical use of fleet assets.[171] As 'flexibility' made its official appearance in the navy's doctrine, the sophistication of the fleet was critical to its reorganisation, allowing a shift in the basic tactical formation from the Cold War-style '8-8' flotilla to a more versatile Escort Division of four units or, as one influential retired admiral defined it, a 'surface mobile force'.[172] Two escort divisions could still be combined together to obtain the full ASW hunting group, and the restructuring was officially implemented in 2007 (Figure 7.9). In addition, each regional force would have to keep at least one destroyer in a constant high level of readiness (Map 3).[173] Compared to the Cold War, the last decade of the twentieth century and

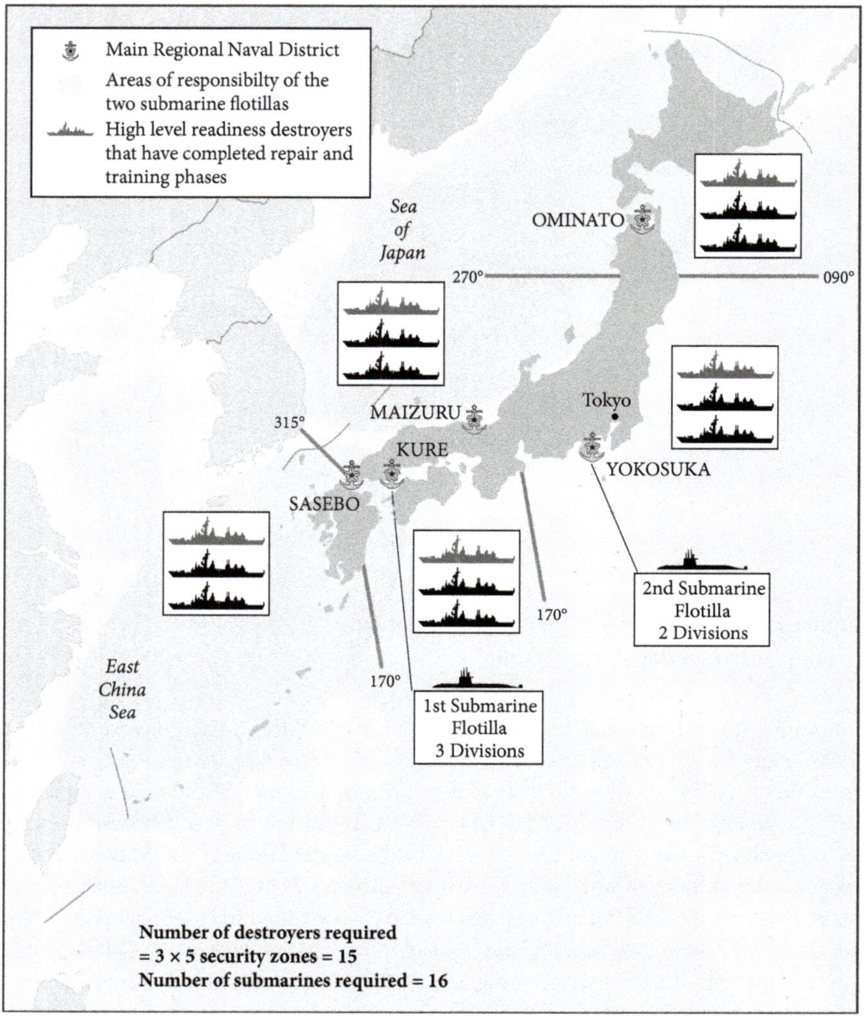

Map 3 Surface fleet structure (2004). Adapted from Japan Ministry of Defence (JMoD), *Defence of Japan* (Tokyo: JMoD, 2013), 124.

the first decade of the new one witnessed an expansion of the JSDF's top operational priorities. They included homeland defence, localised sea control and some measure of expeditionary activities.[174] A flexible force structure and advanced capabilities seemed to remain at the heart of the navy's basic response.

Conclusions

The experience of the war and the initial debates on the organisational aspects of the rearmament set in motion a process that saw the emergence of a navy that was different in doctrine, structure and capabilities from its imperial forerunner. Yet, the professional grammar that underscored the emergence of the Imperial Navy as a highly skilled force manning effective platforms was regarded as ideal to quickly re-establish the new naval professional core. The pre-war assertive seizing of sea control by means of offensive operations was replaced by sea denial missions first, and localised sea control later. The fleet conformed to a defensive strategy but was conceived to employ reactive and aggressive anti-submarine tactics. As a result, operational concepts of imperial origin enabled the JMSDF to build a modern, homogeneous fleet that could cover the full spectrum of its operational undertaking.

The establishment of a unified chain of command that clearly subordinated the fleet to the planning and strategy departments of the navy further helped keeping the development of the fleet and doctrine firmly connected to naval policy. In particular, the informal system of doctrine adopted by the JMSDF promoted broader intellectual ownership within its top brass, along with constant exchanges on the adjustments necessary to pursue relevant capabilities. On the other hand, this doctrinal process, while consolidating the JMSDF's inner cohesiveness, also prompted the service to maintain closer ties with the US Navy, its primary professional partner, than with its sister services.

The extent to which the JMSDF mastered past experience, internalised the legacy of imperial practices and concepts, and developed the ability to renovate policy and doctrine is evident in the measures taken in the 1990s and early 2000s. As Japan's international profile expanded, the service re-evaluated previous preliminary studies in pursuit of new capabilities to increase its strategic lift. The *Ōsumi* class of landing ships was a carefully tailored solution, a prime organisational example of rapid technical and doctrinal response in compliance with shifting national security and foreign agendas. As the JMSDF procured these new capabilities, scholars speculated whether the acquisition of these platforms demonstrated the Japanese willingness to move beyond constitutional precepts in procuring power projection capabilities. In reality, this was not the case. They were an expression of the navy's ambition to give its fleet wider operational 'flexibility', not a move to undermine the foundations of a longstanding strategic posture and doctrinal grammar.

The development of doctrine, fleet and capabilities followed a pattern consistent with other areas of professional significance. While the result was not a 'smaller' Imperial Navy, the imperial legacy offered the JMSDF a pathway to facilitate its evolution into a mature professional force, one that came to see its purpose as an integral part of a national strategy aimed at defending the country's vital economic interests. By endorsing them at the doctrinal level, the JMSDF found the professional principles upon which it developed its will to fight, its readiness and its ability to exercise degrees of sea control. By employing them to develop its capabilities, it created a refined fleet, a reminder on the high seas of the Japanese way of naval warfare

8

Conclusions: The Past and the Future

> *The point is not about how you name the services. I don't like framing the problem in this way. I simply believe that we should instil a military soul into JSDF. So, it's a question of legal status related to the substance of the military institution. We should understand that even if they are called JSDF, ethically and morally we have our personnel understand that they are part of a military institution.*
>
> *I think in the JMSDF we are succeeding in instilling the fighting spirit, the ethics of the imperial navy in our young officers. … When we dispatched the minesweepers to the Gulf ten years ago, the commanders assigned to the squadron together with the chief of the mission, visited Yasukuni, naturally thinking to go and visit the ancestors who devoted their lives to the country. They wanted to talk to them spiritually. This is very natural. This is part of the military spirit.*[1]
>
> Vice Admiral Kaneda Hideaki, JMSDF
> (Commander, Fleet Escort Force, 1998–99)

Outside the context of this book, officers visiting the *Yasukuni* shrine before an important mission overseas to 'talk' to their ancestors 'spiritually' would be cause for concern. For those officers, the visit had a clear aim, but not one designed to make a political statement about the past. Their visit was part of a complex set of traditions and practices aimed at instilling 'a military soul' in the JMSDF to nurture its 'fighting spirit'. Like in any military organisation, those members of the JMSDF were mentally preparing themselves for the stress of an operation. In the literature, depictions of the post-war military presented its members as highly specialised technicians flying air tankers, building bridges, sailing across the archipelago and performing ritualised ceremonies. For them, the past is credited as either a burden, an inconvenient relic of a bygone era daunting today's practices, or else viewed as something of an old uniform preserved with nostalgic affection waiting to be worn to revive a glorious past.

This book's findings demonstrate that these interpretations are the real relics. The history of a military organisation is always controversial for its deals with the terrible drama of war; its preparation and conduct; its human and material costs. In the case of Japan, the mistaken assumption in the literature was that the rejection of the imperial military experience *tout court* was the only way for the post-war JSDF to develop as a professional military force and not to repeat the mistakes of the past. This assumption was tested on a small pool of soldiers over a limited series of interactions and the results were subsequently generalised to the entire military apparatus. The key issue of how post-war military hierarchies and leadership took on the challenge of preparing the JSDF to meet the requirements of national defence remained unaddressed. Similarly important, functional and historical differences among the different branches of the Japanese post-war military remained unaddressed.

This book took a different path. It mobilised previously unavailable documents and combined them with other sources gathered throughout an extended period of time to penetrate the functioning of the JSDF as a military organisation. Its key objective was to understand precisely what the literature had left unaddressed. It focused on the JMSDF to explore how this central component of the Japanese military apparatus reviewed and mobilised the past to understand and articulate its role in Japanese security. The narrative emerging from the pages of this book explains why history is indeed central to the JMSDF's identity. For the JMSDF, a dialogue with the imperial past was essential to rebuild its professional standing, both technically and in terms of ethos. This was a very selective interaction, aimed at addressing core professional issues. The Imperial Navy offered a battle-tested model of seamanship with both operational successes and failures. Thus, the rebuilding of the navy was never about rejecting the past; it was about how its leadership engaged with it. Understanding what enabled success and caused defeat and what was needed to reproduce success contributed to the making of the new navy.

History and the making of the Japanese navy

Two main reasons explain why the post-war navy looked at the past to meet the challenge of the present and one factor underwrites how the navy managed to do so. The first reason pertains to the military nature of the organisation itself. Rebuilding a 'fighting spirit' in the aftermath of complete defeat and under different social and political normative frameworks represented a primary concern for the forerunners of the new organisation. The navy's *esprit de corps* had indeed to be forged within these frameworks, but its leadership still needed to guarantee the cohesiveness and commitment of naval personnel. The navy needed a 'soul' to inspire its personnel, and imperial naval traditions and experience were the primary tools used by the JMSDF to achieve this aim. The new navy considered itself since its inception as a fighting organisation – regardless of its size and normative restrictions. New norms defined the boundaries of the use of force, not the navy's responsibility to have personnel adequate to the task to manage it.

Tactically and operationally, the navy had to instil in its members the will to fight and if necessary, to put their lives at risk to fulfil the task of naval defence. To that end, imperial traditions were instrumental to enhance the navy's pride, morale and corporate spirit. The series of practices, procedures, values and norms which held the keys to the Imperial Navy's staggering success in battle were believed to possess an enduring inspiring value. Ship names, vocabulary and onboard practices all contributed to create in the self-contained environments of a naval unit a microcosm of values and principles meant to instil in sailors and officers the same will to fight possessed by those who had worn the Imperial Navy uniform. In this process, the JMSDF handpicked those elements of the imperial past that had defined the emergence of the Imperial Navy in the Meiji and Taishō eras as a way to inspire the necessary sense of commitment to the pursuit of excellence and operational success. The JMSDF had not been alone in doing that. In fact, the Meiji reformers had originally endeavoured to put in place a similar process when they established the Imperial Navy. The traditions they introduced drew upon Japan's martial and seafaring heritage to create a cohesive national naval force that had no real precedent in the country's history. In turn, the JMSDF referred to the pre-war Imperial Navy to constitute its own fighting spirit.

The second reason for the JMSDF to mobilise the past is strictly connected to the first. The Imperial Navy was not only a source of inspiration to foster fighting spirit. It also represented a valid professional model. The JMSDF drew upon the practices underwriting the pre-war experience to make officers and crews socialise with the type of discipline, teamwork and leadership needed to carry out the new navy's missions. The Imperial Navy's emphasis on seamanship achieved by means of training in a week without rest became a trademark of the JMSDF approach to the naval profession too. Indeed, this contributes to explain why, over the decades, training activities sought to push the boundaries of the safety envelope with occasional accidents occurring between naval vessels and civilian shipping.[2] In terms of leadership, the JMSDF followed the imperial forerunner's pathway, emphasising personal initiative within the navy's values, directives and priorities to favour group cohesiveness. At the tactical level, this was particularly important because a ship needs to remain a single fighting unit, with the captain as its ultimate source of authority. At the operational level, this allowed the JMSDF to be sure that all its captains would act according to the navy's values and procedures. Overall, this understanding of leadership did not depart from those of other modern navies, but the reference to the Imperial Navy had the additional advantage of presenting these notions in the context of continuity with a 'national tradition'.[3]

This, in turn, favoured the JMSDF's need to contextualise past practices in the face of different requirements. The JMSDF was not merely emulating its imperial forerunner. On the contrary, under clear political guidance, structural reforms were introduced in the fields of education and military instruction to address issues related to the elitist imperial character of the pre-war officer corps, its tendency to hold a narrow vision of the military profession, and the profound lack of inter-service dialogue. In naval matters, the JMSDF looked at the best navies of the day to develop answers relevant to its own circumstances. The US Navy offered one such opportunity for improvement. The first generation of JMSDF leaders studied the American higher military education system and adopted some of its solutions to shape the curricula of its own institutions for naval instruction. Concurrently, it made use of American advanced technological know-how to reconstitute and modernise its fleet. In this respect, the Japanese case supports the idea that emulation of foreign militaries is an important driver in military and professional innovation. The specificity of the JMSDF rests on the fact that the imperial legacy operated as a filter to the service's interpretation of how to implement a foreign model and also as a justification for its adoption. Imperial traditions provided the framework through which foreign practices and technology were made relevant to the JMSDF's educational and operational requirements.

Indeed, the imperial experience offered a pathway to justify the introduction of foreign know-how. The *yōsai* formula of imperial flavour helped the JMSDF legitimise the emulation of a successful foreign model and to transform this process into a tool to enhance the 'Japanese' character of the navy. This was a 'traditional' path consistent with previous experience, followed in developing the navy of the second half of the nineteenth century, the navy of the successes in the wars against China and Russia. Thus, for both the Imperial Navy and the JMSDF, foreign technologies and know-how were a necessity of circumstances; for the JMSDF, the existence of previous experience in this context helped to create a perception that eventually transformed a structural weakness into a distinctive organisational trait. The origins of the model or of the specific pieces of military hardware were not of key importance. What mattered was that both Japanese navies were capable of understanding what pieces of hardware and what parts of a foreign educational system would enable them to pursue their goal of a highly sophisticated, smartly manned and well-educated naval force. This was what distinguished the 'Japanese' navy from other organisations inside and outside Japan.

The emergence early in the post-war era of narratives that allowed the new navy to review the imperial experience and embrace its tenets accounts for the fact that it could do so. Public narratives of the Imperial Navy appeared as early as the public and official investigation of the wartime responsibilities themselves. In the widely acknowledged controversial nature of war-related memories, representations of the navy created a stark contrast against Japan's imperial armed services. They emphasised its traditional and modern character, its role as a constraining force against the warmongering impetus of the army, its ability to win wars that balanced political aims and strategic realities and its inability to do so in a war it could not stop. Itō's work as a journalist and Agawa's novels offered convincing narratives that paved the way for the JMSDF to show the existence of an institutional and cultural bond between Japan's two navies. Retired imperial naval officers were never directly involved in the shaping of these narratives, but they actively nurtured ties with individuals like Itō and Agawa that could reinforce an image relevant to their agenda. Moreover, the choice of Agawa's son, Naoyuki, to centre the plot of his novel on two key leaders of the first generation of the JMSDF (both veterans from the Imperial Navy) played to the strengths of this notion of the professional tie between the two organisations. In the midst of growing public attention to the JSDF during the 1990s, Agawa's novel pointed to the relationship between pre- and post-war services as key to the JMSDF's skills.

This was a notion fully embraced by the JMSDF and used by the service as a guiding principle for its self-representation strategies. The network connecting intellectuals and naval aficionados to key naval figures gave the latter an awareness of the complexity of presenting the navy to the public, even in a context where positive images of the past had not been dismissed. Thus, at the beginning, the JMSDF concentrated on *ad hoc* public initiatives like fleet reviews and short cruises which allowed the service 'safe environments' to promote an image that focused on technical characteristics. These public relations activities celebrated professionalism and technical knowledge as much as the positive legacy of the Imperial Navy. In the confined spaces of a warship, or a naval base, the JMSDF could tailor its message to match perceived images that distinguished the Japanese navy: the embodiment of Japan's success in embracing modernisation and transforming a core institution of state – the navy – without losing its 'traditional' self.

The initial decades of initiatives that pre-eminently sought to nurture a 'naval audience' represented an important platform for the increase in public attention of the 1990s and early 2000s. In a changing domestic environment, the JMSDF's longstanding choice to advertise its ties with the Imperial Navy gave it an edge in pitching for the confidence of the Japanese people as a whole. Against a more dynamic and uncertain regional security background, the controversial memories of Japan's aggressive war waged in Asia (further amplified by the 1995 fifty-year commemoration of the end of the Pacific War) made it impossible for the JGSDF to build on the martial spirit and tradition of the Imperial Army to validate its professionalism. For the JASDF, the non-existence of an independent pre-war air force with a battle-hardened tradition (like that of the Royal Air Force in the UK) created a similar problem. Instead, the JMSDF's ability to shield Japan from missile threats or foreign incursions rested on a professional confidence of imperial roots. Accordingly, the JMSDF shifted the focus of its public relations campaigns onto its human fabric; the personnel, their motivation, their skills, all drawing on a longstanding imperial tradition.

It should come as no surprise, therefore, that in 2004, when Japan's national broadcasting television service published the results of its first large-scale documentary project to investigate the origins of the JSDF – partly in response to a growing quest for public information on the identity of the Japanese military – the project focused on the origins of the JMSDF. By then, the JMSDF had already been deployed in the Indian Ocean for almost three years, performing a refuelling mission in support of the US efforts in Afghanistan. The Japanese navy was, in the public sphere, the country's 'senior service', the one that drew upon a strong military tradition to meet Japan's evolving security landscape.

Becoming the 'senior service': Japanese sea power as a national strategy

This leads to the broader argument set forth in this book. The imperial experience not only helped to shape post-war naval identity; it informed the way the navy reviewed its role in national security and argued its case for it. In this sphere, it was not merely the experience of the navy of the Meiji and Taishō eras that informed the relationship with the imperial past. Rather, the Imperial Navy's combat experience as a whole, especially the question of the failures at operational and strategic levels in the last war, became the main focus of the JMSDF's interaction with the past. For the JMSDF, understanding past failures was an essential step in the process of developing policy and strategy.

In terms of naval policy, the study of the actions of the Imperial Navy's foremost strategists across its entire combat history provided (and still provides) the raw materials for reflecting upon how to connect service priorities to national strategy. The examination of the past was instrumental in exposing the catastrophic consequences of the excessive emphasis in the 1930s and early 1940s on the technical preparation for a decisive battle. In particular, the JMSDF sought guidance to widen the 'intellectual horizons' of its key officers, and to discipline them to think in terms of 'maritime' rather than 'naval' strategy. A narrow approach focusing on tactical issues had as a main risk the prioritisation of procurement programmes that benefited the service but did not necessarily prepare the navy to address broader security issues. As a retired JMSDF strategic planner remarked, this was a concern that distinguished the approach of the JMSDF's Operations and Plans Department from the beginning.[4] In operations in the Pacific before 1945, the preparation for a decisive battle with the United States led to a lack of coordination between naval policies and national strategy that proved to be fatal.

How so? Corbett observed that one of the characteristics of naval warfare is that 'over and above the duty of winning battles, fleets are charged with the duty of protecting commerce', because 'financial vigour in war' is vital. To that end, 'the maintenance of the flow of trade has been felt as a paramount consideration'.[5] This was a lesson the JMSDF treasured as it reviewed the imperial wartime experience. The example of Commander Senō's research into Admiral Inoue's unorthodox ideas is a case of the JMSDF contextualising the past to present its contribution to defence policy. The fleet was not simply a tool of war; it contributed to the safety of the wider sea-based economic interests of post-war Japan. The perception of sea lane defence as a strategic imperative in Japanese maritime thinking depended on the JMSDF's full appreciation of the vulnerabilities of Japan's geography. Post-war Japanese economic power rested on maritime trade, and on the archipelago's ability to access primary resources essential to its survival. The JMSDF made sure that its policies and strategic outlook matched this maritime vision. Above all, the JMSDF connected Japan's maritime strategy to the management of the US–Japan alliance. By committing to sea lane defence in the Sea of Japan and the East China Sea, the JMSDF sought to place the navy at the heart of national defence and at the forefront of the alliance requirement to contain the Soviet Union.

In the post-Cold War era, the reliance of the Japanese economy on trade and commerce remained unaltered, as did the political perception of its importance to defence policy. Indeed, the changing strategic environment in East Asia, and the increasingly unstable international arena, did much to reinforce the notion that a maritime-centric defence posture was central to national security. In 1995, access to the maritime arteries transporting the country's resources and trade was restated as a strategic imperative. Concurrently, the JMSDF quickly procured a minimum of strategic lifting capabilities to complement its ASW core and provide the country's foreign policy with the option of joining international efforts in peacekeeping. A decade later, the stability of the countries along 'the SLOCs that run from the Persian Gulf, the Indian Ocean, the Strait of Malacca, the South China Sea, the Bashi Channel, and the east coast of Taiwan' defined the geographic space of Japan's security priorities.[6] By then, Japanese security planners recognised the importance of Japanese contribution to international security, especially in the post-9/11 context. The arc linking the Persian Gulf to the Strait of Taiwan underwrote the prioritisation of national contributions. In 2013, the new NDPG came full circle by paraphrasing Kōsaka's prose to define Japan as 'a maritime state', 'dependent largely on international trade for its supply of food and natural resources'. In the document, 'securing the safety of maritime and air traffic, through strengthening an "Open and Stable Seas" order based upon such fundamental principles as the rule of law and the freedom of navigation', was restated as essential to the country's peace and prosperity.[7]

In this context, defence planners faced the task of increasing the operational flexibility and overall responsiveness of the country's military power to address changes in the security landscape and more constrained budgetary trends. In 2010, the Ministry of Defence adopted a new 'basic concept' for the defence build-up, one that aimed to maintain a 'dynamic' defence force to increase the 'readiness, mobility, flexibility, sustainability, and versatility' of the armed forces.[8] Regionally, the new posture served a geographic shift in the operational focus from the northeast to the southwest part of the archipelago.[9] The emphasis on mobility and readiness, in particular, reflected the genuine logistical requirements to defend the offshore islands in the East China Sea.[10] In that context, Japan had to pursue a 'dynamic deterrence' posture to deny any potential competitor the opportunity to pursue 'fait accompli situations' and 'probing activities' that would endanger the security and integrity of the archipelago. Enhanced readiness and versatility were especially critical to the conduct of intelligence, surveillance and reconnaissance (ISR) activities to avoid 'geographical' and 'time' gaps in the operational posture.[11]

Beyond the confines of Northeast Asia, military diplomacy was becoming an increasing feature of defence policy aimed at reinforcing diplomacy, creating, consolidating and expanding partnerships, as well as promoting international stability. By 2013, the peacetime uses of the JSDF were fully articulated to be part of a 'multi-layered' approach to security to 'ensure the stability of the Asia-Pacific region'.[12] Military exercises, official visits and personnel exchanges were to be enlisted to strengthen ties with key strategic partners like the Republic of Korea and Australia – in addition to the United States. They also sought to promote basic trust and confidence building with regional powers like China and Russia, to explore new relationships in Southeast Asia and with India, and to engage with organisations and countries with major interests in the stability of the oceans and freedom of navigation like the United Kingdom and NATO.[13]

Thus, the navy's response sought to match the evolving requirements of Japanese security. In November 2008, Rear Admiral Takei Tomohisa, then director of the Operations and Planning Department at the MSO, authored what became known as the JMSDF 'new' maritime strategy.[14] In the introduction to the document, Admiral Takei followed his predecessors' footsteps in reaffirming that the very essence of the Japanese navy rested on the premise that the country's 'national survival relies on unimpeded economic activities via sea-lanes of communication'.[15] Accordingly, the navy had endeavoured during the Cold War to prepare itself to protect the sea-lanes in case of an emergency. In the post-9/11 era, the main difference from the past was that 'the freedom of the seas remained a priority during peacetime', and 'it was time for the JMSDF to expand its participation to peacetime activities' and to develop a strategy accordingly.[16] In his view, the navy had to change its approach to sea lane defence. It had to deploy its full versatility to 'provide a wide range of options to achieve national objectives', in peace and war; alone, together with the United States, and with other like-minded partners.[17]

The new strategy proposed a conceptual shift in the understanding of sea lanes. These were no longer to be regarded as 'routes' to protect in case of emergency. They were constructed as part of four wider 'areas' of passage of shipping bound to and from Japan. The specific nature of the potential threats to each one of them (Northeast Asia, Southeast Asia, South Asia and the Middle East) and the available resources to tackle them defined JMSDF activities.[18] Northeast Asia was the neuralgic centre of Japanese maritime operations for three reasons. Within the triangle of Tokyo–Guam–Taiwan (TGT), the defence of sea lanes overlapped with that of the Japanese home waters and included a set of disputed maritime, territorial and potentially resource-rich spaces. The defence of the TGT area was similarly crucial to the ability of the United States to

Map 4 Post-Cold War strategy.

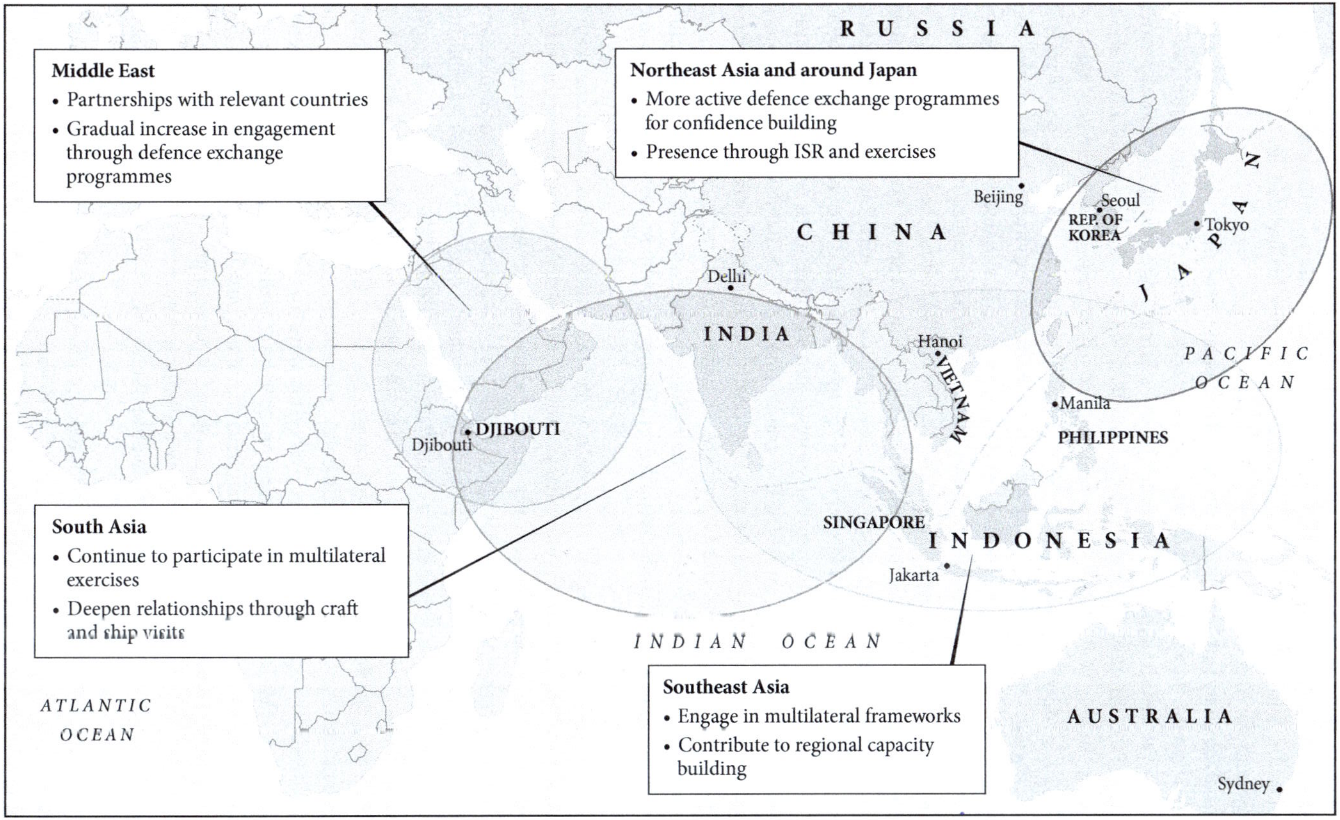

Map 5 Sea lanes as strategic areas. Adapted from Rear Admiral Tomohisa Takei, JMSDF, 'Kaiyō Shinkindai ni okeru Kaijojieitai' (海洋新近代における海上自衛隊 – The JMSDF in the new maritime era), *Hatō* 波涛, 2008:11, 2–29.

project military power in East Asia. In particular, the restructuring of the American military presence in the Korean peninsula and Japan increased the strategic value of Okinawa and Guam as staging platforms for US interventions in the event of a crisis. As such, for Admiral Takei, 'the TGT area was a major bridgehead for U.S. military deployments in East Asia' (Map 4).[19]

The document put a premium on an active naval presence as the JMSDF primary contribution to national security and alliance requirements. It defined the JMSDF peacetime activities as part of a 'commitment strategy', one designed to achieve two objectives: to maintain maritime stability and to deter attacks, seeking to 'win without fighting'.[20] In the TGT area, ISR capabilities and coordination with civilian agencies like the JCG were targeted to help the navy deliver the timely 'detection of missile attacks, incidents of terrorism, and suspicious maritime activities'.[21] To maximise this 'outwardly visible presence', the ISR effort was to be coordinated with the US Navy. Defence exchanges, capacity building, multilateral exercises, port calls and international relief missions all contributed to complete the JMSDF's toolkit.[22] In Southeast Asia, the navy was to help in building strategic partnerships – by means of exercises, exchanges, and capacity building – especially with key partners like Australia. In more distant areas, cooperation with NATO countries in operations like Active Endeavour, or to fight Somali piracy, as well as regular visits to and exercises with countries like India were to be at the forefront of the JMSDF commitment.[23] In Northeast Asia, this multi-layered set of peacetime activities was also central to managing crucial relationships with potential competitors like China. The commitment strategy combined a 'power cancellation' capacity of Chinese naval ambitions in the East China Sea with genuine efforts to enhance mutual understanding and interactions by means of exchanges and visits (Map 5).[24]

In case of aggression against Japanese territorial waters and/or maritime traffic, the JMSDF would rely on a 'contingency strategy'. In spaces closer to the archipelago, the document regarded conflict over maritime interests or territorial sovereignty as possible scenarios, suggesting that the JMSDF take advantage of the peacetime early warning and detection systems for a swift response, concentrating its capabilities on intercepting and anticipating enemy actions. 'The JMSDF must maintain its own strategic defence through its own initiative,' and sea control and straits defence in the TGT area implemented by means of strong ASW, C4ISR (Command, Control, Communications, Computers, Intelligence, Surveillance and Reconnaissance), and at-sea logistical support capabilities were the ways to achieve it.[25] In emergency situations, the JMSDF considered its responses to be coordinated with the US Navy, but it also assumed that it had to be self-sufficient in scenarios (like small scale incursions against remote islands) that would not necessarily prompt an American intervention. This partnership was nonetheless to play a similarly significant role in other security areas, where a threat to maritime trade would likely witness an American involvement or a multinational effort.[26]

By the time the 2010 NDPG was adopted, therefore, the JMSDF had a new strategy in place. This strategy was the result of a debate that evolved as naval missions expanded. Within and outside the naval planning circles, different visions for a future strategy took shape, each building upon different approaches to the navy's military and non-military roles. When Admiral Takei's new vision emerged, its content formalised existing trends in defence policy about the peacetime uses of the armed forces and offered a vision that did not discard the centrality of sea lane defence. On the contrary, the security of shipping lanes enabled the JMSDF to organise the geographic radius of its operational reach and allocate its resources. This strategy was the response of a professional organisation that operated within given boundaries, set by normative restraints and capabilities. In the new strategy, the Imperial Navy's experience was no longer referenced in a direct fashion; yet, its legacy was firmly in the background. It underwrote the principles of the navy's strategic thinking as well as the attention of its senior planners in developing their ideas connecting sea power to national strategy. Corbett wrote that the strategic purpose of a fleet included 'the protection or destruction of commerce', and the 'prevention or securing of alliances'.[27] In that sense, the JMSDF had become Japan's senior service.

Taking the Imperial Naval experience forward: A different navy altogether

The engagement with past imperial naval practices, procedures and strategic thinking, was instrumental for the JMSDF to develop on its own terms. Doctrine, fleet structure and capabilities procurement were the areas where taking the legacy of the Imperial Navy forward brought about the most important differences. The examination in this book of new and previously unavailable documentation pertaining to the development of Japanese naval doctrine and force structure allowed this point to be articulated with unprecedented depth.

In the realm of doctrine, the operational concepts of readiness and prowess, or fighting power, allowed the JMSDF's leadership to set the aspiration of reaching high professional standards and to justify it as part of a process of continuity with the past. The JMSDF simply needed to aim high to match past performance. Conceptually, fighting power and readiness also offered an advantage that suited the different circumstances of post-war naval defence. Constitutional precepts ensured that an offensive strategy to secure command of the sea by means of the annihilation of the opposing fleet was outside the scope of Japanese defence policy. Indeed, until the mid-1970s, Cold War strategy focused on denying the Soviet Pacific fleet based in Vladivostok the chance to threaten Japanese waters. Geography worked to Japan's advantage since the patrolling of the three main straits enabled the navy to bottle up Soviet naval assets.

Yet, by the time the NDPO was adopted in 1976, this strategy was complemented by one aimed at establishing limited sea control to defend trade and shipping in the East China Sea. The core means to achieve this was the ASW hunting group, based on the '8-8' flotilla concept, tasked with the interception of opposing units escaping the surface, underwater and air patrolling net around Japanese straits This posture was operationally defensive, but tactically offensive in that it pro-actively engaged in ASW operations against the enemy. In wartime, convoy escorts based on the same hunting group entailed a tactically defensive posture, the actual defence of merchant vessels, within an overall operationally offensive approach. In the words of the British maritime doctrine, convoys were functional to draw the enemy into an ASW net, forcing units to fight 'in circumstances of one's own choosing'.[28] By the end of the 1970s, fighting power and readiness served a fleet that, like its imperial forerunner, was set to hunt the enemy. This time, however, the aim was the defence of shipping, not just the opposing fleet.

An effective, capable, mobile force at a high level of readiness was instrumental to the navy's ambitions to perform its given combat functions. Doctrinal precepts of imperial flavour were also needed to instil in Japanese crews and officers an aggressive spirit to approach and conduct operations. For the navy, the harsh conditions of life at sea – and war at sea – commanded the need of a highly motivated force, especially one with the aim of performing effective ASW operations. Such an attitude was nonetheless cultivated within the wider context of a different military ethos, one imbued with the democratic values introduced by post-war reformers. The JMSDF was motivated by the commitment to perform its duties to the best of its capabilities, not by the rhetoric of past militarism. In this respect, Japanese choices seem consistent with other naval traditions that sought to train crews to maintain the necessary levels of readiness to perform offensive ASW operations. British maritime doctrine, for example, offers a clear explanation underpinning this argument:

> It has always been highly desirable, and usually essential for victory, that the commander and his subordinates should be endowed with an offensive (or aggressive) mentality: a determination to win whatever the difficulties, a trait in ample evidence in the characters of all the great commanders through history.[29]

By the end of the Cold War, Japanese naval doctrine was evolving together with the rest of the defence posture. The delivery of the operational concepts, especially the enduring presence of fighting power and readiness, continued to offer a sense of continuity in the overall doctrinal context. The concepts themselves, on the other hand, evolved. In particular, fighting power – prowess – evolved in two respects. First, from 1989 onwards, different chiefs of staff made the point that 'real' fighting power was to be measured by the innovative character of the JMSDF leadership. As Admiral Sakuma originally put it, 'When you govern, don't forget to revolt.'[30] A second variation on the notion of fighting power was introduced in 2010. Admiral Sugimoto explained that the key issue for the future of the navy was no longer to merely thinking about how to achieve elevated professional standards and a capable force. For the JMSDF, enhancing fighting power was to be no longer just about material and moral components. It had to focus on how to achieve improvements by striking the appropriate balance among capabilities, martial ethos, and technical knowledge.[31]

In 2003, the introduction of the operational concept 'flexibility' became the primary expression of the JMSDF's ability to take the original imperial tradition forward. The method of delivery and the context – that of the *New Instructions* – were consistent with past practices that could draw their roots from the Imperial Navy. Innovation within the tradition inherited from the Imperial Navy mattered. The concept itself set the JMSDF in the same professional league as the world's top navies, pointing out the navy's need to operationally and tactically increase its flexibility.[32] In March 2008, the then Chief of Staff Admiral Akahoshi Keiji used this notion to contextualise a series of major adjustments that were planned to be enacted a few days after his appointment. The JMSDF was to introduce an upgrade to its software systems, to perform the restructuring of its basic tactical formations and distribution of assets and to commission the first of a new set of multipurpose platforms – the new helicopter destroyer *JDS Hyuga* (DDH 181). This was Japan's first post-war multipurpose through-deck asset designed for missions encompassing ASW, missile defence and Humanitarian Assistance and Disaster Relief (HADR).[33] Two years later, his successor, Admiral Sugimoto, further added that, as an operational concept, 'flexibility' was to underpin the approach to the design of future capabilities. Naval personnel operated in the sky, at sea, and beneath its surface. Yet, only the changes that were currently implemented could guarantee the JMSDF's ability to perform a variety of combat and non-combat missions, alone and with other services, in national and multinational contexts, in the region and beyond it.[34] To achieve these goals, the concepts of 'flexibility', 'fighting power', and 'readiness' were adapting to preserve their function as guiding principles. Far from being forgotten or a viewed as a burden, in the realm of doctrine, history was providing a sense of evolution and continuity to structural and operational changes.

Similar considerations apply to the evolution of fleet structure and capabilities. Throughout the Cold War, the combination of historical circumstances concerning the origins of the JMSDF and the review of the pre-war and wartime experiences were essential to identify the most suitable fleet composition and command structure. At the ship design level, the maximisation of firepower and the harmonisation of speed guided procurement policies. The continuity in the nature of the Cold War missions allowed the navy to employ this logic to expand and improve. The professional understanding developed throughout this period was crucial to review fleet structure and capabilities in the post-Cold War environment. Indeed, in the first decade of the new century, the most significant change to the fleet occurred in its structure. The JMSDF introduced more systematic training cycles to increase readiness and streamlined the command structure for the formation of task forces. A smaller and more versatile Escort Division of four units replaced the original tactical formation based on the '8-8' concept. A similar logic led the navy to restructure the distribution of assets among the different naval districts, where the aim was to have at least one destroyer constantly available for the monitoring and defence of Japanese home waters.[35] With the confirmation in the 2010 NDPG of the ever-increasing requirement for more units to conduct surveillance and patrol in the East China Sea or to contribute to the rotational duties in international missions, the five regional divisions were eliminated altogether. These were replaced by an 'Escort Ship Squadron' including four 'Escort Corps' of four destroyers each, with up to two of them (for a total of eight vessels) on a high level of availability for duties within and beyond Japanese home waters (Map 6).[36]

The fleet restructuring was not an isolated change in the context of improving the fleet's effectiveness. In a step that had no precedent in the pre-war era (in part because no other institution with maritime defence responsibilities existed then), steps were taken to enhance cooperation with the JCG. In 2001, in the wake of the North Korean spy boat incidents off southwest Kyushu, the Coast Guard Law and the Self-Defence Force Law were amended to allow the creation of a liaison system for the sharing of

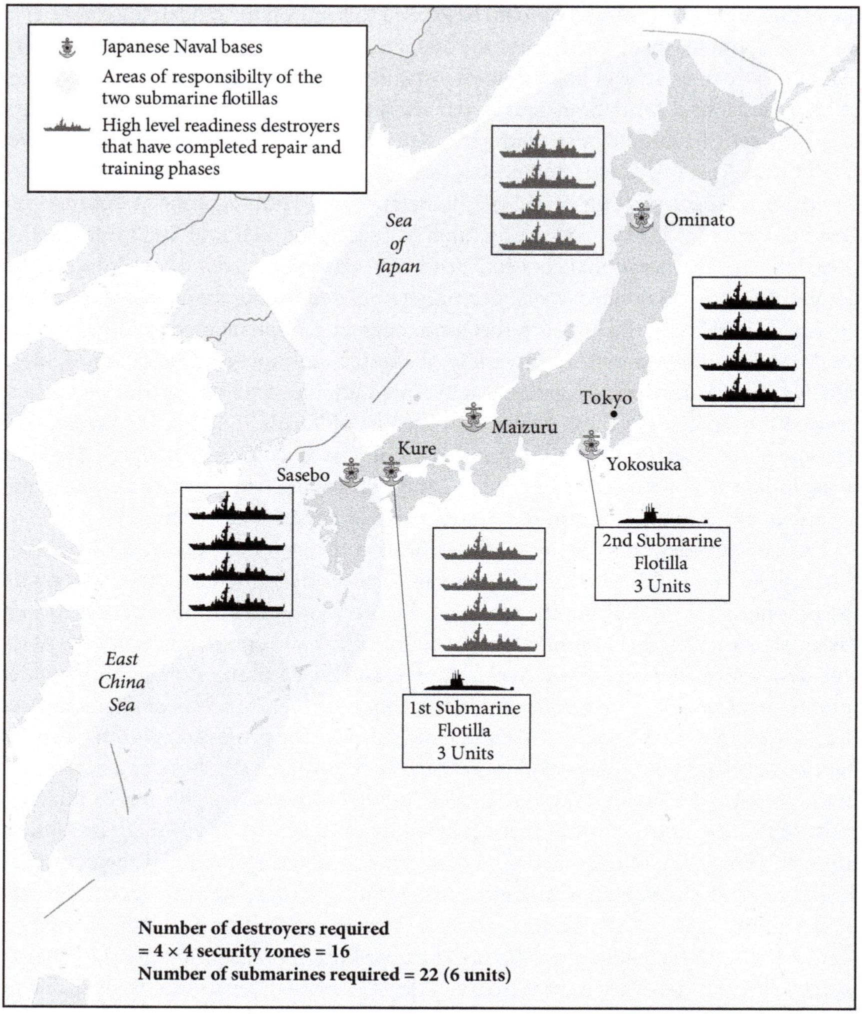

Map 6 Surface fleet structure (2010). Adapted from Japan Ministry of Defence (JMoD), *Defence of Japan* (Tokyo: JMoD, 2013), 124.

information between the JCG and JMSDF. New provisions were created to empower navy commanders with the authority to use weapons in maritime security operations if deemed necessary; the use of advanced photo transmission equipment, flat-nosed shells, high performance 20 mm machine guns and a navy special boarding unit was established.[37] A manual on joint strategies was also developed to determine the division of roles between the two organisations, and joint training and exercises were regularly held to refine procedures for the pursuit and capture of unidentified vessels.[38] Maritime security in the Japanese Exclusive Economic Zone (EEZ) and in contested spaces, notably the Sino Japanese maritime border, and the sovereignty of the Senkaku

Islands (known in Chinese as Diaoyu), was a primary factor in the expansion of the JCG. Yet, its constabulary roles remained complementary to those of the JMSDF, requiring different capabilities from those of the JMSDF – a fact highlighted by the JCG hesitation in acquiring decommissioned warships.[39]

By 2011, the decision to acquire a small logistical base in Djibouti to offer continuous support to the P-3Cs deployed for surveillance activities in the context of the anti-piracy mission proved that the JMSDF was no longer walking in the shadow of the operational achievements of its imperial forerunner. By 2014, the decision to dispatch an officer to the command centre of the international task force (CTF 151) to improve coordination between the two Japanese destroyers and other units in the escort activities further reinforced this point. As of the end of May 2014, Japanese units had escorted 3,461 vessels, while by the end of June of the same year the P-3Cs had flown 1,140 missions for a total of 8,820 flying hours and had identified approximately 92,700 ships.[40] The Japanese were fully engaged in managing international security more than the Imperial Navy ever had been.

Looking ahead …

The strong relationship that the JMSDF entertained and continues to entertain with the imperial past too presents challenges for the navy of today. The continuity in the navy's missions throughout the Cold War created an environment that allowed the JMSDF's to devise a career structure favourable to its organisational priorities. The navy could handpick its best officers and develop their skills in naval politics, strategy and management. Similar to the Imperial Navy, the system aimed at possessing a small core of highly trained and talented officers that could work together and promote innovation in a progressive fashion, emphasising consensus rather than confrontation. This form of management served the JMSDF well.

In the post-Cold War era, however, the navy's inner cohesiveness and personnel management have not eliminated risks or prevented misconducts. Concerning the former, the navy's attention to nurturing young, talented officers from the early stages of their career brought about the risk of being unable to 'replace losses', whether they derived from operational activity or from political considerations. For example, in February 2008, a training accident involving a collision between the destroyer *Atago* and a fishing boat resulted in the resignation of the chief of staff and severe penalties for another eighty-seven officers.[41] The incident proved the extent to which the JMSDF's greater operational and political exposure of the past years might have an impact on the service's future capacity to grant continuity at its top levels in moments of crisis. In terms of misconduct, the navy suffered from a series of personnel scandals. In 2000, a lieutenant commander serving at the National Institute for Defence Studies was caught leaking secret information to an intelligence officer at the Russian Embassy. Similarly, in 2007, a naval instructor at the First Service School in Etajima was involved in the unauthorised circulation of sensitive information concerning the AEGIS combat system.[42]

In terms of fleet, the need to balance the procurement of new capabilities to increase strategic lift and ISR while retaining a cutting-edge ASW core against tighter budgets entailed sacrifices in other areas. The JMSDF remained relatively weak in over-the-horizon air defence in the context of operations requiring deployments outside the land-based air cover provided by the Japan Air Self-Defence Force. The *Kongō* and *Atago* classes of AEGIS destroyers as well as the *Hyūga* and *Izumo* classes of helicopter-carrying destroyers all contributed to improve fleet air defence for ASW operations outside the reach of land-based air cover. Yet, this does not mean that the Japanese navy possesses offensive capabilities in a fashion comparable to the wartime striking force of the *Kidō Butai*.[43] The new *Hyūga* and *Izumo* classes overall deliver superior capabilities to their predecessors. They perform ASW and they are suited for conducting amphibious raids in contested spaces in the southwest part of the Japanese archipelago, as well as peacetime activities, including support in disaster relief and humanitarian missions. Yet, these are not small carriers. They are not designed to acquire or maintain air superiority in a hostile environment. In this respect, on the high seas, outside the confines of the Sea of Japan and the East China Sea, the JMSDF can only operate either as an enabler of diplomatic action to build partnerships and assist in humanitarian crises, or as part of wider coalitions. The lack of over-the-horizon air defence prevents the fleet from operating independently in a high-intensity warfare context.

As this book goes to press, a number of political reforms are ongoing in Japan. The strengthening of the joint functions of the command structure, the easing of restrictions on the defence industry sector and the reinterpretation of the boundaries of Japan's participation in multinational activities are some of the major areas of defence policy under scrutiny. The results of these proposed transformations will require time to fully manifest themselves. Japan might very well become a more pro-active contributor to international security: joining international command structures, embedding units in multinational operational activities, as well as entering bilateral and multilateral procurement programmes. One thing, however, is certain. The process that allowed the imperial past to be reviewed to create the current navy, to motivate its crews and personnel and to inspire change and transformation will guide the future too. This book opened in Etajima, with a description of the graduation ceremony that took place in the year this project started. It seems therefore only appropriate to end with a quotation from the welcoming message of the serving Superintendent of the Officer Candidate School as the journey of this book comes to an end. In describing how Etajima seeks today to prepare the next generation of officers, he stresses that the school

> aims to give students an appreciation for the sea as their work place in the future, and to cultivate a sense of seamanship that they will carry out with initiative and autonomy as young officers. It is a student's duty to devote themselves to training and acquiring enduring stamina and unyielding will power.
>
> In addition I believe it is important for JMSDF officers to faithfully follow orders and give their best effort in all that they do. In that regard, all of our instructors and staff strive to improve the quality of education and training based on three Japanese A-words: *Akiramezu* (never give up), *Anadorazu* (don't make light of

> things), and *Azamukazu* (don't deceive people). Although times have changed, we maintain these principles as the essence of our maritime defense so that we may inherit the good tradition of the Imperial Navy.[44]

Regardless of the reforms currently taking place, one factor will remain certain. The dialogue between the past and present will continue. From *Kaigun* to *Kaiji*.

Notes

Conventions

1 Nengō – 年号.

Chapter 1

1 Laughton, 'The Scientific Study of Naval History', 509.
2 Corbett, *Some Principles of Maritime Strategy*, 15.
3 Corbett, 'The Green Pamphlet. War Course. Strategical Terms and Definitions Used in Lectures on Naval History', 307.
4 Barnett, *Navy Strategic Culture: Why the Navy Thinks Differently*, 79.
5 Author's visit to Etajima at the occasion of the graduation ceremony held on 25 February 2005.
6 Daikōdō (大講堂).
7 Akarenga (赤レンガ). The cadets' building is called Akarenga Seitokan (赤レンガ生徒館).
8 The red bricks were produced and shipped from England, specifically for the new Japanese Naval Academy. One source recently suggested that the bricks were in fact manufactured in Japan to English specifications. Smith, *Fist from the Sky. The Biography of Captain Takashige Egusa, IJN*, 244, ft 27.
9 On the subject of Japan's architectural transformation in the Meiji era, cf. Brunton, *Building Japan, 1868-1876*. The academy is today included in the circuit of principal attractions of regional tourism. 'Etajima de Umi no Otoko wo Tazuneru', *Yomiuri Shimbun*, 23 March 2008.
10 Dean, 'Etajima: Hallowed Halls', 116; Bullock, *Etajima: The Dartmouth of Japan*, 42–6. In the 1882 Imperial Rescript, the Emperor metaphorically describes the nature of the bond with the country's armed forces as follows: 'Soldiers, We are your Commander-in-Chief. Therefore We regard you as Our limbs, and you, on your part, will look upon Us as your head.' Quoted in Ōhara, *Teikoku Riku Kaigun no Hikari to Kage*, 22. English language translations of the Imperial Rescript are available as Appendixes to Lory, *Japan's Military Masters. The Army in Japanese Life*, 239–45, and Bullock, *Etajima*, 128–34.
11 Suikōkai (水交会).
12 Kun'iku (訓育).
13 Marder, *Old Friends, New Enemies: The Royal Navy and the Imperial Japanese Navy, Strategic Illusions, 1936-1941*, 276–7.
14 The Commandant of Kure Naval District made specific reference to the intrusion in Japan's territorial waters of a Chinese nuclear-powered submarine that had occurred

the previous November. Author's attendance to the JMSDF's OCS graduation ceremony, Etajima, 25 February 2005. On the incident, see JDA, *Defence of Japan 2005*, 207–8.

15 US Naval Academy, *Reef Points 2004–5 – The Annual Handbook of the Brigade of Midshipmen*, 29. Burke, 'The Art of Command', 24–8.
16 Bōfure (帽触れ).
17 Kibishii (厳しい).
18 Captain Ōtsuka, conversation with the author, 24 February 2005.
19 For a summary of the ceremony, cf. the documentary video: *Kanbu Kōhosei: Etajima no Seishun*.
20 Kaijōjieitai (海上自衛隊).
21 Speller, *Understanding Naval Warfare*, 43. Mahan's core ideas are set forth in his best known work, *The Influence of Sea Power upon History, 1660-1783*. For a comprehensive introduction to his work, cf. Sumida, *Inventing Grand Strategy and Teaching Command: The Classic Works of Alfred Thayer Mahan*.
22 For definitional clarifications on the adjectives 'naval' and 'maritime', see Speller, *Understanding Naval Warfare*, 5–7.
23 Speller, *Understanding Naval Warfare*, 45; also, Lambert, 'Sea Power', 73–87.
24 Gray, *Strategy and History: Essays on Theory and Practice*, 138.
25 Till, 'Introduction: Sea power and the Rise and Fall of Empires', 2.
26 Patalano and Manicom, 'Rising Tides: Seapower and Regional Security in Northeast Asia', 335–44; Till, *Asia's Naval Expansionism: An Arms Race in the Making?*, especially chapter 1; Cole, *Asian Maritime Strategies: Navigating Troubled Waters*, 1–37.
27 For example, Holmes and Yoshihara, *Red Star Over the Pacific: China's Rise and the Challenge to U.S. Maritime Strategy*; Erickson, 'Rising Tide, Dispersing Waves: Opportunities and Challenges for Chinese Seapower Development', 372–402.
28 J. Schencking, *Making Waves. Politics, Propaganda, and the Emergence of the Imperial Japanese Navy, 1868-1922*, 107; Schencking, 'The Politics of Pragmatism and Pageantry: Selling a National Navy at the Elite and Local Level in Japan, 1890-1913', 21–2.
29 Masayuki Tadokoro, 'Why Did Japan Fail to Become the "Britain" of Asia?', 295.
30 Evans and Peattie, *Kaigun. Strategy, Tactics and Technology in the Imperial Japanese Navy, 1887-1941*, xx.
31 Evans and Peattie, *Kaigun*, xix.
32 In January 2007, the Japan Defence Agency (JDA), or Boeichō (防衛庁), became the Japanese Ministry of Defence (JMoD), or Bōeishō (防衛省).
33 JDA, *Defence of Japan 2005*, 186.
34 Graham, *Japan's Sea Lane Security, 1940-2004. A Matter of Life and Death?*, 8–33. Danielle Demetriou, 'Energy Imports Push Japan Trade Deficit to Record High', *The Telegraph*, 27 January 2014.
35 Shinzo Abe, 'Asia's Democratic Security Diamond', *Project Syndicate*, 27 December 2012.
36 Shinzo Abe, 'Message from Prime Minister Shinzo Abe on the Occasion of "Marine Day"', 13 July 2013.
37 Kitaoka, 'The Strategy of the Maritime Nation Japan: From Yukichi Fukuzawa to Shigeru Yoshida', 46–9; Patalano, 'Japan's Maritime Strategy: The Island Nation Model', 82–9; also, Patalano, 'Introduction: Maritime Strategy and national Security in Japan and Britain', 4–8; Yoshihara and Holmes, 'Japanese Maritime Thought: If not Mahan, Who?', 24–6. On the Yoshida Doctrine, Hughes, *Japan's Re-emergence as a*

'Normal' Military Power, 21–31; Samuels, *Securing Japan: Tokyo's Grand Strategy and the Future of East Asia*, 29–37, 43–8, 57–9.

38 Koda, 'Naval Development in Japan', 54.

39 Kaneda, *Ballistic Missile Defence for Japan*, 73–83; Kaneda, 'Japan's national Maritime Doctrines and Capabilities', 119–22.

40 The most interesting example is the first visit exchange between China and Japan. In November 2007, the Chinese missile destroyer *Shenzhen* visited Yokosuka and the visit had a follow-up in June 2008 when the destroyer *Sazanami* went to Zhanjiang, in the South China Sea, where it delivered 300 blankets and 2,600 emergency food items to victims of the May earthquake in the Sichuan province. 'Japanese Ship's arrival Marks Significant Event', *China Daily*, 24 June 2008.

41 Tow, 'Regional Constraints on the Role of Navies', 43; Reeve, 'The Development of Naval Strategy in the Asia-Pacific Region, 1500-2000', 141; Kim, *Naval Strategy in Northeast Asia. Geostrategic Goals, Policies and Prospects*, 186–8, 193–202; Enders, 'Maritime Security in a Future Asia-Pacific', 7–12; Grove, 'Sea Power in the Asia-Pacific Region', 17–33; Yoshihara and Holmes, *Asia Looks Seaward. Power and Maritime Strategy*, 1–16.

42 Till, *Seapower*, 46; NWDC, *Naval Warfare*, iv; DCDC, *British Maritime Doctrine*, v.

43 Kyle Mizokami, 'PLAN Helicopter "Ignored Orders"? Behold, "Face" in Action', *Japan Security Watch*, 27 April 2010.

44 Kaijōjieitai Kanbu Gakkō (海上自衛隊幹部学校).

45 Laughton, *RUSI Journal*, 508–27; Corbett, 'The Teaching of Naval and Military History', 12–24; Lambert, 'Naval History for Strategists: Sir Julian Corbett and the Development of Strategic Education in the Royal Navy, 1900-1914', 35–43; Grove, *Vanguard to Trident: British Naval Policy since the Second World War*; Hattendorf (ed.), *Ubi Sumus? The State of Naval and Maritime History*; Hattendorf (ed.), *Doing Naval History: Essays toward Improvement*.

46 Agawa, *Umi no Yūjō*; NHK Special Selection, *Kaijojieitai wa Kōshite Umareta*; Masuda, *Jieitai no Tanjō*. For a general overview in English, cf. Maeda, *The Hidden Army: The Untold Story of Japan's Military Forces*.

47 Morris, 'Significance of the Military in Post-war Japan', 3–21; Buck, 'The Japanese Self-Defence Forces', 597–613; Humphreys, 'The Japanese Military Tradition', 21–40; Maeda, *The Hidden Army*, 53–62; Yamaguchi, 'Japan: Completing Military Professionalism', 35–46; Arrington, 'Cautious Reconciliation: The Change in Societal-Military Relations in Germany and Japan since the End of the Cold War', 531–54; Frühstück and Ben-Ari, '"Now We Show It All!" Normalisation and the Management of Violence in Japan's Armed Forces', 1–39.

48 Kinoshita, 'Echoes of Militarism in Japan', 244–51; Huntington, *The Soldier and the State*, 125–6.

49 Frühstück and Ben-Ari, *Journal of Japanese Studies*, 6.

50 Frühstück and Ben-Ari, *Journal of Japanese Studies*, 15–18, 27–30; Frühstück, *Uneasy Warriors*, 152.

51 Frühstück, and Ben-Ari, *Journal of Japanese Studies*, 9

52 John W. Dower, 'The Useful War', *Dedalus*, 50.

53 Gluck, 'The Past in the Present', 65.

54 Barnett, *Navy Strategic Culture*, 9.

55 Barnett, *Navy Strategic Culture*, 15.

56 Hobsbawm and Ranger (eds), *The Invention of Tradition*, 1.

57 Connell and Mack, *Naval Ceremonies, Customs, and Traditions*, 7.

58 Connell and Mack, *Naval Ceremonies, Customs, and Traditions*, 22–42; Speller, *Understanding Naval Warfare*, 16–18, 23–8.
59 Connell and Mack, *Naval Ceremonies, Customs, and Traditions*, 4.
60 Connell and Mack, *Naval Ceremonies, Customs, and Traditions*, 4–5.
61 Guillain, 'The Resurgence of Military Elements in Japan', 211–25; Morris, *Nationalism and the Right Wing in Japan: A Study of Post-War Trends*, 206–65; Searaphim, *War Memory and Social Politics in Japan*, 60–85, Wilson, 'War, Soldier and Nation in 1950s Japan', 187–218.
62 Wilson, 'War, Soldier and Nation in 1950s Japan', 194–6.
63 For example, Saburō Takahashi's *'Senkimono' wo Yomu*. For a thorough investigation of the army 'stragglers' and the publications concerning their experience, see Trefalt, *Japanese Army Stragglers*, especially chapter 4.
64 O'Connell, *Underdogs: The Making of the Modern Marine Corps*, 2.

Chapter 2

1 Quoted in Dean, 'Etajima: Hallowed Halls', 112.
2 The first nucleus of the navy was organised on 8 July 1869, upgraded and further institutionalised in 1871, followed by the official establishment of the Navy Ministry (Kaigunshō, 海軍省) in February 1872. Japanese scholarship generally considers 1871 as the institutional beginning of the Imperial Navy, whereas the standard English language reference on the subject adopts the year 1887, the year the navy first ordered itself as a fleet. Kaigun Rekishi Hozonkai (ed.), *Nihon Kaigunshi*, Vol. 1, 59–60; Schencking, *Making Waves*, 12–15; Evans and Peattie, *Kaigun*, xxi–xxii.
3 Wakon Yōsai (和魂洋才).
4 For an overview of the wakon, yōsai dichotomy, cf. Shūichi Katō, 'Japanese Writers and Modernisation', 425–45.
5 Pyle, *Rising Japan: The Resurgence of Japan's Power and Purpose*, 37.
6 Hirama, 'Japanese Naval Preparations for World War II', 71.
7 Scholarship on the Imperial Navy has illustrated the various political, technological and strategic implications of the service's substantial preoccupations throughout its history with budgetary problems, international naval limitations (in the 1920s and early 1930s) and potential adversaries with superior forces (e.g. Russia, the United States). Schencking, *Making Waves*, especially chapters 6–8; Asada, *Culture Shock and Japanese-American Relations. Historical Essays*, 137–73; Asada, 'From Washington to London: The Imperial Japanese Navy and the Politics of Naval Limitations, 1921-1930', 147–91. Technological and strategic aspects are fully explored in Evans and Peattie, *Kaigun*, chapters 7–9; Evans, 'Japanese Naval Construction, 1878-1918', 22–35; Peattie, 'Japanese Naval Construction, 1919-1941', 93–108.
8 Marder, 'From Jimmu Tennō to Perry: Sea Power in Early Japanese History', 1.
9 Kaikoku Nippon (海国日本 – literally, Maritime Japan).
10 Evans and Peattie, *Kaigun*, 19; Schencking, *Making Waves*, 107–36; Shimazu, 'The Making of a Heroic War Myth in the Russo-Japanese War', 83–96; Shimazu, *Japanese Society at War: Death, Memory and the Russo-Japanese War*, 197–229.
11 Schencking, *Making Waves*, 135.
12 The 'ri' (里) was a system to measure distances adopted in pre-modern Japan which corresponded to approximately 4,000 metres, or 2.44 miles. The character

derives from the combination of the characters for *ta* (田 – field) and *tsuchi* (土 – earth, soil).

13 Marder, 'From Jimmu Tennō to Perry', 1.

14 Ballard, *The Influence of the Sea on the Political History of Japan*, 6; Woolley, *Geography & Japan's Strategic Choice*, 16–17; Kitaoka, *Conflicting Currents*, 39–41.

15 Marder, 'From Jimmu Tennō to Perry', 3.

16 Ise no Kami Kaze (伊勢の神風). Ise, located in the Mie Prefecture, is the place of the Ise Shrine dedicated to the Goddess Amatersu Ōmikami, the most important deity in Shintō, Japan's original religion. The royal family is said to descend from her and traditionally, the high Priest or Priestess of the Shrine has to come from the royal family. According to the myth, Amaterasu sent the typhoon to defend the islands of Japan.

17 Woolley, *Geography & Japan's Strategic Choice*, 2–4; Ballard, *The Influence of the Sea on the Political History of Japan*, 13–41; Marder, 'From Jimmu Tennō to Perry', 12–19; Kiralfy, 'Why Japan's Fleet Avoids Actions', 47.

18 Sakoku (鎖国 – literally, national isolation).

19 Ballard, *The Influence of the Sea on the Political History of Japan*, 42–72; Marder, 'From Jimmu Tennō to Perry', 19–31; Woolley, *Geography & Japan's Strategic Choice*, 27–41. Shōgun (将軍 – Supreme General) of the Tokugawa family ruled Japan from 1600 to 1868; the period from 1853 to 1867 is conventionally called Bakumatsu (幕末). The policies of sakoku were enacted in the 1630s and banned the construction of ocean-going vessels while strictly regulating foreign trade. Gordon, *A Modern History of Japan. From Tokugawa to the Present Times*, 17.

20 Gordon, *A Modern History of Japan*, 61–2.

21 Suigun (水軍).

22 Turnbull, *Pirate of the Far East, 811-1639*. Also, cf. Marder, 'From Jimmu Tennō to Perry', 19–20. Also, Wilson, 'The Sea Battle of Dannoura', 206–22.

23 Sakai, 'The Satsuma-Ryukyu Trade and the Tokugawa Seclusion Policy', 391–403; Hellyer, 'The Missing Pirate and the Pervasive Smuggler: Regional Agency in Coastal Defence, Trade, and Foreign Relations in Nineteenth-Century Japan', 1–24.

24 Asakawa, 'Anglo-Japanese Military Relations, 1800-1900', 22

25 Ballard, *The Influence of the Sea on the Political History of Japan*, 104.

26 Schencking, *Making Waves*, 10–16.

27 Westney, *Imitation and Innovation. The Transfer of Western Organisational Patterns to Meiji Japan*, 18. Also, Matsumura, 'Takaki Kanehiro, 1849-1920: British-trained Medical Pioneer who Became Surgeon General to the Imperial Japanese Navy', 209–22.

28 Kurofune (黒船). The word 'black' refers to the black smoke coming from the steam-powered ships.

29 Evans and Peattie, *Kaigun*, 4–5; Koda, 'The Russo-Japanese war. Primary Causes of Japanese Success', 12–14; Ballard, *The Influence of the Sea on the Political History of Japan*, 102–3; Hamish, 'Towards a Naval Alliance. Some naval Antecedents to the Anglo-Japanese Alliance, 1854-1902', 29.

30 Blond, *Admiral Togo*, 46.

31 Admiral Kawamura had a very influential role in Japanese naval politics for more than a decade, serving first as Vice Navy Minister (1873–77) and then as Navy Minister (1877–80, 1881–85). Saigō Tsugumichi was an equally respected political figure who was drawn into the administration of the navy by Admiral Kawamura. He had no naval background, but throughout his career he encouraged younger officers like Yamamoto Gombei, and was dedicated to the modernisation of the

service. He was Navy Minister three times (1885–86, 1887–90, 1893–98). Admiral Yamamoto had a no less remarkable career and scholars Evans and Peattie compare his actions as innovative reformer to those of Admiral John 'Jackie' Fisher in the Royal Navy. Admiral Yamamoto's influence on the Japanese political and naval landscape of the time is further corroborated by the fact that he served not only as Secretariat to the Navy Minister (1891–96) and Navy Minister (1898–1906), but also as Prime Minister (1913–14, 1923–24). Evans, *The Satsuma Faction and Professionalism in the Japanese Naval Officer Corps of the Meiji Period, 1868-1912*, 114–51; also, Schencking, *Making Waves*, 3, 14–16, 32; Evans and Peattie, *Kaigun*, 20–2.

32 Schencking, *Making Waves*, 10–25.
33 Schencking, *Making Waves*, 33.
34 This was certainly the opinion of a long-time observer of Japanese military affairs, Captain Malcolm D. Kennedy, British Army, in his informed study *The Military Side of Japanese Life*, 316–17. On naval innovation in the late nineteenth century, cf. Herwig, 'The Battlefleet Revolution, 1885-1914', 114–31.
35 Evans and Peattie, *Kaigun*, 8.
36 Kokubō (国防).
37 Kaibō (海防).
38 Evans and Peattie, *Kaigun*, 23–4. Also Asada, *From Mahan to Pearl Harbor*, 293–5; Marder, *Old Friends, New Enemies*, 289–92.
39 Evans, *The Satsuma Faction*, 184–91; Evans, 'The recruitment of Japanese Navy Officers in the Meiji Period', 239–40.
40 Bywater, *Navies and Nations: A Review of Naval Developments since the Great War*, 178–82. Also, Jane, *The Imperial Japanese Navy*, 303.
41 Hara, *Japanese Destroyer Captain. Pearl Harbor, Guadalcanal, Midway – The Great Naval Battles as seen Through Japanese Eyes*, 4.
42 Smith, *Fist From the Sky*, 44.
43 Morris, *The Nobility of Failure. Tragic Heroes in the History of Japan*, 226.
44 Author's cruises on JDS *Kashima* (TV-3508), 10 April 2005; JDS *Kirisame* (DD-104), 27 May 2005; JDS *Chōkai* (DD-176), 25 October 2006; JDS *Sawayuki* (DD-125), 29 July 2007.
45 Riku no Chōshū (陸の長州 – literally, Chōshū of the land).
46 Umi no Satsuma (海の薩摩).
47 In one of its latest popular representations, Saigō's life provided the historical basis for the 2003 motion picture *The Last Samurai*, starring Japanese actor Watanabe Ken as the legendary samurai from Satsuma.
48 Morris, *The Nobility of Failure*, 227–8.
49 The Satsuma Rebellion, known in Japanese as the Seinan Sensō (西南戦争 – South-western War), lasted from January to September 1877 and took place in the part of Kyūshū between the provinces of Kagoshima and Kumamoto. Yates, *Restoration and Rebellion in Satsuma: The Life of Saigō Takamori, 1827-1877*.
50 Keiten Aijin (敬天愛人).
51 Morris, *The Nobility of Failure*, 244–5.
52 Morris, *The Nobility of Failure*, 250.
53 The term kikusui (菊水 – literally, floating chrysanthemum) was used by Saigō and his followers as a password and was reminiscent of the crest of a Japanese samurai of the fourteenth century, Kusunoki Masashige, who fought to restore Emperor Godaigo to power.
54 Morris, *The Nobility of Failure*, 275.

55 Evans, *The Satsuma Faction*, 141.
56 Schencking, *Making Waves*, 31.
57 Captain Fukumoto Izuru, JMSDF, conversation with the author, 28 August 2005.
58 Friday, 'Bushidō or Bull?', 342. Also, Lacoste, 'Japon et Géopolitique', 9–10; Esmein, *Un Demi Plus*, 197–200.
59 Drea, *Japan's Imperial Army: Its Rise and Fall, 1853-1945*, 258.
60 Bullock, *Etajima*, 39.
61 The Imperial Rescript to Soldiers and Sailors (Rikukaigunjin ni Tamawaritaru Chokuyu – 陸海軍人に賜りたる勅諭, or Gunjin Chokuyu – 軍人勅諭) was issued by Emperor Meiji on 4 January 1882. Ōhara, *Teikoku Riku Kaigun no Hikari to Kage*, 19.
62 Chūsetsu (忠節).
63 Reighi (礼儀).
64 Buyū (武勇).
65 Shinghi (信義).
66 Shisso (質素).
67 Dockrill, 'Hirohito, the Emperor's Army and Pearl Harbor', 319–33; Friday, 'Bushidō or Bull?', 339–49.
68 Kokka wo Hogoshi (国家を保護し). Ōhara stressed that the use of this expression helped to define the 'modern' character of the Japanese military, underlying its nature as an instrument of the state, in opposition to the feudal system that emphasised loyalty to a particular warlord. Ōhara, *Teikoku Riku Kaigun no Hikari to Kage*, 23.
69 Ōhara, *Teikoku Riku Kaigun no Hikari to Kage*, 22. Also, Bullock, *Etajima*, 131; Lory, *Japan's Military Masters*, 241–2.
70 See for instance, Parshall and Tully, *Shattered Sword. The Untold Story of the Battle of Midway*, 300; also, Yoshida, 'The Sinking of the Yamato', 493. Yoshida, *Requiem for Battleship Yamato*, 107.
71 The Imperial Navy (like the JMSDF today) was one of the rare navies to never name a ship after a national hero. The Meiji Emperor decided against it in relation to 'heroes' like Saigō who had fought against the government. Captain Ōtsuka Umio, JMSDF, conversation with the author, 20 May 2005.
72 Bywater, *Navies and Nations*, 184.
73 Etajima Kenji no Uta (江田島健児の歌 – The Song of Etajima's Strong Ones), quoted in Bullock, *Etajima*, 127.
74 Gunkan (軍艦 – Battleship), quoted in Marder, *Old Friends, New Enemies*, 272.
75 Hayashi Yoshinaga, 'Nihon no Shokugyō Gunjin Ishiki – 1500 Nen no Gunjishi wo Furikaette', *Senshibu Nenpō*, 2005:8, 127–51.
76 Evans, Peattie, *Kaigun*, 25–7.
77 Gluck, *Japan's Modern Myths. Ideology in the Late Meiji Period*, 53–5, 78–9.
78 The preference for vertical forms of interactions is conveyed through a seniority system called Sempai-Kōhai (先輩後輩). Davies and Ikeno, *The Japanese Mind. Understanding Contemporary Japanese Culture*, 187–92.
79 After the Meiji restoration, Shintō (神道 – literally, the way of the Gods) became a state religion and its influence extended to stylistic solutions adopted in the Rescript.
80 Ōhara, *Teikoku Riku Kaigun no Hikari to Kage*, 22; Bullock, *Etajima*, 131–2; Lory, *Japan's Military Masters*, 242. In particular, Lory uses the word 'propriety' instead of 'courtesy'.
81 Ōhara, *Teikoku Riku Kaigun no Hikari to Kage*, 23–4; Bullock, *Etajima*, 132–3; Lory, *Japan's Military Masters*, 243–4. In the case of the third tenet, Bullock renders it as 'courage' rather than 'valour'.

82 Kyōiku Seishin (教育精神).
83 Quoted in Asada, *From Mahan to Pearl Harbor*, 163.
84 Bullock, *Etajima*, 14–15.
85 Getsugetsukasuimokukinkin (月月火水木金金).
86 Hirama, 'Japanese Naval Preparations for World War II', 66.
87 Kendō (剣道).
88 Jūdō (柔道).
89 Jukenjutsu (銃剣術).
90 Kyūdō (弓道).
91 Marder, *Old Friends, New Enemies*, 268–70; Bullock, *Etajima*, 22–3, 25.
92 Bullock, *Etajima*, 28–9.
93 Go Fun mae Kōdo (五分前コード). On Japanese warships too communications concerning routine activities (e.g. morning raising of the flag) were passed on always 'five minutes before'. This practice is still in use today in the JMSDF. Author's cruise, JDS *Sawayuki* (DD-125), 29 July 2007.
94 Defune (出船).
95 Bullock, *Etajima*, 53.
96 KurasuKai (クラス会).
97 Negaimasu (願います – literally, I wish).
98 Toshio Yoshida, *Kaigun no Kokoro* (Tokyo: Bungei Shunjū, 2000), 90.
99 Yoshida, *Requiem for Battleship Yamato*, 152.
100 Kōkoku no Kōhai Kono Issen ni Ari, Kakuin Issō Funrei Doryoku Seyo (皇国の興廃この一戦に在り、各員一層奮励動力せよ).
101 Perry, 'Great Britain and the Emergence of Japan as Naval Power', 306–8.
102 Perry, *Monumenta Nipponica*, 310. Also, Gow, 'The Douglas Mission (1873-1879) and Meiji Naval Education', 144–57. For instance, in 1865, nineteen students were 'illegally' sent by the domain of Satsuma to study in Britain. Cobbing, *The Japanese Discovery of Victorian Britain. Early Travel Encounters in the Far East*, 22–4.
103 Perry, 'Great Britain and the Emergence of Japan as Naval Power', 311–16; Evans and Peattie, *Kaigun*, 11–13; Kennedy, *Some Aspects of Japan and Her Defences*, 34–42; Ikeda, 'The Silent Admiral: Tōgō Heihachirō (1848-1934) and Britain', 106–20.
104 Asada, *Culture Shock and Japanese-American Relations*, 139; Checkland, '"Working at Their Profession": Japanese Engineers in Britain Before 1914', 45–53.
105 Evans and Peattie, *Kaigun*, 135–6; Peattie, 'Akiyama Saneyuki and the Emergence of Modern Japanese Naval Doctrine', 60–9.
106 Marie Conte-Helm, 'Armstrong's, Vickers and Japan', 92–105.
107 During the Russo-Japanese War, British naval observers were granted special status with privileged access to the fleet. Cf. Towle, 'British Naval and Military Observers of the Russo-Japanese War', 158–69. Also, Corbett, *Maritime Operations of the Russo-Japanese War, 1904-1905*, xii, xxv–xxvi.
108 For an overview of the politico-diplomatic aspects, cf. Nish, 'Britain and Japan: Long-Range Images, 1900-1952', 149–61; Nish, 'The Historical Significance of the Anglo-Japanese Alliance', 40–7; Nish and Kibata (eds), *The History of Anglo-Japanese Relations, 1600-2000. Volume II: The Political-Diplomatic Dimension, 1931-2000.*
109 Ferris, 'A British "Unofficial" Aviation Mission and Japanese Naval Developments, 1919-1929', 416–39; Best, 'Lord Sempill (1893–1965) and Japan, 1921-1941', 375–82; Colonel The Master of Sempill, 'The British Aviation Mission in Japan', 37–50.
110 Asada, *Culture Shock and Japanese-American Relations*, 137–73; Asada, *From Mahan to Pearl Harbor*, especially Chapters 7, 9 and 10; Aizawa, 'The Path Towards an "Anti-British" Strategy by the Japanese Navy Between the Wars', 59–98; Ferris, 'Double-

Edged Estimates: Japan in the Eyes of the British Army and the Royal Air Force, 1900–1939', 91–108.

111 Oyatoi Gaikokujin (お雇い外国人 – literally, foreign employees).

112 Ikeda, *Kaigun to Nihon*, 148. On the *oyatoi* system, cf. Shinohara, *Nihon Kaigun Oyatoi Gaijin* Muramatsu, *Westerners in the Modernization of Japan*.

113 The *Jeune Ecole* (Young School) pertains to a movement developed in France in the 1870s which proposed the procurement of new weapons such as torpedoes, mines and large numbers of torpedo boats and fast cruisers to oppose preponderant British naval power. It was a strategy conceived to appeal to weaker naval powers. Hill, *War at Sea in the Ironclad Age*, 94–5. On Emile Bertin's working experience with Japan, Takahashi Kunitarō, *Oyatoi Gaikokujin 6. Gunji*, 231–5.

114 Rikugun Daigaku (陸軍大学). Ikeda, *Kaigun to Nihon*, 149.

115 Marder, *Old Friends, New Enemies*, 272.

116 Marder, *Old Friends, New Enemies*, 148. Also, cf. Nomura, *Nihon Kaigun no Rekishi*, 16–17; Gow, 'The Douglas Mission (1873-1879) and Meiji Naval Education', 149–56. Captain Ingles' role as adviser to the staff college (Kaigun Daigaku – 海軍大学) was fundamental in the technical and tactical advancement of the navy's professionalism. Evans and Peattie, *Kaigun*, 12–13.

117 Perry, 'Great Britain and the Emergence of Japan as Naval Power', 312.

118 Douglas, *Life of Admiral Sir Archibald Lucius Douglas*, 41.

119 Douglas, *Life of Admiral Sir Archibald Lucius Douglas*, 57, 65.

120 Gow, 'The Douglas Mission (1873-1879) and Meiji Naval Education', 151.

121 Ikeda, *Kaigun to Nihon*, 149–50.

122 Marder, *Old Friends, New Enemies*, 278–85.

123 Marder, *Old Friends, New Enemies*, 283.

124 Jane, *The Imperial Japanese Navy*, 257–8; Bullock, *Etajima*, 12.

125 Financial compensation was commensurate to their status. Auer, *The Post-war Rearmament of Japanese Maritime Forces*, 20. Also, Jane, *The Imperial Japanese Navy*, 267–72.

126 Hara, *Japanese Destroyer Captain*, 4; Smith, *Fist from the Sky*, 45–7.

127 Hidenori Takahashi, 'Kaigun Heigakkō no Kyōiku Kikan Enchō to Seishin Kagaku Dōnyū', *Gunji Shigaku*, Vol. 34, 1998:1, 23–4.

128 Sempill, 'The British Aviation Mission in Japan', 43.

129 Jane, *The Imperial Japanese Navy*, 279.

130 Jane, *The Imperial Japanese Navy*, 284–5.

131 Marder, *Old Friends, New Enemies*, 266; Bullock, *Etajima*, 122. Captain Ōtsuka Umio, JMSDF, conversation with the author, 25 February 2005.

132 Bullock, *Etajima*, 126.

133 Auer, *The Post-war Rearmament of Japanese Maritime Forces*, 20.

134 Marder, *Old Friends, New Enemies*, 283–5.

135 The 'treaty faction' (or administrative group, Gunsei Ha – 軍政派) was composed of officers headed in later years by the 'triumvirate': Admiral Yonai Mitsumasa, Rear Admiral Inoue Shigeyoshi and Admiral Yamamoto Isoroku. The 'fleet faction' (or command group, Kantai-ha – 艦隊派) was led by Admiral Katō Kanji, Admiral Suetsugu Nobumasa and Admiral Ōsumi Mineo. Asada, *From Mahan to Pearl Harbor*, 164–6; Asada, 'The Japanese Navy's Road to Pearl Harbour, 1931–1941', 137–73.

136 Takahashi, 'Kaigun Heigakkō no Kyōiku Kikan Enchō to Seishin Kagaku Dōnyū', 24.

137 Kageyama, *Kaigun Heigakkō no Kyōiku*, 226–7.

138 Kaigun Heigakkō Kyōiku Hōshin (海軍兵学校教育方針 – Teaching Criteria of the Naval Academy).

139 Kageyama, *Kaigun Heigakkō no Kyōiku*, 228.
140 Ōhara, *Teikoku Riku Kaigun no Hikari to Kage*, 60, 64–5.
141 Bullock, *Etajima*, 58.
142 Kyōiku Sankōkan (教育参考館).
143 Author's visits to Etajima, 24 February 2005 and 1 June 2008.
144 Admiral Sakuma Makoto, JMSF (Ret.), interview with the author, 11 October 2005.
145 Go Sei (五省).
146 Ōhara, *Teikoku Riku Kaigun no Hikari to Kage*, 61–3.
147 Courtesy of Captain Ōtsuka Umio, JMSDF, Japan Ministry of Defence.
148 Admiral Furushō Kōichi, JMSDF (Ret.), interview with the author, 02 September 2005; Admiral Sakuma, interview with the author, 11 October 2005.
149 Parshall and Tully, *Shattered Sword*, 76.
150 Parshall and Tully, *Shattered Sword*, 76.
151 Reiter, 'Nationalism and Military Effectiveness: Post-Meiji Japan', 27–54; Nish, 'Japan, 1914-1918', 229–48; Boyd, 'Japan Military Effectiveness: The Interwar Period', 131–68; Coox, 'The Effectiveness of the Japanese Military Establishment in the Second World War', 1–40.
152 Parshall and Tully, *Shattered Sword*, 77.
153 Oitsuku, Oikosu (追い付く追い越す).
154 Ittō Koku (一等国). Samuels, *Machiavelli's Childern*. 12.

Chapter 3

1 'Memorandum of 14 October 1964' in Ishii et al., *Documents on United States Policy toward Japan, Documents Related to Diplomacy and Military Matters 1964, Volume 7*, 56.
2 Nisohachi, 'Riku Kaigun wo Meguru Ōkina Nazo', 38–9.
3 Dower, *Embracing Defeat*, 443–84. Also, Futamura, *War Crimes Tribunals and Transitional Justice*, and Futamura, 'Individual and Collective Guilt: Post-war Japan and the Tokyo War Crimes Tribunal', 471–83.
4 Comyns Carr, 'The Tokyo War Crimes Trial', 113.
5 Yoshida, *The Yoshida Memoirs*, 278.
6 The Japanese case stands in sharp contrast with that of Italy, where harsh critiques of the military decision-making in preparation for and during the war applied indiscriminately to all of the armed services. As one popular publication of the 1980s suggested, Italians should have 'executed the Admirals' for their responsibilities. Rocca, *Fucilate Gli Ammiragli: La Tragedia Della Marina Italiana nella Seconda Guerra Mondiale*.
7 In 2006, on the occasion of the 61st anniversary of the end of Pacific War, the *Yomiuri Shimbun* published a series of articles highlighting the Imperial Army's larger share of responsibility for the country's aggressive war; Auer, *Who Was Responsible?*. In 2007, however, this view was challenged in a special issue of a popular monthly magazine where critics reflected on the navy's failure to prevent the war, the isolated nature of its anti-war group, and its strategic blunders. Kendō et al., *Shōwa no Kaigun Erīto Shūdan no Eikō to Shittsui*, 142–86.
8 In the 1960s, award-winning writer Shiba Ryōtarō had a substantial influence on memorialising the Imperial Navy of the Meiji era. His serial historical novel *A Cloud at the Top of the Slope* (Saka no Ue no Kumo – 坂の上の雲) was instrumental in this process. The novel dealt with the adventures of Akiyama

Yoshifuru and Saneyuki, two brothers serving in the army cavalry and in the navy, respectively, during the Russo-Japanese War. Chiba, 'Shifting Contours of Memory and History, 1904-1980', 374–5; Nakao, 'The Legacy of Shiba Ryotaro', 99–115; Keene, *Five Modern Japanese Novelists*, 85–100. In the 1980s, *manga* creator Kawaguchi Kaiji introduced iconic Japanese naval figures, assets and events from both the imperial navy and the JMSDF in popular culture with the multi-volume series *The Silent Service* (Chinmoku no Kantai – 沈黙の艦隊), and *Zipang* (ジパング). *The Silent Service* featured an invincible Japanese nuclear submarine symbolically named *Yamato*; *Zipang* detailed the story of a JMSDF's *Aegis* destroyer that travels back in time right before the Battle of Midway. In 2009, *Zipang* boasted an animated cartoon version, while *The Silent Service* appeared on television and as a PlayStation game. The original volumes have sold over 2,500,000 copies. Nakao, 'The Legacy of Shiba Ryotaro', 110.

9 The parts of this chapter concerning Itō Masanori appeared in a different version in Patalano, '"A Symbol of Tradition and Modernity": Itō Masanori and the Legacy of the Imperial Navy in the Early Post-war Rearmament Process', 1–22.

10 Sonnō Jōi (尊王攘夷).

11 For biographical data on Itō Masanori, see Usui et al., *Nihon kindai jinmei jiten*, 95; 'Saigo no kaigun kisha Itō Masanori', 106.

12 FPC, *Japan's Mass Media*, 11–12.

13 'Gogatsu nijūnananichi no tama yo yomigaere'; 'Setsusetsu to kaigun o omou'.

14 FPC, *Japan's Mass Media*, 11.

15 'Seishin de musubareta ai'; 'Gogatsu nijūnananichi no tama yo yomigaere'.

16 The volumes in the Sankei archive corresponded to the period from 1951 to 1962 and contained some 1,121 articles, taken from a variety of daily, weekly, national and local publications. In almost all cases, the articles presented war-related issues which Itō subsequently developed in his books.

17 *Fude no chikara* (筆の力), attributed to him in 'Kaigun to Itō Masanori'. In the archive, this article was just a photocopy with no page references, so the page number cannot be provided in this case.

18 Instead of the character 'ren' (連) he used (聯). 'Saigo no kaigun kisha Itō Masanori', 105.

19 Buruma, *Wages of Guilt*, 34.

20 In pre-war Japan, it was not uncommon, and not only among those who had a passion for naval matters, for individuals to know the names of entire classes of Japanese capital ships by heart. Kizu Tōru, Editor in Chief/Director, *Sekai no Kansen* (Ships of the World), interview with the author, 30 May 2003.

21 'Saigo no kaigun kisha Itō Masanori', 106; 'Setsusetsu to kaigun o omou', 21.

22 'Nihon no Senshishitsu: Itō Masanori', 82–3.

23 Nihon no Senshishitsu: Itō Masanori', 82.

24 Itō's informed assessments and characterisations of the main protagonists of the naval treaties are still employed by leading Japanese scholars on the subject. Asada, *From Mahan to Pearl Harbor*, 54, 70, 73.

25 Reportedly, at the Washington Naval Conference (1921–22), Itō was one of the few who confidently 'predicted' the IJN's request for a 70 per cent ratio for its fleet vis-à-vis the Royal Navy and the US Navy; the *Washington Post*, for example, claimed that Japan intended to ask for a little over 60 per cent. Itō's grasp of the conference and of the 1927 Geneva Conference is well documented in Gow, *Military Intervention in Pre-war Japanese Politics*, 115, 130, 140–1, 164.

26 'Setsusetsu to kaigun o omou', 21.

27 Itō, *The End of the Imperial Japanese Navy*, 177–9.
28 'Itō Masanori Shi'. Itō was on good terms with journalists and editors from popular foreign publications such as *The Morning Post* and the *New York Times*, and with leading naval journalists with expertise on Pacific Affairs, like Hector C. Bywater. 'Nihon no Senshishitsu: Itō Masanori', 82; Itō, *The End of the Imperial Japanese Navy*, 7–8.
29 Allen, 'Notes on Japanese Historiography', 134.
30 Allen, 'Notes on Japanese Historiography'. A reviewer of the English version of his works described his style as 'racy, succinct, and never dull'. Thomas, 'The End of the Imperial Japanese Navy', 180.
31 Editorial Department, 'Seishin de musubareta ai'.
32 Itō, *The End of the Imperial Japanese Navy*, 2.
33 Itō, *The End of the Imperial Japanese Navy*.
34 Roskill, 'The End of the Imperial Japanese Navy', 644.
35 For a brief overview on Japan's convoy escort problem, see Graham, *Japan's Sea Lane Security*, 63–89.
36 Editorial Department, 'Itō Masanori Shi'.
37 Itō, *The End of the Imperial Japanese Navy*, 10–11.
38 Itō, *The End of the Imperial Japanese Navy*, 3.
39 Itō, *The End of the Imperial Japanese Navy*, 19–20, 216–28. Inter-service disputes and military factionalism in Japan are also comprehensively treated in Itō's three-volume work *Gunbatsu kōbō shi*.
40 Itō, *The End of the Imperial Japanese Navy*, 221.
41 Admiral Yamamoto Isoroku, Yōnai Mitsumasa and Inoue Shigeyoshi played a primary role in arguing against war. Asada, *From Mahan to Pearl Harbor*, 212–19, 256, 275–8; Evans and Peattie, *Kaigun*.
42 Evans and Peattie, *Kaigun*, 173–4.
43 Evans and Peattie, *Kaigun*, 11.
44 Evans and Peattie, *Kaigun*, 179. The expression was used by Admiral Kurita in an interview he gave to Itō.
45 Evans and Peattie, *Kaigun*, 228.
46 For an understanding of the concerns concerning the ethos of the JSDF at the time of Itō's writing, see Morris, *Nationalism and the Right Wing in Japan*, 235–6.
47 The January series was titled 'Kokubō no kadode ni okuru' (approximately, In Honour of the Shouldering of [the task of] National Defence). The first instalment appeared on 1 January 1954.The second series was titled (significantly) 'Jieigun o mukaete' (Welcoming the Self-Defence Military), and the first instalment appeared on 4 July 1954, three days after the inauguration of the JSDF.
48 From September to December 1953, Prime Minister Yoshida sought the cooperation of the Reform Party to amend the existing *Safety Agency Law* (Hōantaihō). A special committee was instructed to study the various legal, constitutional and economic ramifications of the proposed amendments, and by January 1954 the new bills were nearly completed. They were submitted to the Diet on 11 March 1954, with the JDA and the JSDF officially inaugurated on 1 July 1954. Auer, *The Post-war Rearmament of Japanese Maritime Forces*, 98–9.
49 For an in-depth analysis of the debate, see Samuels, *Securing Japan*, 29–37.
50 Itō, 'Rikkoku no seishin wasuruna'; Itō, 'Guntai wa kokumin no sanbutsu'.
51 Morris, *Nationalism and the Right Wing in Japan*, 236.
52 Itō, 'Kyōhei to gunkokushugi no betsu'.

53 Itō, 'Kokumin no kokubō o satoru koto'.
54 Itō, 'Kokumin no kokubō o satoru koto'
55 Itō, 'Guntai wa kokumin no sanbutsu'.
56 *Jieigun* (Self-Defence Military), and *Jieitai* (JSDF). It must be noted that the series were published after the official creation of the JSDF.
57 Gun (軍).
58 Hatoyama, Kishi and other conservative politicians used the term *jieigun* to emphasise the autonomous character they wished to give to the Japanese post-war military. Samuels, *Securing Japan*, 35.
59 Itō, 'Guntai wa kokumin no sanbutsu'.
60 Itō, 'Kokumin no kokubō o satoru koto'.
61 Itō, 'Kokumin no kokubō o satoru koto'; 'Guntai wa kokumin no sanbutsu'.
62 'Saigo no kaigun kisha Itō Masanori', 106; 'Senkan *Mikasa* to Itō Masanori'.
63 Peter C. Smith, 'A Naval View of Anglo-Japanese Relations', *Mainichi Shinbun*, 28 May 1998. The Mikasa Preservation Society was established in 1924 to restore the battleship which had reported severe damage during the Great Kantō Earthquake of 1923. The inaugural ceremony was held on 12 November 1926 in the presence of the Prince Regent Hirohito. Mikasa Preservation Society, *Memorial Ship Mikasa*, 20.
64 Kinoshita, 'Echoes of Militarism in Japan', 244.
65 Itō, 'Gaikoku wa imamo kinensu'.
66 Potter, *Nimitz*, 466.
67 '*Mikasa* kanjō de zōtei shiki'.
68 Itō, 'Gaikoku wa imamo kinensu'.
69 Itō, 'Sekai kūzen no senshō'.
70 Author's visit to the memorial ship *Mikasa*, 16 August 2007. For details on the exhibition, cf. Mikasa Preservation Society, *Memorial Ship Mikasa*, 25; and http://www.kinenkan-mikasa.or.jp/siryou/index.html (accessed 20 July 2008). In English, see Powers, 'Mikasa: Japan's Memorial Battleship', 69–77.
71 Tanki Gen'eki Shikan Seido, or Tangen (短期現役士官制度, or 短現).
72 Biographical details in Yasuoka, *Watashi no Rirekisho. Dai San no Shinjin*, 113–221.
73 Professor Agawa Naoyuki, Keio University, interview with the author, 24 October 2006.
74 Dower, *Embracing Defeat*, 180.
75 Dower, *Embracing Defeat*, 406–19.
76 Rubin, 'From Wholesomeness to Decadence', 74.
77 Magazines continue to prosper to the present day. In 2002 some 3,489 magazines were published, including 106 weekly titles, and approximately 3,000,000 were sold throughout the year. FPC, *Japan's Mass Media*, 71.
78 Dower, *Embracing Defeat*, 182.
79 Rubin, 'From Wholesomeness to Decadence', 74–5.
80 Yamagiwa, 'Literature and Politics in the Japanese Magazine, Sekai', 254.
81 Rubin, 'From Wholesomeness to Decadence', 74–80.
82 Darakuron (堕落論).
83 Rubin, 'From Wholesomeness to Decadence', 78; Dower, *Embracing Defeat*, 154–62.
84 Quoted in Dower, *Embracing Defeat*, 156.
85 Dower, *Embracing Defeat*, 186–7.
86 Yamagiwa, 'Literature and Politics in the Japanese Magazine, Sekai', 254–68.
87 Agawa, 'Nennen Saisai' (年年歳歳 – Year after Year), 124–43.
88 Rubin, 'From Wholesomeness to Decadence', 89.

89 For instance, Yokochi Samuel, 'A Cat, a Man, and Two Women by Jun'ichiro Tanizaki (trans. Paul McCarthy); Citadel in Spring by Hiroyuki Agawa (trans. Lawrence Rogers); The Bomb by Makoto Oda (trans. D. H. Whittaker)', 949.
90 Lifton, *Death in Life. Survivors of Hiroshima*, 391.
91 Haru no Shiro (春の城), translated in English by Lawrence Rogers.
92 Kumo no Bohyō (雲の墓標), translated in English by Teruyo Shimizu.
93 Also known as Special Attack Corps, or Tokkōtai Kamikaze (特攻隊神風). The word 'kamikaze' literally means 'divine wind' and refers to the typhoons in 1274 and 1281 which severely damaged Mongolian fleets which were attempting to invade Japan.
94 Among other famous recipients of this prize, controversial author Mishima Yukio (1957, 1961), and more recently, the popular writer Murakami Haruki (1996).
95 Professor Agawa Naoyuki, Keio University, interview with the author, 20 July 2007.
96 Maruyama's expression is presented in Dower, *Embracing Defeat*, 233–9.
97 Hiroyuki Agawa, *Devil's Heritage*, X.
98 Agawa, *Burial in the Clouds*, 27.
99 Dower, *Embracing Defeat*, 415.
100 Agawa, interview with the author, 20 July 2007.
101 Rear Admiral Yōichi Hirama, JMSDF (Ret.), interview with the author, 15 April 2005; Commander Takahiro Ishihara, JMSDF, interview with the author, 14 June 2005.
102 Professor Akio Watanabe, Research Institute for Peace and Security – RIPS, interview with the author 9 May 2005; Commander Naoto Yagi, JMSDF, International Institute for Policy Studies – IIPS, interview with the author, 19 May 2005.
103 Suikōkai (水交会).
104 Naoyuki Agawa, *Umi no Yūjō*, 28.
105 Naoyuki Agawa, *Umi no Yūjō*, 36–7.
106 A group of radical middle echelons from the Imperial Army entered the capital with troops from the 1st Division and murdered members of the Cabinet, demanding the appointment of more sympathetic political leaders. Gordon, *A Modern History of Japan*, 196–8.
107 Agawa, interview with the author, 20 July 2007.
108 Agawa, interview with the author, 20 July 2007.
109 Agawa, *The Reluctant Admiral: Yamamoto and the Imperial Navy*, 100
110 Agawa, *The Reluctant Admiral: Yamamoto and the Imperial Navy*, 188–9.
111 Agawa, *The Reluctant Admiral: Yamamoto and the Imperial Navy*, 192–3.
112 The battleship *Nagato* was laid down in the Kure dockyards in 1917 and was commissioned in 1919. In 1936, it underwent a major refit and subsequently served throughout the entire war, serving as flagship of the Combined Fleet until February 1942. The *Nagato* was eventually sunk in March 1946 during the American nuclear tests conducted on the Bikini atoll. Hiroyuki Agawa, *Gunkan Nagato no Shōgai.*
113 Yoshida's book was censored in 1946 and 1948 and appeared only abridged in 1949. It was fully published only after the end of the occupation. Dower, *Embracing Defeat*, 416.
114 At the request of a friend, Agawa was recruited as testimonial for a 1982 Japanese advertisement for a famous international coffee brand. In the short promotional video, both his reputation as a 'naval writer' and his professional experience as a former naval officer (emphasised by two cartoon images, one featuring two IJN officers drinking coffee, the other representing a group of sailors on a cutter rowing

energetically as part of their training activity) are key to 'validate' the characteristics of the product. Sophistication of taste, high quality (due to the blend of the best coffee beans worldwide) and energising capabilities, all delivered with a flavour for tradition, are the attributes that the advertisement seeks to convey to the potential customer. The video is available on the internet, http://www.youtube.com/watch?v=Xl0dMaNaKl4, accessed 27 July 2008.

115 Shimazu, 'Popular Representations of the Past: The Case of Post-war Japan', 112.

116 In the 1970s, there was a growing trend in Japanese mass culture to emphasise elements of continuity between the past and the present. One of the most interesting examples on the subject is the Japanese national railways advertisement campaign 'Discover Japan'. This has been described as one of 'the largest and longest-running ad campaign(s) in Japanese history' and had a primary goal of stimulating travelling around Japan by promoting an idea of spatial continuity between the rural, traditional areas of the country and the more modern and developed urban landscapes. Ivy, 'Formation of Mass Culture', 251–2. For an overview of Japan's social changes in the 1960–80 period, cf. Gordon, *A Modern History of Japan*, 264–9, 304–9.

117 Fowler, 'Rendering Words, Traversing Cultures: On the Art and Politics of Translating Modern Japanese Fiction', 15.

118 Asada, *Culture Shock and Japanese-American Relations*, 134–5; Asada, *From Mahan to Pearl Harbor*, 150–1; Hata, 'Admiral Yamamoto's Surprise Attack and the Japanese Navy's War Strategy', 68–9; Aizawa, *Kaigun no Sentaku*, 10.

119 Annotated Bibliography available at the authors' webpage, http://www.combinedfleet.com/biblio.htm, accessed 27 July 2008.

120 Bunka Kunshō (文化勲章).

121 The Asahi Shimbun, *Japan Almanac 2004*, 234.

122 Commander Senō Sadao, JMSDF (Ret.), interview with the author, 5 August 2005. Commander Senō studied at the Naval Academy under Admiral Inoue and, after the war, remained close to the admiral in his late years.

123 Agawa, interview with the author, 20 July 2007.

124 Agawa, interview with the author, 24 October 2006.

125 From April 1979 to September 1988, Commander James Auer, USN, was assigned as Japan Desk officer at the Office of the Secretary of Defence. In 1983, he retired from the USN and continued to serve in that capacity as a political appointee of the Reagan Administration. Auer's first encounters with Admiral Uchida occurred in 1970, when he spent a year in Japan to conduct research for his PhD doctoral thesis on the history of the JMSDF, which was sponsored by the USN and supervised by Professor Edwin O. Reishauer. Over the years, Dr Auer remained in close contact with his Japanese naval acquaintances. Koji Murata, 'James Auer Oral History Interview', March 1996, http://www.gwu.edu/~nsarchiv/japan/auerohinterview.htm, accessed 20 March 2007; Dr James Auer, Vanderbilt University, interview with the author, 30 June 2007.

126 The character 'awa' is used in the adjective 'awai' (淡い – pale, light). When repeated twice, its reading is 'Tantan' (淡淡, or 淡々 – philosophical indifferent). Agawa, interview with the author, 24 October 2006.

127 Agawa, interview with the author, 24 October 2006. Also, Agawa, *Umi no Yūjō*, 9–10.

128 Agawa, interview with the author, 24 October 2006.

129 Every year, the Education Division and the Public Affairs Office of the JMSDF invite a small group of civilians from a variety of fields (Japanese media, university

professors, distinguished businessmen, foreign officials, etc.) to attend the ceremony at the academy as a way to introduce them to the traditions and history of the JMSDF. Captain Ōtsuka Umio, JMSDF, conversation with the author, 24 February 2005.

130 Admiral Furushō Kōichi eventually was appointed as 27th Chief of Maritime Staff, JMSDF, serving in that capacity from 2003 to 2005.

131 Agawa, interview with the author, 20 July 2007. For instance, Naoyuki mentioned a 2000 visit as a guest speaker to the Japan Naval Association branch in the Kansai area where he was welcomed by then Rear Admiral Furushō, Commander of the Regional Forces in Hanshin (Osaka-Kobe area). Agawa, *Umi no Yūjō*, 293.

132 The invitation to attend the graduation ceremony had no connection with the *Tan Tan Kai* meetings; rather with the role as an academic and a consultant to the Japanese Ministry of Foreign Affairs. Professor Agawa Naoyuki, Keio University, interview with the author, 15 April 2010.

133 Agawa, *American Royā no Tanjō*; Agawa, *America ga Kirai Desuka?*; Agawa, *Daitōryō wo Uttaemasuka?*.

134 Agawa, interview with the author, 24 October 2006; Agawa, interview with the author, 20 July 2007.

135 Agawa, *Umi no Yūjō*, 49.

136 Agawa, *Umi no Yūjō*, chapters 2–3.

137 Agawa, interview with the author, 20 July 2007.

138 Agawa, interview with the author, 24 October 2006.

139 Professor Agawa Naoyuki, email to the author, 25 April 2010. By Western standards, these figures might sound impressive, but they do not qualify the book as a bestseller on the Japanese book market. However, it must be noted that it was a successful product since it went through a second edition (the first edition numbering 15,000 copies) and, given the decline of the publishing business in the country, it maintained a steady circulation.

140 Agawa, interview with the author, 24 October 2006.

141 Dower, *Embracing Defeat*, 175–7, 186. For an overview of the role of Kodansha culture, cf. also Maruyama, *Thoughts and Behaviour in Modern Japanese Politics*, 304, 307–8.

142 It is worth noting that both Itō and Agawa did not elaborate on the IJN's main strategic misgiving, namely the navy's lack of flexibility to adapt to the requirements of a protracted war, as was demonstrated for instance by its failure to organise appropriate convoy escorts in a timely manner.

143 Agawa, *Burial in the Clouds*, 217.

144 CDSC, *The Council on Security and Defence Capabilities Report: Japan's Visions for Future Security and Defence Capabilities*, 1.

Chapter 4

1 Admiral Kōichi Furushō, CMS, JMSDF, 'Bridge to Babylon', in Shibata, *Arabia no Umi*.

2 Namae nomi (名前のみ). Anonymous Lt Commander, JMSDF, 20 August 2005.

3 Yōi Shūtō (用意周到).

4 Kōmyaku Kōka (鉱脈硬化).

5 Yūmou Kakan (勇猛果敢).

6 Shirimetsuretsu (支離滅裂).
7 NHK Special Selection, *Kaijōjieitai wa Kōshite Umareta*, 32.
8 Yuigadokuson (唯我独尊).
9 Dentō Bokushu (伝統墨守).
10 Corbett, 'The teaching of Naval and Military History', 15.
11 In 1952, following the termination of the Allied occupation and the coming into effect of the Peace Treaty and the Security Treaty, the National Police Reserve (Keisatsu Yobitai – 警察予備隊) which had been established in 1950, was reorganised as a National Safety Force (Hoantai – 保安隊). The new organisation included also a maritime component (Keibitai – 警備隊). In 1954, the enactment of the Defence Agency Establishment Bill and the Self-Defence Law led to the renaming of the police reserve in Japan Self-Defence Forces. Japan Ministry of Defence (JMoD), *Defence of Japan 2007*, 158–60. Maeda, *The Hidden Army*, 1–79; on the maritime forces, see Auer, *The Post-war Rearmament of Japanese Maritime Forces*, 69–89.
12 Yoshida, *The Yoshida Memoirs*, 9–10.
13 United States Strategic Bombing Survey (USSBS), *Interrogations of Japanese Officials*, 330–1.
14 Asada, *From Mahan to Pearl Harbor*, 166–9, 213–14, 220–1.
15 Shizuo Nakamori, *Bōei Daigakkō no Shinjitsu*, 28–9.
16 Auer, *The Post-war Rearmament of Japanese Maritime Forces*, 203; Maeda, *The Hidden Army*, 53.
17 Nakamori, *Bōei Daigakkō no Shinjitsu*, 24–5.
18 Hoan Daigakkō (保安大学校). The Defence Academy assumed its present name in 1953. Academic activities started in April 1953, and the first class graduated in March 1957. Matsumoto, '"Bōei Daigakkō Go Jū Nenshi" wo Yonde', 1
19 Yoshida, *The Yoshida Memoirs*, 190–1.
20 Matsumoto, '"Bōei Daigakkō Go Jū Nenshi" wo Yonde', 5. The academy is located uphill at the easterly end of Yokosuka, conveying to both visitors and locals a distinctive sense of separation from the rest of the city. The area is nonetheless well served by public transport and to date, almost all faculty members commute on a daily basis from residential areas in Tokyo and Yokohama. Professor Kawano Hitoshi, conversation with the author, 5 September 2005.
21 Nakamori, *Bōei Daigakkō no Shinjitsu*, 26–7.
22 Maeda, *The Hidden Army*, 56.
23 Professor Nishihara Masashi, interview with the author, 29 June 2007. Former Japan Defence Agency Director General Nakatani Gen is an example of an academy graduate who pursued a career as a civil servant after resigning from the JGSDF.
24 Over the decades, the number of graduates declining to join the JSDF stabilised on approximately twenty students per graduating class. In 2007, only ten did not enter the armed forces and in 2008, twenty-six, the highest number of the past decade One of the reasons credited for this rise concerned the scandals involving top officials from the JMoD, and the February 2008 collision between a JMSDF destroyer and a fishing boat. Editorial Department, 'Academy Grads Told to Repair SDF Image', *The Japan Times*, 24 March 2008.
25 Maeda, *The Hidden Army*, 58; Auer, *The Post-war Rearmament of Japanese Maritime Forces*, 204–5.
26 Discipline, politeness and a smart appearance are still given high consideration. Masashi Nishihara, 'Gakusei yo, Iyoku wo Motte, Jōnetsu wo Moyase', 21.

27 Maeda, *The Hidden Army*, 56. After the war, Admiral Inoue retired to his house in Yokosuka.
28 Colonel Tsuji, a Diet member by the time the academy started this activity, is said to have interrupted the first formal ball dance and accused the attendees of being feeble womanisers (onnatarashi – 女誑し), rather than military officers. Maki had subsequently to offer a formal explanation for his decision to organise the event. Nishihara, interview with the author, 29 June 2007.
29 Nakamori, *Bōei Daigakkō no Shinjitsu*, 67–8.
30 Nishihara, interview with the author, 29 June 2007; Professor Tadokoro Masayuki, conversation with the author, 28 May 2008. Cf. also, Nakamori, *Bōei Daigakkō no Shinjitsu*, 62–98, in which the author defines Maki's long-term influence as 'Maki-ism'.
31 Jieikan no Kokorogamae (自衛官の心構え - The Attitude of the JSDF's Personnel). An English version of the text is presented in JMoD, *Defence of Japan 2007*, 584–6.
32 Bōōei Kenkyūkai, *Jieitai no Kyōiku to Kunren*, 46–60.
33 Bōōei Kenkyūkai, *Jieitai no Kyōiku to Kunren*, 57. For an earlier assessment of the JSDF's ethos, see Osamu Inagaki, 'Jieitai Seishin Kyōiku', 142–52; the article appeared in English too as 'The Jieitai: Military Values in a Pacifist Society', *The Japan Interpreter*, 1–15.
34 JMoD, *Defence of Japan 2007*, 585.
35 Bōei Kenkyūkai, *Jieitai no Kyōiku to Kunren*, 12–13. Also, JMoD, *Defence of Japan 2007*, 585–6.
36 Kengaku no Seishin (建学の精神).
37 Matsumoto, '"Bōei Daigakkō Go Jū Nenshi" wo Yonde', 6.
38 Matsumoto, '"Bōei Daigakkō Go Jū Nenshi" wo Yonde', 12–14. Also, 'Bōōei Daigakkō de Naniga Manaberuka', 10; Nishihara, interview with the author, 29 June 2007.
39 One case that contributed to keeping the national debate over the JSDF military identity going was the incident of the 'Three Arrow Strategic Plan' (Mitsuya Sakusen Keikaku – 三ツ矢作戦計画). In February 1965, a Diet member of the socialist party, Okada Haruo, ignited a heated political debate revealing that he had gained possession of a war exercise plan according to which the JSDF would set up a military government in case of war. Details released about the plan informed public debate on the JSDF well into the following decade. Ike Nobutaka, 'Japan Twenty Years after Surrender', 25–6; Inagaki, 'The Jieitai: Military Values in a Pacifist Society', 3.
40 Matsumoto, '"Bōei Daigakkō Go Jū Nenshi" wo Yonde', 12.
41 The departments are: Liberal Arts and General Education, Humanities and Social Sciences, Applied Sciences, Electrical and Computer Engineering, Systems Engineering, Defence Studies.
42 For an updated overview of the NDA's programmes, see Editorial Department, 'Bōei Daigakkō de Naniga Manaberuka', 11–13.
43 'Miccyaku! Korega Bōei Daigakkō no Gakusei Seikatsuda', 14–19.
44 Author's cruise on JDS *Kashima* (TV-3508), 10 April 2005; author's visit to JDS *Kashima* (TV-3508), 23 July 2008.
45 Nakamori, *Bōei Daigakkō no Shinjitsu*, 162–8. Professor Kawano Hitoshi and Assistant Professor Hikotani Takako, conversation with the author, 5 September 2005.
46 Shōtai (小隊).
47 Daitai (大隊).
48 Nishihara, interview with the author, 29 June 2007; Kōda, interview with the author, 17 August 2007; Vice Admiral Ōta Fumio, JMSDF (Ret.), interview with the author,

28 April 2005; Admiral Sakuma Makoto, JMSDF (Ret.), interview with the author, 21 October 2005.
49 Vice Admiral Fumio Ōta, JMSDF, 'Jointness in the Japanese Self-Defence Forces', 57.
50 Ota, interview with the author, 28 April 2005.
51 For instance, in 2005, while the details of the transformation were debated, the three chiefs of staff of the JSDF were all former Defence Academy classmates. Reportedly, meetings unfolded in a rather informal atmosphere that favoured the discussions. This is far from being an unusual situation, and it often recreates itself at lower departmental levels. Admiral Saitō Takashi, JMSDF, interview with the author, 2 September 2005; Kōda, interview with the author, 17 August 2007.
52 Vice Admiral Ota, interview with the author, 28 April 2005.
53 'Y' Iinkai (Y 委員会). For a brief overview of the proceedings of the Committee, see Auer, *The Post-war Rearmament of Japanese Maritime Forces*, 83–6; Maeda, *The Hidden Army*, 50–2. For a comprehensive presentation of the subject, NHK Special Selection, *Kaijojieitai wa Kōshite Umareta*, especially Chapters 4–8; Sōbei Suzuki, *Kikisho: Kaijojieitai Shiwa*, 59–85; Masuda, *Jieitai no Tanjō*, 128–37.
54 Suzuki, *Kikisho: Kaijojieitai Shiwa*, 79–84; NHK Special Selection, *Kaijōjieitai wa Kōshite Umareta*, 139.
55 See for instance, Admiral Toyoda Soemu's comments in USSBS, *Interrogations of Japanese Officials*, 318, 325.
56 The USN had a leading role in this transformation. Cf. Baer, *One Hundred Years of Seapower*, 284–313, 332–66. For similar considerations concerning the Royal Navy, cf. Grove, *Vanguard to Trident*, Chapters 3–6. Also, Polmar, *Aircraft Carriers*, Chapters 2–8; Polmar and Moore, *Cold War Submarines*, Chapters 2–6.
57 Admiral Teiji Nakamura, JMSDF (Ret.), *Nakamura Teiji: Ōraru Hisutorī - Gekan*, 226.
58 Suzuki, *Kikisho: Kaijojieitai Shiwa*, 107.
59 Vice Admiral Kenichi Kitamura, JMSDF (Ret.), 'The Dawn of the New Japanese Navy: The Story of a Japanese Officer's Attendance at the US Naval War College', 108–9
60 Auer, *The Post-war Rearmament of Japanese Maritime Forces*, 208; Kitamura, 'The Dawn of the New Japanese Navy', 108–9.
61 For instance, in January 1955, nine officers and seventy-two petty officers and sailors, who were to become members of the first crew of the *Kuroshio*, arrived in New London and joined the school's training programmes for the following six months. Tsukudo, 'Kaijōjieitaihatsu no Sensuikan "Kuroshio" Kaisōki', 103.
62 Patalano, '"If You Can't Beat Them, Join Them": US-Japan Military Exchanges and the Development of the Japanese Post-war Submarine Force, 1955-2005'.
63 JMSDF, *Kaijōjieitai Gojū Nenshi*, 58–60.
64 Jutsuka Gakkō (術科学校).
65 The 1st Service school was initially located in Taura, and in 1956 when two structures were opened, it was moved to Etajima as a branch of the Yokosuka school. JMSDF, *Kaijōjieitai Gojū Nenshi*, 56.
66 JMSDF, *Kaijōjieitai Gojū Nenshi*, 56–7. Also, Auer, *The Post-war Rearmament of Japanese Maritime Forces*, 207–8.
67 Admiral Nakayama Sadayoshi, JMSDF, *Chakuninni Saishi Kunji*, 8 August 1961.
68 Admiral Uchida Kazuomi, JMSDF, *Chakuninni Saishi Kunji*, 1 July 1969.
69 Admiral Ōga Ryōhei, JMSDF, *Chakuninni Saishi Kunji*, 1 September 1977.
70 Captain Ōtsuka Umio, JMSDF, interview with the author, 14 March 2005.

71 Sakuma, interview with the author, 21 October 2005.
72 Nishihara, interview with the author, 29 June 2007. Captain Ojima G., JMSDF, interview with the author, 14 March 2005.
73 Nakamura, *Nakamura Teiji: Ōraru Hisutorī - Gekan*, 226–7.
74 Nakamura, *Nakamura Teiji: Ōraru Hisutorī - Gekan*, 227–8.
75 Nakayama, *Chakuninni Saishi Kunji*, 8 August 1961.
76 Admiral Sugie Kazumi, JMSDF, *Chakuninni Saishi Kunji*, 7 January 1963.
77 Seimeisen (生命線). Admiral Nakamura Teiji, JMSDF, *Chakuninni Saishi Kunji*, 16 March 1976.
78 Chinmoku Shōjin (沈黙精進).
79 Seiei Butai (精鋭部隊).
80 Uchida, *Chakuninni Saishi Kunji*, 1 July 1969.
81 Admiral Hayashizaki Chiaki, JMSDF, *Chakuninni Saishi Kunji*, 1 July 1993. For an overview of the JMSDF's contribution to the three operations see, JMSDF, *Kaijōjieitai Gojū Nenshi*, 467–86, 492–6, 498–500.
82 From 1953 to 1956, officers' training was carried out in Yokosuka. JMSDF, *Kaijōjieitai Gojū Nenshi*, 58.
83 Auer, *The Post-war Rearmament of Japanese Maritime Forces*, 205; Dean, 'Etajima: Hallowed Halls', 112.
84 Etajima Taifū (江田島台風).
85 JMSDF, *Kanbu Kōhosei: Etajima no Seishun* (DVD).
86 Lt Commander Kitagawa, JMSDF, 14 September 2005.
87 Dean, 'Etajima: Hallowed Halls', 113–15.
88 Lt Commander Kitagawa, JMSDF, 14 September 2005; Commander Ikeuchi T., JMSDF, 20 September 2005.
89 Nylander, 'Etajima Educated the Instructor', 10.
90 Auer, *The Post-war Rearmament of Japanese Maritime Forces*, 206; JMSDF, *Kaijōjieitai Gojū Nenshi*, 82–4.
91 JMSDF, *Kaijōjieitai Gojū Nenshi*, 84–5. On Prime Minister Ikeda's trip to Europe and Japanese diplomacy, see Bert Edström (ed.), *The Japanese and Europe: Images and Perceptions*, 213–14; Edström, *Japan's Evolving Foreign Policy Doctrine. From Yoshida to Miyazawa*, 46–56.
92 JMSDF, *Kaijōjieitai Gojū Nenshi – Shiryōhen*, 239–40.
93 Cabins are designated as Shikan Shitsu (士官室 – Officer's Cabin). The Japanese term used to indicate JSDF's officers is Jieikan (自衛官 – Self-Defence Official).
94 Shuho (酒舗).
95 Author's cruises on JDS *Kashima* (TV-3508), 10 April 2005; JDS *Kirisame* (DD-104), 27 May 2005; JDS *Chōkai* (DD-176), 25 October 2006; JDS *Sawayuki* (DD-125), 29 July 2007.
96 Kitamura, 'The Dawn of the New Japanese Navy', 109
97 JMSDF, *Kaijōjieitai Kanbu Gakkō Gojū Nenshi*, 1–3.
98 Academikku furīdamu (アカデミックフリーダム).
99 JMSDF, Kaijōjieitai Kanbu Gakkō Gojū Nenshi, 11. Author's group discussion with staff college students, 22 August 2005.
100 Author's group discussion with staff college students, 22 August 2005, 2.
101 Akiyama became an instructor at the NSC in 1900, at the specific request of its president, Admiral Sakamoto Toshiatsu. There, he reorganised the core course into three main areas of study: strategy, tactics and 'conduct of war' (which included logistics, communications and training). According to Mark Peattie, the last notion, while it became a standard area of interest for navies worldwide,

was dominant in Japanese higher naval education at that time of its introduction. The operational concepts developed by Akiyama were instrumental to Japan's naval successes in the Russo-Japanese War and continued to influence naval doctrine and planning well into the 1930s and early 1940s. Mark R. Peattie, 'Akiyama Saneyuki and the Emergence of Modern Japanese Naval Doctrine', 60–9; Evans and Peattie, *Kaigun*, 70–7. For a comprehensive overview of Akiyama's NSC's lectures and writings, cf Kazushige Todaka, *Akiyama Saneyuki Senjutsu Ronshū*.

102 When it was first instituted in 1954, the school was a rather modest institution, with a sixteen-personnel strong faculty. By 1957, staff numbers had increased and one of the two research divisions was tasked with the study of history-related matters. In October 2004, the faculty had reached 125 members, including 102 uniformed men. JMSDF, *Kaijōjieitai Kanbu Gakkō Gojū Nenshi*, 7–10.

103 In the second half of the 1980s, the study of wars of the past came to include even recent conflicts such as the 1971 Indo-Pak War and the 1982 conflict in the Falklands. JMSDF, *Kaijōjieitai Kanbu Gakkō Gojū Nenshi*, 19, 35.

104 On Admiral Yamanshi's lectures, Haruko Fukuda, 'The Peaceful Overture: Admiral Yamanashi Katsutoshin (1877–1967)', in Hugh Cortazzi and Gordon Daniels (eds), *Britain and Japan, 1859-1991. Themes and Personalities*, 198–213.

105 Yagi, conversation with the author, 19 May 2005; Commander Ishihara Takahiro, JMSDF, interview with the author, 14 June 2005; Lieutenant Commander Hirano Ryūji, JMSDF, conversation with the author, 12 July 2007.

106 The staff college was moved to the Meguro facilities in 1994 JMSDF, *Kaijōjieitai Kanbu Gakkō Gojū Nenshi*, 5.

107 This account is based on the author's numerous visits to the college during spring and summer 2005, 2007, 2009, 2011 and 2012.

108 The three colleges are identical in both organisation and distribution of classes and offices. Each of them features at its entrance decorations of various kinds, including flags of the countries represented at the college, commemorative plaques and photos of hosted events. This memorabilia contributes to put on 'display' the colleges' prestige. By placing the statue of Admiral Akiyama at the centre of this space, the maritime staff college (unlike the ground staff college) seeks to stress the significance of the intellectual bond between its educational emphasis and the pre-war naval tradition. Yagi, conversation with the author, conversation with the author, 19 May 2005; Hirano, conversation with the author, 12 July 2007.

109 The questionnaire was followed by a lengthy discussion held on 22 August 2005 with a group of officers who had answered the questions. The officers joining the group discussion included two male and one female JMSDF officers along with the two foreign officers. In the text, the presentation of the results of the questionnaire and the interviews refers to the Japanese students only, unless otherwise indicated.

110 The group of respondents was composed by thirteen 'surface' officers, seven supply officers, one submariner, three helicopter pilots, and one P-3C operator. The two foreign officers were both from the surface branches of their respective services.

111 In detail, eleven students (equal to 45.8 per cent) indicated a preference for the sea and technical jobs as the first reasons for joining the service, five (equal to 20.8 per cent) added the willingness to gain experience travelling abroad.

112 Agawa, *Umi no Yūjō*, 6.

113 Aikokushin (愛国心 – literally patriotism, love for one's country).

114 Indicated with the term Zasei (犠牲) which in Japanese implies the idea of sacrifice at risk of one's life.

115 On the basis of twenty-three responses, seventeen officers (equal to 73.9 per cent) evaluated the 'ability to take decisions' as critical; similar views were expressed in regard to the 'commitment to defend the country' (fifteen students, equal to 62.5 per cent) and in relation to the importance of 'discipline' (twelve students, equal to 52.1 per cent).
116 Only five officers considered 'technical skills' as a vital component of the officer's professional profile, though for all of them it was at least 'particularly relevant'. For twelve of them (equal to 50 per cent), the 'will to take risks' was seen as a 'crucial' asset.
117 During the group discussion, the JMSDF female officer subsequently pointed out that these traits are most desirable regardless of the officer's gender. In her opinion, the lessons she had drawn from imperial naval officers concerned moral qualities, the ability to lead a team and to command; therefore, they had a universal application. Group discussion, 22 August 2005.
118 There are two additional reasons that informed the author's decision to focus on these admirals. First of all, a preliminary selection of specific historical figures, while imposing a limitation on the respondent's personal choices, favoured a comparative analysis of the different answers. Secondly, these admirals were chosen by the author on the basis of their wide popularity in order to create favourable conditions for the respondents to elaborate in greater details on their answers.
119 On this subject, cf. Asada, *From Mahan to Pearl Harbor*, 111–12, 127, 132, 143–4, 155; Asada, *Culture Shock and Japanese-American Relations*, 128, 132; Gow, *Military Intervention in Pre-war Japanese Politics*, 220–1, 268–73.
120 Evans and Peattie, *Kaigun*, 482–6. Commander Sadao Senō, JMSDF, 'A Chess Game with no Checkmate: Admiral Inoue and the Pacific War', 26–39.
121 Admiral Inoue's memorandum is explained in Senō, 'A Chess Game with no Checkmate', 31–5.
122 Evans and Peattie, *Kaigun*, 485–6; Senō, 'A Chess Game with no Checkmate', 35–7.
123 Paul S. Dull, *A Battle History of the Imperial Japanese Navy, 1941-1945*, 134.
124 Vice Admiral Kaneda Hideaki, JMSDF (Ret.), interview with the author, 5 August 2005.
125 Reportedly, Admiral Yamamoto received a considerable number of letters and postcards from Japanese people across the country on a daily basis. Some of his attendants later reported that he habitually slept only four hours at night, taking the rest of the time to answer all the mail from his fellow citizens. Agawa, *The Reluctant Admiral*, 41–2.
126 More specifically, thirteen students (equal to 54.1 per cent) were of this opinion. Similar views were restated during the group session. Group discussion, 22 August 2005.
127 Group discussion, 22 August 2005.
128 In this regard, the more recent experience of the Royal Navy offers striking similarities. Cf. Eric Grove, 'The Discovery of Doctrine. British Naval Thinking at the Close of the Twentieth Century', 184–5.
129 Both foreign students when asked whether they thought their Japanese colleagues were 'naval' or 'self-defence' officers, they both answered that the two are in fact the same.
130 Anonymous Lt. Commander, JMSDF, 20 September 2005.
131 In some cases, the JMSDF pushed the safety envelope in operational training to extremes, resulting in collateral damage to civilian shipping. The most dramatic accident occurred in July 1988, when a new submarine, *Nadashio*, collided with a pleasure fishing boat, killing thirty passengers. In November 2006, the submarine *Asashio* collided with a Panama-registered chemical tanker, but the incident had

no repercussions apart from minor structural damage sustained by the boat and the tanker. 'Sub Skipper Admits Fault in Collision', *The Japan Times*, 12 June 2007.

132 One of the most recent examples of how these factors contribute to affect the JMSDF's operational activity is the 19 February 2008 collision of the AEGIS destroyer *Atago*, which resulted in two missing civilians. Preliminary results of the investigation pointed to human errors due to a reduced complement and limited training. 'Probe: Atago Crew Missed Boat though Radar Saw It', *The Yomiuri Shimbun*, 8 June 2008.

133 Morris Janowitz, *The Professional Soldier: A Social and Political Portrait*, 127.

Chapter 5

1 Captain Toshiyuki Itō, JMSDF, interview with the author, 20 May 2005

2 JMSDF, *Kaijōjieitai Gojū Nenshi – Shiryōhen*, 252.

3 JMSDF, *Umi no Mamori Gojū Nen*, 112.

4 JMSDF, *Kaijōjieitai Gojū Nenshi*, 96.

5 On left-wing political opposition to the JSDF, see Mendel, 'Public Views of the Japanese Defence System', in Buck, *The Modern Japanese Military System*, 155, 161; Kliman, *Japan's Security Strategy in the Post-9/11 World*, 86–7, 134; Samuels, *Securing Japan*, 118–19.

6 JDA, *Defence of Japan 2005*, 397.

7 Literature on the question of Japanese public perception of the JSDF as a whole is extensive. For the period from the 1950s to the early 1970s, Mendel, 'Public Views of the Japanese Defence System', 149–80. For later years, Midford, *Japanese Public Opinion and the War on Terrorism*; Kliman, *Japan's Security Strategy in the Post-9/11 World*, 42–66.

8 Masuhara, *A Review of Japan's Defence Strength*, 14; JMSDF, *Kaijōjieitai Gojū Nenshi – Shiryōhen*, 278; Auer, *The Post-war Rearmament of Japanese Maritime Forces*, 82, 156.

9 Kankanshiki (観艦式).

10 JMSDF, *Kaijōjieitai Gojū Nenshi*, 96.

11 Author's attendance to the rehearsal of the JMSDF Fleet Review 2006 onboard JDS *Chōkai* (DDG176), held on 25 October 2006.

12 The 2006 edition had five full-scale rehearsals and an audience of some 10,000 people. More than 30,000 people applied online months in advance to receive tickets for any of the available dates. Public Affairs Office (PAO) member of staff, JMSDF, interview with the author, 9 August 2007. On the JGSDF and the JASDF main public events, Frühstück and Ben-Ari, '"Now We Show It All!"', 18–19; Frühstück, *Uneasy Warriors*, 138–48.

13 Shibata Mitsuo, interview with the author, 2 June 2005.

14 Nihonkai Kaisen (日本海海戦).

15 Gunkan (軍艦).

16 JDA, *Defence of Japan 1984*, 86.

17 Admiral Tōru Ishikawa, JMSDF, 'Greetings from CMS, JMSDF', *2002 International Fleet Review Information Booklet* (Tokyo: Maritime Staff Office – MSO, October 2002), courtesy of the JMSDF's PAO.

18 Frühstück and Ben-Ari, 'Now We Show It All!', 1–39; Frühstück, *Uneasy Warriors*, 116–48.

19 Kōhōshitsu (広報室).
20 Captain Itō Toshiyuki, JMSDF, interview with the author, 20 May 2005.
21 Wakamiya, 'SDF's star on the rise in turbulent times', *The Asahi Shimbun*, 31 July 2003.
22 Midford, *Japanese Public Opinion and the War on Terrorism*, 5, 17–20, 44–5, 49; Kliman, *Japan's Security Strategy in the Post-9/11 World*, 50–2; Hughes, *Japan's Re-emergence as a 'Normal' Military Power*, 58–9; Samuels, *Securing Japan*, 71–82.
23 Morris, *Nationalism and the Right Wing in Japan*, 207; Auer, *The Post-war Rearmament of Japanese Maritime Forces*, 183.
24 Nakamoto, 'Young Japanese Unwilling to be Soldiers', *Financial Times*, 7 September 1990; Schoenberger, 'Military in Japan Gets No Respect', *Los Angeles Times*, 10 September 1990.
25 Quoted from a JMSDF Promotional video, JDA, April 2005, courtesy of JMSDF's PAO, MSO.
26 For instance, JMSDF members of staff from the PAO expressed very moderate sympathies for Prince Pickles as it did not advertise any of the 'navy's values'. It is worth noting that while Prince Pickles could be purchased as a plastic doll or as a mobile phone string in shops at the JMoD or other major JSDF facilities, its appearance on the shelves of the JMSDF's souvenir shops in museums or on the temporary stands before a major naval parade was rare. In these places of distinctive 'naval advertising', more classic dolls wearing the JMSDF's blue jacket or navy hat-wearing penguin puppets are the items that replace it in the role of 'selling the navy'. PAO member of staff, JMSDF, interview with the author, 9 August 2007; author's visits to JMSDF's museums in Etajima (February 2005, May 2008), Sasebo (July 2005), Kanoya (August 2005), Kure (August 2007); author's attendance to the JMSDF's 2006 Fleet Review, 26 October 2006.
27 As of 2007, the official JMSDF website included three video clips to pinpoint different professional attributes that more easily reconcile the service's identity with the different interests of a junior high school child, a potential recruit with a high school educational background, or a university undergraduate student. On this subject see also, Philip Brasor, 'Imagine All the Soldiers and Sailors Singing and Dancing in Harmony', *The Japan Times*, 22 April 2007, http://search.japantimes.co.jp/cgi-bin/fd20070422pb.html.
28 In the 1990s, the public affairs divisions of all civilian and military branches of the JDA were reinforced. Katzenstein, *Cultural Norms and National Security*, 108.
29 Frühstück and Ben-Ari, 'Now We Show it All', 18.
30 Itō, interview with the author, 20 May 2005; Captain Ōseto Isao, JMSDF, interview with the author, 20 June 2007.
31 Frühstück, *Uneasy Warriors*, 118.
32 Chief Petty Officer, JMSDF, interview with the author, 14 August 2007.
33 Itō, interview with the author, 20 May 2005.
34 'SDF's 3 Arms Battle for Hits on Web Sites', *Yomiuri Shinbun*, 6 January 2006, http://www.yomiuri.co.jp/dy/national/20060106TDY02002.htm.
35 Data concerning the period from January to July 2007, courtesy of the JMSDF's PAO, Tokyo.
36 *Bōei Nenkan*, 577.
37 Furushō, interview with the author, 2 September 2005.
38 Lieutenant Commander Hirose Takeo was only twenty-five years old when he was promoted posthumously to the rank of commander and the Imperial Navy's official historian, First-Lieutenant (later Rear Admiral) Ogasawara Naganari, endeavoured to raise him to the status of 'military god' (Gunshin – 軍神). As an officer, Hirose

was a charismatic leader, keen not only on his duty but on the well-being of his subordinates, nurturing an almost brother-like bond with them. His abnegation to his crew members was epitomised by a tragic death in an explosion while searching for Superior Warrant Officer Sugino Magoshichi on board the sinking *Fukimaru*, one of the block-ships employed in the second attempt to blockade Port Arthur on 27 March 1904. Shimazu, 'The Making of a Heroic War Myth in the Russo-Japanese War', 83–96.

39 *Bōei Nenkan*, 577; Admiral Furushō, interview with the author, 2 September 2005

40 Umi no Bujin (海の武人). Considerations based on the author's interviews and conversations with several middle rank and senior JMSDF's officers, May, August and September 2005.

41 Auer, *The Post-war Rearmament of Japanese Maritime Forces*, 49–52.

42 Auer, *The Post-war Rearmament of Japanese Maritime Forces*, 62–8, 159; NHK Special Selection, *Kaijōjieitai wa Kōshite Umareta*, 250–5; Hirama, 'Japan's Value in the Korean War: Issues Surrounding the Dispatch of Minesweepers', http://www.bea.hi-ho.ne.jp/hirama/yh_e_top.html.

43 Maeda, *The Hidden Army*, 43–4.

44 Considerations based on the author's interviews and conversations with several middle rank and senior JMSDF officers, May, August and September 2005.

45 Samuels, *Securing Japan*, 66–7; Hughes, *Japan's Re-emergence as a 'Normal' Military Power*, 41–2; also, Takashi, 'Japan's Response to the Gulf Crisis: An Analytical Overview', 257–73.

46 'Sōkaitei Kyō Syukkō', *Asahi Shinbun*, 26 April 1991. Also, JMSDF, *Kaijōjieitai Gojū Nenshi*, 474–80.

47 Woolley, *Japan's Navy*, 89–109.

48 Vice Admiral Kaneda, interview with the author, 19 October 2005; Woolley, *Japan's Navy*, 101; Woolley, 'Japan's 1991 Minesweeping Decision', 813–14.

49 Admiral Sakuma, JMSDF, *Chakunin ni Saishi Kunji*, 31 August 1989.

50 It must be noted that minesweeping is seen in Japan as one of the arms of the JMSDF of great public utility for the clearing from territorial waters of sea mines planted during the Pacific War. Reportedly, 99 per cent of the archipelago is now clear of these devices, though the service is continuously engaged in the destruction and removal of dangerous explosives at the request of local authorities. As late as 2004, minesweepers removed 32,153 explosives including two mines (almost 618 explosives a week on average), totalling about 100 tons of volume. JDA, *Defence of Japan 2005*, 397.

51 Midford, *Japanese Public Opinion and the War on Terrorism*, 16–17. In 1992 the Japanese Diet passed a legislation (the International Peace Cooperation Law) to allow the participation of the JSDF in UN PKO. Since its enactment, SDF personnel participated in UN missions in Cambodia (1992), Mozambique (1993), Zaire (1994), the Golan Heights (1996) and East Timor (2002). More recently, the SDF were dispatched to Indonesia (2004), as part of the international emergency assistance provided in the wake of the tsunami in the Indian Ocean and to Haiti (2010) as part of the UN relief mission after the earthquake.

52 Furushō, 'Kaijōjieitai no Kirai Senbutai: Sono Genjō to Syōrai', 141–5; Hino, 'Chūmoku no Perusyawan Haken Sōkaibutai', 168–71.

53 Reference to the Naval Academy in Etajima and to its museum as 'holy places' occurred on more than one occasion in conversations and interviews with JMSDF's flag officers when they explained its spiritual value to service's identity. Kaneda, interview with the author, 5 August 2005; Kōda, JMSDF, interview with the author, 17 August 2007.

54 Agawa, *Umi no Yūjō*, 4.
55 Agawa, interview with the author, 20 July 2007.
56 It is significant that officially they are classified as 'Reference Places' for education (Shiryōkan – 資料館) and in fact, the organisation of the exhibitions and the arrangement of the displays is supervised by the Education and Planning Divisions of the MSO.
57 This paragraph draws on information collected during a visit to the Naval Aviation Museum and the Naval Aviation Base in Kanoya on 27 and 28 August 2005 and on 10 and 11 April 2010.
58 Gunjin Seishin (軍人精神).
59 Tokubetsu Kōgeki Tai (特別攻撃隊), or Tokkōtai (特攻隊). The Naval Aviation Museum should not be confused with the nearby museum in Chiran, which also memorialises the history of Tokkōtai, but is not connected to the JSDF.
60 For the content of the letter, Auer, *Who Was Responsible?*, 164–5.
61 Director of the Naval Aviation Museum, interview with the author, 27 August 2005.
62 This paragraph draws on the materials gathered during a one-day visit to the Naval Historical Museum in Sasebo on 31 July 2005 and on 8 April 2010. According to the officer who guided this author through the museum, the volume of visitors is similar to Kanoya, though visitors are primarily Japanese.
63 JDA, *Defence of Japan 1999*, 170.
64 Captain Ōtsuka Umio, JMSDF, interview with the author, 14 March 2005.
65 Shibata, interview with the author, 2 June 2005.
66 Itō, interview with the author, 20 May 2005. Captain Itō further explained that this approach was at the basis of his involvement in the development of the main characters for the two fiction films *Bōkoku no Aegis* (亡国のイージス – The Country-less Aegis) and *Otokotachi no Yamato* (男たちの大和 – The Men of the Yamato). Both movies did well at the box office, the former placed on the 12th position in the 2005 list of most successful films, the latter 6th for 2006 (Motion Picture Producers Association Japan, http://www.eiren.org/boxoffice_e/2005.html, http://www.eiren.org/boxoffice_e/2006.html). Captain Itō was also the model for the lead character of prime time TV drama aired by the network TBS in 2005. 'Jieitai Tōjō Suru Kono Shīn', 12–15.
67 JMSDF, *Kanbu Kōhosei: Etajima no Seishun* (DVD).
68 Midford, *Japanese Public Opinion and the War on Terrorism*, 20–45; on shifts in public opinion's perceptions of the JSDF and defence policy in relation to North Korea and China, cf. Kliman, *Japan's Security Strategy in the Post-9–11 World*, 55–60.
69 Midford, *Japanese Public Opinion and the War on Terrorism*, 24–8.
70 JDA, *Defence of Japan 2003*, 295–6.
71 JMSDF, *Kaijōjieitai Gojū Nenshi*, 681–2.
72 JMSDF, *Kokusai Kankan Shiki 2002.*
73 Author's attendance to the JMSDF's Commemoration of the Battle of Tsushima onboard of JDS *Kirisame* (DD-104), 28 May 2005.
74 The DVD version of *Otokotachi no Yamato* contained 'extras' including a long video interview with Captain Itō explaining the JMSDF's material contribution to the production of the film and more importantly, the ethical and cultural ties between the pre- and post-war service in terms of discipline, teamwork and camaraderie.
75 Nao Shimoyaki, 'Admiral Proposes SDF less Run by Civilians', *The Japan Times*, 3 July 2004, http://search.japantimes.co.jp/cgi-bin/nn20040703a1.html.
76 Furushō, interview with the author, 2 September 2005.
77 Admiral Furushō, *Chakunin ni Saishi Kunji*, 28 January 2003.

78 Kokumin no Me ni Yoru Hyōka (国民の目による評価). Admiral Furushō, *Chakunin ni Saishi Kunji*, 28 January 2003.
79 Admiral Furushō, *Chakunin ni Saishi Kunji*, 28 January 2003.

Chapter 6

1 Tsunoda, Uchida, 'The Pearl Harbor Attack: Admiral Yamamoto's Fundamental Concept with Reference to Paul S. Dull's, *A Battle History of the Imperial Japanese Navy (1941-1945)*', 88.
2 Masashi Nishihara, 'Maritime Japan Should Reinforce Maritime Defence Capability', 17 July 2008, http://www.jiia.or.jp/en_commentary/200807/17-1.html, accessed 20 October 2008.
3 Kaijōjieitai Sōkai Butai, *Nihon no Sōkaishi: Chōsen Dōran Tokubetsu Sōkaishi*, 13–19.
4 Kaijōjieitai Sōkai Butai, *Nihon no Sōkaishi: Chōsen Dōran Tokubetsu Sōkaishi*, 12; Auer, *The Post-war Rearmament of Japanese Maritime Forces*, 66.
5 Kaijōjieitai Sōkai Butai, *Nihon no Sōkaishi: Chōsen Dōran Tokubetsu Sōkaishi*, 46–9. Also, NHK Special Selection, *Kaijōjieitai wa Kōshite Umareta*, 250–3.
6 Nomura, 'Memorandum 6', 31 January 1951, Mauch, *The Occupation-era Correspondence of Kichisaburo Nomura*, 135–6.
7 Till, *Maritime Strategy and the Nuclear Age*, 224–5.
8 Corbett, *Some Principles of Maritime Strategy*, 14.
9 Corbett, *Some Principles of Maritime Strategy*, 15.
10 USSBS, *Interrogations of Japanese Officials*, 318. This assessments were confirmed by later scholarship, for examples, Evans and Peattie, *Kaigun*, 398–401; Asada, *From Mahan to Pearl Harbor*, 287–9.
11 USSBS, *Interrogations of Japanese Officials*, 394.
12 Mauch, *Sailor Diplomat: Nomura Kichisaburō and the Japanese-American War*, 218.
13 For example, Evans, *The Japanese Navy in World War II*.
14 Yokoi 'Thoughts on Japan's Naval Defeat', 68.
15 Schencking, *Making Waves*, 8, 125–8, 145–60; Asada, *From Mahan to Pearl Harbor*, 47–51, 178–82, 293–5; Asada, *Culture Shock and Japanese-American Relations*, 106–36; Yokoi, 'Thoughts on Japan's Naval Defeat', 71–2.
16 Evans and Peattie, *Kaigun*, Chapters 7 and 8. Also, Hirama, 'Japanese Naval Preparations for World War II', 63–81.
17 Yokoi, 'Thoughts on Japan's Naval Defeat', 69.
18 Yokoi, 'Thoughts on Japan's Naval Defeat', 74–5. Toyama, 'Lessons from the Past', 62–9.
19 Until 1945, the Imperial Navy required approximately 3 million tons of fuel yearly. For instance, at the Battle of the Leyte Gulf, the Japanese fleet consumed 15,000 tons of oil in less than a week. Parillo, 'The Imperial Navy in World War II', 64.
20 Parillo, *The Japanese Merchant Marine in World War II*, 215, 247.
21 Blair, *Silent Victory: The U.S. Submarine War against Japan*, 900–83.
22 Blair, *Silent Victory: The U.S. Submarine War against Japan*, 966–75.
23 Toyama, 'Lessons from the Past', 68–9; Atsushi Oi, 'Why Japan's Antisubmarine Warfare Failed', 385–414. Also, Nomura, *Kaisenshi ni Manabu*, 236–50; Graham, *Japan's Sea Lane Security*, 77–89.
24 Goralski and Freeburg, *Oil & War: How the Deadly Struggle for Fuel in WWII Meant Victory or*, 246–7; Winton, *Convoy: The Defence of Sea Trade, 1890-1990*, 314; Blair, *Silent Victory*, 878–9.

25 Quoted in Blair, *Silent Victory*, 879.
26 Koda, 'A Commander's Dilemma', 70–4; Parshall and Tully, *Shattered Sword*, 402–15.
27 Mauch, *Sailor Diplomat*, 227.
28 Mauch, *Sailor Diplomat*, 227.
29 Auer, *The Post-war Rearmament of Japanese Maritime Forces*, 70.
30 Mauch, *The Occupation-era Correspondence of Kichisaburo Nomura*, 129–55, 185–9.
31 Auer, *The Post-war Rearmament of Japanese Maritime Forces*, 83–9.
32 Mauch, *Sailor Diplomat*, 247.
33 Nomura Kichisaburō, 'Japan After Independence', 3 July 1952, in Mauch, *The Occupation-era Correspondence of Kichisaburo Nomura*, 213.
34 Yahuda, *The International Politics of the Asia-Pacific*, 20–5; Buckley, *The United States in the Asia-Pacific since 1945*, 49–82; Cohen, *East Asia at the Centre: Four Thousand Years of Engagement with the World*, 375–6.
35 The Constitution of Japan, http://www.kantei.go.jp/foreign/constitution_and_government_of_japan/constitution_e.html.
36 Yoshida's views, though not officially formalised, substantially informed his successors' policies and for this reason, they are frequently referred to as the 'Yoshida Doctrine', or 'Yoshida's Line'. Hughes, *Japan Re-Emergence as a 'Normal' Military Power*, 21–7; Samuels, *Securing Japan*, 29–37; Graham, *Japan's Sea Lane Security*, 92–8; Nakajima Shingo, *Sengo Nihon no Bōei Seisaku. 'Yoshida Rosen' wo Meguru Seiji, Gaikō, Gunji*.
37 Masataka Kosaka, 'Japan's Major Interests and Policies in Asia and the Pacific', *Orbis*, Vol. 24, 1975:3, 793–808.
38 Seido Chōsa Iinkai (制度調査委員会).
39 Auer, *The Post-war Rearmament of Japanese Maritime Forces*, 154.
40 Keibitai (警備隊).
41 Kaijōkōtsūhogo (海上交通保護).
42 It must be noted that at the time of the drafting of this first proposal, the defence of maritime transportation was not a pressing issue as Japan's economy was still recovering from the war disaster. In 1955, the Japanese economy was equal to 7 per cent of that of the United States and ranked below major European countries. Gordon, *A Modern History of Japan*, 246.
43 Auer, *The Post-war Rearmament of Japanese Maritime Forces*, 154; Graham, *Japan's Sea Lane Security*, 100.
44 Nomura, 'Memorandum 6', 31 January 1951, in Mauch, *The Occupation-era Correspondence of Kichisaburo Nomura*, 136.
45 Military Assistance and Advisory Group Japan (MAAG-J), 'Requirements for the Naval Defence of Japan', 14 November 1956, in Ishii and Ono, *Documents on the United States Policy towards Japan. Documents related to Diplomatic and Military Matters 1956, Volume 4*, 398–405.
46 Later drafts produced after 1955 attributed to naval defence increasingly modest tonnage allocations, ranging from 81,000 to 143,000 tons. Auer, *The Post-war Rearmament of Japanese Maritime Forces*, 155.
47 From a broader strategic point of view, the next war was expected to involve the two superpowers (i.e. the United States and the USSR) and to be atomic and of limited duration, in which case the navy would have little or no role to play. On the other hand, in the less likely case of a prolonged conventional conflict, Japan would rely heavily on American naval operations to keep sea lanes open. JMSF, *Kaijōjieitai Gojū Nenshi*, 26; Baer, *One Hundred Years of Seapower*, 332–3.

48 William J. Sebald to Secretary of State, 28 January 1955, and MAAG-J to Secretary of State, 18 March 1955 in Ishii and Ono, *Documents on the United States Policy towards Japan. Documents related to Diplomatic and Military Matters 1955, Volume 2*, 27, 95.

49 From 1955 to 1973, Japan's economy grew at a staggering rate, reaching the third position in the world after the United States and the Soviet Union, with its GNP climbing to approximately one-third of the US total. Gordon, *A Modern History of Japan*, 246–7.

50 *Bōei Ryoku Seibi Keikaku* (防衛力整備計画). These plans were also known as *Jibō* (次防).

51 Masuhara, *A Review of Japan's Defence Strength*, 19.

52 *Hondohe no Cyokusetsu Shinryakuni Taisuru Kaijō Bōei* (本土への直接侵略に対する海上防衛).

53 JMSF, *Kaijōjieitai Gojū Nenshi*, 29–30.

54 Vice Admiral Yōji Kōda, JMSDF, interview with the author, 27 May 2008.

55 Akihiro Sadō, *Sengo Seiji to Jieitai*, 84–7.

56 Within the Liberal Democratic Party, the strengthening of Japanese naval and air defences represented a long-term goal supported by a politicians like Vice Admiral Hoshina. References by Admiral Hoshina to this idea can be found as early as 1957, and were restated by Funada Naka in 1969, though his emphasis was more on the general question of the qualitative build-up of Japan's military potential. Hoshina Zenshiro, 'Opinion Regarding Adjustment of American-Japanese Relations from the Strategic Standpoint of the East and West', 12 February 1957, in Ishii and Ono, *Documents on the United States Policy towards Japan. Documents related to Diplomatic and Military Matters 1957, Volume 5*, 134–5.

57 Embassy Tokyo to Department of State, 'The Funada Plan for Post-Okinawa Reversion Security', 22 August 1969, in Ishii, Gabe, and Miyazato, *Documents on the United States Policy towards Japan. Documents related to Diplomatic and Military Matters 1969, Volume 7*, 29.

58 For one authoritative American naval observer, Japan's naval policies were producing very limited results, since 'nothing much seems to have changed as far as the number of ships built, percentage of budget, and continued strengthening of the already capable minesweeping force'. Auer, *The Post-war Rearmament of Japanese Maritime Forces*, 161.

59 JMSDF, *Kaijōjieitai Gojū Nenshi*, 31. In 1968, 99.4 per cent of crude oil consumed in Japan was imported, and 91 per cent of it came from the Middle East. Crude oil constituted more than 30 per cent of Japan's total imports. Sekino, 'Japan and her Maritime Defence', 115.

60 Nagata, 'Shīrēn Bōei', 78.

61 *Kōrotai* (航路帯).

62 *Nansei Kōrotai* (南西航路帯).

63 *Nantō Kōrotai* (南東航路帯).

64 Sadō, *Sengo Seiji to Jieitai*, 146; Graham, *Japan's Sea Lane Security*, 101. These lines later became referred to as the 'Nakamura lines', as Admiral Nakamura Teiji was said to have been one of the first to draw them. Agawa, *Umi no Yūjō*, 214.

65 JDA, *Defence of Japan 1977*, 100.

66 Kaiyō Kokka (海洋国家).

67 Tsūshō Kokka (通商国家).

68 Kōsaka, 'Kaiyō Kokka Nihon no Kōsō', *Chūō Kōron*, 48–80; Kōsaka, 'Tsūshō Kokka Nippon no Unmei', 116–40.

69 Kōsaka, *Options for Japan's Foreign Policy*, 3.
70 Professor Kōsaka was one of Prime Minister Yoshida Shigeru's most authoritative biographers and the first to use the term 'doctrine' in reference to Yoshida's political legacy. Cf. his *Saishō Yoshida Shigeru ron*.
71 JMSDF, *Kaijōjieitai Gojū Nenshi*, 121.
72 Maeda, *The Hidden Army*, 230.
73 Sekino, 'Japan and her Maritime Defence', 98–121. Sekino, 'Waga Kuni no Kaijō Goei Monday', 64–6.
74 Sekino, 'Japan and her Maritime Defence', 103.
75 For a detailed summary of the debate, cf. Graham, *Japan's Sea Lane Security*, 102–9.
76 Kaihara, 'Shīrēn Bōei Mondai wo Kangaeru: Jissai Mondai Toshite Fukanō', *Sekai no Kansen*, 130–1.
77 In the literature, Nakasone – who later served as Prime Minister – is generally described as a political maverick that adds to the difficulty of assessing the extent of his commitment to naval affairs. During the Pacific War, Nakasone served as junior officer in the Imperial Navy through the *Tangen* system, and in its aftermath, he never hesitated to admit his affiliation with the imperial service and remained in contact with the Japan Naval Association. Sadō, *Sengo Seiji to Jieitai*, 87–96; Graham, *Japan's Sea Lane Security*, 102–4.
78 Graham, *Japan's Sea Lane Security*, 121.
79 The Advisory Panel on Reconstruction of the Legal Basis for Security, *Report of the Advisory Panel on Reconstruction of the Legal Basis for Security* (Tokyo, 14 May 2014), 7.
80 Watanabe, 'Has Japan Crossed the Rubicon?', 241–4. Also, Hughes, *Japan Re-Emergence as a 'Normal' Military Power*, 67–8.
81 Kibanteki Bōeiryoku Kōsō (基盤的防衛力構想).
82 For a description of these types of missions, see Turner, 'Missions of the U.S. Navy', 94.
83 Watanabe, 'Has Japan Crossed the Rubicon?', 242–3.
84 For an in-depth analysis of Japan's dependence on shipping for trade and energy security from the mid-1970s to the second half of the 1980s, cf. Akaha, 'Japan's Response to Threats to Shipping Disruptions in Southeast Asia and the Middle East', 255–9.
85 Shin Gumbi Keikaku Ron (新軍備計画論).
86 Senō, 'A Chess Game with no Checkmate: Admiral Inoue and the Pacific War', 26–39. Also Evans and Peattie, *Kaigun*, 482–6.
87 Senō, interview with the author, 5 August 2005.
88 Commander Senō remained on friendly terms with Inoue Shigeyoshi until the time of the admiral's death. Senō, interview with the author, 5 August 2005.
89 Vice Admiral Stanfield Turner, USN, letter to Commander Senō, 1973. Courtesy of Commander Senō.
90 Graham, *Japan's Sea Lane Security*, 127.
91 JDA, *Defence of Japan 1977*, 64–5.
92 Graham, *Japan's Sea Lane Security*, 136; also Matsumae, *The Limits of Defense: Japan as an Unsinkable Aircraft-Carrier*, 38.
93 Kimura, 'The Soviet Military Build-up: Its Impact on Japan and its Aims', in Solomon and Kōsaka, *The Soviet Far East Military Build-up. Nuclear Dilemmas and Asian Security*, 107. Also, Maeda, *The Hidden Army*, 199–200.
94 Term used to describe a naval force capable of operating across the deep waters of open oceans, as opposed to green and brown water navies, which operate within coastal areas to 200 NM.

95 Polmar, *Guide to the Soviet Navy – Third Edition*, 20.
96 Polmar, *Guide to the Soviet Navy – Third Edition*, 21.
97 Polmar, *Guide to the Soviet Navy – Third Edition*, 21.
98 Polmar, *Guide to the Soviet Navy – Third Edition*, 25. For reference to Admiral Long, cf. Graham, *Japan's Sea Lane Security*, 126.
99 JDA, *Defence of Japan 1977*, 17, 29.
100 Ranft and Till, *The Sea in Soviet Strategy*, 120.
101 Polmar, *Guide to the Soviet Navy – Third Edition*, 20–1.
102 Uchida, 'Naval Cooperation and Security in East Asia', in Alford, *Sea Power and Influence: Old Issues and New Challenges*, 107.
103 Polmar, *Guide to the Soviet Navy – Third Edition*, 40–1, 43.
104 Sekino, 'Japan and her Maritime Defence', 119.
105 Senior Japanese naval officers often used this metaphor to describe the JMSDF's role in the Cold War when addressing an American audience; see for example Ishikawa, '"A Half-Century's Partnership": Japan Maritime Self-Defence Force's Enduring Relationship with the U. S. Navy', 32.
106 Uchida, 'Naval Cooperation and Security in East Asia', 107.
107 Sadō, *Sengo Seiji to Jieitai*, 144.
108 Maeda, *The Hidden Army*, 207–8.
109 Maeda, *The Hidden Army*, 208.
110 Maeda, *The Hidden Army*, 209.
111 In this respect, as early as 1973, Admiral Uchida was voicing in a lecture at the US Naval War College the importance that the JMSDF attributed to its navy-to-navy relation with the USN and its intention to strengthen it. Uchida, 'The Rearmament of the Japanese Maritime Forces', 41–8.
112 JMSDF, *Kaijōjieitai Gojū Nenshi*, 141–2.
113 Sadō, *Sengo Seiji to Jieitai*, 160–2; Watanabe, 'Has Japan Crossed the Rubicon?', 248; Graham, *Japan's Sea Lane Security*, 132.
114 Korb, 'The Erosion of American Naval Pre-eminence, 1962-1978', in Hagan, *In Peace and War: Interpretations of American Naval History, 1775-1978*, 338; also, Korb, *The Fall and Rise of the Pentagon: American Defense Policies in the 1970s*, 34, 37.
115 Korb, *The Fall and Rise of the Pentagon*, 42.
116 Marolda, *Ready Seapower: A History of the U.S. Seventh Fleet*, 89.
117 Baer, *One Hundred Years of Seapower*, 404.
118 Marolda, *Ready Seapower*, 89–90.
119 Quoted in Maeda, *The Hidden Army*, 234.
120 Baer, *One Hundred Years of Seapower*, 424–6.
121 Baer, *One Hundred Years of Seapower*, 430.
122 IISS, *The Military Balance 1992-1993*, 150–1.
123 Hughes, *Japan's Remilitarisation*, 24–5; JMoD, *Defence of Japan 2009*, 119.
124 Nishikawa, *Nihon no Anzen Hoshō Seisaku*, 163–4.
125 Hughes, *Japan's Remilitarisation*, 25.
126 Kaihara, 'Shīrēn Bōei Mondai wo Kangaeru: Jissai Mondai Toshite Fukanō', 131–3; Matsumae, *The Limits of Defense*, 139–40.
127 Yamaguchi, 'Balancing Threat Perceptions and Strategic Priorities: Japan's Post-war Defence Policy', in Patalano, *Maritime Strategy and National Security in Japan and Britain. From the First Alliance to Post 9/11*, 89–90.
128 Quoted in Yamaguchi, 'Balancing Threat Perceptions and Strategic Priorities', 90.
129 Quoted in Kimura, 'The Soviet Military Build-up: Its Impact on Japan and its Aims', 110.

130 Watanabe, 'Has Japan Crossed the Rubicon', 239.
131 Sadō Akihiro maintains that international criticisms against Japan's lack of initiative represented a 'trauma' for the country's political circles. Sadō, *Sengo Seiji to Jieitai*, 170.
132 As a first step to address this issue in August 1992, the Japanese Diet passed a legislation (the International peace Cooperation Law) to allow the participation of the JSDF in UN PKOs. Shortly after, the government of Japan dispatched JSDF units to Cambodia (UNTAC, September 1992) and Mozambique (ONUMOZ, May 1993).
133 Samuels, *Securing Japan*, 66–7; Pyle, *Japan Rising*, 290–3.
134 Woolley, *Japan's Navy*, 101; Woolley, 'Japan's 1991 Minesweeping Decision: An Organizational Response', *Asian Survey*, 804–17.
135 Woolley, *Japan's Navy*, 101.
136 Woolley, *Japan's Navy*, 101.
137 Editorial Department, 'Sōkaitei Kyō Syukkō', *Asahi Shinbun*, 26 April 1991. For a comprehensive account, see JMSDF, *Kaijōjieitai Gojū Nenshi*, 474–80.
138 JMSDF, *Kaijōjieitai Gojū Nenshi*, 469–70.
139 JMSDF, *Kaijōjieitai Gojū Nenshi*, 478–80.
140 Marolda and Schneller, *Shield and Sword: The United States Navy and the Persian Gulf War*, 322–5.
141 Vice Admiral Yōji Kōda, 'From Alliance to Coalition, then Where? Japan and the US Navy Cooperative Strategy for the Twenty-First Century', in Patalano, *Maritime Strategy and National Security in Japan and Britain*, 218.
142 'Japan, by Sending Minesweepers to the Gulf, Takes Step Toward Broader World Role', *Wall Street Journal*, 25 April 2001, 10.
143 Akaha, 'Japan's Response to Threats to Shipping Disruptions in Southeast Asia and the Middle East', 270–5.
144 Admiral Okabe Fumio, *Chakunin ni Saishi Kunji*, 1 July 1991.
145 Mulloy, *Japan Self-Defense Forces' Overseas Dispatch Operations in the 1990s*, 134.
146 JMSDF, *Kaijōjieitai Gojū Nenshi*, 441.
147 In Japanese, the 1995 NDPO was named *Shin Bōei Keikaku no Taikō*, or *Shin Taikō* (新防衛計画の大綱). The word 'shin' means 'new' and it was used to distinguish it from the previous edition. In this text, however, 'new' is used in reference to the latest version of the document, published in 2004.
148 Advisory Group on Defence Issues, *The Modality of the Security and Defence Capability of Japan*, 6; JDA, *Defence of Japan 1996. Response to a New Era*, 70, 78–9.
149 Kawano, 'Japan's Military Role: Allied Recommendations for the Twenty-First Century', 9–21.
150 Advisory Group on Defence Issues, *The Modality of the Security and Defence Capability of Japan*, 4–5; JDA, *Defence of Japan 1996*, 29, 42, 45; Kawano, 'Japan's Military Role: Allied Recommendations for the Twenty-First Century', 10–11; Watanabe, 'Has Japan Crossed the Rubicon', 239–41; Hughes, *Japan Re-Emergence as a 'Normal' Military Power*, 68–70.
151 JMSDF, *Kaijōjieitai Gojū Nenshi*, 568–70.
152 JDA, *Defence of Japan 1996*, 81.
153 Advisory Group on Defence Issues, *The Modality of the Security and Defence Capability of Japan*, 22.
154 Kawano, 'Japan's Military Role: Allied Recommendations for the Twenty-First Century', 18.
155 Kibin (機敏).
156 Tekikaku (的確).

157 Natsukawa, *Chakunin ni Saishi Kunji*, 25 March 1996.
158 Hughes, *Japan Re-Emergence as a 'Normal' Military Power*, 108–11.
159 Hughes, *Japan Re-Emergence as a 'Normal' Military Power*, 109–10.
160 Yamaguchi, 'Balancing Threat Perceptions and Strategic Priorities', 96–9.
161 Yamaguchi, 'Balancing Threat Perceptions and Strategic Priorities', 100.
162 JDA, *Defence of Japan 1996*, 45.
163 JDA, *Defence of Japan 1996*, 87, 93.
164 Patalano, 'Shielding the "Hot Gates": Submarine Warfare and Japanese Naval Strategy in the Cold War and Beyond (1976-2006)', 886.
165 JMoD, *Defence of Japan 2009*, 481.
166 The Council on Security and Defence Capabilities, *Japan's Visions for Future Security and Defence Capabilities*, 11–13; JDA, *Defence of Japan 2005*, 118–19; NIDS, 'Japan – Responding to the Changing Security Environment', 228–9.
167 NIDS, 'Japan – Responding to the Changing Security Environment', 229–30.
168 In March 2001, months before the 9/11 attacks, Admiral Ishikawa called for the personnel of the JMSDF to focus on professionalism built on the legacy of the Imperial Navy, to meet the challenges of the evolving regional security. In his speech, he referred to the suspicious boat incident that took place off the Noto Peninsula, when units of the JMSDF and Japan Coast Guard (JCG) fired warning shots against the vessel. Ishikawa, *Chakunin ni Saishi Kunji*, 27 March 2001.
169 Ishikawa, '"A Half-Century's Partnership": Japan Maritime Self-Defence Force's Enduring Relationship with the U.S. Navy', 33.

Chapter 7

1 Admiral Furushō, *Chakunin ni Saishi Kunji*, 28 January 2003.
2 Lieutenant Commander Kitagawa Keizo, JMSDF, 14 September 2005.
3 JMoD, *Defence of Japan*, 151–4.
4 Grove, 'The Discovery of Doctrine: British Naval Thinking at the Close of the Twentieth Century', 182; Hattendorf, *US Naval Strategy in the 1990s. Selected Documents*, 3.
5 Rear Admiral Kawano Katsutoshi, JMSDF, interview with the author, Tokyo, 26 June 2007.
6 For example, enhancing inter-service cooperation and understanding was a primary aim in the Royal Navy's 1995 *The Fundamentals of British Maritime Doctrine* (BR1806) and one of the two aims of the current doctrine. Grove, 'The Discovery of Doctrine', 189; DCDC, *British Maritime Doctrine*, v.
7 Ike, *Japan's Decision for War: Records of the 1941 Policy Conferences*, 106.
8 Hirama, 'Japanese Naval Preparations for World War II', 64–71; Koda, 'A Commander's Dilemma: Admiral Yamamoto and the "Gradual Attrition" Strategy', 66–9; Evans and Peattie, *Kaigun*, 282–5.
9 Dull, *A Battle History of the Imperial Japanese Navy, 1941-1945*, 353–4.
10 Peattie, 'Japanese Naval Construction, 1919-1941', 103.
11 Peattie, 'Japanese Naval Construction, 1919-1941', 103–4.
12 Koda, 'Introduction', 3.
13 Yokoi, 'Thoughts on Japan's Naval Defeat', 71. Asada, *From Mahan to Pearl Harbor*, 26–44; Asada, *Culture Shock*, 71–80. Also, Dingman, 'Japan and Mahan', 49–66.
14 Yokoi, 'Thoughts on Japan's Naval Defeat', 71. Also, Evans and Peattie, *Kaigun*, 38–41, 92–3.

15 Evans and Peattie, *Kaigun*, 59–60.
16 Taikan Kyuhōshugi (大艦巨砲主義). Evans and Peattie, *Kaigun*, 150–1.
17 Yokoi, 'Thoughts on Japan's Naval Defeat', 73. Also, cf. Itō, *The End of the Imperial Japanese Navy*, 3.
18 Kaisen Yōmurei (海戦要務令). The Battle Instructions were issued for the first time in 1901 and revised in 1910, 1912, 1920, 1928 and 1934 and comprised the core of the tactical doctrine. Evans and Peattie, *Kaigun*, 550 footnote 44.
19 Quoted in Evans and Peattie, *Kaigun*, 282.
20 USSBS, *Interrogations of Japanese Officials*, 325.
21 Passage from Battle Instructions quoted in Asada, *From Mahan to Pearl Harbor*, 163.
22 Hirama, 'Japanese Naval Preparations for World War II', 63–4; Koda, 'A Commander's Dilemma', 66; Asada, *From Mahan to Pearl Harbor*, 281; Asada, *Culture Shock and Japanese-American Relations*, 143–4; Hata, 'Admiral Yamamoto's Surprise Attack and the Japanese Navy's War Strategy', 58–62; Evans and Peattie, *Kaigun*, 479–82.
23 Yasengun (夜戦群).
24 Yokoi, 'Thoughts on Japan's Naval Defeat', 73; Hirama, 'Japanese Naval Preparations for World War II', 64–71; Koda, 'A Commander's Dilemma', 66–9; Evans and Peattie, *Kaigun*, 282–95.
25 Yasen Butai (夜戦部隊), or Zenshin Butai (Advance Force – 前進部隊). Evans and Peattie, *Kaigun*, 275–6.
26 Peattie, *Sunburst*, 79–85.
27 Hirama, 'Japanese Naval Preparations for World War II', 73.
28 Nagata, 'Shīrēn Bōei', *Sekai no Kansen*, 76.
29 Far East Command, Military History Section, Special Staff, General Headquarters, *The Imperial Japanese Navy in World War II: A Graphic Presentation of the Japanese Naval Organisation and List Of Combatant and Non-Combatant Vessels Lost or Damaged in the War*, 1
30 Lambert, 'Seapower 1939-1940: Churchill and the Strategic Origins of the Battle of the Atlantic', 86–108.
31 Kaibōkan (海防艦).
32 Oi, 'Why Japan's Antisubmarine Warfare Failed', 396. Also, Evans and Peattie, *Kaigun*, 438–40.
33 Maiolo, 'The Knockout Blow against the Import System: Admiralty Expectations of Nazi Germany's Naval Strategy, 1934-9', 202–28. Also, Lambert, 'Seapower 1939-1940', 90–5.
34 USSBS, *Interrogations of Japanese Officials*, 394.
35 Hirama, 'Japanese Naval Preparations for World War II', 67; Koda, 'A Commander's Dilemma', 68; Evans and Peattie, *Kaigun*, 266–72.
36 Peattie, 'Japanese Naval Construction, 1919-1941', 102–3.
37 Peattie, 'Japanese Naval Construction, 1919-1941', 103.
38 Gray, *The Leverage of Seapower*, 21.
39 Kaigunshō (海軍省).
40 Gunreibu (軍令部).
41 Asada, *From Mahan to Pearl Harbor*, 161. Also, Evans and Peattie, *Kaigun*, 26–7.
42 Asada, *From Mahan to Pearl Harbor*, 169–74.
43 Jōyaku-ha (条約派). The opposing group was known as 'fleet faction', or Kantai-ha (艦隊派).
44 Asada, *From Mahan to Pearl Harbor*, 173.
45 Auer, *The Post-war Rearmament of Japanese Maritime Forces*, 49–52, 69–70.

46 Kaijō Hoanchō (海上保安庁). In 2000, the English name was changed to Japan Coast Guard (JCG).
47 Auer, *The Post-war Rearmament of Japanese Maritime Forces*, 39–41, 52.
48 Naoyuki Agawa, James E. Auer, 'Pacific Friendship', http://www.vanderbilt.edu/VIPPS/VIPPSUSJ/publications/friendship.htm, accessed 10 August 2004.
49 Auer, *The Post-war Rearmament of Japanese Maritime Forces*, 64. Also Maeda, *The Hidden Army*, 45–6.
50 Maeda, *The Hidden Army*, 45. Kaijōjieitai Sōkai Butai, *Nihon no Sōkaishi: Chōsen Dōran Tokubetsu Sōkaishi*, 13–19, 46–9. Also, NHK Special Selection, *Kaijojieitai wa Kōshite Umareta*, 250–3.
51 Auer, *The Post-war Rearmament of Japanese Maritime Forces* 68.
52 Keisatsu Yobitai (警察予備隊).
53 Maeda, *The Hidden Army*, 3, Auer, *The Post-war Rearmament of Japanese Maritime Forces*, 72–3.
54 Auer, *The Post-war Rearmament of Japanese Maritime Forces* 72–3.
55 Auer, *The Post-war Rearmament of Japanese Maritime Forces*, 80.
56 Auer, *The Post-war Rearmament of Japanese Maritime Forces*, 73.
57 Auer, *The Post-war Rearmament of Japanese Maritime Forces*, 83–4; Maeda, *The Hidden Army*, 50–1; Masuda, *Jieitai no Tanjō*, 129–36; NHK Special Selection, *Kaijojieitai wa Kōshite Umareta*, 158–80. Also, Suzuki, *Kikisho: Kaijojieitai Shiwa*, 59–62.
58 Auer, *The Post-war Rearmament of Japanese Maritime Forces*, 80–2; Maeda, *The Hidden Army*, 51–2; NHK Special Selection, *Kaijojieitai wa Kōshite Umareta*, 157; Suzuki, *Kikisho: Kaijojieitai Shiwa*, 68–74.
59 Suzuki, *Kikisho: Kaijojieitai Shiwa*, 73–6; JMSDF, *Kaijōjieitai Gojū Nenshi*, 56.
60 Kaijō Keibitai (海上警備隊).
61 Maeda, *The Hidden Army*, 49.
62 Auer, *The Post-war Rearmament of Japanese Maritime Forces*, 86.
63 Maeda, *The Hidden Army*, 68.
64 Keibitai (警備隊). Auer, *The Post-war Rearmament of Japanese Maritime Forces*, 85–6.
65 Hoanchō (保安庁).
66 JMSDF, *Kaijōjieitai Gojū Nenshi*, 56.
67 JMSDF, *Kaijōjieitai Gojū Nenshi*, 58. Today, the Self-Defence Fleet is under the command of a Vice Admiral (three stars), and the Chief of Staff is a full Admiral (four stars). Editorial Department, 'Kaijōjieitai 2008-2009', 162.
68 JMSDF, *Kaijōjieitai Gojū Nenshi – Shiryōhen*, 66–7.
69 Auer, *The Post-war Rearmament of Japanese Maritime Forces*, 40.
70 Asada, *From Mahan to Pearl Harbor*, 161.
71 Sadō, *Sengo Nihon no Bōei to Seiji*, 82. For a presentation of bureaucratic control, see Hirose, *Kanryō to Gunjin*.
72 Maeda, *The Hidden Army*, 27.
73 Naibu Bukyoku (内部部局), or Naikyoku (内局).
74 Nakajima, *Sengo Nihon no Bōei Seisaku*, 34–6.
75 Nakajima, *Sengo Nihon no Bōei Seisaku*, 38–9. Nakajima distinguishes between 'Civilian Control' – Bunmin Tōsei (文民統制) – and Bureaucratic Supremacy – Bunkan Yūi (文官優位). Feaver, Hikotani and Narine, 'Civilian Control and Civil-Military Gaps in the United States, Japan, and China', *Asian Perspectives*, 233–71.
76 Class ranking upon graduation from the Naval Academy was an important factor in the career promotion system of the Imperial Navy too. Evans, 'The Satsuma Faction', 210–12; Asada, *From Mahan to Pearl Harbor*, 163.

77 Vice Admiral Kōda, interview with the author, 5 July 2007.
78 Captain Ōtsuka, interview with the author, 17 February 2005; author's conversations with Captain Ike, August 2005, and Captain Terada, February 2008.
79 Senpai Kōhai (先輩後輩).
80 Vice Admiral Kōda Yōji, JMSDF, interview with the author, 5 July 2007; author's conversations with senior staff officers including former CMS Admiral Furushō Kōichi, JMSDF (Ret.), Rear Admiral Kawano, Captain Ike Tarō, Yamashita Kazuki and Ōtsuka Umio, JMSDF, Tokyo, May, June and September 2005.
81 Woolley, *Japan's Navy: Politics and Paradox, 1971-2000*, 24.
82 Captain Yamashita Kazuki, JMSDF, interview with the author, Tokyo, 19 August 2007.
83 Kachō (課長).
84 Ishihara, *Kengen no Dai Idō*. For a brief examination in English, Shinoda, *Koizumi Diplomacy*, 23–5.
85 Vice Admiral Kaneda, interview with the author, 21 July 2009.
86 Hendry, *Understanding Japanese Society*, 151.
87 Seikyō (精強).
88 Sokuou (即応).
89 *Chinmoku Shōjin* (沈黙精進).
90 Admiral Uchida, *Chakunin ni Saishi Kunji*, 1 July 1969.
91 Shōsū seiei shugi (少数精鋭主義).
92 Throughout the JMSDF's history, the officer corps represented no more than 20 per cent of the entire personnel strength. From 1989 to 2001, the percentage was between 19.9 (1993) and 20.8 (2001). JMSDF, *Kaijōjieitai Gojū Nenshi – Shiryōhen*, 110.
93 The JMSDF emphasis on intense training led the service at times to push the safety envelope to extremes, resulting in collateral damage to civilian shipping. The most dramatic accident occurred in July 1988, when the submarine *Nadashio* (SS-577) collided with a pleasure fishing boat, killing thirty passengers. Patalano, 'Shielding the "Hot Gates"', 869, 890–1. In February 2008, the brand new Aegis destroyer *Atago* (DDG-177) was similarly involved in a night collision with a fishing boat, leaving two fishermen missing and presumed dead. Editorial Department, 'Probe: Atago Crew Missed Boat though Radar Saw It', *The Yomiuri Shimbun*, 8 June 2008.
94 Kaneda, interview with the author, 5 August 2005.
95 *Guntai no Yōwa Sentōni Ari* (軍隊の用は戦闘にあり).
96 Admiral Nakamura, *Chakunin ni Saishi Kunji*, 16 March 1976.
97 Admiral Maeda, *Chakunin ni Saishi Kunji*, 16 February 1981.
98 Kyōkona Seishin (強固な精神).
99 Jinkaku no Tōya (人格の陶冶).
100 Admiral Itaya, *Chakunin ni Saishi Kunji*, 30 April 1966.
101 In 2001, Admiral Ishikawa preferred the expression 'to act with pure heart', or 'Magokoro wo Tsukusu' (真心を尽くす), for he wished to point out that the navy risked paying too much attention to knowledge-acquisition processes and vague 'spiritual education', or 'Seishin Kyōiku' (精神教育). As a result, young people in the ranks of the navy lacked common sense and failed in 'educating their hearts' to the higher values of the military profession. Admiral Ishikawa, *Chakunin ni Saishi Kunji*, 27 March 2001. Admiral Ishikawa's emphasis on the moral values of the profession partly reflected the circumstances of the time. In 2000, news of a JMSDF officer admitting to having passed sensitive information to personnel of the Russian

Embassy in Tokyo affected the navy's reputation and ethical status. '"Conduct exposed the people to danger": Officer admits giving secrets to Russian spy', *The Japan Times*, 28 November 2000.

102 Admiral Yoshida, *Chakunin ni Saishi Kunji*, 26 April 1983.
103 Sōikufū (創意工夫): Originality/Creativity (Literally: Original Device).
104 Admiral Itaya, *Chakunin ni Saishi Kunji*, 30 April 1966
105 Chini Ite Ran wo Wasuresu (治にいて乱をわすれす). Admiral Sakuma, *Chakunin ni Saishi Kunji*, 31 August 1989.
106 Shimei no Jikaku (使命の自覚).
107 Uteba Hibiku (打てば響く).
108 Sono Tokini Natte, Nantoka Narō (その時になって、何とかなろう).
109 Sono Tokini Natte, Nantomo Dekinakatta (その時になって、何ともできなかった). Admiral Yada, *Chakunin ni Saishi Kunji*, 15 February 1980.
110 Renkei (連係).
111 Admiral Ōga, 'Kaijōjieitai to Watashi', 176–7; JMSDF, *Kaijōjieitai Gojū Nenshi*, 141–2.
112 Yada, *Chakuninni Saishi Kunji*, 15 February 1980.
113 BeiKaigun Oyobi – Riki – Kū – Jieitai tono Renkei no kyōka (米海軍及び· 陸· 空· 自衛隊との連係の強化).
114 Admiral Nagata, *Chakunin ni Saishi Kunji*, 1 August 1985.
115 Kyōdō Taisei (共同態勢).
116 Admiral Fukuchi, *Chakunin ni Saishi Kunji*, 15 December 1994.
117 Kyōkona Danketsu (強固な団結).
118 Onaji Kama no Meshi wo Kū (同じ釜の飯を食う).
119 Kiritsu (規律).
120 Yoshida, *Chakunin ni Saishi Kunji*, 26 April 1983.
121 Jūnansei (柔軟性).
122 Furushō, *Chakunin ni Saishi Kunji*, 28 January 2003
123 Admiral Yamamoto, *Chakunin ni Saishi Kunji*, 13 October 1997.
124 *Hataraku Jitai* (働く時代).
125 *Ishizue wo Kizuku Jidai* (礎を築く時代); *Seijuku no Jidai* (成熟の時代). Admiral Ishikawa, *Chakunin ni Saishi Kunji*, 27 March 2001.
126 Mark P. Parillo, 'The Imperial Navy in World War II', 61.
127 Evans, 'Japanese Naval Construction, 1878-1918', 25; Peattie, 'Japanese Naval Construction, 1919-1941', 96–101. The *Mogami* class of 'heavy light cruisers' was one symptomatic example of this design process. When completed in 1935, it was extremely fast and heavily armoured, but the excessive top weight gave her dangerous instability. Evans and Peattie, *Kaigun*, 239.
128 In the official vocabulary of the JDA/JMoD, 'denial capabilities', or Bōshiryoku (防止力).
129 Goei Kantai (護衛艦隊). Kaneda, interview with the author 5 August 2005.
130 Nagata, 'Shīrēn Bōei', *Sekai no Kansen*, 76–7.
131 Sekino, 'Japan and her Maritime Defence', 105.
132 Until 1971, the JMSDF's offensive use of mine warfare to blockade the straits was minimal. Sekino reports that the service possessed only two small ships for mine-laying, *Tsugaru* (ARC-481) and *Erimo* (ARC-491), with plans for the acquisition of another vessel. Sekino, 'Japan and her Maritime Defence', 107.
133 Sekino, 'Japan and her Maritime Defence', 120. Also, Sekino 'Waga Kuni no Kaijō Goei Monday', 66–8.

134 JMSDF, *Kaijōjieitai Gojū Nenshi*, 27. In the late 1950s, different abbreviations existed in reference to aircraft carriers, and in all of them 'V' was the fixed-wing designator. In the late 1940s, the US Navy modified some of its aircraft carriers to operate ASW aircraft, and these ships were sometimes referred to as CVEK ('CVE' used for escort carriers, and 'K' indicating their hunter-killer capability). The abbreviation CVH did not follow any of the conventions of the time and existing evidence is insufficient to shed light on the JMSDF's reasons for employing it. Polmar, *Aircraft Carriers*, 95–7.
135 Chief, Operations Division, MSO, JMSDF to Chief, Navy Section, MAAG-J, 12 July 1960, in Ishii and Ono, *Documents on the United States Policy towards Japan. Documents of the Joint Chiefs of Staff of the United States, 1953-1961, Volume 11*, 71–3.
136 Vice Admiral Kōda Yōji, JMSDF, interview with the author, 27 May 2008.
137 Polmar, and Moore, *Cold War Submarines*, especially Chapters 2–4.
138 Terada, '"Oyashio" Kenzō no Omoide', 98.
139 JMSDF, *Kaijōjieitai Gojū Nenshi*, 30.
140 JMSDF, *Kaijōjieitai Gojū Nenshi*, 102–3. Sekino, 'Waga Kuni no Kaijō Goei Monday', 67.
141 JMSDF, *Kaijōjieitai Gojū Nenshi – Shiryōhen*, 294.
142 Sekino, 'Japan and her Maritime Defence', 104.
143 Auer, *The Post-war Rearmament of Japanese Maritime Forces*, 159.
144 Sekino, 'Japan and her Maritime Defence', 103.
145 JMSF, *Kaijōjieitai Gojū Nenshi - Shiryōhen*, 298.
146 JMSF, *Kaijōjieitai Gojū Nenshi*, 103.
147 JMSF, *Kaijōjieitai Gojū Nenshi*, 31–2
148 JMSF, *Kaijōjieitai Gojū Nenshi*, 33.
149 Prior to the procurement of the *Atsumi* class, the JMSDF's amphibious component was centred on the two USN-leased Second World War vintage landing ships, rechristened as *Ōsumi* class.
150 JMSF, *Kaijōjieitai Gojū Nenshi – Shiryhen*, 278–82
151 JDA, *Defence of Japan 1977*, 64.
152 JMSF, *Kaijōjieitai Gojū Nenshi*, 157–8.
153 Kōda, interview with the author, 27 May 2008.
154 Kōda, interview with the author, 27 May 2008.
155 JMSF, *Kaijōjieitai Gojū Nenshi*, 158
156 JMSF, *Kaijōjieitai Gojū Nenshi*, 539.
157 In the following years, the JMSDF progressively moved from CODOG engines to CODAG (Combined Diesel and Gas Turbine), followed by the adoption of COGOC (Combined Gas Turbine or Gas Turbine) and finally, COGAC (Combined Gas Turbine and Gas Turbine) systems. JMSF, *Kaijōōjieitai Gojū Nenshi*, 161. According to Japanese sources, gas turbines provide high-speed capability, and are more fuel efficient and silent compared to diesel engines. *Goeikan Pāfekuto Gaido*, 44–8. Nonetheless, an authoritative 1990 study pointed out that they represented an expensive choice compared to CODAG and all diesel (CODAD) solutions adopted in main European navies. Grove, *The Future of Seapower*, 121–3.
158 JMSF, *Kaijōōjieitai Gojū Nenshi*, 159.
159 JMSF, *Kaijōōjieitai Gojū Nenshi*, 163–71; *Goeikan Pāfekuto Gaido*, 50–67.
160 Ugaki, 'Kaijōjieitai no Atarashī Ījisukan Unyō Kōsō', *Sekai no Kansen*, 85.
161 Sigur, jr., 'Proposed sale of Aegis Weapons System to Japan', *Department of State Bulletin*, 13.

162 *Goeikan Pāfekuto Gaido*, 36–9.
163 JMoD, *Defence of Japan 2007*, 146; 'Kaijōjieitai 2008-2009', 31.
164 Yamazaki, 'Kaijōjieitai wa BMD ni Dōtori Kumu Bekika', 80–1; Ugaki, 'Kaijōjieitai no Atarashī Ījisukan Unyō Kōsō', 85–7; Nishikawa, 'Japan's BMD', JDA's unpublished paper presented at National Graduate Institute for Policy Studies (GRIPS), Tokyo, March 2005; *Goeikan Pāfekuto Gaido*, 22–5. Also, JDA, *Defence of Japan 2006*, 156–64; JDA, *Defence of Japan 2003*, 131.
165 Nagata, '21Seiki no Kaijōjieitai: 21Seiki no Jieikan wa Kōnaru', 88–93; JMSDF, *Kaijōjieitai Gojū Nenshi*, 299.
166 The first group focused on the implementation of technologies related to active sonar and noise reduction while the second committee chiefly dealt with a new tactical integrated fire control system. Jane's Information Group, 'Japan Launches Latest Harushio', *Jane's Defence Weekly*, 20 February 1993, 14.
167 JMSDF, *Kaijōjieitai Gojū Nenshi*, 564. Patalano, 'Shielding the "Hot Gates"', 879–82.
168 Originally, options were examined for a 7,000–8,000-ton landing ship based on the model of the Italian San Marco class to facilitate the redeployment of elements of the Western Army from Honshu to Hokkaido. Kōda, interview with the author, 17 August 2007.
169 Technical data from 'Kaijōjieitai 2007-2008', 68–9.
170 Ishii, 'Dōnaru!? Nayami Ōi Kaijōjieitai no Dejitaruka', 87; Vice Admiral Ōta Fumio, interview with the author, 28 April 2005.
171 Kaneda, 'Jieitai ni Tarinai Mono wa?', 88–91; Kaneda, '21Seiki ni Okeru Jieikan no Missyon', 124–9.
172 Kaneda, 'Japan's National Maritime Doctrines and Capabilities', 128.
173 Editorial Department, 'Kaijōjieitai 2007-2008', 151.
174 JMoD, *Defence of Japan 2007*, 185, 204–63.

Conclusions

1 Kaneda, interview with the author, 19 October 2005.
2 On this subject, see for example Patalano, '"Shielding the Hot Gates"', 869.
3 Speller, *Understanding Naval Warfare*, 27–8.
4 Vice Admiral Yōji Kōda, JMSDF (Ret.), interview with the author, 1 August 2014.
5 Corbett, *Some Principles of Maritime Strategy*, 162.
6 CSDCNE, *Japan's Visions for Future Security and Defense and Capabilities in the New Era*, 12.
7 JMoD, *National Defense Program Guidelines for FY 2014 and Beyond*, 4.
8 JMoD, *Defense of Japan* (Tokyo, 2013), 115.
9 JMoD, *National Defense Program Guidelines for FY 2011 and Beyond*, 10; James R. Kendall, 'Deterrence by Presence to Effective Response: Japan's Shift Southward', 603–14.
10 NIDS, 'Japan: Toward the Establishment of a Dynamic Defense Force', 253–6.
11 CSDCNE, *Japan's Visions for Future Security and Defense and Capabilities in the New Era*, 24; NIDS, 'Japan: The Adoption of the New National Defense Program Guidelines – Toward a More Dynamic Defense Force', 243; NIDS, 'Japan: The Adoption of the New National Defense Program Guidelines', 256.
12 CSDCNE, *Japan's Visions for Future Security and Defense and Capabilities in the New Era*, 15, 30–5; also, NIDS, 'Japan – Toward More Effective International

Cooperation', 240–6; JMoD, *National Defense Program Guidelines for FY 2014 and Beyond*, 8.

13 JMoD, *National Defense Program Guidelines for FY 2011 and Beyond*, 8–9; CSDCNE, *Japan's Visions for Future Security and Defense and Capabilities in the New Era*, 18–20; JMoD, *National Defense Program Guidelines for FY 2014 and Beyond*, 10–13.

14 Rear Admiral Tomohisa Takei, JMSDF, 'Kaiyō Shinkindai ni okeru Kaijōjieitai', 2–29.

15 Rear Admiral Tomohisa Takei, JMSDF, 'Kaiyō Shinkindai ni okeru Kaijōjieitai', 6.

16 Rear Admiral Tomohisa Takei, JMSDF, 'Kaiyō Shinkindai ni okeru Kaijōjieitai', 8, 11–12.

17 Rear Admiral Tomohisa Takei, JMSDF, 'Kaiyō Shinkindai ni okeru Kaijōjieitai', 15–16.

18 JMSDF Staff College, seminar discussion with the author, 20 September 2011.

19 Takei, 'Kaiyō Shinkindai ni okeru Kaijōjieitai', 19. On the strategic importance of Okinawa in a Northeast Asian crisis, Michishita, 'Changing Military Strategies and the Future of the U.S. Marine Presence in Asia', 70–6. The author is grateful to Professor Michishita for providing a copy of this study.

20 Tatakawazushite Katsu (戦わずして勝つ). Takei, 'Kaiyō Shinkindai ni okeru Kaijōjieitai', 17.

21 Takei, 'Kaiyō Shinkindai ni okeru Kaijōjieitai', 18.

22 Takei, 'Kaiyō Shinkindai ni okeru Kaijōjieitai', 20–1.

23 Takei, 'Kaiyō Shinkindai ni okeru Kaijōjieitai', 22.

24 Takei, interview with the author, 12 September 2012.

25 Takei, interview with the author, 12 September 2012. Also, Takei, 'Kaiyō Shinkindai ni okeru Kaijōjieitai', 23–4, 26.

26 Takei, 'Kaiyō Shinkindai ni okeru Kaijōjieitai', 24.

27 Corbett, Some Principles of Maritime Strategy, 317.

28 Royal Navy, *BR 1806: British Maritime Doctrine* (Second Edition, London: HMSO, 1999), 45–6.

29 Royal Navy, *BR 1806: British Maritime Doctrine* (Second Edition, London: HMSO, 1999), 45.

30 Admiral Sakuma Makoto, JMSDF, *Chakunin ni Saishi Kunji*, 31 August 1989.

31 Admiral Sugimoto Masahiko, JMSDF, *Chakunin ni Saishi Kunji*, 26 July 2010.

32 J. Conway, G. Roughhead and T. Allen, 'Cooperative Strategy for 21st Century Seapower', 17 October 2007, http://www.navy.mil/maritime/MaritimeStrategy.pdf, accessed 10 September 2008; Ministry of Defence, *BR 1806: British Maritime Doctrine*, 22–4.

33 Admiral Akahoshi Keiji, JMSDF, *Chakunin ni Saishi Kunji*, 24 March 2008.

34 Admiral Sugimoto, JMSDF, *Chakunin ni Saishi Kunji*, 26 July 2010.

35 JDA, *Defense of Japan 2006*, 110.

36 JMoD, *Defense of Japan 2011*, 123–4.

37 JDA, *Defence of Japan 2005*, 211.

38 JMoD, *Defence of Japan* (Tokyo, 2009), 201.

39 James Simpson, 'Coast Guard to Pick Up Retiring Hatsuyuki-Class Destroyers?', *Japan Security Watch*, 2 April 2013, http://jsw.newpacificinstitute.org/?p=10821.

40 JMoD, *Defence of Japan 2014*, http://www.mod.go.jp/e/publ/w_paper/pdf/2014/DOJ2014_3-3-3_1st_0730.pdf.

41 'Japanese Navy Chief Fired over Collision and Scandals', *International Herald Tribune*, 21 March 2008.

42 'MSDF Officer Arrested, Admits Spying for Russia', *The Japan Times*, 9 September 2000; 'MSDF Officer Held in Aegis Secrets Leak', *The Japan Times*, 14 December 2007.

43 Kidō Butai (機動部隊) was the designation used by the IJN for its carrier striking force.

44 Rear Admiral Ike Taro, JMSDF, 'Welcome from the Superintendent', *Maritime Officer Candidate School*, 26 June 2012, http://www.mod.go.jp/msdf/mocs/mocs/about/sub02/.

Bibliography

Primary material

Unpublished

A) Official documents

Chakuninni Saishi Kunji (着任に際し訓示 – Official Instructions, Tokyo: Maritime Staff Office, Japan Defence Agency, 1961–2005).

B) Private correspondence, diaries and memoirs, collections of speeches, pamphlets

Japan Missile Promotion Research Team, 'Total Missile Defence for Japan', unpublished working paper, September 2006.

Kaneda, Hideaki, Vice Admiral JMSDF (Ret.), 'Japan's perspective on Missile Defence: Facing Realistic Missile Threats from China and North Korea', unpublished paper presented at the Laughton Naval History Seminar Series, King's College London, 25 September 2006.

Kannō, Tsubasa, Captain JMSDF, 'Japan's Maritime Strategy after 9/11', unpublished paper presented at the Laughton Naval History Seminar Series, King's College London, 16 November 2006.

Kazumi, Nishikawa, 'Japan's BMD', unpublished paper presented at National Graduate Institute for Policy Studies (GRIPS), Tokyo, March 2005.

Kazumine, Akimoto, Rear Admiral JMSDF (Ret.), 'Sea Lane Defence in the Eurasia Blue Belt', unpublished policy paper, Tokyo: Ocean Policy Research Foundation, 2007.

O'Connell, John, Captain USN, 'Discussion of JMSDF Submarine Requirements', unpublished discussion paper presented to Vice Admiral Abe Katsuo, JMSDF, Tokyo, 6 August 1980.

Turner, Stanfield, Vice Admiral USN, letter to Commander Senō, 1973.

Published

A) Official documents, government publications

Foreign Press Centre Japan (FPC), *Japan's Mass Media* (Tokyo: FPC).

Ishii, Osamu (ed.), *Documents on the United States Policy towards Japan. Documents Related to Diplomatic and Military Matters, 1959-1960* (9 Volumes, Tokyo: Kashiwashobo, 1996).

Ishii, Osamu (ed.), *Documents on the United States Policy towards Japan. Nixon Presidential Materials – White House Special Files and Central Files* (10 Volumes, Tokyo: Kashiwashobo, 2008).

Ishii, Osamu and Hideki Uemura (eds), *Documents on the United States Policy towards Japan. Documents of the Joint Chiefs of Staff of the United States, 1948-1953* (16 Volumes, Tokyo: Kashiwashobo, 2000).

Ishii, Osamu, Masaaki Gabe, and Seigen Miyazato (eds), *Documents on the United States Policy towards Japan. Documents Related to Diplomatic and Military Matters, 1964* (10 Volumes, Tokyo: Kashiwashobo, 2001).

Ishii, Osamu, Masaaki Gabe, and Seigen Miyazato (eds), *Documents on the United States Policy towards Japan. Documents related to Diplomatic and Military Matters, 1964-1971* (Multi-volume Collection, Tokyo: Kashiwashobo, 2001–3).

Ishii, Osamu, Masaaki Gabe, and Seigen Miyazato (eds), *Documents on the United States Policy towards Japan. Documents Related to Diplomatic and Military Matters, 1965* (9 Volumes, Tokyo: Kashiwashobo, 2001).

Ishii, Osamu, Masaaki Gabe, and Seigen Miyazato (eds), *Documents on the United States Policy towards Japan. Documents Related to Diplomatic and Military Matters, 1966* (9 Volumes, Tokyo: Kashiwashobo, 2002).

Ishii, Osamu, Masaaki Gabe, and Seigen Miyazato (eds), *Documents on the United States Policy towards Japan. Documents Related to Diplomatic and Military Matters, 1967* (11 Volumes, Tokyo: Kashiwashobo, 2002).

Ishii, Osamu, Masaaki Gabe, and Seigen Miyazato (eds), *Documents on the United States Policy towards Japan. Documents Related to Diplomatic and Military Matters, 1968* (9 Volumes, Tokyo: Kashiwashobo, 2003).

Ishii, Osamu and Naoki Ono (eds), *Documents on the United States Policy towards Japan. Documents of the Joint Chiefs of Staff of the United States, 1953-1961* (Multi-volume Collection, Tokyo: Kashiwashobo, 2000).

Ishii, Osamu and Naoki Ono (eds), *Documents on the United States Policy towards Japan. Documents Related to Diplomatic and Military Matters, 1955* (9 Volumes, Tokyo: Kashiwashobo, 1999).

Ishii, Osamu and Naoki Ono (eds), *Documents on the United States Policy towards Japan. Documents related to Diplomatic and Military Matters, 1955-1963* (Multi-volume Collection, Tokyo: Kashiwashobo, 1998–99).

Ishii, Osamu and Naoki Ono (eds), *Documents on the United States Policy towards Japan. Documents Related to Diplomatic and Military Matters, 1956* (10 Volumes, Tokyo: Kashiwashobo, 1999).

Ishii, Osamu and Naoki Ono (eds), *Documents on the United States Policy towards Japan. Documents Related to Diplomatic and Military Matters, 1957* (10 Volumes, Tokyo: Kashiwashobo, 1998).

Ishii, Osamu and Naoki Ono (eds), *Documents on the United States Policy towards Japan. Documents Related to Diplomatic and Military Matters, 1958* (7 Volumes, Tokyo: Kashiwashobo, 1998).

Ishii, Osamu and Naoki Ono (eds), *Documents on the United States Policy towards Japan. Japanese Internal Affairs as Seen by the American Diplomats, 1960* (9 Volumes, Tokyo: Kashiwashobo, 1997).

Japan Defence Agency, *A Review of Japan's Defence Strength* (Tokyo: Japan Defence Agency, 1956).

Japan Defence Agency, *Defence of Japan* (Tokyo: *The Japan Times*, Urban Connection, Intergroup, 1970, 1977–2007).

Japan Defence Agency, *Jieitai Nenkan* (自衛隊年鑑 – Yearbook of the JSDF, Tokyo, 1961–2005).

Japan Maritime Self-Defence Force, *Kaijōjieitai Gojū Nenshi* (海上自衛隊五十年史 – JMSDF's Fifty Year History, Tokyo, 2003).

Japan Maritime Self-Defence Force, *Kaijōjieitai Gojū Nenshi – Shiryōhen* (海上自衛隊五十年史、資料編 – JMSDF's Fifty Year History – Data, Tokyo, 2003).

Japan Maritime Self-Defence Force, *Kaijōjieitai Hakodate Kichitai Gojū Nenshi* (海上自衛隊函館基地隊五十年史 – JMSDF's Hakodate Naval Base Fifty Year History, Hakodate, 2003).

Japan Maritime Self-Defence Force, *Kaijōjieitai Kanbu Gakkō Gojū Nenshi* (海上自衛隊幹部学校５０年史 – Fifty Year History of the JMSDF's MSC, Tokyo, 2005).

Japan Maritime Self-Defence Force, *Kaijōjieitai Kure Chihōtai Nijūgo Nenshi* (海上自衛隊呉地方隊二十五年史 – JMSDF's Kure Naval District Twenty-Five Year History, Kure, 1981).

Japan Maritime Self-Defence Force, *Kaijōjieitai Yokosuka Chihōtai Gojū Nenshi* (海上自衛隊横須賀地方隊五十年史 – JMSDF's Yokosuka Naval District Fifty Year History, Yokosuka, 2003).

Ministry of Foreign Affairs, *Diplomatic Bluebook* (Tokyo: Ministry of Foreign Affairs, Urban Connection, 1988–2005).

National Institute for Defence Studies, *East Asia Strategic Review* (Tokyo: *The Japan Times*, 1996–2009).

Royal Navy, *BR 1806: British Maritime Doctrine* (Second Edition, London: HMSO, 1999).

Royal Navy, *Ethos: The Spirit to Fight and Win* (London: Royal Navy Graphic Centre, 2006).

The Advisory Panel on Reconstruction of the Legal Basis for Security, *Report of the Advisory Panel on Reconstruction of the Legal Basis for Security* (Tokyo: May 2014).

The Council on Defence and Security Capabilities, *The Council on Security and Defence Capabilities Report: Japan's Visions for Future Security and Defence Capabilities* (Tokyo: October 2004).

The Council on Defence and Security Capabilities, *The Modality of the Security and Defence Capability of Japan* (Tokyo: August 1994).

U.S. Naval Academy, *Reef Points 2004-2005 – The Annual Handbook of the Brigade of Midshipmen* (99th edition, Annapolis, MA: U.S. Naval Academy, 2004).

United States Department of State, *Department of State Bulletin* (Washington, DC, 1955–88).

United States Navy, United States Coast Guard, United States Marine Corps, *A Cooperative Strategy for 21st Century Seapower* (http://www.navy.mil/maritime/MaritimeStrategy.pdf, October 2007).

United States Strategic Bombing Survey (USSBS), *Interrogations of Japanese Officials* (2 Volumes, Naval Analysis Division, Washington, DC: Government Printing Office, 1946).

B) Official photographic, video and online reference materials

Japan Maritime Self-Defence Force, *2006 Kaijōjieitai Kankan Shiki: Kono Umi to Kimi wo Mamoru* (２００６海上自衛隊観艦式：この海と君を守る – 2006 JMSDF's Fleet Review: Protecting You and this Sea, DVD, Tokyo: Maritime Staff Office, Japan Defence Agency, 2006).

Japan Maritime Self-Defence Force, *Headline of JMSDF* (DVD, Tokyo: Maritime Staff Office, Japan Defence Agency, 2006).

Japan Maritime Self-Defence Force, *Umi no Mamori Gojū Nen* (海の護り５０年 – 50 Years of Defence at Sea: Pictorial History of the JMSDF, Tokyo: Maritime Staff Office, Japan Defence Agency, 2003).

The following websites are in English unless otherwise stated:
Japan Air Self-Defence Force: http://www.mod.go.jp/asdf/english/index.html.
Japan Ground Self-Defence Force: http://www.mod.go.jp/gsdf/.
Japan Maritime Self-Defence Force: http://www.mod.go.jp/msdf/formal/english/index.html.
Japan Ministry of Defence (JMoD): http://www.mod.go.jp/e/index.html.
Joint Staff, JMoD: http://www.mod.go.jp/jso/english_top.htm.
JMSDF Kanoya Museum: http://www.mod.go.jp/msdf/kanoya/(Japanese only).
JMSDF Kure Museum: http://www.jmsdf-kure-museum.jp/en/index.php.
JMSDF Sasebo Museum: http://www002.upp.so-net.ne.jp/jl6wgo/(Japanese only).
JMSDF Videos: http://www.mod.go.jp/msdf/formal/gallery/cm/index.html.

C) Private correspondence, diaries and memoirs, collections of speeches, pamphlets

Japan Maritime Self-Defence Force, *2002 International Fleet Review Information Booklet* (Tokyo: Maritime Staff Office, October 2002).
Kaihara, Osamu, *Watashi no Bōei Jisho* (私の防衛白書 – My Defence White Paper, Tokyo: Jiji Press, 1975).
Kaneda, Hideaki, Vice Admiral JMSDF (Ret.), *Ballistic Missile Defence for Japan* (Tokyo: The Okazaki Institute/The Ballistic Missile Defence Group, 2003).
Kurisu, Hirōmi, *Watashi no Bōeiron* (私の防衛論 – My View of the Problem of National Defence, Tokyo: Takagishobo, 1978).
Murata, Koji, 'James Auer Oral History Interview', March 1996, http://www.gwu.edu/~nsarchiv/japan/auerohinterview.htm, accessed 20 March 2007.
Nakamura, Teiji, Admiral JMSDF (Ret.), *Nakamura Teiji: Ōraru Hisutorii* (中村悌次：オーラルヒストリー– Nakamura Teiji: Oral History, 2 Volumes, Tokyo: Bōei Kenkyūjo, 2006).
Sakuma, Makoto, Admiral JMSDF (Ret.), *Sakuma: Ōraru Hisutorii* (佐久間：オーラルヒストリー – Sakuma: Oral History, 2 Volumes, Tokyo: KINS, 2008).
Sankei Shimbun Tōkyō Honsha Chōsabu: Itō Masanori (産経新聞東京本社調査部：伊藤正徳 – Sankei Shimbun Archive, Tokyo Headquarters: Itō Masanori, SSAIM. This is a seven-volume collection of Itō's articles organised roughly along chronological lines).

Interviews

Agawa, Naoyuki, Professor, Keio University, Tokyo, 22 June 2005, 24 October 2006, 20 July 2007.
Auer, James E., Professor, New Sanno Hotel, Tokyo, 30 June 2005, 22 June 2007.
Furushō, Kōichi, Admiral JMSDF (Ret.), NTT Data Corporation, Tokyo, 9 September 2005.
Hikotani, Takako, Professor, National Defence Academy, Yokosuka, 5 September 2005.
Hirama, Yōichi, Rear Admiral JMSDF (Ret.), Japan Naval Association, Tokyo, 15 April 2005.
Ishibashi, Tokuetsu, Captain JMSDF, Maritime Staff College, Tokyo, 13 May 2005, and Intelligence Division, Joint Staff Office, Tokyo, 14 July 2007.
Ishihara, Takahiro, Commander JMSDF, Maritime Staff College, Tokyo, 14 June 2005.
Itō, Toshiyuki, Captain JMSDF, Public Affairs Office, Maritime Staff Office, Japan Ministry of Defence, Tokyo, 20 May 2005.

Kaneda, Hideaki, Vice Admiral JMSDF (Ret.), Mitsubishi Research Institute, Tokyo, 18 January 2005, 5 August 2005, 21 October 2006, 25 July 2007, and London, 25 September 2006.
Kawano, Hitoshi, Professor, National Defence Academy, Yokosuka, 5 September 2005.
Kawano, Katsutoshi, Rear Admiral JMSDF, Maritime Staff Office, Japan Ministry of Defence, 26 June 2007.
Kazumine, Akimoto, Rear Admiral JMSDF (Ret.), Ocean Policy Research Foundation, Tokyo, Japan, 13 January 2005, 5 June 2005, 3 July 2007, and London, 30 September 2006.
Kōda, Yōji, Vice Admiral JMSDF, HQ Self-Defence Fleet, Yokosuka, 5 July 2007, 17 August 2007, 27 May 2008.
Kōta, Greg Katsuo, Captain JMSDF (Ret.), *Mikasa* Battleship Museum, Yokosuka, 17 August 2007.
Nishihara, Masashi, Professor, Research Institute for Peace and Security, Tokyo, 29 June 2007.
Ōjima, G., Captain JMSDF, Maritime Staff Office, Japan Ministry of Defence, Tokyo, 14 March 2005.
Ōseto, Isao, Captain JMSDF, Public Affairs Office, Maritime Staff Office, Japan Ministry of Defence, 20 June 2007.
Ōta, Fumio, Vice Admiral JMSDF (Ret.), National Defence Academy, Yokosuka, 28 April 2005.
Ōtsuka, Umio, Captain JMSDF, Maritime Staff Office, Japan Ministry of Defence, Tokyo, 17 February 2005, 14 March 2005, 19 June 2005, and 21st Destroyer Division Command, Yokosuka, 21 July 2007.
Saitō, Takashi, Admiral JMSDF, Maritime Staff Office, Japan Ministry of Defence, 2 September 2005.
Sakuma, Makoto, Admiral JMSDF (Ret.), Japan Naval Association, Tokyo, 21 October 2005.
Satō, Ken, Mr, Institute for International Policy Studies, Tokyo, 5 August 2007.
Senō, Sadao, Commander JMSDF (Ret.), Japan Naval Association, Tokyo, 3 August 2005, and *Mikasa* Battleship Museum, Yokosuka, 20 August 2005.
Shibata, Mitsuo, Mr, Maritime Staff Office, Japan Ministry of Defence, 2 June 2005.
Tōru, Kizu, Mr, Maritime Staff Office, Japan Ministry of Defence, 30 May 2008.
Watanabe, Akio, Professor, Research Institute for Peace and Security, Tokyo, 9 May 2005.
Yagi, Naoto, Commander JMSDF, International Institute for Policy Studies – IIPS, interview with the author, 19 May 2005
Yamaguchi, J., Captain JMSDF (Ret.), Research Institute for Peace and Security, Tokyo, 27 January 2005.
Yamaguchi, Noboru, Major General JGSDF, National Institute for Defence Studies, Tokyo, 26 July 2005.
Yamamoto, Yasumasa, Admiral JMSDF (Ret.), *Mikasa* Battleship Museum, Yokosuka, 20 August 2005.

Informal conversations

A) JMSDF personnel

Admirals: Yamamoto, Yasumasa (Ret.); Furushō, Kōichi (Ret.).
Vice Admirals: Doke, Kazunari; Kuramoto, Kenichi; Oka, Toshihiko; Yamazaki, Makoto

Rear Admirals:	Adachi, Takāshi; Fukumoto, Izuru; Kawano, Katsutoshi; Izumi, Sansei; Izumi, Tōru; Matsuoka, Sadayoshi; Miyaura, Hiroji; Shibata, Masahiro; Takahashi, Tadayoshi; Takashima, Hiromi; Yakei, Tomohisa; Yoshida, Masanori.
Captains:	Hatano, Shunichi; Hori, Hiroyuki; Hosoya, Masao; Ike, Tarō; Isomichi, Shingo; Itō, Hiroshi; Iwasaki, Yōichi; Kannō, Tsubasa; Kitagawa, Fumiyaki; Kunii, Masashi; Mizuna, Takaki; Nakata, Yoshiki; Ōtsuka, Umio; Sekiguchi, Yuki; Shinomura, Yasuhiko; Sonoda, Naoki; Tada, Minoru; Yamamura, Hiroshi; Yamashita, Kazuki.
Commanders:	Asanuma, Hiromi; Mototaka, Hogaki; Sato, Fumio; Yutaka, Fujisawa.
Lt. Commanders:	Kuramitsu, Keisuke; Nishida, Katsutoshi; Kitagawa, Keizo.
Lieutenants:	Osamura, Hisamitsu.
NCOs:	Yokoe Mitsuyasu.

B) Civil servants, academics, corporate and media executives

Akagi, Kanji (Keio University, Tokyo, Japan).
Ashizuka, Osamu (Ministry of Defence, Tokyo, Japan).
Bolat, Jean-Pierre, Commander US Navy (US Forces Yokota, Japan).
Chelton, Simon, Captain Royal Navy (British Embassy, Tokyo, Japan).
Derrick, Gareth, Captain Royal navy (British Embassy, Tokyo, Japan).
Dujarric, Robert (Temple University, Tokyo, Japan).
Duram, Elisabeth (Government Account Office, Washington, DC, USA).
Fish, Tim (Jane's Information Group, London, Japan).
Gellel, Tim, Lt. Colonel Australian Army (National Institute for Defence Studies, Tokyo, Japan).
Graham, Euan (Foreign and Commonwealth Office, London, UK).
Hague, Mark O., Lt. Colonel US Army (US Forces, Yokota, Japan).
Ishizu, Tomoyuki (National Institute for Defence Studies, Tokyo, Japan).
Iwama, Yoko (National Institute for Policy Studies, Tokyo, Japan).
Katahara, Eichi (National Institute for Defence Studies, Tokyo, Japan).
Katsuya, Tsukamoto (National Institute for Defence Studies, Tokyo, Japan).
Kobayashi, Kakumi (Kyodo News, Tokyo, Japan).
Kotani, Ken (National Institute for Defence Studies, Tokyo, Japan).
Kotani, Tetsuo (Ocean Policy Research Foundation, Tokyo, Japan).
Mastrorocco, Elio, Captain Italian Navy (Italian Embassy, Tokyo, Japan).
Michishita, Narushige (National Institute for Policy Studies, Tokyo, Japan).
Mochizuki, Masahiko (Mizuho International plc., London, UK).
Morris, Anne R., Colonel US Air Force (US Forces, Yokota, Japan).
Mulloy, Garren (Daito Bunka University, Tokyo, Japan).
Murai, Tomohide (National Defence Academy, Yokosuka, Japan).
Neill, Alexander (Royal United Services Institute for Defence and Security Studies, London, UK).
Nishimoto, Koji (National Institute for Policy Studies, Tokyo, Japan).
Ono, Keishi (National Institute for Defence Studies, Tokyo, Japan).
Oros, Andrew L. (Washington College, MD, USA).
Ota, Masakatsu (Kyodo News, Tokyo, Japan).
Papadopulos, Randy (US Naval Historical Center, Washington, DC, USA).
Piro, Giuseppe, Rear Admiral Italian Navy (Italian Embassy, Tokyo, Japan).
Shiga, Sahoko (Ministry of Defence, Tokyo, Japan).
Shimazu, Naoko (Birkbeck University, London, UK).

Spurlock, Kenneth, Commander US Navy (National Institute for Defence Studies, Tokyo, Japan).
Staples, Mark T. (Lockheed Martin, Tokyo, Japan).
Tadokoro, Masayuki (Keio University, Tokyo, Japan).
Takagi, Seiichiro (Aoyama Gakuin University, Tokyo, Japan).
Takesada, Hideshi (National Institute for Defence Studies, Tokyo, Japan).
Tokuchi, Hideshi (Ministry of Defence, Tokyo, Japan).
Tōmatsu, Haruo (Tamagawa University, Tokyo, Japan).
Yukie, Yoshikawa (Reishauer Center for East Asian Studies, Washington, DC, USA).

Secondary sources

Monographs and articles

A) Japanese language

Agawa, Hiroyuki, *Gunkan Nagato no Shōgai* (軍艦長門の生涯 – The Life of the Battleship *Nagato*, 2 Volumes, Tokyo: Shinchōsha, 1975).
Agawa, Hiroyuki, *Inoue Seibi* (井上成美 – Inoue Seibi, 2 Volumes, Tokyo: Shinchōsha, 1986).
Agawa, Hiroyuki, *Yamamoto Isoroku* (山本五十六 – Yamamoto Isoroku, Tokyo: Shinchōsha, 1965).
Agawa, Hiroyuki, *Yonai Mitsumasa* (米内光政 – Yonai Mitsumasa, 2 Volumes, Tokyo: Shinchōsha, 1978).
Agawa, Naoyuki, *Umi no Yūjō* (海の友情 – Friendship at Sea, Tokyo: Chūōkōronsha, 2001).
Asahi Shimbun, *Jieitai: Shirarezaru Henyō* (自衛隊：知られざる変容 – The JSDF: Understanding the Transformation, Tokyo: Asahi Shimbunsha, 2005).
Bōei, Kenkyūkai, *Bōeishō Jieitai* (防衛庁自衛隊 – The Japan Defence Agency and the JSDF, Tokyo: Kaya Shobō, 1990).
Bōei, Kenkyūkai, *Jieitai no Kyōiku to Kunren* (自衛隊の教育と訓練 – The Education and Training of the JSDF, Tokyo: Kaya Shobō, 1996).
Bōei Kensyūjo Senshishitsu [presently Bōei Kenkyūjo Senshibu], *Kaigunshō Nenpō* (海軍省年俸 – Yearbook of the Navy Ministry, Various Years, Tokyo: Bōei Kensyūjo, 1983).
Editorial Department, *Goeikan Pāfekuto Gaido* (護衛艦パーフェクトガイド – JMSDF's Destroyer Perfect Guide, Rekishi Gunzo Series, Tokyo: Gakken, 2006).
Editorial Department, 'Jieitai Tōjō Suru Kono Shīn' (自衛隊登場するこのシーン – The JSDF Appear in This Scene), *Securitarian*, 2005:5, 12–15.
Editorial Department, 'Kaijōjieitai 2008-2009' (海上自衛隊２００８－２００９ – Ships and Aircraft of the JMSDF), *Sekai no Kansen* 世界の艦船, 2008:7.
Editorial Department, 'Miccyaku! Korega Bōei Daigakkō no Gakusei Seikatsuda' (密着！これが防衛大学校の学生生活だ – Stick firmly! This is the student's life at the NDA), *Securitarian*, 2004:5, 14–19.
Fukushima, Shingo, *Nihon no 'Bōei' Seisaku* (日本の「防衛」政策 – Japan's Defence Policy, Tokyo: Tokyo Daigaku Shuppankai, 1978).
Furushō, Kōichi, Captain JMSDF, 'Kaijōjieitai no Kirai Senbutai: Sono Genjō to Syōrai' (海上自衛隊の機雷戦部隊：その現状と将来 – Present and Future of the JMSDF Mine Warfare Force), *Sekai no Kansen* 世界の艦船, 1991:7, 141–5.
Hikotani, Takako, 'Shibirian Contrōru no Shōrai' (シビリアンコントロールの将来 – The Future of Japan's Civil-Military Relations), *Kokusai Anzen Hoshō* 国際安全保障, Vol. 32, 2004:1, 21–48.

Hino, Keiichi, 'Chūmoku no Perusyawan Haken Sōkaibutai' (注目のペルシャ湾派遣掃海部隊 – Japanese Minesweepers Leave for the Gulf), *Sekai no Kansen* 世界の艦船, 1991:7, 168–71.

Hiroshi, Masuda, *Jieitai no Tanjō* (自衛隊の誕生 – The Origins of the Self-Defence Forces, Tokyo: Chūōkōronsha, 2004).

Hoshino, Yasusaburō, *Jieitai* (自衛隊 – The Self-Defence Forces, Tokyo: San Ichi Shobo, 1969).

Ikeda, Kiyoshi, *Kaigun to Nihon* (海軍と日本 – The Navy and Japan, Tokyo: Chūokōronsha, 1981).

Inagaki, Osamu, 'Jieitai Seishin Kyōiku' (自衛隊精神教育 – The JSDF's Spiritual Education), *Tenbō* 展望, 1974:5, 142–52.

Ishiba, Shigeru, *Kokubō* (国防 – National Defence, Tokyo: Shinchōsha, 2005).

Ishihara, Nobuo, *Kengen no Dai Idō* (権限の大異動 – The Major Transfer of Authority, Tokyo: Kanki Shuppan, 2001).

Ishii, Koyu, 'Dōnaru!? Nayami Ōi Kaijōjieitai no Dejitaruka' (どうなる！？悩み多い海上自衛隊のデジタル化 – JMSDF's Digital Technology), *Sekai no Kansen* 世界の艦船, 2005:2, 84–9.

Ishii, Koyu, 'Heisei no Hinomaru Kūbo '16 DDH' no Operēshon' (平成の日の丸空母「１６DDH」のオペレーション - Operations of the JMSDF's New '16 DDH'), *Sekai no Kansen* 世界の艦船, 2005:4, 106–9.

Itō, Masanori, *Gunbatsu Kōbō Shi* (軍閥興亡史 – A History of the Rise and Fall of the Military Cliques, 3 Volumes, Tokyo: Bungei Shunju Shinsha, 1958).

Itō, Masanori, *Rengō Kantai no Eikō* (連合艦隊の栄光 – Glories of the Combined Fleet, Tokyo: Bungei Shunju Shinsha, 1962).

Itō, Masanori, *Rengō Kantai no Saigo* (連合艦隊の最後 – The End of the Combined Fleet, Tokyo: Bungei Shunju Shinsha, 1956).

Itō, Masanori, *Teikoku Rikugu no Saigo* (帝国陸軍の最後 – The end of the Imperial Japanese Army, 5 Volumes, Tokyo: Bungei Shunju Shinsha, 1959–61).

Kageyama, Noboru, *Kaigun Heigakkō no Kyōiku* (海軍兵学校の教育 – Education at the Naval Academy, Tokyo, 1978).

Kaigun Rekishi Hozonkai (ed.), *Nihon Kaigunshi* (日本海軍史 - A History of the Japanese navy, 10 Volumes, Tokyo: Hatsubai Dai Ichi Hōki Shuppan Kabushiki Kaisha, 1996).

Kaihara, Osamu, 'Shīrēn Bōei Mondai wo Kangaeru: Jissai Mondai Toshite Fukanō' (シーレーン防衛問題を考える：実際問題として不可能 – On the Sea Lane Defence Problem in Dispute: Such a Mission is Impossible), *Sekai no Kansen* 世界の艦船, 1982:12, 130–1.

Kaneda, Hideaki, Vice Admiral JMSDF (Ret.), '21Seiki ni Okeru Jieikan no Missyon' (２１世紀における自衛艦のミッション – Missions of the JMSDF's Destroyers for the 21st Century), *Sekai no Kansen* 世界の艦船, 2005:1, 124–9.

Kaneda, Hideaki, Vice Admiral JMSDF (Ret.), 'Jieitai ni Tarinai Mono wa?' (海上自衛隊に足りないものは – Subjects for Tomorrow's JMSDF), *Sekai no Kansen* 世界の艦船, 2003:6, 88–91.

Kawano, Hitoshi, 'Taishō Shōwa ki Gunji Rlite no Keisei Katei' (大正・昭和期軍事エリートの形成過程 – The Formation Process of the Military Elite in the Taishō and Shōwa Eras) in Kiyotada (ed.), *'Kindai Nippon' no Rekishi Shakaigaku*, 95–140.

Kendō, Katsutoshi, Ikuhiko Hata, Katsushige Todaka, Katsuya Fukuda, and Hirama Yōichi, *Shōwa no Kaigun Erīto Shūdan no Eikō to Shittsui* (昭和の海軍エリート集団の栄光と失墜 – Glories and Abasements of the Elite Group of the Shōwa Navy), *Bungei Shunjū* 文芸春秋, 2007:8, 142–86.

Kiyotada, Tsuitsui (ed.), *'Kindai Nippon' no Rekishi Shakaigaku* (近代日本の歴史社会学 – Historical Sociology of 'Modern Japan', Tokyo: Bokutakusha, 1990).
Kobayashi, Hiroaki, *Bōei no Ronri* (防衛の論理 – The Logic of National Defence, Tokyo: Nippon Kōgyō Shinbunsha, 1981).
Kobayashi, Hiroaki, *Jiei no Ronri* (自衛の論理 – The Logic of Self-Defence, Tokyo: Tairyūsha, 1990).
Kōsaka, Masataka, 'Kaiyō Kokka Nihon no Kōsō' (海洋国家日本の構想 – The Concept of Japan as Maritime State), *Chūō Kōron* 中央公論, 1964:09, 48–80.
Kōsaka, Masataka, *Saishō Yoshida Shigeru ron* (宰相吉田茂論 – On Prime Minister Yoshida Shigeru, Tokyo: Chūō Kōronsha, 1968).
Kōsaka, Masataka, 'Tsūshō Kokka Nippon no Unmei' (通商国家日本の運命 – The Fate of Japan as a Trading State), *Chūō Kōron* 中央公論, 1975:11, 116–40.
Maeda, Tetsuo, *Jieitai wo Dōsuruka?* (自衛隊をどうするか – What is next for The JSDF?, Tokyo: Iwanami Shōten, 1992).
Matsumoto, Saburō, '"Bōei Daigakkō Go Jū Nenshi" wo Yonde. Bōei Daigakkō ni okeru Shikan Kyōiku' (「防衛大学校五十年史」を読んで。防衛大学校における士官教育 - Reading the "Fifty-year History of the NDA". Officers Education at the NDA), *Bōeigaku Kenkyū* 防衛学研究, No. 31, 2004:7, 1–15.
Nagata, Hiroshi, Admiral JMSDF (Ret.), '21Seiki no Kaijōjieitai: 21Seiki no Jieikan wa Kōnaru' (２１世紀の海上自衛隊：２１世紀の自衛艦はこうなる – The JMSDF in the 21st Century: Thinking about 21st Century Ships), *Sekai no Kansen* 世界の艦船, 1995:12, 88–93.
Nakajima, Shingo, 'Sengo Nihongata Seigunkankei no Keisei' (戦後日本型政軍関係の形成 – The Creation of Post-war Japanese Civil-Military Relations) *Gunji Shigaku* 軍事史学, Vol. 34, 1998:1, 22–39.
Nakajima, Shingo, *Sengo Nihon no Bōei Seisaku. 'Yoshida Rosen' wo Meguru Seiji, Gaikō, Gunji* (戦後日本の防衛政策。「吉田路線」をめぐる政治、外交、軍事 – Japan's Post-War Defence Policy. Politics, Foreign Policy and Military Affairs about the 'Yoshida's Line', Tokyo: Keiō Gijuku Daigaku Shuppankai, 2005).
Nakamori, Shizuo, *Bōei Daigakkō no Shinjitsu* (防衛大学校の真実 – The Reality of the National Defence Academy, Tokyo: Keizaikai, 2004).
NHK Special Selection, *Kaijojieitai wa Kōshite Umareta* (海上自衛隊はこうして生まれた - The Way The Maritime Self-Defence Force Was Born, Tokyo: Nihon Hōsō Shuppan Kyōkai, 2003).
Nishihara, Masashi, 'Gakusei yo, Iyoku wo Motte, Jōnetsu wo Moyase' (学生よ、意欲を持って、情熱を燃やせ – Students, Bring your Motivation, Burn of Passion), *Securitarian*, 2004:5, 20–1.
Nishiuchi, Tadashi, *Nihon no Bōei* (日本の防衛 – Japan's National Defence, Tokyo: Nippon Kyōbunsha, 1970).
Nisohachi, Hyōdō, 'Riku Kaigun wo Meguru Ōkina Nazo' (陸海軍を巡る大きな謎 – The Army-Navy Share, A Big Mistery), *Seiron* 正論, 2005:5, 38–9.
Nomura, Minoru, *Kaisenshi ni Manabu* (海戦史に学ぶ – Learning from the History of Naval Battles, Tokyo: Bungei Shunjū, 1985).
Nomura, Minoru, *Nihon Kaigun no Rekishi* (日本海軍の歴史 – The History of the Japanese Navy, Tokyo: Yoshikawa Kōbunkan, 2002).
Ōga, Ryōhei, Admiral JMSDF (Ret.), 'Kaijōjieitai to Watashi' (海上自衛隊と私 - My Experience with the JMSDF), *Sekai no Kansen* 世界の艦船, 1999:1, 176–8.
Ōhara, Yasuo, *Teikoku Riku Kaigun no Hikari to Kage* (帝国陸海軍の光と影 – 'Lights' and 'Shadows' of the Imperial Japanese Army and Navy, Tokyo: Tentensha, 2005. First Edition: 1982).

Ōtake, Hideo, *Nihon no Bōei to Kokunai Seiji* (日本の防衛と国内政治 – Japan's National Defence and Domestic Politics, Tokyo: San Ichi Shobo, 1983).

Sadō, Akihiro, *Sengo Seiji to Jieitai* (戦後政治と自衛隊 – Post-war Politics and the JSDF, Tokyo: Yoshikawa Bunkan, 2006).

Sekino, Hideo, 'Waga Kuni no Kaijō Goei Monday' (わが国の海上護衛問題 – Ocean Escort Problems of Japan), *Sekai no Kansen* 世界の艦船, 1973:8, 64–6.

Shinohara, Hiroshi, *Nihon Kaigun Oyatoi Gaijin* (日本海軍お雇い外人 – The Navy's Foreign Employees, Tokyo: Chūo Kōronsha, 1988).

Sōbei, Suzuki, *Kikisho: Kaijojieitai Shiwa* (聞書：海上自衛隊史話 – Memories of the Maritime Self-Defence Forces, Tokyo: Suikōkai, 1989).

Tachikawa, Kyōichi, Tomoyuki Ishizu, Narushige Michishita, and Katsuya Tsukamoto (eds), *Shii Pawaa* (シーパワー – Seapower, Tokyo: Fuyō Shobō, 2008).

Takahashi, Hidenori, 'Kaigun Heigakkō no Kyōiku Kikan Enchō to Seishin Kagaku Dōnyū' (海軍兵学校の教育期間延長と精神科学の導入 – The Introduction of Spiritual Education at the Japanese Naval Academy During the Interwar Period), *Gunji Shigaku* 軍事史学, Vol. 34, 1998:1, 2–24.

Takahashi, Kunitarō, *Oyatoi Gaikokujin 6. Gunji* (お雇い外国人６． 軍事 – Foreign Employees 6. Military Affairs, Tokyo: Kajima Kenkyūjo Shuppankai, 1968).

Terada, Akira, '"Oyashio" Kenzō no Omoide' (「おやしお」建造の思い出 – Memories of the Construction of the Construction of "Oyashio"), *Sekai no Kansen* 世界の艦船, 1997:5, 96–101.

Todaka, Kazushige, *Akiyama Saneyuki Senjutsu Ronshū* (秋山真之戦術論集 – Collection of Essays on Tactics by Akiyama Saneyuki, Tokyo: Chūō Kōron Shinsha, 2005).

Tsukudo, Tatsuo, 'Kaijōjieitaihatsu no Sensuikan "Kuroshio" Kaisōki' (海上自衛隊初の潜水艦「くるしお」回想記 – Recollections from the First Submarine of the JMSDF, "Kuroshio"), *Sekai no Kansen* 世界の艦船, 1997:5, 102–5.

Ugaki, Taisei, 'Kaijōjieitai no AtarashīĪjisukan Unyō Kōsō' (海上自衛隊の新しいイージス艦運用構想 – New Operational Concept of JMSDF's Aegis Ships), *Sekai no Kansen* 世界の艦, 2001:4, 84–7.

Usui, Katsumi, Naosuke Takamura, Yasushi Toriumi, and Masaomi Yui, *Nihon Kindai Jinmei Jiten* (日本近代人名辞典 – Japanese Modern Biographical Dictionary, Tokyo: Yoshikawa Kōbunkan, 2001).

Yamazaki, Makoto, Vice Admiral JMSDF (Ret.), 'Kaijōjieitai wa BMD ni Dōtori Kumu Bekika' (海上自衛隊はBMDにどう取り組むべきか – BMD and the JMSDF in the Near Future), *Sekai no Kansen* 世界の艦船, 2003:9, 76–81.

Yasuoka, Shōtarō, *Watashi no Rirekisho. Dai San no Shinjin* (私の履歴書。第三の新人 – My resume. Third Volume of Newcomers, Tokyo: Nippon Keizai Shimbusha, 2007).

Yoshida, Toshio, *Kaigun no Kokoro* (日本海軍のこころ – The Heart of the Japanese Navy, Tokyo: Bungei Shunjū, 2000).

Yoshinaga, Hayashi, 'Nihon no Shokugyō Gunjin Ishiki – 1500 Nen no Gunjishi wo Furikaette' (日本の職業軍人意識－１５００年の軍事史を振り返って – The Japanese Military Professionalism: Overview through the 1500-year long Japanese Military History), *Senshibu Nenpō* 戦史部年俸, 2005:8, 127–51.

B) Other languages (monographs and edited volumes)

Agawa, Hiroyuki, *Citadel in Spring: A Novel of Youth Spent at War* (Tokyo: Kodansha International, 1990).

Agawa, Hiroyuki, *Devil's Heritage* (Tokyo: The Hokuseido Press, 1957).

Agawa, Hiroyuki, *The Reluctant Admiral: Yamamoto and the Imperial Navy* (Tokyo: Kodansha International, 1979).

Akaha, Tsuneo, *Japan in Global Ocean Politics* (Honolulu, HI: University of Hawai Press, 1985).

Alagappa, Muthiah (ed.), *Coercion and Governance: The Declining Political Role of the Military in Asia* (Stanford, CA: Stanford University Press, 2001).

Alagappa, Muthiah (ed.), *Military Professionalism in Asia: Conceptual and Empirical Perspectives* (Honolulu, HI: East-West Centre, 2001).

Alagappa, Muthiah, (ed.), *Asian Security Practice: Material and Ideational Influences* (Stanford, CA: Stanford University Press, 1998).

Andrew, Cobbing, *The Japanese Discovery of Victorian Britain: Early Travel Encounters in the Far East* (Richmond, Surrey: The Japan Library, 1998).

Asada, Sadao, *Culture Shock and Japanese-American Relations. Historical Essays* (Columbia, MO: University of Missouri Press, 2007).

Asada, Sadao, *From Mahan to Pearl Harbor. The Imperial Japanese Navy and the United States* (Annapolis, MD: Naval Institute Press, 2006).

Auer, James E., *The Post-war Rearmament of Japanese Maritime Forces, 1945-71* (New York, Washington, London: Preager, 1973).

Auer, James E. (ed.), *Who Was Responsible? From Marco Polo Bridge to Pearl Harbour* (Tokyo: *The Yomiuri Shimbun*, 2006).

Austin, Greg, *China's Ocean Frontier: International Law, Military Force and National Development* (Canberra: Allen & Unwin, 1998).

Axelbank, Albert, *Black Star over Japan: Rising Forces of Militarism* (London: Hill & Wang, 1972).

Baer, George W., *One Hundred Years of Seapower: The U.S. Navy, 1890-1990* (Stanford, CA: Stanford University Press, 1994).

Balbi, Bartolomeo, *La Psiche e la Virtù Bellica del Popolo Giapponese* (Naples, IT: Casa Editrice Italo-Cino-Giapponese, 1916).

Baldwin, Christopher, *Seaborne Trade Flows in the Asia Pacific. Present and Future Trends* (Working Paper No. 9, Canberra: Royal Australian Navy, Sea Power Centre, 2001).

Ballard, George A., *The Influence of the Sea on the Political History of Japan* (London: John Murray, 1921).

Barnett, Robert W., *Beyond War: Japan's Concept of Comprehensive National Security* (Washington, DC: Brassey's, 1984).

Beeler, John F., *British Naval Policy in the Gladstone-Disraeli Era, 1866-1880* (Stanford, CA: Stanford University Press, 1997).

Bell, Christopher M., *The Royal Navy, Seapower and Strategy Between the Wars* (Basingstoke, Hampshire: Macmillan, 2000).

Blair, Clay Jr., *Silent Victory: The U.S. Submarine War against Japan* (Annapolis, MD: Naval Institute Press, 2001. First edition 1975).

Blond, Georges, *Admiral Togo* (trans. by Edmond Hyams, New York: Macmillan, 1960).

Booth, Ken and Russell Trood (eds), *Strategic Cultures in the Asia Pacific Regions* (London: Macmillan, 1999).

Booth, Kenneth, *Navies and Foreign Policy* (London: Croom Helm, 1977).

Borg, Dorothy and Shumpei Okamoto (eds), *Pearl Harbour as History: Japanese-American Relations, 1931-41* (New York: Columbia University Press, 1973).

Boyce, Robert and Esmond Robertson (eds), *Paths to War: New Essays on the Origins of the Second World War* (New York: St. Martin Press, 1989).

Brunton, Richard H., *Building Japan, 1868-1876* (Folkestone, Kent: The Japan Library, 1991).

Buck, James H. (ed.), *The Modern Japanese Military System* (Beverly Hills, CA: Sage, 1975).

Buckley, Roger, *The United States in the Asia-Pacific since 1945* (Cambridge: Cambridge University Press, 2002).
Bullock, Cecil, *Etajima: The Dartmouth of Japan* (London: Sampson Low, Marston & Co., 1942).
Buruma, Ian, *Wages of Guilt: Memories of War in Germany and Japan* (London: Jonathan Cape, 1994).
Bywater, Hector C., *Navies and Nations: A Review of Naval Developments since the Great War* (London: Constable and Co, 1927).
Bywater, Hector C., *Seapower in the Pacific: A Study of the American-Japanese Naval Problem* (Boston, New York: Houghton Mifflin Co, 1921).
Cable, James, *The Political Influence of Naval Force in History* (Basingstoke, Hampshire: Macmillan, 1998).
Caforio, Giuseppe (ed.), *Handbook of the Sociology of the Military* (New York: Springer, 2006).
Caforio, Giuseppe (ed.), *The European Cadet: Professional Socialisation in Military Academies* (Baden-Baden: Nomos, 1998).
Chapman, John W. M., *Japan's Quest for Comprehensive Security* (New York: St. Martin Press, 1983).
Chinworth, Michael W., *Inside Japan's Defence: Technology, Economics and Strategy* (Washington, DC, New York: Brassey's, 1992).
Cole, Bernard, *The Great Wall at Sea: China's Navy Enters the 21st Century* (Annapolis, MD: Naval Institute Press, 2001).
Corbett, Julian S., *Maritime Operations of the Russo-Japanese War, 1904-1905* (Annapolis, MD: Naval Institute Press, 1994).
Corbett, Julian S., *Some Principles of Maritime Strategy* (London: Longmans, Green & Co., 1911).
Cortazzi, Hugh (ed.), *Britain and Japan: Biographical Portraits, Volume IV* (London: The Japan Library, 2002).
Cortazzi, Hugh (ed.), *Britain and Japan: Biographical Portraits, Volume V* (Folkestone, Kent: Global Oriental, 2005).
Cortazzi, Hugh and Gordon Daniels (eds), *Britain and Japan, 1859-1991. Themes and Personalities* (Abingdon, OX: Routledge, 1991).
Cullen, L. M., *A History of Japan, 1582-1941: Internal and External Worlds* (Cambridge: Cambridge University Press, 2003).
Davies, Roger J. and Osamu Ikeno, *The Japanese Mind. Understanding Contemporary Japanese Culture* (North Clarendon, VT: Tuttle Publishing, 2002).
Dockrill, Saki (ed.), *From Pearl Harbour to Hiroshima: The Second World War in Asia and the Pacific, 1941-45* (New York: St. Martin Press, 1994).
Douglas, Archibald C., *Life of Admiral Sir Archibald Lucius Douglas* (Totnes, Devon: Mortimer Bros., 1938).
Dower, John W., *Embracing Defeat, Japan in the Wake of World War II* (New York: W.W. Norton & Co., 1999).
Dower, John W., *Empire Aftermath: Yoshida Shigeru and the Japanese Experience, 1878-1954* (Cambridge: Harvard University Press, 1979).
Drea, Edward J., *Japan's Imperial Army: Its Rise and Fall, 1853-1945* (Lawrence, KS: University Press of Kansas, 2009).
Drifte, Reinhard, *Arms Productions in Japan: The Military Application of Civilian Technology* (London: Westview, 1986).
Drifte, Reinhard, *Japan's Foreign Policy in the 1990s: From Economic Superpower to What Power?* (Basingstoke, Hampshire: Macmillan, 1996).

Drifte, Reinhard, *Japanese-Chinese Territorial Disputes in the East China Sea – Between Military Confrontation and Economic Cooperation* (Asia research Centre Working Paper 24, London: London School of Economics and Social Science, 2008).
Duk-Ki, Kim, *Naval Strategy in Northeast Asia. Geostrategic Goals, Policies and Prospects* (London: Frank Cass, 2000).
Dull, Paul S., *A Battle History of the Imperial Japanese Navy, 1941-45* (Annapolis, MD: Naval Institute Press, 1978).
Dyer, Henry, *Japan in World Politics* (London: Blackie & Son, 1909).
Edgerton, Robert B., *Warriors of the Rising Sun* (Boulder, CO: Westview Press, 1997).
Edström, Bert, *Japan's Evolving Foreign Policy Doctrine. From Yoshida to Miyazawa* (Basingstoke, Hampshire: MacMillan, 1999).
Edström, Bert (ed.), *The Japanese and Europe: Images and Perceptions* (Richmond, Surrey: Japan Library, 1999).
Esmein, Jean, *Un Demi Plus* (Paris: Fondation pour les Etudes de Defence Nationale, 1983).
Estrange, Michael G., *The Internationalization of Japan's Security Policy: Challenges and Dilemmas for a Reluctant Power* (Berkeley, CA: University of California, 1990).
Evans, David C. (ed.), *The Japanese Navy in World War II: In the Words of Former Japanese Naval Officers* (Annapolis, MD: Naval Institute Press, 1986. First edition 1969).
Evans, David C. and Mark R. Peattie, *Kaigun. Strategy, Tactics and Technology in the Imperial Japanese Navy, 1887-1941* (Annapolis, MD: Naval Institute Press, 1997).
Evans, David C., The Satsuma Faction and Professionalism in the Japanese Naval Officer Corps of the Meiji Period, 1868-1912 (Unpublished PhD Dissertation, Stanford University, 1978).
Falk, Edwin A., *Togo and the Rise of Japanese Sea Power* (London: Longmans, Green & Co., 1936).
Farrell, Theo and Terry Terriff, *The Source of Military Change* (Boulder, CO: Lynne Rienner, 2002).
Friedman, George and Meredith Le Bard, *The Coming War with Japan* (New York: St. Martin's Press, 1991).
Friedman, Norman, *Seapower as Strategy: Navies and National Interests* (Annapolis, MD: Naval Institute Press, 2001).
Frühstück, Sabine, *Uneasy Warriors: Gender, Memory, and Popular Culture in the Japanese Army* (Berkeley and Los Angeles, CA: University of California Press, 2007).
Fukushima, Akiko, *Japanese Foreign Policy: The Emerging Logic of Multilateralism* (New York: St. Martin Press, 1999).
Futamura, Madoka, *War Crimes Tribunals and Transitional Justice: The Tokyo Trial and the Nuremberg Legacy* (London: Routledge, 2007).
Gluck, Carol, *Japan's Modern Myths: Ideology in the Late Meiji Period* (Princeton: Princeton University Press, 1985).
Goldman, Emily O. and Leslie C. Eliason (eds), *The Diffusion of Military Technology and Ideas* (Stanford, CA: Stanford University Press, 2003).
Gordon, Andrew, *A Modern History of Japan: From Tokugawa to the Present Times* (Oxford: Oxford University Press, 2003).
Gordon, Andrew (ed.), *Postwar Japan as History* (Berkeley, Los Angeles, Oxford: University of California Press, 1993).
Gordon, Andrew, *The Rules of the Game: Jutland and British Naval Command* (London: John Murray, 1996).
Gordon, Andrew and Merle Goldman, *Historical Perspectives on Contemporary East Asia* (Cambridge, MA: Harvard University Press, 2000).

Gow, Ian, *Military Intervention in Pre-war Japanese Politics. Admiral Katō Kanji and the 'Washington System'* (London, New York: Routledge Curzon, 2004).
Gow, Ian, Yōichi Hirama, and John Chapman (eds), *The History of Anglo-Japanese Relations, 1600-2000. Volume III: The Military Dimension* (Basingstoke, Hampshire: Palgrave Macmillan, 2003).
Graham, Euan, *Japan's Sea Lane Security, 1940-2004. A Matter of Life and Death?* (Nissan Institute/Routledge Japanese Studies Series, London and New York: Routledge, 2006).
Gray, Colin S., *The Leverage of Seapower: The Strategic Advantage of Navies in War* (New York: Free Press, 1992).
Green, Michael J., *Arming Japan* (New York: Columbia University Press, 1995).
Green, Michael J. (ed.), *The New Security Agenda: a Global Survey* (Tokyo, New York: JCIE, 1998).
Green, Michael J. and Patrick Cronin (eds), *The US-Japan Alliance: Past, Present and Future* (New York: Council on Foreign Relations Press, 1999).
Grove, Eric, *The Future of Seapower* (Annapolis, MD: Naval Institute Press, 1990).
Grove, Eric, *Vanguard to Trident: British Naval Policy since the Second World War* (London: Bodley Head, 1987).
Halloran, Richard, *Chrysanthemum and Sword Revisited: Is Japanese Militarism Resurgent?* (Honolulu, HI: East-West Centre, 1991).
Hara, Tameichi, Captain IJN (Ret.), *Japanese Destroyer Captain. Pearl Harbor, Guadalcanal, Midway – The Great Naval Battles as seen Through Japanese Eyes* (trans. T. Hara, Fred Saito, and Roger Pineau. Annapolis, MD: Naval Institute Press, 1967).
Hashimoto, Mochitsura, *Sunk: The Story of the Japanese Submarine Fleet* (New York: Henry Holt, 1954).
Hattendorf, John B. (ed.), *Doing Naval History: Essays toward Improvement* (New Port, RI: Naval War College Press, 1995).
Hattendorf, John B. (ed.), *Mahan on Naval Strategy: Selections from the Writings of Rear Admiral Alfred Thayer Mahan* (Annapolis, MD: Naval Institute Press, 1991).
Hattendorf, John B. (ed.), *Ubi Sumus? The State of Naval and Maritime History* (New Port, RI: Naval War College Press, 1994).
Hattendorf, John B. (ed.), *US Naval Strategy in the 1990s: Selected Documents* (Newport Paper 27, New Port, RI: Naval War College Press, 2006).
Hendry, Joy, *Understanding Japanese Society* (London: Routledge, 1995. First edition 1987).
Herwig, Holger H., *'Luxury' Fleet: The Imperial German Navy, 1888-1918* (London: Allen and Unwin, 1980).
Hicks, George, *Japan's War Memories: Amnesia or Concealment?* (Brookfield, VT: Ashgate, 1997).
Hill, Richard, *Maritime Strategy for Medium Powers* (Annapolis, MD: Naval Institute Press, 1986).
Hill, Richard, *War at Sea in the Ironclad Age* (London: Cassell, 2000).
Hoare, J. E. (ed.), *Britain and Japan. Biographical Portraits, Volume III* (Richmond, Surrey: The Japan Library, 1999).
Hobsbawm, Eric and Terence Ranger (eds), *The Invention of Tradition* (Cambridge: Cambridge University Press, 1983).
Holland, Harrison, *Managing Defense: Japan's Dilemma* (Lanham, MD: University Press of America, 1988).
Hook, Glenn D., *Militarization and Demilitarization in Contemporary Japan* (London: Routledge, 1996).

Hoyt, Edwin P., *The Militarists. The Rise of Japanese Militarism Since WWII* (New York: Donald I. Fine, 1985).
Hugh, Smith and Anthony Bergin (eds), *Naval Power in the Pacific: Toward the Year 2000* (Boulder, CO: Lynne Rienner, 1993).
Hughes, Christopher W., *Japan's re-emergence as a 'Normal' Military Power* (Adelphi Paper No. 368–9, Oxford for IISS, 2004).
Hughes, Christopher W., *Japan's Remilitarisation* (London: IISS/Routledge, 2009)
Hughes, Christopher W., *Japan's Security Agenda: Military, Economic & Environmental Dimensions* (Boulder, CO: Lynne Rienner, 2004).
Humphreys, Leonard A., *The Way of the Heavenly Sword* (Stanford, Stanford University Press, 1995).
Huntington, Samuel P., *The Soldier and the State* (Cambridge, MA Belknap Press of Harvard University Press, 1954).
Inoguchi, Takashi, *Japan's Foreign Policy in an Era of Global Change* (London: Printer Publishers, 1993).
Jane, Frederick T., *The Imperial Japanese Navy* (London: Conway Maritime Press, 1984. First published 1904).
Janowitz, Morris, *The Professional Soldier: A Social and Political Portrait* (New York: The Free Press, 1960).
Jansen, Marius (ed.), *Changing Japanese Attitudes toward Modernisation* (Princeton: Princeton University Press, 1965).
Jansen, Marius B., Madoka Kanai, and Danis Twitehett (eds), *The Cambridge History of Japan* (6 Volumes, Cambridge, MA: Cambridge University Press: 1988–91).
Jonhston, Alastair I., *Cultural Realism: Strategic Culture and Grand Strategy in Chinese History* (Princeton, NJ: Princeton University Press, 1995).
Jordan, David, James D. Kiras, David J. Lonsdale, Ian Speller, Christopher Tuck, and C. Dale Walton, *Understanding Modern Warfare* (Cambridge: Cambridge University Press, 2008).
Kane, Thomas M., *Chinese Grand Strategy and Maritime Power* (London: Frank Cass, 2002).
Katahara, Eiichi, *The Politics of Japanese Defence Policy* (Unpublished PhD Dissertation, Griffith University, 1990).
Kataoka, Tetsuya, *Waiting for a 'Pearl Harbour': Japan Debates Defence* (Stanford: Hoover Institution Press, 1980).
Katxenstein, Peter J., *Rethinking Japanese Security* (Abingdon, OX, New York: Routledge, 2008).
Katzenstein, Peter J., *Cultural Norms and National Security: Policy and Military in Post-war Japan* (Ithaca, NY: Cornell University Press, 1996).
Katzenstein, Peter J. and Nobuo Okawara, *Japan's National Security* (Ithaca, NY: Cornell University Press, 1993).
Kawano, Hitoshi, *A Comparative Study of Combat Organisations: Japan and the United States During World War II* (Unpublished PhD Dissertation, Evaston, IL: Northwestern University, 1996).
Kearsley, Harold J., *Maritime Power and the Twenty-first Century* (Aldershot: Dartmouth, 1991).
Keddell, Joseph P., *The Politics of Defence in Japan: Managing Internal and External Pressures* (Armonk, New York: M. E. Sharpe, 1993).
Keene, Donald, *Five Modern Japanese Novelists* (New York: Columbia University Press, 2003).

Kehr, Eckart, *Battleship Building and Party Politics in Germany, 1894-1901* (Chicago, IL: Chicago University Press, 1973).

Kennedy, Gregory C. and Keith Neilson (eds), *Military Education. Past, Present, and Future* (Westport, CT: Preager, 2002).

Kennedy, Malcolm D., *Some Aspects of Japan and Her Defences* (London: Kegan Paul, Trench, Trubner & Co., 1928).

Kennedy, Malcolm D., *The Military Side of Japanese Life* (London: Constable & Co., 1924).

Kier, Elisabeth, *Imagining War: French and British Military Doctrine between the Wars* (Princeton, NJ: Princeton University Press, 1997).

Kliman, Daniel M., *Japan's Security Strategy in the Post-9/11 World* (Westport, CT: Praeger for CSIS, 2006).

Koda, Yoji, *The Rise of Naval Powers in Asia and Europe's Decline* (Oslo Files on Defence and Security, Oslo: Norwegian Institute for Defence Studies, 2012).

Kondapalli, Srikanth, *China's Naval Power* (Delhi: Institute for Defence Studies and Analyses, 2001).

Kōsaka, Masataka, *Options for Japan's Foreign Policy* (Adelphi Papers No. 97, London: International Institute for strategic Studies, 1973).

Lambert, Andrew D., *The Foundations of Naval History. John Knox Laughton, the Royal Navy and the Historical Profession* (London: Chatham, 1998).

Lambert, Andrew D., *War at Sea in the Age of Sail* (London: Cassell, 2000).

Lifton, Robert J., *Death in Life. Survivors of Hiroshima* (Chapel Hill, NC: North Carolina University Press, 1991).

Lim, Robin, *The Geopolitics of East Asia: The Search for Equilibrium* (London: Routledge, 2003).

Lory, Hillis, *Japan's Military Masters: The Army in Japanese Life* (Westport, CO: Greenwood Press, 1943).

Love, Robert W. Jr. (ed.), *Changing Interpretations and New Sources in Naval History: Papers form the Third United States Naval Academy History Symposium* (New York: Garland Publishing, 1980).

MacArthur, Douglas, *Reminiscences* (New York: McGraw-Hill, 1964).

Macgregor, Knox and Williamson Murray (eds), *The Dynamics of Military Revolution, 1300-2050* (Cambridge: Cambridge University Press, 2001).

McIntosh, Malcolm, *Japan Re-Armed* (New York: St. Martin Press, 1986).

Maeda, Tetsuo, *The Hidden Army: The Untold Story of Japan's Military Forces* (Chicago: Edition Q, 1995).

Mahan, Alfred T., *The Problem of Asia and its Effects upon International Policies* (London: Sampson, Low, Marston, 1900).

Marder, Arthur J., *Old Friends, New Enemies: The Royal Navy and the Imperial Japanese Navy, Strategic Illusions, 1936-1941* (Oxford: Oxford University Press, 1981).

Maruyama, Masao, *Thoughts and Behaviour in Modern Japanese Politics* (ed. Ivan Morris, London: Oxford University Press, 1963).

MasWood, Javed S., *Japanese Defence: The Search for Political Power* (Pasir Panjang: Regional Studies Programme of the Institute of South-East Asian Studies – (ISEAS), 1990).

Matthews, Ron and Keisuke Matsuyama (eds), *Japan's Military Renaissance?* (New York: St. Martin Press, 1993).

Mazzei, Franco, *Japanese Particularism and the Crisis of Western Modernity* (Venice: University of Venice, Ca' Foscari, 1997).

Mendl, Wolf, *Japan's Asia Policy: Regional Security and Global Interests* (New York, London: Routledge, 1995).

Midford, Paul, *Japanese Public Opinion and the War on Terrorism: Implications for Japan's Security Strategy* (Washington, DC: East-West Centre Washington, 2006).
Miller, Stephen E. and Stephen Van Evera, *Naval Strategy and National Security* (Princeton, NJ: Princeton University Press, 1988).
Millet, Allan R. and Williamson Murray (eds), *Military Effectiveness, Volume I: The First World War* (Boston, MA: Allen and Unwin, 1988).
Millet, Allan R. and Williamson Murray (eds), *Military Effectiveness, Volume II: The Interwar Period* (Boston, MA: Allen and Unwin, 1988).
Millet, Allan R. and Williamson Murray (eds), *Military Effectiveness, Volume III: The Second World War* (Boston, MA: Allen and Unwin, 1988).
Morris, Ivan I., *Nationalism and the Right Wing in Japan: A Study of Post-War Trends* (Oxford: Oxford University Press, 1960).
Morris, Ivan I., *The Nobility of Failure. Tragic Heroes in the History of Japan* (New York: Meridian Book, 1975).
Muramatsu, Teijirō, *Westerners in the Modernization of Japan* (Tokyo: Hitachi, 1995).
Murray, Williamson, MacGregor Knox, and Alvin Bernstein (eds) *The Making of Strategy. Rulers, States, and War* (Cambridge: Cambridge University Press, 1999. First edition 1994).
Murray, Williamson and Tomoyuki Ishizu (eds), *Conflicting Currents. Japan and the United States in the Pacific* (Santa Barbara, CA: Praeger Security International, 2010).
Nish, Ian (ed.), *Britain and Japan. Biographical Portraits* (Folkestone, Kent: The Japan Library, 1994).
Nish, Ian and Yōichi Kibata (eds), *The History of Anglo-Japanese Relations, 1600-2000: Volume II: The Political-Diplomatic Dimension, 1931-2000* (Basingstoke, Hampshire: Palgrave Macmillan, 2000).
Nishi, Osamu, *The Constitution and National Defence Law System in Japan* (Tokyo: Seibundo, 1987).
O'Brien, Philips P. (ed.), *Technology and Naval Combat in the Twentieth Century and Beyond* (London: Frank Cass, 2001).
O'Brien, Phillips P. (ed.), *The Anglo-Japanese Alliance, 1902-1922* (London: Routledge, 2004).
Okazaki, Hisahiko, *A Grand Strategy for Japanese Defence* (Lanham, MD: University Press of America, 1986).
Oros, Andrew L., *Normalizing Japan: Politics, Identity, and the Evolution of Security Practice* (Stanford, CA: Stanford University Press, 2008).
Paine, S. C. M., *The Sino-Japanese war of 1894-1895. Perceptions, Power and Primacy* (Cambridge: Cambridge University Press, 2003).
Parillo, Mark P., *The Japanese Merchant Marine in World War II* (Annapolis, MD: Naval Institute Press, 1993).
Parshall, Jonathan and Anthony Tully, *Shattered Sword: The Untold Story of the Battle of Midway* (Washington, DC: Potomac Books, 2005).
Peattie, Mark R., *Ishiwara Kanji and Japan's Confrontation with the West* (Princeton, NJ: Princeton University Press, 1975).
Peattie, Mark R., *Nan'yō: The Rise and Fall of the Japanese in Micronesia, 1885-1945* (Honolulu, HI: University of Hawaii Press, 1987).
Polmar, Norman, *Aircraft Carriers: A History of Carrier Aviation and its Influence on World Events, Volume II* (Washington, DC: Potomac Books, 2008).
Polmar, Norman and K. J. Moore, *Cold War Submarines* (Washington, DC: Potomac Books, 2004).

Polomka, Peter, *Japan as Peacekeeper: Samurai State or New Civilian Power?* (Canberra: Canberra Papers on Strategic Defence, 1992).
Prabhakar, Lawrence W., Joshua H. Ho, and Sam Bateman (eds), *The Evolving Maritime Balance of Power in the Asia-Pacific: Maritime Doctrines and Nuclear Weapons at Sea* (Singapore: Institute of Defence and Strategic Studies, 2006).
Pyle, Kenneth B., *Rising Japan: The Resurgence of Japan's Power and Purpose* (Century Foundation Book, New York: Public affairs, 2007).
Ranft, Brian and Geoffrey Till, *The Sea in Soviet Strategy* (Annapolis, MD: Naval Institute Press, 1983).
Renwick, Neil, *Japan's Alliance Politics and Defence Production* (Basingstoke, Wiltshire: MacMillan in association with St. Anthony's College, 1995).
Rocca, Gianni, *Fucilate gli Ammiragli: La Tragedia della Marina Italiana nella Seconda Guerra Mondiale* (Milan: Mondatori, 1987).
Rupert, Smith, *The Utility of Force: The Art of War in the Modern World* (London: Penguin, 2006).
Russell, Edward, *The Knights of Bushido: A Shocking History of Japanese War Atrocities* (New York: E.P. Dutton, 1958).
Sadkowich, James J. (ed.), *Reevaluating Major Naval Combatants of World War II* (Westport, CO: Greenwood Press, 1990).
Samuels, Richard J., *Machiavelli's Childern: Leaders & Their Legacy in Italy and Japan* (Ithaca, NY, London: Cornell University Press, 2003).
Samuels, Richard J., *'Rich Nation, Strong Army': National Security and the Technological Transformation of Japan* (Ithaca, NY: Cornell University Press, 1994).
Samuels, Richard J., *Securing Japan. Tokyo's Grand Strategy and the Future of East Asia* (Ithaca, NY: Cornell University Press, 2007).
Schencking, Charles J., *Making Waves: Politics, Propaganda, and the Emergence of the Imperial Japanese Navy, 1868-1922* (Stanford, CA: Stanford University Press, 2005).
Seaton, Philip A., *Japan's Contested War Memories* (Abingdon, OX, New York: Routledge, 2007).
Shambaugh, David, *Modernising China's Military: Progress, Problems, and Prospects* (Berkeley, Los Angeles, London: University of California Press, 2003).
Shimazu, Naoko, *Japanese Society at War: Death, Memory and the Russo-Japanese War* (Cambridge: Cambridge University Press, 2009).
Shinoda, Tomohito, *Koizumi Diplomacy: Japan's Kantei Aproach to Foreign and Defence Affairs* (Seattle, WA: University of Washington Press, 2007).
Shulman, Mark, *Navalism and the Emergence of American Seapower* (Annapolis, MD: Naval Institute Press, 1995).
Shurman, David M., *The Education of a Navy. The Development of British Strategic Thought, 1867-1914* (Chicago, IL: Chicago University Press, 1965).
Sims, Richard, *Japanese Political History since the Meiji Restoration 1868-2000* (London: Hurst & Co., 2001).
Smith, Hugh and Anthony Bergin (eds), *Naval Power in the Pacific: Toward the Year 2000* (Boulder, CO: Lynne Rienner, 1993).
Smith, Peter C., *Fist From the Sky: The Biography of Captain Takashige Egusa, IJN* (Manchester: Crécy Publishing, 2006).
Solomon, Richard H. and Masataka Kōsaka (eds), *The Soviet Far East Military Build-up. Nuclear Dilemmas and Asian Security* (Dover, MA: Auburn House Publishing Company, 1986).
Stanley-Mitchell, Elizabeth A. and Risa Brooks (eds), *Creating Military Power: The Sources of Military Effectiveness* (Stanford, CA: Stanford University Press, 2007).

Starrs, Roy (ed.), *Japanese Cultural Nationalism at Home and in the Asia Pacific* (Folkestone, Kent: Global Oriental, 2004).
Sumida, John T., *In Defence of Naval Supremacy: Finance, Technology, and British Naval Policy1889-1914* (Boston, MA: Unwin Hyman, 1989).
Tangredi, Sam J. (ed.), *Globalization and Maritime Power* (Washington, DC: National Defence University Press, 2002).
Taylor, Paul D. (ed.), *Asia and the Pacific: US Strategic Traditions and Regional Realities* (Newport, RI: Naval War College Press, 2001).
Till, Geoffrey, *Maritime Strategy and the Nuclear Age* (London: Macmillan, 1982).
Till, Geoffrey, *Seapower: A Guide for the Twenty-First Century* (London: Frank Cass, 2004), 158.
Till, Geoffrey (ed.), *Seapower at the Millennium* (Phoenix Mill, Gloucestershire: Sutton Publishing, 2001).
Vlastos, Stephen (ed.), *Mirror of Modernity: Invented Traditions of Modern Japan* (Berkeley: University of California Press, 1998).
Weinstein, Martin, *Japan's Post-war Defence Policy, 1947-1968* (New York: Columbia University Press, 1971).
Westney, Eleanor D., *Imitation and Innovation: The Transfer of Western Organisational Patterns to Meiji Japan* (Cambridge, MA: Harvard University Press, 1987).
Wilson, Sandra (ed.), *Nation and Nationalism in Japan* (London: Routledge, 2002).
Wolff, David, S. G. Marks, D. Schimmelpenninck ven der Oye, J. W. Steinberg, and Y. Shinji (eds), *The Russo-Japanese War in Global Perspective – World War Zero* (2 Volumes, Leiden, Boston: Brill, 2007).
Woolley, Peter J., *Geography & Japan's Strategic Choice* (Washington, DC: Potomac Books, 2005).
Woolley, Peter J., *Japan's Navy: Politics and Paradox, 1971-2000* (Boulder, CO: Lynne Rienner, 2000).
Yates, Charles L., *Restoration and Rebellion in Satsuma: The Life of Saigō Takamori, 1827-1877* (Unpublished PhD dissertation, Princeton University: 1987).
Yoshida, Mitsuru, *Requiem for Battleship Yamato* (Annapolis, MD: Naval Institute Press, 1999).
Yoshida, Shigeru, *The Yoshida Memoirs* (London, Melbourne, Toronto: Heinemann, 1961).
Yoshihara, Toshi and James R. Holmes (eds), *Asia Looks Seaward. Power and Maritime Strategy* (Westport, CO: Praeger Security International, 2008).

C) Other languages (articles and book chapters)

Agawa, Naoyuki and James E. Auer, 'Pacific Friendship', *US Naval Institute Proceedings*, Vol. 122, 1996:10, http://www.vanderbilt.edu/VIPPS/VIPPSUSJ/publications/friendship.htm, accessed 10 August 2004.
Aizawa, Yoshio, 'The Path Towards an "Anti-British" Strategy by the Japanese Navy Between the Wars', in Ian Gow, Yōichi Hirama, and John Chapman (eds), *The History of Anglo-Japanese Relations, 1600-2000 Volume III: The Military Dimension* (Basingstoke, Hampshire: Palgrave Macmillan, 2003), 139–50.
Akaha, Tsuneo, 'Japan's Response to Threats of Shipping Disruptions in Southeast Asia and the Middle East', *Pacific Affairs*, Vol. 59, 1986:2, 255–77.
Amano, Yasukasu, 'Peace and Anti-war: The Postwar Peace Movement', *AMPO Japan Asia Quarterly Review*, Vol. 24, 1997:2, 39–46.
Arrington, Aminta, 'Cautious Reconciliation: The Change in Societal-Military Relations in Germany and Japan since the End of the Cold War', *Armed Forces and Society*, Vol. 28, 2002:4, 531–54.

Arthur J. Marder, 'From Jimmu Tennō to Perry: Sea Power in Early Japanese History', *The American Historical Review*, Vol. LI, 1945:1, 1–34.
Arthur S. Comyns Carr, 'The Tokyo War Crimes Trial', *Far Eastern Survey*, Vol. 18, 1949:10, 109–14.
Asada, Sadao, 'From Washington to London: The Imperial Japanese Navy and the Politics of Naval Limitations, 1921-1930', *Diplomacy and Statecraft*, Vol. 4, 1993:3, 147–91.
Asakawa, Michio, 'Anglo-Japanese Military Relations, 1800-1900', in Ian Gow, Yōichi Hirama, and John Chapman (eds), *The History of Anglo-Japanese Relations, 1600-2000. Volume III: The Military Dimension* (Basingstoke, Hampshire: Palgrave Macmillan, 2003), 13–34.
Auer, James E., Lieutenant Commander USN, 'Japan's Maritime Self-Defence Force: An Appropriate maritime Strategy?', *Naval War College Review*, Vol. 23, 1971:4, 3–20.
Barnhart, Michael A., 'Japan's Economic Security and the Origins of the Pacific War', *Journal of Strategic Studies*, Vol. 4, 1981:1, 97–124.
Berger, Thomas U., 'From Sword to Chrysanthemum: Japan's Culture of Anti-Militarism', *International Security*, Vol. 17, 1993:4, 119–50.
Best, Anthony, 'Lord Sempill (1893–1965) and Japan, 1921-1941', in Hugh Cortazzi (ed.), *Britain and Japan: Biographical Portraits, Volume IV* (London: The Japan Library, 2002), 375–82.
Boyd, Carl, 'Japan Military Effectiveness: The Interwar Period', in Allan R. Millet and Williamson Murray (eds), *Military Effectiveness, Volume II: The Interwar Period* (Boston, MA: Allen and Unwin, 1988), 131–68.
Broadbridge, Seymour, 'Shipbuilding and the State in Japan since the 1850s', *Modern Asian Studies*, 1977:4, 601–13.
Buck, James H., 'The Japanese Self-Defence Forces', *Asian Survey*, Vol. 7, 1967:9, 597–613.
Burke, Arleigh A., Admiral USN (Ret.), 'The Art of Command', *Naval War College Review*, Vol. 23, 1972:10, 24–8.
Checkland, Olive, '"Working at Their Profession": Japanese Engineers in Britain Before 1914', in Ian Nish (ed.), *Britain and Japan: Biographical Portraits* (Folkestone, Kent: The Japan Library, 1994), 45–53.
Colonel, The Master of Sempill, 'The British Aviation Mission in Japan', *Transactions and Proceedings of the Japan Society - London*, Vol. 22, 1925, 3rd–4th Sessions, 37–50.
Conte-Helm, Marie, 'Armstrong's, Vickers and Japan', in Ian Nish (ed.), *Britain and Japan: Biographical Portraits* (Folkestone, Kent: The Japan Library, 1994), 92–105.
Coox, Alvin D., 'The Effectiveness of the Japanese Military Establishment in the Second World War', in Allan R. Millet and Williamson Murray (eds), *Military Effectiveness, Volume III: The Second World War* (Boston, MA: Allen and Unwin, 1988), 1–40.
Corbett, Julian S., 'The teaching of Naval and Military History', *History*, 1916: April, 12–24.
David, Arase, 'A Militarised Japan?', *The Journal of Strategic Studies*, Vol. 18, 1995:3, 84–103.
Dean, Ralph J., Lieutenant USN, 'Etajima: Hallowed Halls', *US Naval Institute Proceedings*, Vol. 109, 1983:3, 110–16.
Dockrill, Saki, 'Hirohito, the Emperor's Army and Pearl Harbor', *Review of International Studies*, Vol. 18, 1992, 319–33.
Edström, Bert, 'Yoshida Shigeru and the Yoshida Doctrine', *The Stockholm Journal of East Asian Studies*, 1993:4, 85–140.
Erickson, Andrew S., 'Can China become a Maritime Power?', in Toshi Yoshihara and James R. Holmes (eds), *Asia Looks Seaward: Power and Maritime Strategy* (Praeger Security International, 2008), 70–110.

Evans, David C., 'Japanese Naval Construction, 1878-1918', in Philips P. O'Brien (ed.), *Technology and Naval Combat in the Twentieth Century and Beyond* (London: Frank Cass, 2001), 22–35.

Evans, David C., 'The recruitment of Japanese Navy Officers in the Meiji Period', in Robert W. Love Jr. (ed.), *Changing Interpretations and New Sources in Naval History: Papers from the Third United States Naval Academy History Symposium* (New York: Garland Publishing, 1980), 229–45.

Farrell, Theo, 'The Dynamics of British Military Transformation', *International Affairs*, Vol. 84, 2008:4, 777–807.

Feaver, Peter D., Takako Hikotani, and Narine Shaun, 'Civilian Control and Civil-Military Gaps in the United Sates, Japan, and China', *Asian Perspective*, Vol. 29, 2005:1, 233–71.

Ferris, John, 'A British "Unofficial" Aviation Mission and Japanese Naval Developments, 1919-1929', *The Journal of Strategic Studies*, Vol. 5, 1982:3, 416–39.

Ferris, John, 'Double-Edged Estimates: Japan in the Eyes of the British Army and the Royal Air Force, 1900-1939', in Ian Gow, Yōichi Hirama, and John Chapman (eds), *The History of Anglo-Japanese Relations, 1600-2000. Volume III: The Military Dimension* (Basingstoke, Hampshire: Palgrave Macmillan, 2003), 91–108.

Friday, Karl F., 'Bushidō or Bull? A Medieval Historian's Perspective on the Imperial Army and the Japanese Warrior Tradition', *The History Teacher*, Vol. 27, 1994:3, 339–49.

Frühstück, Sabine and Eyal Ben-Ari, '"Now We Show It All!" Normalisation and the Management of Violence in Japan's Armed Forces', *Journal of Japanese Studies*, Vol. 28, 2002:1, 1–39.

Fukuda, Haruko, 'The Peaceful Overture: Admiral Yamanashi Katsutoshin (1877-1967)', in Hugh Cortazzi and Gordon Daniels (eds), *Britain and Japan, 1859-1991: Themes and Personalities* (Abingdon, OX: Routledge, 1991), 198–213.

Futamura, Madoka, 'Individual and Collective Guilt: Post-war Japan and the Tokyo War Crimes Tribunal', *European Review*, Vol. 14, 2006:4, 471–83.

Gluck, Carol, 'The Past in the Present', in Andrew Gordon (ed.) *Postwar Japan as History* (Berkeley, Los Angeles, Oxford: University of California Press 1993), 64–95.

Gow, Ian, 'Civilian Control of the Military in Post-war Japan', in Ron Matthews and Keisuke Matthews (eds), *Japan's Military Renaissance?* (New York: St. Martin Press, 1993), 50–68.

Gow, Ian, 'The Douglas Mission (1873–1879) and Meiji Naval Education', in J. E. Hoare (ed.), *Britain and Japan: Biographical Portraits, Volume III* (Richmond, Surrey: The Japan Library, 1999), 144–57.

Green, Michael J., 'Japan is Back: Why Tokyo's New Assertiveness is Good for Washington', *Foreign Affairs*, Vol. 86, 2007:2, 142–7.

Grisson, Adam, 'The Future of Military Innovation Studies', *The Journal of Strategic Studies*, Vol. 29, 2006:5, 905–34.

Grove, Eric, 'Sea Power in the Asia-Pacific Region', in Lawrence W. Prabhakar, Joshua H. Ho and Sam Bateman (eds), *The Evolving Maritime Balance of Power in the Asia-Pacific: Maritime Doctrines and Nuclear Weapons at Sea* (Singapore: Institute of Defence and Strategic Studies, 2006), 17–33.

Grove, Eric, 'The Discovery of Doctrine. British Naval Thinking at the Close of the Twentieth Century', in Geoffrey Till (ed.), *The Development of British Naval Thinking: Essays in Memory of Brian Ranft* (Abingdon, OX: Routledge, 2006), 184–5.

Guillam, Robert, 'The Resurgence of Military Elements in Japan', *Pacific Affairs*, Vol. 25, 1952:3, 211–25.

Halloram, Richard, 'Is Japan a Military Threat to Asia?', *Arms Control Today*, Vol. 24, 1994, 12–17.

Hata, Ikuhiko, 'Admiral Yamamoto's Surprise Attack and the Japanese Navy's War Strategy', in Saki Dockrill (ed.), *From Pearl Harbour to Hiroshima: The Second World War in Asia and the Pacific, 1941-45* (New York: St. Martin Press, 1994), 55–71.

Hattendorf, John B., 'The Conundrum of Military Education in Historical Perspective', in Gregory C. Kennedy and Keith Neilson (eds), *Military Education. Past, Present, and Future* (Westport, CT: Preager, 2002), 1–12.

Heginbotham, Eric, 'The Fall and Rise of Navies in East Asia: Military Organisations, Domestic Politics, and Grand Strategy', *International Security*, Vol. 27, 2002:2, 86–125.

Heginbotham, Eric and Richard J. Samuels, 'Japan's Dual Hedge', *Foreign Affairs*, Vol. 81, 2002:5, 110–21.

Heginbotham, Eric and Richard J. Samuels, 'Mercantile Realism and Japanese Foreign Policy', *International Security*, Vol. 22, 1998:4, 171–203.

Hellyer, Robert I., 'The Missing Pirate and the Pervasive Smuggler: Regional Agency in Coastal Defence, Trade, and Foreign Relations in Nineteenth-Century Japan', *The International History Review*, Vol. XXVLL, 2005:1, 1–24.

Herwig, Holger H., 'The Battlefleet Revolution, 1885-1914', in Knox Macgregor and Williamson Murray (eds), *The Dynamics of Military Revolution, 1300-2050* (Cambridge: Cambridge University Press, 2001), 114–31.

Hirama, Yōichi, Rear Admiral JMSDF (Ret.), 'Japan's Value in the Korean War: Issues Surrounding the Dispatch of Minesweepers', *The Third Korean-Japan Security Shuttle Paper* (Seoul: The Okazaki Institute, 1997), http://www.bea.hi-ho.ne.jp/hirama/yh_e_top.html, accessed 20 July 2006.

Hirama, Yōichi, Rear Admiral JMSDF (Ret.), 'Japanese Naval Preparations for World War II', *Naval War College Review*, Vol. 94, 1991:2, 63–81.

Holmes, James R. and T. Toshi Yoshihara, 'China's Naval Ambitions in the Indian Ocean', *The Journal of Strategic Studies*, Vol. 31, 2008:3, 367–94.

Holmes, James R. and T. Toshi Yoshihara, 'Japan's Post-Mahanian Maritime Strategy', paper presented at the annual meeting of the *International Studies Association*, San Diego, CA, March 2006, http://www.allacademic.com/meta/p99656_index.html.

Howard, Michael, 'The Forgotten Dimension of Strategy', *Foreign Affairs*, Vol. 57, 1979:5, 975–86.

Hughes, Christopher W., 'Not Quite the "Great Britain of the Far East": Japan's Security, the US-Japan Alliance and the "War on Terror" in East Asia', *Cambridge Review of International Affairs*, Vol. 20, 2007:2, 325–38.

Hughes, Christopher W. and Ellis S. Krauss, 'Japan's New Security Agenda', *Survival*, Vol. 49, 2007:2, 157–76.

Humphreys, Leonard A., 'The Japanese Military Tradition', in James H. Buck (ed.), *The Modern Japanese Military System* (Beverly Hills, CA: Sage, 1975), 21–40.

Ikeda, Kiyoshi, 'The Silent Admiral: Tōgō Heihachirō (1848-1934) and Britain', in Ian Nish (ed.), *Britain and Japan: Biographical Portraits* (Folkestone, Kent: The Japan Library, 1994), 106–20.

Inagaki, Osamu, 'The Jieitai: Military Values in a Pacifist Society', *The Japan Interpreter*, Vol. 10, 1975:1, 1–15.

Ion, Hamish, 'Towards a Naval Alliance. Some naval Antecedents to the Anglo-Japanese Alliance, 1854-1902', in Phillips Payson O'Brien (ed.), *The Anglo-Japanese Alliance, 1902-1922* (London: Routledge, 2004), 26–47.

Ishikawa, Tōru, Admiral JMSDF, 'Japan maritime Self-Defence Force's Enduring Relationship with the U.S. Navy', *Seapower*, 2002: December, 31–3.

Jeans, Roger B., 'Victims or Victimisers? Museums, Textbooks, and the War Debate in Contemporary Japan', *The Journal of Military History*, Vol. 69, 2005: January, 149–95.

Jonhston, Alastair Iain, 'Thinking about Strategic Culture', *International Security*, Vol. 19, 1995:4, 32–64.

Kaneda, Hideaki, Vice Admiral, JMSDF (Ret.), 'Japan's national Maritime Doctrines and Capabilities', in Lawrence W. Prabhakar, Joshua H. Ho, and Sam Bateman (eds), *The Evolving Maritime Balance of Power in the Asia-Pacific. Maritime Doctrines and Nuclear Weapons at Sea* (Singapore: Institute of Defence and Strategic Studies, 2006), 117–32.

Kaneda, Hideaki, Vice Admiral JMSDF (Ret.), 'The Rise of Chinese Sea Power', http://www.project-syndicate.org/commentary/kaneda7, accessed 20 September 2006.

Katō, Shūichi, 'Japanese Writers and Modernisation', in Marius Jansen (ed.), *Changing Japanese Attitudes Toward Modernisation* (Princeton: Princeton University Press, 1965), 425–45.

Katsutoshi, Kawano, Captain JMSDF, 'Japan's Military Role: Allied Recommendations for the Twenty-First Century', *Naval War College Review*, Vol. 51, 1998: Autumn, 9–21.

Katzenstein, Peter J. and Nobuo Okawara, 'Japan's National Security: Structures, Norms and Policies', *International Security*, Vol. 17, 1993:4, 84–118.

Kier, Elizabeth, 'Culture and Military Doctrine', *International Security*, Vol. 19, 1995:4, 65–93.

Kinoshita, Hanji, 'Echoes of Militarism in Japan', *Pacific Affairs*, Vol. 26, 1953:3, 244–51.

Kiralfy, Alexander, 'Japan's Strategic Problem', *Far Eastern Survey*, Vol. 10, 1941:2, 15–20.

Kiralfy, Alexander, 'Why Japan's Fleet Avoids Action', *Foreign Affairs*, Vol. 22, 1943:1, 45–58.

Kitamura, Kenichi, Vice Admiral JMSDF (Ret.), 'The Dawn of the New Japanese Navy: The Story of a Japanese Officer's Attendance at the US Naval War College', *Naval War College Review*, Vol. 37, 1984: September–October, 108–16.

Kitaoka, Shinichi, 'The Strategy of the Maritime Nation Japan: From Yukichi Fukuzawa to Shigeru Yoshida', in Williamson Murray and Tomoyuki Ishizu (eds), *Conflicting Currents. Japan and the United States in the Pacific* (Santa Barbara, CA: Praeger Security International, 2010), 46–9.

Koda, Yoji, Captain JMSDF, 'A Commander's Dilemma: Admiral Yamamoto and the "Gradual Attrition" Strategy', *Naval War College Review*, Vol. 46, 1993: Autumn, 63–74.

Koda, Yoji, Vice Admiral JMSDF, 'The Russo-Japanese war. Primary Causes of Japanese Success', *Naval War College Review*, Vol. 58, 2005:2, 12–14; 10–44.

Koda, Yoji, 'Naval Development in Japan', in Bjørn Terjesen and Øystein Tunsjø (eds), *The Rise of Naval Powers in Asia and Europe's Decline* (Oslo Files on Defence and Security, Oslo: Norwegian Institute for Defence Studies, 2012), 53–66.

Kosaka, Masataka, 'Japan's Major Interests and Policies in Asia and the Pacific', *Orbis*, Vol. 24, 1975:3, 793–808.

Kotani, Tetsuo, 'Presence and Credibility: Homeporting the USS Midway at Yokosuka', *The Journal of American-East Asian Relations*, Vol. 15, 2008, 51–82.

Lambert, Andrew D., 'Naval History for Strategists: Sir Julian Corbett and the Development of Strategic Education in the Royal Navy, 1900-1914', *Osservatorio dell'Istituto di Studi Marittimi Militari*, 2007:139, 35–43.

Lambert, Andrew D., 'Sea Power', in G. Kassimeris and J. Buckley (eds), *The Ashgate Research Companion to Modern Warfare* (Surrey: Ashgate, 2010), 73–87.

Laughton, John K., 'The Scientific Study of Naval History', *RUSI Journal*, Vol. 18, 1875, 508–27.

Lind, Jennifer M., 'Pacifism or Passing the Buck?', *International Security*, Vol. 29, 2004:1, 92–121.

Louis, Allen, 'Notes on Japanese Historiography: Wolrd War II', *Military Affairs*, Vol. 35, 1971:4, 133–8.

McNelly, Theodore, 'The renunciation of war in the Japanese Constitution', *Armed Forces and Society*, Vol. 13, 1986:1, 81–106.

Matsumura, Jerry K., 'Takaki Kanehiro, 1849-1920: British-trained Medical Pioneer who Became Surgeon General to the Imperial Japanese Navy', in Hugh Cortazzi (ed.), *Britain and Japan. Biographical Portraits, Volume V* (Folkestone, Kent: Global Oriental, 2005), 209–22.

Midford, Paul, 'Japan's Leadership role in East Asian Security Multilateralism: The Nakayama Proposal and the Logic of Reassurance', *Pacific Review*, Vol. 13, 2000:3, 367–97.

Morris, Ivan I., 'Significance of the Military in Post-war Japan', *Pacific Affairs*, Vol. 31, 1958:1, 3–21.

Nakao, Hidehiro, 'The Legacy of Shiba Ryotaro', in Roy Starrs (ed.), *Japanese Cultural Nationalism at Home and in the Asia Pacific* (Folkestone, Kent: Global Oriental, 2004), 99–115.

Nish, Ian, 'Britain and Japan: Long-Range Images, 1900-1952', *Diplomacy and Statecraft*, Vol. 15, 2004:1, 149–61.

Nish, Ian, 'Japan, 1914-1918', in Allan R. Millet and Williamson Murray (eds), *Military Effectiveness, Volume I: The First World War* (Boston, MA: Allen and Unwin, 1988), 229–48.

Nish, Ian, 'The Historical Significance of the Anglo-Japanese Alliance', *Studies in the Anglo-Japanese Alliance, 1902-1923* (Discussion Paper No.IS/03/443, London: London School of Economics, 2003), 40–7.

Nishihara, Masashi, 'Maritime Japan Should Reinforce Maritime Defence Capability', *The Association of Japanese Institutes of Strategic Studies (AJISS) – Commentary*, No. 37, 17 July 2008, http://www.jiia.or.jp/en_commentary/200807/17-1.html, accessed 20 October 2008.

Nylander, John, Lieutenant Commander USN (Ret.), 'Etajima Educated the Instructor', *JANAFA Bullettin*, 2005:28, 9–15.

Osaki, Eriko and Michael Penn (trans.), 'Japan's New Blue Water Navy: A Four-year Indian Ocean mission recasts the Constitution and the US-Japan alliance', *Japan Focus*, November 2005, http://japanfocus.org/products/topdf/1812, accessed 20 April 2007.

Ōta, Fumio, Vice Admiral JMSDF, 'Jointness in the Japanese Self-Defence Forces', *Joint Forces Quarterly*, 2000–1: Winter, 57–60.

Parillo, Mark P., 'The Imperial Navy in World War II', in James J. Sadkowich (ed.), *Reevaluating Major Naval Combatants of World War II* (Westport, CO: Greenwood Press, 1990), 61–78.

Patalano, Alessio, '"If You Can't Beat Them, Join Them": US-Japan Military Exchanges and the Development of the Japanese Post-war Submarine Force, 1995-2005', paper presented at the Naval History Symposium, Annapolis, MD, 20–22 September 2007.

Patalano, Alessio, 'Shielding the "Hot Gates": Submarine Warfare and Japanese Naval Strategy in the Cold War and Beyond (1976-2006)', *The Journal of Strategic Studies*, Vol. 31, 2008:6, 859–95.

Peattie, Mark R., 'Akiyama Saneyuki and the Emergence of Modern Japanese Naval Doctrine', *US Naval Institute Proceedings*, Vol. 103, 1977:1, 60–9.

Peattie, Mark R., 'Japanese Naval Construction, 1919-1941', in Philips P. O'Brien (ed.), *Technology and Naval Combat in the Twentieth Century and Beyond* (London: Frank Cass, 2001), 93–108.

Perry, John Curtis, 'Great Britain and the Emergence of Japan as Naval Power', *Monumenta Nipponica*, Vol. 21, 1966:3/4, 305–21.

Powers, William M., 'Mikasa: Japan's Memorial Battleship', *US Naval Institute Proceedings*, Vol. 102, 1976:4, 69–77.

Reeve, John, 'The Development of Naval Strategy in the Asia-Pacific Region, 1500-2000', in Geoffrey Till (ed.), *Seapower at the Millennium* (Phoenix Mill, Gloucestershire: Sutton Publishing, 2001), 134–44.

Reiter, Dan, 'Nationalism and Military Effectiveness: Post-Meiji Japan', in Elizabeth A. Stanley-Mitchell and Risa Brooks (eds), *Creating Military Power: The Sources of Military Effectiveness* (Stanford, CA: Stanford University Press, 2007), 27–54.

Roskill, Stephen W., Captain RN (Ret.), 'The End of the Imperial Japanese Navy by Itō Masanori, Roger Pineau, Andrew Y. Kuroda', *International Affairs*, Vol. 39, 1963:4, 643–4.

Saeki, Kiichi, 'The Rebuilding of Japan's Self-Defence Force', *Japan Quarterly*, Vol. IV, 1957, 101–10.

Sakai, Robert K., 'The Satsuma-Ryukyu Trade and the Tokugawa Seclusion Policy', *The Journal of Asian Studies*, Vol. 23, 1964:3, 391–403.

Schencking, Charles J., 'Navalism, Naval Expansion and War: The Anglo-Japanese Alliance and the Japanese Navy', in Phillips Payson O'Brien (ed.), *The Anglo-Japanese Alliance, 1902-1922* (London: Routledge, 2004), 122–39.

Sekino, Hideo, Commander Imperial Japanese Navy (Ret.), 'Japan and her Maritime Defence', *US Naval Institute Proceedings*, Vol. 97, 1971:5, 98–121.

Senō, Sadao, Commander JMSDF, 'A Chess Game with no Checkmate: Admiral Inoue and the Pacific War', *Naval War College Review*, Vol. 26, 1974: January–February, 26–39.

Shimazu, Naoko, 'Popular Representations of the Past: The Case of Post-war Japan', *Journal of Contemporary History*, Vol. 38, 2003:1, 101–16.

Shimazu, Naoko, 'The Making of a Heroic War Myth in the Russo-Japanese War', *Waseda Journal of Asian Studies*, Vol. 25, 2004, 83–96.

Soeters, Joseph L., Donna J. Winslow, and Alise Weibull, 'Military Culture', in Giuseppe Caforio (ed.), *Handbook of the Sociology of the Military* (New York: Springer, 2006), 237–54.

Soeya, Yoshihide, 'Japan: Normative Constraints versus Structural Imperatives', in Muthiah Alagappa (ed.), *Asian Security Practice: Material and Ideational Influences* (Stanford, CA: Stanford University Press, 1998), 198–233.

Speller, Ian, 'Delayed Reaction: UK Maritime Expeditionary Capabilities and the Lessons of the Falklands Conflict', *Defence & Security Analysis*, Vol. 18, 2002:4, 363–78.

Speller, Ian, 'Naval Warfare', in David Jordan, James D. Kiras, David J. Lonsdale, Ian Speller, Christopher Tuck, and C. Dale Walton (eds), *Understanding Modern Warfare* (Cambridge: Cambridge University Press, 2008), 122–77.

Summers, Harry, 'Reluctant samurai', *Defence & Diplomacy*, Vol. 9, 1991:1–2, 7–11.

Takai, Sususmu and Kazumine Akimoto, 'Ocean-Peace Keeping and New Roles for Maritime Force', *NIDS Security Reports*, 2000:1, March, 57–79.

Tanter, Richard, 'Japan's Indian Ocean Naval Deployment: Blue water militarization in a "normal country"', *Japan Focus*, May 2006, http://japanfocus.org/products/topdf/1700, accessed 20 April 2007.

Tanter, Richard, 'Japanese Militarization and the Bush Doctrine', *Japan Focus*, February 2005, http://www.japanfocus.org/products/details/1989, accessed 21 November 2007.

Tanter, Richard and Masaru Honda, 'Does Japan Have a National Strategy?', *Japan Focus*, May 2006, http://www.japanfocus.org/products/details/1938, accessed 18 November 2007.

Tow, William T., 'Regional Constraints on the Role of Navies', in Hugh Smith and Anthony Bergin (eds), *Naval Power in the Pacific: Toward the Year 2000* (Boulder, CO: Lynne Rienner, 1993), 43–64.

Towle, Philip, 'British Naval and Military Observers of the Russo-Japanese War', in J. E. Hoare (ed.), *Britain and Japan: Biographical Portraits, Volume III* (Richmond, Surrey: The Japan Library, 1999), 158–69.

Toyama, Saburo, 'Lessons from the Past', *US naval Institute Proceedings*, Vol. 108, 1982:9, 62–9.

Tsunoda, Jun and Kazutomi Uchida, Admiral JMSDF (Ret.), 'The Pearl Harbor Attack: Admiral Yamamoto's Fundamental Concept with Reference to Paul S. Dull's *A Battle History of the Imperial Japanese Navy (1941-1945)*', *Naval War College Review*, Vol. 31, 1978: Fall, 83–8.

Turner, Stansfield, 'Missions of the U.S. Navy', *Naval War College Review*, Vol. 51, 1998:1, 87–103 (first published in 1974).

Uchida, Kazutomi, Admiral JMSDF (Ret.), 'The Rearmament if the Japanese Maritime Forces', *Naval War College Review*, Vol. 26, 1973:3, 41–8.

Watanabe, Akio, 'Has Japan Crossed the Rubicon? Defence Policy since the Higuchi Report', *Japan Review of International Affairs*, 2003: Winter Issue, 238–54.

Weste, John L., 'Staging a Comeback: Rearmament Planning and Kyūgunjin in Occupied Japan, 1945-1952', *Japan Forum*, Vol. 11, 1999:2, 165–78.

Wilson, W. R., Captain USN (Ret.), 'The Sea Battle of Dannoura', *American Neptune*, Vol. 28, 1968, 206–22.

Wimbush, S. Enders, 'Maritime Security in a Future Asia-Pacific', *Headmark: Journal of the Australian Naval Institute*, 2006:119, 7–12.

Woolley, Peter J., 'Japan's 1991 Minesweeping Decision: An organizational Response', *Asian Survey*, Vol. 36, 1996:8, 804–17.

Woolley, Peter J., 'Japan's Sea Lane Defence Re-visited', *Strategic Review*, Vol. XXIV, 1996, 49–58.

Woolley, Peter J., 'The Kata of Japan's Naval Forces', *Naval War College Review*, Vol. 49, 1996: Spring, 59–69.

Yamagiwa, Joseph K., 'Literature and Politics in the Japanese Magazine Sekai', *Pacific Affairs*, Vol. 28, 1955:3, 254–68.

Yamaguchi, Noboru, Major General, JGSDF, 'Japan: Completing Military Professionalism' in Muthiah Alagappa (ed.), *Military Professionalism in Asia: Conceptual and Empirical Perspectives* (Honolulu, HI: East-West Centre, 2001), 35–46.

Yokoi, Toshiyuki, Rear Admiral IJN (Ret.), 'Thoughts on Japan's Naval Defeat', *US Naval Institute Proceedings*, Vol. 86, 1960:10, 68–75.

Yoshihara, Toshi and James R. Holmes, 'Command of the Sea with Chinese Characteristics', *Orbis*, Vol. 49, 2005:4, 685–7.

Yoshihara, Toshi and James R. Holmes, 'Japanese Maritime Thought: If not Mahan, Who?', *Naval War College Review*, Vol. 59, 2006:3, 23–51.

Photographic and video reference materials

DVD: *Bōkoku no Aegis* (亡国のイージス – The country-less Aegis, Geneon Video, 2005).

DVD: *Otokotachi no Yamato* (男たちの大和 – The Men of the Yamato, Tōei Video, 2006).

Japan Maritime Self-Defence Force, *Kaijōjieitai Kankan Shiki 2003* (海上自衛隊観艦式２００３ – JMSDF's Fleet Review 2003, DVD, Tokyo: WAC, 2004).

Japan Maritime Self-Defence Force, *Kanbu Kōhosei: Etajima no Seishun* (幹部候補生：江田島の青春 – The Officer Candidate Student: The Youth of Etajima, DVD, Tokyo: WAC, 2004).
Japan Maritime Self-Defence Force, *Kokusai Kankan Shiki 2002* (国際観艦式２００２ – International Fleet Review 2002, DVD, Tokyo: WAC, 2003).
Mikasa Preservation Society website: http://www.kinenkan-mikasa.or.jp/index.htm.
Mikasa Preservation Society, *Memorial Ship Mikasa* (Photographic Booklet, Yokosuka: Mikasa Preservation Society, 2007).
Mitsuo Shibata, *Arabia no Umi* (アラビアの海 – The Arabian Sea, Photographic Book, Tokyo: NESCO, 2004).
Museum of the Meiji Restoration: http://www.ishinfurusatokan.info/index.html (Japanese only).

Index

Ingram Content Group UK Ltd.
Milton Keynes UK
UKHW020152140323
418539UK00007B/147

9 781350 011083